PARTICULAR
PLACES

PARTICULAR PL*a*CES

AN ORANGE FRAZER ROADBOOK

Library of Congress Catalog Card
Number: 90-61654

ISBN 0-9619637-9-4

Published by
Orange Frazer Press, Inc.
Main Street, Box 214
Wilmington, Ohio 45177

Acknowledgements

Grateful acknowledgement to Roy Wolford and *Ohio Magazine*, for the generous permission to use selected pieces from the magazine's stalwart inventory, notably material on Lake Erie (*Ohio Magazine*, July, 1991), and Morgan County (*Ohio Magazine*, May, 1991).

Also to: Tracy C. Alleman, The Delta Queen Steamboat Co.; John Barton, Sports Editor, *Piqua Daily Call*; Cynthia Beach, Logan County Convention & Tourist Bureau; Scott C. Brown; Barbara Burch, The Delta Queen Steamboat Co.; Lynn Cook, Delaware, Ohio; Albert Grimm, Spirit of '76 Museum, Wellington; Dr. Arnold Lewis, the College of Wooster; Ellen Maurer, the Milan Historical Museum; Jim Oda, Piqua Historical Museum; Melody Snure, the *Daily Record*, Wooster.

Project Editors/Damaine Vonada, Marcy Hawley

Contributing Writers/Damaine Vonada, Marcy Hawley, Bob Batz, Jr., Jane Ware, Sue Gorisek

Designer and illustrator/Brooke Wenstrup

Cover/painting by Christopher O'Leary

Typography/Designer Set, Wilmington, Ohio

Contents

DELTA QUEEN   262

■ The world's last working paddle wheel steamboat is the Grande dame of the Ohio River, a floating first class hotel that transports overnight passengers in luxurious and historic style.

ADAMS COUNTY   276

■ Its lineage more noble than known, rural Adams offers the careful tourist sophisticated overnights, Amish craftsmen—and some of   the state's richest vistas and natural areas.
Map/page 290

Foreword

We've been at it again. Mr. Orange Frazer's intrepid writers have been traveling about Ohio; checking out the best bed and breakfasts; breaking bread at hometown eateries from hamburger joints to gourmet restaurants; tromping through museums, historic sites, and scenic spots; and rubbing shoulders with intriguing Ohioans past and present—architects, astronomers, naturalists, pioneers, soldiers, sailors, sculptors, artisans, Indians, inventors, and innkeepers. Ever since the first volume of *Particular Places* proved so popular with our readers (thank you *very* much), we've been gathering material about additional Ohio towns with exciting attractions and worthy places to eat and sleep. About a year ago, we took to the road to see for ourselves exactly what *is* out there on the Buckeye byways and highways, and the result of our journeys is this new guidebook to seventeen different areas of the state.

We at Orange Frazer think of ourselves as pathfinders who travel ahead into what for most folks is uncharted Ohio territory, where we explore and evaluate the local interests, amusements, and accommodations. Of course, since we're editorial pathfinders, you'll find us quite opinionated—and selective—about the places we've included in *Particular Places II*. As was the case with Volume I, none of the establishments reviewed herein paid to appear in this book; they were chosen solely because of their excellence, uniqueness, grassroots renown, or merit as a steadfast fixture in the local culture and society.

Since we believe that the best, most interesting travel books are about people, you'll find a lot of local color—and characters—in *Particular Places II*. Museums, monuments, and amusements are the framework of any guidebook, but we like to flesh out places by exploring not only *what* is in an area, but *how* and *why* it got there. The "Asides" that supplement the text are practically our trademark, and we've sprinkled them liberally throughout the chapters to enhance your travel experience by putting the particular places we've visited in context—historically, geographically, and biographically.

Even while you're reading this page, Mr. Orange Frazer and his writers have begun working on his next travel book, *Particular Places III*. For that guide, we'll be journeying to Ohio's big seven: Cincinnati, Columbus, Cleveland, Dayton, Toledo, Akron, and Youngstown. Do look for us in your city. We'll be the footsore folks unfolding maps, juggling notebooks, tracking down attractions, investigating inns, doggedly asking questions, and, of course, getting the answers.

The Editors

P.S. A fact of the food and lodging business is that hours and prices tend to change frequently, so please take the precaution of calling ahead to check. The cost of bed and breakfasts and other lodgings mentioned in this book averages around $50 per night, double occupancy. Since most of them require reservation, which means you'll be calling anyway, we did not include prices for these establishments.

P.P.S. With regard to restaurant price ranges, "inexpensive" means less than $6 for a meal. "Moderate" means $6-$12, and "expensive" means anything more than $12.

The Delta

Queen

Delaware County Courthouse

Delaware

The prettiest approach to Delaware is via State Route 315, which intersects Interstate 270 just north of Columbus and dead ends on U.S. 23 just south of Delaware. Also known as the Olentangy River Road, State Route 315 skirts that meandering stream for twenty or so miles between downtown Columbus and downtown Delaware. North of the interstate, the road is wooded, and it winds past small country churches, neat farms, and the new upscale housing developments of southern Delaware County to provide a green and refreshing transition between the twentieth century concrete towers of Columbus and the quaint nineteenth century brick buildings of Delaware. ¶ Although it is a small town, Delaware is the largest community in Delaware County, which happens to be the fastest growing county in Ohio. The population explosion has happened largely because of suburban encroachment by moneyed Columbusites who appreciate the county's accessibility to the city as well as the beauty of its gentle hills and open spaces. Most of the development, however, has stayed south of Delaware proper, leaving that town of 20,000 an amiable county seat with wide streets, interesting shops, and a plethora of beautifully maintained Victorian houses and downtown buildings on the National Register of Historic Places. In spite of the BMWs parked beside the expensive houses only a few miles away, Delaware has not gone Yuppie yet. There is nothing ersatz, artificial, or contrived about the place. Delaware still has a real, working downtown, where residents can actually get their hair cut, buy groceries, have their shoes repaired, and patronize a hardware store. Agriculture continues to be an economic mainstay of the fertile till plains in the surrounding countryside, and Delaware's most famous annual event – the nationally known Little Brown Jug harness race – remains firmly grounded in the county fairgrounds on the north edge of town. ¶ If there is a single influential presence – other than the courthouse – in Delaware, it is Ohio Wesleyan University, a private liberal arts school with a Methodist foundation, a strong tradition of community service, and an excellent academic reputation. OWU has produced a string of distinguished alumni, including the powerful positive thinker Norman Vincent Peale, the syndicated columnist/humorist/social commentator Dave Berry, and baseball's legendary Branch Rickey, who integrated the modern major leagues by signing Jackie Robinson to the Brooklyn Dodgers in 1947. Although the University is small, its impact in Delaware is considerable. The campus

is located only a five minute walk from the heart
of town, and two of Delaware's most venerable
institutions – Perkins Observatory and Garth's
Auctions – were founded, respectively, by a
professor and an alumnus. When classes are in
session, its 2,000 students swell the town's
population by ten percent, and on rainy days, a
flotilla of red and black – the OWU colors –
umbrellas on downtown streets attests to Ohio
Wesleyan's local economic importance. ¶ The
University and Delawareans have also worked
hand in hand to make the town a blossoming
center for the arts in central Ohio. Thanks largely
to joint town-gown organizations that promote
the arts, Delaware has a lively cultural life of its
own. Comprised of both campus and community
musicians, the Central Ohio Symphony Orchestra
has an annual concert series and gives holiday
concerts that play to standing-room-only crowds,
while the Delaware Theatre Association recruits
local talent for dramas and musicals performed
on campus. The University's Performing Arts/
Lecture Series brings renowned entertainers to
Delaware; its National Colloquium features
weekly lectures by distinguished speakers on
public policy issues; and every May, scores of
artisans and craftspeople from throughout Ohio
gather in downtown Delaware for a weekend of
exhibits at the popular Spring Arts Festival. Even
the circa 1915 Strand Theatre on East Winter
Street has a film series that allows local folks to
see classic motion pictures on a wide screen at
the same time that OWU students fulfill their fine
arts course requirements by viewing genre films.
Delaware may have a typical small town feel and

gentleness of pace, but its cultural ambiance is quite atypical for communities its size. Although the town is located less than half an hour away from Columbus, Delaware is carving a unique niche for itself as a pleasant and pleasing Chautauqua on the Olentangy.

VAN DEMAN HOUSE — Judge John Van Deman built a big Italianate house on a hill in the 1860s, and his descendants kept it in the family for almost a hundred years. Now it is owned by Bob and Connie Roser, a chemist and nurse by profession, who moonlight as building renovators and have transformed the grand old home into a comfortable bed and breakfast that is only a short walk from downtown Delaware. Guests can relax in the rocking chairs on the rambling front porch, have a swim in the inground pool in the backyard, or socialize in their own private sitting room upstairs. For folks who don't like to carry suitcases, there is even a small elevator to take them up to the second floor bedrooms.
339 North Sandusky Street; 614/363-2963. MC, V.

Long View Farm

LONGVIEW FARM — The family photos displayed in the dining room provide a pictorial history of John and Shirley Humes's family, which has been farming in the Delaware area since the 1830s. The farmhouse where the couple now welcomes bed and breakfast guests was built in the 1920s by John's grandfather, whose original clawfoot tub still dominates the shared bathroom in the upstairs hall. Though the farmhouse is only a ten minute drive from Delaware, it is part of a working dairy farm with a resident herd of Jersey cows and calves that "beller" in the morning. Guests often enjoy exploring the farm, but

John says that so far nobody has gotten up early enough in the morning to help him with the milking. The view – and it is a l-o-o-o-ng one across miles of cornfields – is best seen from the private porch adjacent to the "Blue" guest room. On weekends when there are sporting or other events at Ohio Wesleyan, the simply furnished rooms fill up quickly, and the Humes have hosted a mix of foreign students, parents, physicians, and chamber musicians. Their most memorable guest, however, was a woman from New York City who was so unaccustomed to fresh air and open spaces that she was afraid to drive her car down the road through the tall corn.

3780 Bowtown Road; 614/362-0387. Open Mar-Nov. No smoking. No pets. No young children.

Bun's Restaurant

BUN'S — A bakery as well as a restaurant, Bun's has been a Delaware institution since George Frederick Hoffman opened a bake shop in 1863. Several generations of Hoffmans – all of whom were named George, but had apropos nicknames such as Bun and Biscuit – expanded the bakery to include a sit-down restaurant. They were such enterprising fellows that they managed to smuggle baked goods into the no-men-allowed women's dormitories at Ohio Wesleyan by having coeds lower baskets out of the windows on ropes. The Hoffman family sold the business a few years ago, but the landmark "Bun's Restaurant" sign still arcs high over West Winter Street, making it virtually impossible to not be able to find the place. The decor is traditional, and the menu accordingly features "American Classics" – roast turkey, pork chops, grilled ham, and country fried steak served with side dishes such as real whipped potatoes, buttered corn, and pickled eggs and beets. The soups are all homemade, and, of course, so are the desserts.

6 West Winter Street; 614/363-3731. Tu-Sat 7:30 a.m.-8 p.m. Lunch, moderate. Dinner, moderate-expensive. MC, V.

HAMBURGER INN — The wood counters and chrome stools have been well worn by several generations of Delawareans, but every time owners Larry and Bev King talk about remodeling, their customers protest and tell them to leave the Hamburger Inn exactly the way it is. If you grew up in the 1950s, you probably remember hamburger joints where you could get a good, greasy burger and a real milkshake mixed by a soda fountain machine and poured from a shiny metal shaker. Rejoice, for the Hamburger Inn is still one of those places. It's not fancy, but as a favorite community gathering spot, it's common ground — ahem — beef for what one veteran waitress calls Delaware's "doctors, lawyers, and Indian chiefs." The inn is known for its thick, spicy chili, but you can also get a roast beef dinner with mashed potatoes and two side dishes for less than $4. Larry himself gets up in the wee hours of the morning to make all of the buns, rolls, pies, and doughnuts, and just because his customers enjoy them so much, the inn is one of the few places anywhere where you can get freshly baked mincemeat and pumpkin pie all year round.
16 North Sandusky Street; 614/369-3850. Mon-Th 6 a.m.-7 p.m., Fri 6 a.m.-8 p.m., Sat 6 a.m.-7 p.m., Sun 6 a.m.-2 p.m. Inexpensive.

THE BROWN JUG RESTAURANT — The Brown Jug Restaurant has been a Delaware institution as long as the town's Little Brown Jug horse race. Both began in 1946, and the "racy" decor — displays of sulkies and booths that mimic horse stalls — of this friendly downtown eatery and watering hole emphasizes their joint position at the starting gate. Stromboli, spaghetti, and veal parmesan give the menu's standard chicken, beef, and chops an Italian accent, and the food is well-prepared and served. And every afternoon at 3 p.m. and 6 p.m., folks gather at the bar to watch replays of the previous day's races at Scioto Downs.
13-15 West William Street; 614/369-3471. Mon-Sat 11 a.m.-11:30 p.m. Inexpensive-expensive. AE, MC, V.

HEARTLAND CAFE & GRILLE — If ever there were a *country* bistro, the Heartland is it. Quilts used as tablecloths and lanterns hanging along the walls set the tone for the Heartland's rustic, almost old-fashioned atmosphere, yet the eclectic menu offers up-to-date selections such as chargrilled chicken breast, barbecued shrimp kabob, and tortellini with pesto sauce. Even a dish as ordinary as meat loaf is dressed up with fresh herbs. On chilly evenings, you can get hot spiced red wine from the bar, and on weekends, there is always evening entertainment — a strolling magician who performs table side tricks on Friday and a jazz band on Saturday.
19 East Winter Street; 614/363-0860. Breakfast Mon-Fri 7-10:30, Sat 7-11:30. Lunch Mon-Fri 11-2:30, Sat 12-2:30. Dinner, Fri-Sat 5-10. Inexpensive-expensive. MC, V.

THE BRANDING IRON — This steak house with its western motif is a local favorite. Chickens slowly rotate on spits, and a glass-fronted meat case near the entrance displays the prime rib and T-bones that the patrons will be having for dinner. The breads, salad dressings, and barbecue sauce are all homemade, and several of the entrees — a whole roasted chicken, a 24-ounce sirloin, a three-pound slab of ribs — are big enough for two. The raisin bread is especially tasty, and the

round, crispy potato Texas fries nicely complement the barbecued meats.
1400 Stratford Road; 614/363-1846. Tu-Th 5-9:30, Fri-Sat 5-10:30, Sun noon-8. Moderate-expensive. MC, V.

TALL PINES — The small, but pleasant dining room has a fireplace and looks out into the sweeping pine trees surrounding this restaurant located in an old home just outside of Delaware. The very traditional menu emphasizes chicken, beef, ribs, and fish. All of the dinners are served with homemade sourdough bread and cinnamon rolls, and at lunch time, you can enjoy your cooked-to-order hamburgers with mouthwatering, homemade potato chips that are thin, crunchy, and cooked with the peel still on them.
1185 U.S. 23 north of Delaware; 614/369-0254. Mon-Th 11-9, Fri 11-10, Sat 4-10. Moderate-expensive. AE, MC, V.

FORK & FINGERS — The bar is busy; the juke box blares; the lighting is low; and the food is excellent at this Mexican restaurant. Although you'll find most of the expected Mexican entrees – tacos, burritos, enchiladas-here, the diverse menu includes such unusual items as hot chiles stuffed with beef and onions or Pedro's Pies, a meat and vegetable dish in pastry topped by cheese and enchilada sauce. If you're counting calories, have a cup of the Cafe Fiesta – hot coffee with a dash of coffee liqueur and cinnamon – for dessert. If you're not, have the churros, a scrumptiously warm and crunchy cruller-type pastry covered with sugar and whipped cream.
377 London Road; 614/363-3077. Mon-Th 11 a.m.-10 p.m., Fri 11 a.m.-midnight, Sat noon-midnight. Inexpensive-expensive. MC, V.

ASIDE Rutherford B. Hayes, nineteenth President of the United States, was born in Delaware on October 4, 1822. Unfortunately, his birthplace, a brick house on East William Street, was torn down long ago. A gasoline station now stands on the historic site, which is marked only by a small stone monument. Like President Bill Clinton, Hayes was born to a single mother who had been widowed shortly before his birth. Ironically, the desk that Clinton, like Kennedy before him, chose for the Oval Office is the "Resolute Desk" that had originally been used by Hayes. It was made from the timbers of *H.M.S. Resolute* and given to President Hayes by Queen Victoria in 1880.

WALKING TOUR OF DELAWARE — In the early 1800s, founding father Moses Byxbe laid out the streets of Delaware in a system of grids around a central business district that theoretically promotes walking. His plan has worked well, for Delaware today has many pretty, tree-lined streets – especially in the northwest section of town – that are a pleasure to stroll because of their historically and architec-turally interesting sites. The **Delaware County Courthouse** (corner of Sandusky Street and Central Avenue) and the adjacent **Sheriff's Residence and Jail** (corner of Central Avenue and Franklin Street) comprise an historically significant area in downtown Delaware. A splendid example of Queen Anne architecture, the combination

Sheriff's Residence
Delaware

residence/jail reflects one of the ideas that Rutherford B. Hayes had
about prison reform when he was Governor of Ohio in the 1870s. It is
one of only a handful of structures left in Ohio where the sheriff and
his family lived only a wall away from the prisoners. The **Asbury
United Methodist Church** (corner of Lincoln and Franklin) is a
stunning Romanesque building with a huge Tiffany art glass window
installed in walls made of the beautiful blue limestone that is plentiful
in the Delaware area. **Winter Street** west of Franklin Street was
Delaware's first residential area and home to physicians, bankers,
businessmen, and college presidents. Someone once fancied West
Winter to be the most beautiful street in the world, and the array of
well-kept buildings in architectural styles ranging from Federal to Art
Deco make it is easy to see why. Many of the former residences now
serve as fraternity and sorority houses for Ohio Wesleyan students, and
the far west end of the street includes **Monnett Lawn**, which is part
of the university's lovely arboretum. Built of blue limestone in 1844,
the Gothic-style **St. Peter's Episcopal Church**, 45 West Winter, is
modeled after the parish churches of Great Britain. Its plans were
imported by Philander Chase, the bishop who founded Kenyon
College. Between Franklin and Sandusky streets, Winter Street is
commercial, and businesses occupy the nineteenth century buildings.
The **iron arch** that so beautifully transcends Winter Street was
installed by merchants in the 1920s and used to have electric lights.
When the lights were no longer needed, the arch was going to be
dismantled, but George "Bun" Hoffman came to the rescue, and it has
been pointing the way to Bun's restaurant ever since.
*Walking tour maps and information are available at the Delaware
County Historical Museum (see entry below) or at the Delaware
Area Chamber of Commerce, 27 West Winter Street; 614/369-6221.
Mon-Fri 9-5.*

ASIDE Delaware is named for the Indian tribe that came to the area in the 1700s after the Iroquis drove them out of the Delaware Valley on the east coast. The Delawares had a sizable village on the site where the town of Delaware now stands, and their cornfields covered most of what is the present day downtown.

THE ARTS CASTLE — With its picturesque tower, stalwart blue limestone walls, and lofty location, the Arts Castle is a wonderful ending to the pretty parade homes on West Winter Street. A Delaware landmark, this magnificent old house was built in 1846 by business-man William Little as a wedding present for his daughter Elizabeth and her groom, George Campbell. Mr. Campbell was an avid horticulturist who planted vineyards in the surrounding property and developed the Delaware wine grape in the castle's greenhouses. On a trip to China, he also brought back a ginkgo tree and planted it on the West Winter Street side of the castle lawn, where more than 140 years later, it is still alive and well and shading the old iron fence with its fan-shaped leaves. Considered very rare because of its age and Chinese origin, the tree is said to be worth more than the castle and the grounds put together. For many years, Ohio Wesleyan used the castle as its fine arts building, but it eventually fell into private hands and disrepair. Then in 1988, community volunteers renovated and revitalized the castle, giving it a new and exciting life as a local cultural arts center where dozens of classes, workshops, exhibits, concerts, performances, and receptions are held throughout the year. In October, the castle's Arts A Fair celebration features personal appearances by regional artists who work in a variety of media. The castle also has a small, but excellent shop featuring a wide selection – textiles, glass, pottery, porcelain, jewelry, baskets – of original, juried items by Midwest artists. Everything in the shop is reasonably priced, and many of the works are one of a kind. If the volunteers who work at the castle have time, they'll cheerfully give you a tour of the studios and recital rooms that were once the Campbells' living quarters. Take special note of the narrow, but beautiful spiral staircase that stretches from the bottom to the top of the tower. If you stand with your chin over the newell post and look up, the steps create the illusion of being an architectural nautilus shell as they wind toward the sky.
190 West Winter Street; 614/363-1486. Call for dates and times of classes, workshops, exhibits, performances, and tour availability. Office open Mon-Fri 9-4. Gallery Shop open Tu-Sat 11:30-4. MC, V.

OHIO WESLEYAN UNIVERSITY CAMPUS AND ARBORETUM — Located in the heart of Delaware, Ohio Wesleyan's lovely, 200-acre campus is notable for its diverse buildings – eleven of which are on the National Register of Historic Places – and trees. The campus is divided into two parts separated by Sandusky Street: the academic and athletic buildings on the east side, and the dormitories, Greek houses, and student union on the west side. Until 1877, the present east campus was the province of male students at Ohio Wesleyan, while the west campus belonged to the women attending Ohio Wesleyan Female College. The two schools merged in 1877, creating one of the

The Arts Castle
Delaware County Cultural Arts Center

first nation's early coeducational campuses. The university's show-
piece and seminal building is **Elliot Hall**, which was originally used as
a resort hotel for people taking "the cure" at a sulphur spring now
located behind Phillips Hall on the west campus. Hard times forced
the hotel to close, and the Methodist Church turned it into a college.
When Ohio Wesleyan was chartered in 1842, the entire school —
eleven students, dormitory, classrooms, administration, chapel — was
housed in Elliott Hall. **University Hall**, built in 1893, holds most
administrative offices and Gray Chapel, an auditorium boasting
outstanding acoustics and the largest of only six German-made Klais
organs in the United States. The flags hanging in the hall's foyer
represent the home countries of foreign students, and the huge mirror
with its impressively carved fruit-and-flower motif belonged to Lucy
Webb Hayes. An alumna of the Ohio Wesleyan Female College, Mrs.
Hayes used it in the White House when her husband was President.
Modern **Beeghly Library** is the second largest library in a private
Ohio College and has a fine collection of manuscripts and memorabilia
from Walt Whitman and Robert and Elizabeth Barrett Browning.
Slocum Hall, which contains the Office of Admissions, has a lovely
second floor mezzanine with stained glass windows and portraits of
important historical figures. **Selby Stadium**, where the football, track,
and lacrosse teams play, is a wonderful art deco style structure built in
1929 — Ohio Wesleyan beat Miami University 20-12 in the opening
game — that harkens to the days when Wesleyan's "Battling Bishops"
played the likes of Ohio State and the University of Michigan on the
gridiron. Ohio Wesleyan football games are not merely campus, but
community events that bring town and gown together. At one of the
first home games every fall, the University hosts a sports day for
Delawareans with a picnic and carnival outside the stadium and free
admission to the football game. On the east campus, the **Hamilton-
Williams Campus Center**, (popularly called the "GRUB," meaning
"Green-Roofed Union Building"), is the hub of student activities and
organizations. It has a bookstore for buying Ohio Wesleyan T-shirts
and souvenirs; a bakery that sells fresh cookies, cakes, and croissants;

and a chapel on the third floor with the best view in Delaware of both the town and the campus.

The **Jane Decker Arboretum** covers virtually the entire Ohio Wesleyan campus, although the trees are most prevalent in the academic area east of Sandusky Street, and at far west end of Winter Steet near Sanborn Hall on the old Female College campus. Touring the trees is a novel and relaxing way to see the campus, which is especially pretty around Mother's Day, when the university tradition-ally holds its graduation and many of the trees and aromatic lilac bushes are in full bloom. Started in the 1860s by Delaware minister Joseph Creighton, the arboretum is named for the distinguished Ohio Wesleyan botany professor Jane Decker. It boasts more than a hundred species of trees from around the world, and most of them have been labeled with markers giving their popular and scientific names. Two of the trees that the Reverend Creighton planted more than a century ago have literally become landmarks on the west side of the campus: the bald cyprus just east of the sulphur spring behind Phillips Hall, and the Ginkgo tree behind Slocum Hall. The Ginkgo is so revered that the 1960s, the decision was made to not make Slocum Hall bigger because it would have meant cutting down that tree. Instead, the university built a new library.

Arboretum and campus tour information and maps are available at the Office of Admissions in Slocum Hall; 614/368-3020. Mon-Fri 8-5 during the academic year, 8:30-4:30 during the summer.

ASIDE Lucy Webb Hayes of Chillicothe, Ohio, was the first wife of a U.S. President to have a college degree, having been graduated — with honors — from Ohio Wesleyan Female College in 1850. Although she was popularly dubbed "Lemonade Lucy" for banning liquor from White House parties, she was also the first "First Lady." In an account of the Hayes inauguration, a reporter referred to Mrs. Hayes as "the first lady of the land," and the sobriquet stuck not only to her, but also to the wives of succeeding Presidents. Mrs. Hayes's road to the White House, by the way, supposedly began on the Ohio Wesleyan campus. Tradition has it that she met Rutherford B. Hayes while he was visiting the sulphur spring and that he subsequently proposed to her on the picturesque steps of Elliott Hall.

DELAWARE COUNTY HISTORICAL MUSEUM — As the headquarters for the Delaware County Historical Society, the museum focuses on local history with displays and archives located in a period house that has an adjacent Annex and Library. The **Nash House** was built in the 1870s and is furnished with interesting items that reflect life in Delaware County from 1870-1890. The **Annex and Library** building houses an excellent collection of genealogy research materials and artifacts pertaining to Rutherford B. Hayes, the Little Brown Jug, and other aspects of the community's proud past.

157 East William Street; 614/369-3831. Open mid-March-mid-November. Nash House Museum is open Wed and Sun, 2-4:30. Annex and Library are open Wed, Th, and Sun, 2-4:30. Tours and winter hours by appointment. Closed major holidays. Free, but donations accepted.

Perkins Observatory

PERKINS OBSERVATORY — Located on a splendid secluded site abounding with woods and wildlife, this observatory is operated by two universities, Ohio Wesleyan and Ohio State, but it was created in the 1920s according the vision of one man, Hiram Perkins. And what a vision he had: the building that supports the gleaming observatory dome is absolutely beautiful. Perkins, a professor of mathematics and astronomy at Ohio Wesleyan, both planned and paid for the observatory, which in its form and function elegantly combines art and science. Architecturally, the building is a combination of Italian Renaissance styles punctuated with extraordinary artistic and symbolic details. The names of astronomers from antiquity to modern times are engraved in gold on marble slabs along the top of the building; the signs of the zodiac appear above columns on the exterior walls; angels clutching celestial spheres stand watch at the entrance; and a splendid frieze over the doorway depicts the Greek god Helios giving water to his horses after a day of pulling the sun across the heavens. One of the world's few curved friezes, it is a copy of one that was commissioned in the 1700s by a Cardinal in Paris and is now part of the French National Archives. Inside, the ceiling of the foyer is decorated with recessed stars designed by Perkins himself, and a wonderful floating staircase leads to the dome and telescope on the second floor. The observatory library, with its original oak tables, brass reading lamps, and vintage bookcases, is handsomely frozen in time. It also houses one of the world's largest collections of astronomy books, many of them autographed by Perkins, whose portrait and family Bible are prominently displayed there. When the observatory opened in 1931, it boasted a telescope with a 69-inch diameter reflecting mirror that was the third largest in the world. That telescope was dispatched to Arizona in the 1960s, because, alas, central Ohio is one of the cloudiest places in the nation. The present 32-inch telescope is used by astronomers for photometric and spectroscopic research, but its larger purpose has become the one that Perkins had always intended: letting the public see "the glory of God through the Glory of God's creation." Astronomy programs at the Perkins include tours, slide shows, lectures, and, of course, peeking at stars and planets through the telescope. The "32-incher," by the way, has the distinction of being the second-largest telescope in Ohio. The largest is at the University of Toledo. However, Toledo is not only almost as cloudy as Delaware, but also suffers, astronomically speaking, from considerably more artificial lights at night. Thus, asserts the ever-enthusiastic staff member Tom Burns, Perkins is the observatory with the largest *usable* telescope in Ohio.

3199 State Route 23 south of Delaware; 614/363-1257. Open to visitors Mon-Fri 2-3. Open several nights each month for public programs and viewings through the telescope; call for specific dates and times. Closed holidays. Group tours and programs by appointment. Free, but donations are accepted.

ASIDE Since Hiram Perkins flunked the Army physical, he didn't have to fight in the Civil War. Instead, he raised pigs and made a fortune selling meat to feed Union soldiers. But Perkins felt guilty about making so much money from the death and suffering of others, so he never spent it and lived quietly as a university professor in Delaware. In his final years, Perkins decided to use the money to build an observatory, and he was 90 years old when he lifted the first shovel of earth at the 1923 groundbreaking. A year later, he was dead and thus never got to see the observatory dome open up to the sky or look through the telescope. Some people say that the strange sounds heard by astronomers working late at night in the observatory are not the groans of an old building, but rather the haunting spirit of Hiram Perkins trying to study the stars from beyond the grave.

GARTH'S AND STRATFORD AUCTION CENTER — After Garth Oberlander was graduated from Ohio Wesleyan in 1938, he bought a house and barn on 210 acres just south of Delaware and started farming and buying antiques. By 1952, he was holding antique auctions and building a business that specializes in top quality Early American, English, and Continental antiques. Garth died many years ago, but two of his protégés, Tom and Carolyn Porter – they got interested in antiques as newlyweds because they couldn't afford new furniture – took over his auction house. They have maintained Garth's international reputation and hold auctions regularly at his old farm. Garth's Auctions features eighteenth and nineteenth century antiques, while Stratford Auction Center focuses on Victorian items and twentieth century collectibles. The huge barns have exposed beams and cement floors, but they are clean and well kept and provide plenty of space to hang Oriental carpets and display antiques. Garth's agents scout out antiques from all over the country, and the auction house is well-known for its handling of personal collections and estates. Although rarities such as a beaded American Indian pipe bag have sold for as high as $17,000, Tom Porter says that most of the auctioned items sell for bids between $150 and $200. Obviously, Garth's attracts plenty of serious collectors. But if you want to browse instead of buy, you can go into the barns and view everything during each auction's preview, which is held for several hours before the bidding begins.

2690 Stratford Road; 614/362-4771, 614/369-5085. Calls for times and dates of auctions. Auction catalogs for sale on site or upon request.

THE LITTLE BROWN JUG — Harness racing began informally on the country roads of Ohio, Kentucky, and Tennessee in the late 1800s, and the competition eventually moved to county fairs and then commercial tracks. The last major harness racing event still held at a county fairgrounds is the Little Brown Jug, which draws international attention – and more than 50,000 people – to the Delaware County Fair every September as the main event in five days of Grand Circuit races. Named for a famous horse that once raced on the back roads after church on Sunday, the race's official song is, of course, "Little Brown Jug," and its official trophy is a plain, but highly prized brown jug with a bronze plaque. Since the Jug began in 1946, it has grown into *the* major race for three year old pacers, and the crown jewel in harness racing's Triple Crown. A win – or loss – on Jug Day can make – or break – a horse's career. Although it is the most prestigious event in the world of harness racing, the classic is very much a Delaware event, albeit one that has been masterfully promoted by the community. Considered the fastest half-mile track in the world, the Little Brown Jug racetrack was the work of a local man, R.K. McNamara; the first Jug was won by Ensign Hanover, driven by Delaware's own Wayne "Curly" Smart; and the sights and sounds of the county fair provide a very homegrown and festive backdrop for the manicured track and its crisp white buildings. But perhaps the most telling local element of all is the tradition that Delawareans have of reserving a spot along the track by chaining lawn chairs to the fence and leaving them there from one year's Jug to the next.
At the Delaware County Fairgrounds off of U.S. 23 north; 614/363-6000. Little Brown Jug race is held the third Thursday after Labor Day.

OLENTANGY INDIAN CAVERNS — The Indians used these caverns for shelter, and Chief Leatherlips, who befriended the white men coming into the area, was put to death near the cave entrance by fellow tribesmen who took umbrage with his social connections. It is said that Leatherlips dressed himself in fancy beaded buckskin and ate a last meal of deer meat before succumbing to a tomahawk. Visitors can take tours of labyrinth-like caverns, and the underground river that formed these blue limestone caverns still flows deep beneath the rocks. There is an adjacent campground that accommodates recreational vehicles.
1779 Home Road (off of State Route 315, about six miles south of Delaware); 614/548-7917. Open Apr-Oct. Daily 9:30-5. Admission fee.

THE MARTIN-PERRY HOMESTEAD/POWELL — After rescuing this 1880s house from the path of a developer's bulldozer, The Powell-Liberty Historical Society restored and filled it with Victorian period furnishings. The homestead is the only house left in Powell in almost-original condition. It was "modernized" with electricity in 1928, but still lacks a furnace and indoor bathroom.
103 East Olentangy Street; 614/848-6210. Open the fourth weekend of every month, 1-4. Free, but donations accepted.

SHOPPING IN THE DELA-WARE AREA — Thanks to a diversity of retail shops as well as trees and flowers planted along the main commercial area on Sandusky Street, downtown Delaware is an interesting and pleasant place to visit. On the last Friday of every month, the merchants sponsor a Shop Hop featuring sales and special events such as magic shows, perfor-mances by folks singers, an Easter egg hunt, and a Christmas open house. All the shops stay open until 8 p.m. and a horse-drawn carriage takes folks for rides around town.

The Courtyard — With a lot of "blood, sweat, tears, and money," Ann Cashman trans-formed a deteriorated warehouse — it was full of opossums and had three inches of water on the floor — into an attractive emporium of furniture, home accessories, apparel, and gifts. With a tasteful eye and consider-able research, she has collected unusual wicker, brass, wood, paper, and textile items from around the world. The styles range from Shaker to Oriental, and she sells almost everything at significantly less than big city prices. *66 North Sandusky Street; 614/369-7727. Mon-Sat 10-6, Sun noon-5. MC, V.*

Rare Earth — Nicole Winston was a geology major who has turned her hobby into a retail business featuring earthly artifacts such as rocks, gems, minerals, and fossils. Much of the jewelry on display is made in the shop, and there is a fine selection of crystals, beads, pearls, and settings if you want to design your own earrings or necklace. *51 North Sandusky Street; Mon-Fri 10-6, Sat 10-5:30. AE, Discover, MC, V.*

Coffee & Tea Exchange — The coffee here comes from Central and South America, Africa, Hawaii, and Indonesia, and the green beans are roasted on the premises a pound at a time every day. Bob and Sandi Hopp's best-seller is an aromatic Colombian coffee, but you'll also find such rare coffees as Costa Rica's La Minita Tarrazu, of which no more than 700 bags are imported into the U.S. each year. You can select coffees to take home (each pound yields about 150 cups) or treat yourself to a cup of fresh cappuccino and a freshly baked biscotti in the intimate, attractive cafe located in a quiet corner of the store. *49 North Sandusky Street; 614/363-9229. Mon-Fri 9-7, Sat 9-6. MC, V.*

Essentials by C.C. Hoffman — Ms. Hoffman has filled her shop with a charming and eclectic blend of quality American antiques and personal boutique items that include cards, gifts, toiletries, clothing, and hand-crafted jewelry. She only handles antiques that are "affordable, livable, and practical," and a carefully selected stock of reference books on such subjects as antiques, furniture, and gardening lends substance to her very stylish inventory. *43 North Sandusky Street; 614/369-7003. Mon-Th 10-6, Fri 10-8, Sat 10-6, Sun noon-5. AE, MC, V.*

The Global Village Collection — Operated by volunteers with the support of local community groups and churches, this nonprofit retail store provides a marketplace for goods made by craftsmen in 35 developing countries around the world. Everything is handmade, and the selection — including silver, brass, pottery, leather, wood, and paper items — is always exotic, unusual, and diverse. *37 North Sandusky Street; 614/363-6267. Tu-Fri 11-6, Sat 10-6, Sun noon-4.*

Nectar Candyland — Anthony Zanetos's family has been making candy for about a hundred years, and the copper kettles where he makes nut brittles are the same ones that his grandfather used at the turn of the century. The selection of molded chocolates is vast and varied — you'll find novelties from dinosaurs to baseball bats — but several generations of Delawareans have satisfied their sweet tooth with the hand dipped nut clusters and barks that are still made from Zenatos family recipes. *23 North Sandusky Street; 614/362-0931. Mon-Th 9-6, Fri 9-9, Sat 9-6. Extended hours during holiday seasons.*
In areas nearby Delaware, there are also a number of intriguing places for shoppers.

The Seraph — A "high country" furniture and accessories store, The Seraph sells reproductions of American country home furnishings from the 1780-1839 time period. Owner Alexandra Pifer designs the historically correct furniture that is manufactured in The Seraph's own workshops, and many of the accessories and fabrics are supplied by craftspersons under exclusive contract to the store. *5606 State Route 37 east of Delaware; 614/369-1817. Mon-Sat 10-5. MC, V.*

"Antique District" in Powell — Powell is a village located about ten miles south of Delaware. Although new housing developments are everywhere in and around Powell, the heart of the village still retains its original rural character. Many of the old

buildings — houses, a former hardware store, even the railroad depot — along Olentangy and Liberty streets have been turned into antique and specialty shops that feature more than 100 dealers in everything from furniture and jewelry to glass and collectibles. Because the shops are concentrated in a small area, you can park along the street and walk to any of them. *State Route 750 west of State Route 315. Hours of the shops vary, but almost all are open Tu through Sun and closed Mon. Some accept MC, V.*

Groll Fine Furniture/ Waldo — If your interest is in the new rather than the old, you might want to visit this top name brand furniture store in the village of Waldo, about ten miles north of Delaware on U.S. 23. Groll's has been in business since the 1800s, and its showrooms and warehouses are spread out over so many buildings in the village — there are even have displays in an old church — that Waldo sometimes seems to be part of Groll's rather than vice versa. Bargain hunters should look in the warehouse behind the church for reduced prices on discontinued, damaged, and returned items. *149 North Marion Street; 614/726-2131. Mon, Wed, Fri 9-5:30, Tu, Th, Sat 9-9, Sun 12-5. MC, V.*

G&R TAVERN/WALDO — Although the G&R is a sports bar where Ohio State football posters set the tone for the very casual decor, the place is famous in central Ohio for its balogna. The balogna, which is specially made for the G&R, has a slight, but sassy garlic taste, and you can order it two ways: either as balogna salad similar to ham salad or as a sandwich consisting of a thick, fried slice of balogna served with a slab of onion. Both ways taste great with a cold beer and a side order of the G&R's almost-as-famous curly fries – potatoes sliced so thin they actually do curl when they're cooked.
103 Marion Street; 614/726-9685. Mon-Fri 6:30 a.m.-1 a.m., Sat 6:30 a.m.-midnight. Inexpensive.

SHAMROCK VINEYARDS/WALDO — Though all of his equipment came from Italy and he is of Irish stock, Tom Quilter has taken on the challenge of growing wine grapes in one of Ohio's colder areas. He is succeeding. Visitors to the farmland that he has turned into a vineyard and small winery will get a tour of the wine making process from grapes – Tom has 2,500 well and lovingly tended vines – to glass – his wife Mary presides at tastings in the dining room of an old farmhouse. The Quilters are knowledgeable and affable hosts, and the tastings are a leisurely and pleasantly convivial way to sample their very good wines, which are made entirely of their own hand-picked fruit. They even provide a score sheet so that visitors can rank their favorites, ranging from a very dry, oak-fermented seyval to a sweet apple dessert wine.
Rengert Road (from U.S. 23 north of Delaware, turn east on Waldo-Fulton Road, then north on Gearhiser Road, then east on Rengert Road and watch for the Shamrock Vineyard sign shortly after the Marion-Morrow County Line); 614/726-2883. Mon-Sat 1-6.

DELAWARE STATE PARK — Although it has been eclipsed in recent years by the newer, larger Alum Creek State Park, Delaware State Park remains a favorite with boaters – especially families – who appreciate its calmer, quieter waters and less crowded beach. One of the state's prettiest and best-maintained parks, Delaware has an adjacent wildlife area that harbors all manner of flora and fauna and provides plenty of green and scenic views along the east shore of the 1300-acre lake. Thanks to the efforts of local schoolteacher Richard Tuttle who built and installed breeding boxes, the park is brightened by hundreds of bluebirds with their beautiful azure and peach coloring. An extensive system of trails make all areas of the park – lake shore, campgrounds, picnic areas – easily accessible by foot or bicycle, and both boat and dock rentals are available.
5202 U.S. 23 north of Delaware; 614/369-2761 (office), 614/363-4561 (campground), 614/363-6102 (marina).

ALUM CREEK STATE PARK — With the largest – 3000 feet – inland beach in Ohio and a 3387-acre lake, Alum Creek is a very recreation-oriented and popular park that attracts millions of people every year. The lake is most heavily used south of the U.S. 36 causeway. There, a huge open zone is perfect for unlimited horsepower boating and water skiing, and the beach attracts up to 40,000 sunbathers and swimmers on a sunny weekend afternoon. The marina where boats can be rented, picnic sites, and campgrounds – with their own beach and boat ramp – are also located in this area. North of the causeway, the lake narrows and becomes more wooded and scenic. Plenty of coves around a no wake zone make it a haven for fishermen, while extensive bridle trails and primitive campsites for horsemen are located along the shore.

3615 South Old State Road; 614/548-4631.

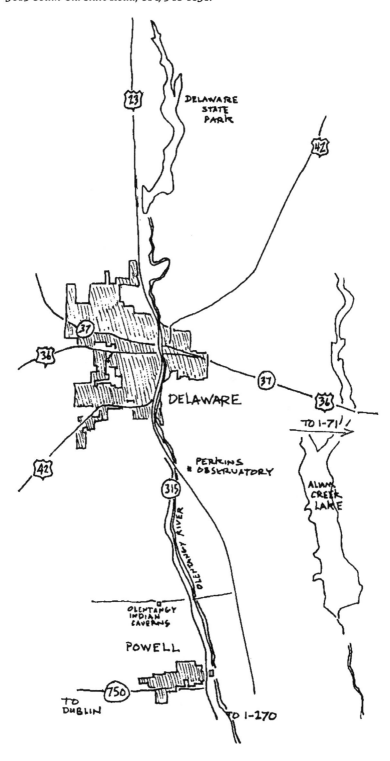

The Logan County Historical Museum

Mad River Country: Urbana, West Liberty, & Bellefontaine

Indians called the Mad River country the "smiling valley," which was — and still is — a tellingly appropriate name for this most pleasantly pretty place. Where once there was a buffalo trail, however, there is now State Route 68, which intersects Interstate 70 at Springfield and heads northward up the middle of the broad, gentle Mad River valley through the small towns of Urbana, West Liberty, and Bellefontaine. It is a singularly enjoyable drive with rolling hills poking softly at the sky, rural vistas in every direction, and surprises all along the way — a spectacular natural bog near the start; deep caverns and tall castles waiting amid the cornfields on the side roads; and Indian Lake, one of Ohio's largest and most popular recreational lakes, offering a refreshing finish at the far northern leg of the journey. ¶ The beauty of this land began during the Ice Age, when glaciers destroyed the mighty Teays River and filled its sweeping valley with vast deposits of rich silt that would make many a farmer in Champaign and Logan counties prosperous in the nineteenth and twentieth centuries. But before the land was tamed by plowshares and factories that made farm machinery, the valley belonged to the Indians. Even today, every nook and cranny of the Mad River country seems to resound with Indian lore and the legends of frontier Ohio. It was here that the rugged Indian fighter Simon Kenton ran the gauntlet; that Issac Zane, the first white man to settle in Logan County, lived with his lovely Indian princess; that Moluntha presided with his Grenadier Squaw as the Shawnee Chief of Chiefs; that General Benjamin Logan's army destroyed the *Mac ac ocheek* towns of the Shawnee and murdered Moluntha near present day West Liberty; and that the war chief Blue Jacket, who would be defeated by "Mad" Anthony Wayne at the famous Battle of Fallen Timbers, had his Shawnee town at the place now known as Bellefontaine. ¶ Historical markers seem to be everywhere, which is most convenient – and informative – for tourists unaware of the significance of this stream or that street. The number of visitors who come to Logan County every year make it one of the top ten counties in Ohio for tourism. Not only does the area have considerable scenic beauty, but it also has the good fortune to be the location for an assortment of attractions – the Top of Ohio and Cardinal Trail bicycle routes, a ski resort, the Piatt Castles, the first concrete street, the world's shortest street, the highest place in the state (Campbell Hill), and two of the lowest (the Ohio Caverns and Zane Caverns). ¶ As appealing as the outdoor and tourist attractions may be, however, the towns of the Mad River country are in and of themselves well worth a visit. Urbana, West Liberty, and Bellefontaine are pleasing to look at as well as be in, characterized by small, but lively downtowns where nineteenth century buildings harbor a wonderful variety of specialty clothing stores, fine gift shops, galleries, antique stores, and gourmet tea and coffee shops. All of Urbana's central business district is on the National Register of Historic Places, and some of the older merchants still maintain the tradition of closing their doors at noon on Wednesday. The town's focus is Monument Square with its statue of a somewhat forlorn looking Union soldier looking northward toward home. The Man on the Monument was made from melted down Confederate cannons and dedicated in 1871 by the then-governor of Ohio, Rutherford B. Hayes. The Urbana area was such an important mustering point during the Civil War – Champaign County had a total population of only 23,000, but more than 3200 of its men served in the Union army – that Lincoln's funeral train stopped there three times. In the decades after the war, retired officers joined well-to-do farmers and businessmen in building the beautiful homes that still grace Scioto Street with a smorgasbord – Queen Anne, Italianate, Gothic Revival – of architectural styles. ¶ The conservative influence of the local Mennonite community has made West Liberty, which lies midway between Urbana and Bellefontaine on State Route 68, a "dry" village. Its quaint downtown is only one block long, but is filled with interesting shops in spic-and-span Italianate buildings. Children ride bicycles on the sidewalks, in spite of plenty of signs admonishing them not to do so, and the windows at the bank sport hand-lettered posters that advertise community events such as a church chili supper. Though it is small, West Liberty has a mighty location, for it is very near to the popular castles and caverns.

¶ Bellefontaine, which means "beautiful fountain" in French and got its name because of the numerous springs in the vicinity, has been the Logan County seat since 1820. There are shade trees along the downtown sidewalks and plenty of park benches for people-watching in front of the Logan County Courthouse. Strategically located near the courthouse fountain, the eternal flame memorializing the county's war dead, and the nation's first concrete street, the benches make an especially good place to munch a sandwich at noon and take in such uniquely small town touches as the sign posted by one proprietor on the door of her store: "If the weather gets nasty, and the roads get bad, I go home."

AT HOME IN URBANA/URBANA — Shirley Ingersoll believes that coffee and tea always taste better in a china cup, and thus her bed and breakfast guests always drink from cups in her collection of English bone china. She and her husband Grant, a hospice chaplain, live in a beautifully restored house built in 1842 that is on the National Register of Historic Buildings. They peeled as many as eight layers of wallpaper off the ceiling, but the result of their hard work — and her good taste — are bright, welcoming rooms impeccably furnished with family antiques and Shirley's charming floral arrangements. The impressive bedroom set in the pretty Peach Bedroom once belonged to Grant's grandparents, and his father made the cherry desk in the foyer from a tree on the old family homestead near Urbana. A local history buff, Grant can direct visitors to the area's most significant sites, and Shirley is such a gracious hostess that she even provides a formal parlor where her guests can entertain their guests. But as good as Shirley's hospitality may be, her cooking is even better. She stages luncheons and candlelit dinners for small groups on the cherry sun porch, and she is famous for the inventive flapjacks — piña colada with fresh pineapple and rum sauce, ginger with lemon topping, and pumpkin with a sauce of mulled cider — that she serves at breakfast.

301 Scioto Street; 800/800-0970. AE, MC, V. No smoking.

Douglas Inn

DOUGLAS INN/URBANA — As Urbana's most deluxe restaurant, the inn is located in a former hotel that is a local landmark on the town square. Although its very Victorian facade dates to the 1880's, the inn actually consists of what once were several buildings constructed between 1820 and 1858. The quiet and subdued dining room is pleasantly accented by fretwork, old-fashioned chandeliers, and antique plates displayed on the walls. Although the menu offers fairly standard fare such as steaks, chicken, and pasta, local foods are featured. The source for the popular pan fried trout is Freshwater Farms of Ohio, and the house salad dressing — raspberry vinaigrette — comes from Rothschild Berry Farm, as does the raspberry mustard used on the pork tenderloin. Folks with a thirst might also want to visit the adjacent pub, the Simon Kenton Tavern.

111 Miami Street; 513/653-5585. Mon-Th 11:30-2 and 5-9; Fri 11:30-2 and 5-10; Sat 5-10. Moderate-expensive. AE, MC, V.

MUMFORD'S POTATO CHIPS AND DELI/URBANA — Folks in Champaign County have known and loved these crispy, wafer-thin chips since 1932, when Asa Mumford started cooking potatoes in an open kettle in the back of an Urbana grocery store. Today, the chips are still being made by Marilyn Leopard, who first went to work for the Mumford family back in 1957. She not only continues to use Asa's kettle-cooked process, but also has installed a deli where customers can enjoy soups and sandwiches along with the freshly-made potato chips. You can buy them by the bag, but the light, flavorful chips are so addictive that you'll probably end up buying them in bulk by the pound.
325 North Main Street; 513/653-3491. Mon-Sat 9-6.

FRESHWATER FARMS OF OHIO/URBANA — This is the one farm in Ohio where you won't find plowed fields and combines. What you will find are huge tanks of water where well-bred fish are pampered from the time they're hatched until they're served in some of the state's finest restaurants. Freshwater Farms is Ohio's only trout farm, and the farmer who harvests this uncommon crop is David Smith, a marine biologist with a doctorate in fish nutrition. He and his engineer father devised the system of raceways and tanks that uses fresh water from wells to produce some of the most wholesome, mildly-flavored fish available anywhere. His "herd" of more than 400,000 fish a year truly leads a sheltered life, for Freshwater Farms is the only place in the nation where rainbow trout are commercially raised indoors in tanks of recirculated water that has been cleaned, filtered, and oxygenated. Fed a special diet, the trout are raised under controlled conditions in a solar-heated hatchery that was once a chicken house. There, customers can not only view the tanks from which small fry will become big fish in gravel "ponds" fed by spring water, but also savor their flavor in a small retail area, where delicious, smoked trout fillets and easy-to-cook, frozen trout patties are sold.
2624 State Route 68 north; 513/652-3701. Retail store open Mon-Fri 1-6, Sat 10-6. MC, V. Group tours of the farm by appointment.

ROTHSCHILD BERRY FARM/URBANA — You may have read about Robert Rothschild's raspberry salsa in *Bon Appetit* magazine or seen his premium raspberry products at gourmet and specialty food shops throughout the United States. The source of all those absolutely delicious preserves, sauces, syrups, mustards, and salad dressings is the Rothschild family farm, where the exceptionally large and flavorful Heritage variety of red raspberries is grown in sunny fields only about three miles from Urbana. In the 1970s, Rothschild left the San Francisco area and his profession as a construction engineer for 176 acres in Ohio's Mad River Valley. He and his wife Sara now preside over not only the largest raspberry patch and herb garden in the state, but also a 25,000-square foot manufacturing facility where all of the Rothschild products are made. Rothschild foods are known for their artful packaging as well as their top-quality ingredients, and the entire gourmet line is sold in a small retail shop located on the farm. The very accommodating staff will help you make selections and will even put together customized gift baskets with delicacies such as raspberry chocolates and whole raspberries in liqueur, which are elegantly bottled in imported European glass jars and decanters. Visitors to the farm can also go into the fields to pick herbs in the summer or raspberries during late August and September. At the height of the harvest season every September, the Rothchilds host Raspberry Sunday on the farm grounds. This one-day country festival is an epicurean feast with wine tastings, a catered gourmet buffet, art exhibits, and live music by performers that have ranged from folk singers and jazz duos to the Kingston Trio.

3143 U.S. 36 East; 513/653-7397. Retail store is open Mon-Fri 8-5, Sat 9-noon. Dates vary for public herb and raspberry picking; call ahead. Admission and food tickets for September's Raspberry Sunday sell out quickly; call early for prices, date, and specific information. MC, V. Tours available for groups of 20 or more by appointment.

MAIN GRAPHICS AND URBANA VISITORS' CENTER/URBANA – Almost twenty years ago, visual artist Michael Major came to Champaign County from New York as the state's first Art-in-Residence under a program sponsored by the Ohio Arts Council. He liked the people and way of life he found in Ohio so much that he decided to stay and raise his family in the Urbana area. Today, this talented painter, illustrator, and printmaker operates a commercial design and printing business that does double – and perhaps triple – duty as a small publishing house, tourist information center, and outlet for regional books. With his great sense of history and keen interest in lithographs and etchings, Mike himself has produced several books of excellent drawings about Champaign County and other areas of Ohio. He is a fine source of information about things that have happened and are happening in Urbana, and his shop sells history books as well as historical calendars about notable locals and landmarks. Visitors will also find maps and historical walking tours of Urbana, plus wonderful postcards and notecards illustrated by Mike's own hand.

113 North Main Street; 513/653-3334. Mon-Fri 8:30-5, Sat 10-noon. MC, V.

ASIDE Although he never achieved the widespread fame of his friend and fellow frontiersman Daniel Boone, the life of Simon Kenton was inextricably bound with the history of white settlement in western Ohio and Kentucky. Indeed, by the time Kenton had taken his last breath in Zanesfield in 1836, his adventures and experiences constituted a veritable summation of the events that had overpowered the native Indians, ejected the British, and led to the development of the nation's first frontier beyond the Allegheny Mountains. Kenton served as a scout during Lord Dunmore's War, George Rogers Clark's expeditions, and "Mad" Anthony Wayne's campaigns. He fought to subdue the Indians at the Battle of Fallen Timbers in 1794, and he was at the Battle of the Thames, where Tecumseh died and the British were defeated in the War of 1812. Captured by the Indians, Kenton reportedly ran the gauntlet eight times and escaped being burned at the stake three times. He even saved Daniel Boone's life during an Indian raid on Boonesborough, Kentucky. In between battles with the Indians and the British, Kenton also fathered two broods of children by two wives; was a founder of Maysville, Kentucky; planted corn; built houses and barns; operated a store; and otherwise labored to bring civilization to the wilderness. Kenton County, Kentucky, and the city of Kenton, Ohio, are both named in honor of the man, who, ironically, left his native state of Virginia and first went west at age 16 only because he mistakenly believed he had killed a man in a fight over a girl. For the full details of Kenton's truly legendary life, consult the historical novel *The Frontiersman*, in which the noted Bellefontaine author Allen Eckert recounts how the Ohio west was won — and lost by the Indians — the author interweaving the lives and times of Kenton and Tecumseh with those of their comrades, contemporaries, friends, and foes.

OAK DALE CEMETERY/URBANA – The entrance to this old cemetery is distinguished by an Ohio Historical Society marker that identifies it as the final resting place of Simon Kenton. Take the first right turn after you go through the stone gateposts and follow the signs to reach Kenton's grave. But along the way, you will first pass by the grave of John Quincy Adams Ward, the "Father of American Sculpture." His tomb is easily recognized because it is marked by a bronze sculpture, "Indian Hunter," which is a replica of the one that Ward designed for New York's Central Park. Ward's grandfather was in business with Simon Kenton, and almost five decades after the venerable frontiersman's death in 1836, Ward was commissioned by the State of Ohio to produce a suitable memorial. The result is the impressive monument – appropriately adorned with the images of an Indian and various wild animals – that now marks Kenton's grave with a fitting phrase that aptly summarizes his life, "Full of Honors, Full of Years."
Off State Route 54 just southeast of Urbana; 7:30 a.m. until dark daily.

ASIDE When John Quincy Adams Ward's original "Indian Hunter" and "The Freedman" were displayed at the International Exhibition in Paris in 1867, they not only cemented his reputation as a first-rate artist but also secured his highly successful career as a sculptor. Born near Urbana in 1830, Ward was the grandson of William Ward, who had founded the town in 1805. Ward studied and had his studio in New York, and he was the first American sculptor whose training was totally in the United States. His outdoor statues-"Pilgrim" and "Private of the Seventh Regiment" in Central Park; "Good Samaritan" in the Boston Public Gardens; the pediment of the New York Stock Exchange — brought him popular recognition, but Ward also did busts and statues of many well-known people, including Horace Greeley and Henry Ward Beecher in New York; the Marquis de Lafayette in Burlington, Vermont; General John Reynolds in Gettysburg, Pennsylvania; and General Israel Putnam in Hartford, Connecticut. Ward had a near-obsession for accurate anatomical details, a professional standard perhaps best exhibited in his "Statue of Washington" at Federal Hall in New York City. Unveiled in 1883, it is considered one of the foremost likenesses of George Washington.

CEDAR BOG NATURE PRESERVE/URBANA — According to on-site naturalist Terry Jaworski, visiting Cedar Bog is like seeing Ohio as the mastodons saw it at the end of the Ice Age. Cedar Bog is frozen in time, a remnant of the last glacier, which destroyed the ancient Teays River and filled with limestone gravel the valley where it once flowed. Cool ground water rising to the surface of the gravel in much the same way that water bubbles from a leak in a garden hose formed the swampy "bog," which is actually a fen through which water flows rather than accumulates. Cedar Bog was Ohio's first nature preserve, and the cool, sweet water supply — the temperature is a constant 54F all year round — makes it the only fen in the state that is still surrounded by an Ice Age community of woody plants that includes northern white cedar and dwarf birch. Cedar Bog is a National Natural Landmark, and public access is limited in order to safeguard this unique, 10,000-year-old geologic and botanical area. Guided tours, however, are conducted via a well-designed boardwalk that takes visitors over the bog and past the plants and animals (many of which are rare and endangered) that it harbors — lady's-slipper orchids that bloom in the spring, yellow cinquefoil, blue fringed gentians, Milbert's tortoise shell butterflies, spotted turtles, massasauga rattlesnakes, sedges (which have edges), and grasses (which are round).
980 Woodburn Road; 513/484-3744. Apr-Sept, public tours Sat and Sun at 1 and 3; group tours by appointment. Oct-Mar, tours by appointment only.

LIBERTY HOUSE BED AND BREAKFAST/WEST LIBERTY — Sue Peterson is such a good hostess — and cook — that she has been known to get up at 5 a.m. to prepare a full breakfast for an early-rising guest. Sue, who has a baker's license, is known for the homemade breads that she sells as well as serves at breakfast. But she also prepares elegant lunches and candlelight dinners — chicken breasts in wine cream sauce, for example, accompanied by a platter of mushroom caps, candied carrots, and sautéed leeks — for small groups. Liberty House is a comfortable, turn-of-the-century home with an inviting wrap-around porch and bedrooms furnished with family antiques and brightly-colored quilts, many of which Sue makes herself. It's close to most of the area's tourist attractions and downtown West Liberty is only a short walk away, but many of Sue's guests are content to just walk through her gardens, which provide a colorfully profuse display of bulbs and flowers from April through October.
208 North Detroit Street; 513/465-1101, 800-437-8109. Lunches and dinners by pre-arrangement only. Children welcome. No smoking. No pets.

OHIO CAVERNS/WEST LIBERTY — Carved by an ancient underground river, these caverns are not only the largest in Ohio, but arguably the most colorful in the nation. Yet they were unknown until 1897, when a teenage farmhand noticed a sinkhole in a field and started digging. The slow drip of surface water through the limestone caverns over tens of millions of years has produced spectacular accumulations of calcite crystals on the floor (stalagmites) and ceiling (stalactites). These milky white formations provide a striking contrast to the colorful cavern walls, where stunning shades of red, orange, and yellow plus purple, brown, and black have been produced by oxides of iron and manganese found in the earth above the caverns. At just a shade under five feet long, the caverns' carrot-shaped, 400-pound Crystal King is the largest stalactite in Ohio. Since the caverns' crystals are still "growing" at the rate of about one cubic inch every 500 to 1000 years, the 250,000-year-old Crystal King should reach its full five foot length in several decades. The caverns also have the nation's only dual formations, consisting of both iron oxide and calcite producing individual stalactites. Touching the beautifully preserved stalactites and stalagmites is prohibited because they are quite fragile, but the tour guides do have a six-and-a-half pound, 4,000-year-old specimen called the pet rock for visitors who want to get a feel for the crystals. Tours usually last about an hour, during which you'll descend 103 feet under the ground along well-lighted passages that take full advantage of the caverns' natural beauty. Since the temperature inside the caverns is a constant 54 degrees all year, take along a sweater or jacket, even in the summer. For most of this century, the caverns have been owned by members of the Smith-Evans family, who have done a remarkable job of preserving the beauty of both the caverns and the park-like grounds where they are located. The grassy, 35-acre hilltop setting is open to the public during daylight hours and has pavilions where people can picnic or simply enjoy a fine, pastoral view of the countryside.

2210 East State Route 245; 513/465-4017. Apr 1-Oct 31 Mon-Sun 9-5; Nov 1-Mar 31 Mon-Sun 9-4. Closed Thanksgiving and Christmas Day. Admission fee. Guided tours daily.

Castle Mac-O-Chee

PIATT CASTLES/WEST LIBERTY – After the Civil War, General Abram Piatt and his brother Colonel Donn Piatt returned to their extensive estates in Ohio and built themselves neighboring castles in the countryside as a testament to both the wealth of their lands and their own success. The Shawnees who once lived in the area called it *Mac ack ocheek,* which meant "the smiling valley," and thus Abram named his castle Mac-A-Cheek, while Donn christened his Mac-O-Chee. Both of these grand structures are located in beautiful, wooded settings overlooking a lovely, still-smiling valley. Graced by tall towers, they are made of the same Columbus gray limestone that is found in the nearby Ohio Caverns and was used to construct the Ohio Statehouse. With the exception of several decades when Donn's castle was owned – and, incredibly, at one time used as barn – by outsiders, the castles have been in the Piatt family for seven generations. Abram, a gentleman farmer, patterned his castle after a Norman French chateau. His "moat" was originally a millrace, and he even provided a built-in house – which is still there – for the castle dog. Donn, who was a diplomat, editor, and writer, built his castle to mimic a Flemish chateau, and legend has it that the Hoosier poet James Whitcomb Riley was inspired to write his much-loved "When the Frost Is on the Punkin" poem while he was a guest there in the late 1800s. But as impressive as the exteriors of the castles may be, it is the interiors that are truly amazing. With the exception of the glass in the windows and the slate on the roof, all of the materials used to build Castle Mac-A-Cheek were found on the Piatt property, and the woodwork made from Abram's own oak, walnut, cherry, ash, and pine trees is extraordinary. Intricate parquet floors display several different patterns within one room, while the walls are adorned with Gothic-like arches and ten-foot tall panels made from a single piece of wood. The carved woodwork and flooring in Mac-O-Chee are similarly striking, and both castles have wonderful frescoes painted by a Frenchman who incorporated the likeness of Donn's first wife into one of the ceiling designs. The incomparable furnishings in Mac-A-Cheek have been collected by the Piatts over hundreds of years, and a massive glass-fronted display case in the drawing room still contains ancient artifacts ranging from a mastodon tooth to Native American arrowheads that were found on the property. Although its original family pieces are gone, Mac-O-Chee is nonetheless beautifully furnished with European and Asian antiques. Abram and Donn, by the way, still maintain a vigilance of sorts over their castles and small fiefdom in Ohio. They are buried side by side on a hillside in the family cemetery just 100 yards to the east of Castle Mac-A-Cheek on Township Road 47.

Two miles east of West Liberty on State Route 245; 513/465-2821. Open Mar, Sat-Sun, noon-4; Apr, Mon-Sun, noon-4; May-Sept, Mon-Sun 11-5; Oct, Mon-Sun noon-4. Groups tours by appointment. Admission fee.

ASIDE Although the decidedly different architectural vision of Abram and Donn Piatt has dazzled visitors for more than a century and a half, their castles were not opened to public tours until about 1912. The story goes that curious people doing business at the estate repeatedly asked Abram's son, William, if they could go inside to see Mac-A-Cheek. Since that man's castle really was his home, William repeatedly turned them down. Eventually, the requests got so bothersome that William decided he could discourage his friends and neighbors by asking them for money when they wanted to see the castle. Much to his surprise, they paid willingly, and the castle tour business was born.

PIONEER HOUSE/WEST LIBERTY – In 1828, Benjamin Piatt bought 1700 acres along the banks of the pretty Macochee Creek and built a 17-room log home for his family. He was the Piatt patriarch in west central Ohio, a farmer, businessman, and federal judge who had served as Quartermaster General in the War of 1812. He built mills on his land, while his wife Elizabeth constructed a Catholic church and made their hinterland mansion a stop on the Underground Railroad. Her abolitionist activities were illegal, of course, and as a circuit court judge, her husband was obliged to enforce the law. But Elizabeth supposedly "fooled" Judge Piatt by only sheltering runaway slaves when he was not at home. Two of the Piatt's children, Abram and Donn, built the famous nearby castles, but the historic house where they grew up had largely been forgotten until the 1970s, when David and Jane Younkman bought 25 acres of land and were astonished to discover the badly deteriorated, but venerable log building tucked back in the woods on their property. They spent many years and dollars to authentically restore the Piatt manse, and today the old fireplaces and black walnut stairs provide a delightful setting for the fine gift shop that Jane operates. She has filled the charming rooms with select antiques, folk art, toys, baskets, dried flowers, herbs, everlastings, candles, quilts, and handmade items from the local Mennonite community. Even the upstairs room where runaways were once hidden has been outfitted with candles in the window, soft sculpture "slaves," and a door. Yes, a door...just so folks won't have to enter by crawling through the attic as they did before the Civil War. *10245 Township Road 47 (just east of Castle Mac-a-Cheek); 513/465-4801. Open May 1-Dec 31. Mon-Sat 11-5, Sun 1-5. MC, V. Tours by pre-arrangement.*

MAD RIVER THEATER WORKS/WEST LIBERTY – The history, folklore, and storytelling tradition of the rural Midwest is the inspiration for the original plays written and produced by the Mad River Theater Works. Founded more than a decade ago by the multi-talented actor, writer, producer, and director Jeff Hooper, this professional company of actors and musicians not only premiers new works every summer at its theater facility near West Liberty, but also includes a touring ensemble that performs a repertoire of plays throughout the nation. Employing music as well as drama to portray regional stories and events, the very creative productions have included *Shooting Star*, which was about Ohio's own legendary Annie Oakley, and *Freedom Bound*, the true story of how the people of Mechanicburg, Ohio, armed themselves with knives and pitchforks to prevent federal authorities from returning runaway slave Addison White to his Kentucky master. The audience can also participate in pre and post performance events such as dinners, receptions, and meetings with the cast and crew. And on the Fourth of July, the theater works hosts a "non traditional" Independence Day celebration featuring folk music and poetry readings given by the light of a huge bonfire. *Six miles east of West Liberty on State Route 287 (follow the signs from downtown West Liberty and look for the tent theater); 513/465-1580. Performances mid-June through mid-August. Wed-Sun at 8 p.m. Reservations strongly recommended. MC, V.*

THE MARKET PLACE/WEST LIBERTY – Housed in a beautifully renovated barn more than 100 years old, this unusual shop is as big on quality as well as it is on floor space. Proprietor Jane Vourlas has tapped the talents of more than 70 local artisans, who supply The Market Place with top notch gift and decorative items. From potpourri and jewelry to the bears made from old quilts, virtually everything in the shop is handmade and charmingly displayed on numerous antiques in the barn's attractive white oak and stone interior. Jane also sells "country" foods such as fresh produce, sorghum, cider, and Amish-made baked goods, meats, and cheese. And folks with a sweet tooth will want to have a piece of "the world's best baklava," which Jane's daughter makes from scratch every day.
One mile south of West Liberty on U.S. 68; 513/465-8728. Open May 1-Oct 31. Mon-Sun 10-6. Christmas Open House, first weekend in Nov, Fri 5-9, Sat-Sun 10-6. Open winter weekends mid-Nov-mid-Dec, Fri-Sun 10-6. MC, V.

GLOBAL CRAFTS/WEST LIBERTY – A rural village is an unlikely place to find whistles and flutes from Cameroon or filigree jewelry made in Nepal, but the Mennonite Central Committee sponsors one of the most international shops in Ohio in West Liberty's tiny downtown. Global Crafts is a sales outlet for low-income craftspeople in developing countries through a Mennonite self-help program that has put needy people to work for almost 50 years. Since some 35,000 craftspeople in more than 30 countries participate in the program, Global Crafts is a true world bazaar. Staffed by volunteers, the shop abounds with unusual and exotic items – untold kinds of baskets from Bangladesh, paintings by Haitian artists, rattan trays and tables woven in Laos, and a handsome, ten-foot tall giraffe made in Kenya. Even the greeting cards are individually designed on handmade paper.
106 North Detroit Street; 513/465-3077. Mon, Tu, Th, Fri 10-5; Wed, Sat 10-4. Closed Sunday. Discover, MC, V.

MARIE'S CANDIES/WEST LIBERTY – The chocolates at Marie's are so addictive that a lot of people claim that they can't even drive through West Liberty without stopping for a pound of smooth raspberry creams or a box of the caramel and pecan turkins. Marie King began making candy in the 1940s as gifts for kindly friends and neighbors who had helped during her husband Winfred's bout with polio. Marie's peppermint chews were such a success that she and her husband started a candy business, which their son Jay now operates in the modest red brick house where Marie once lived. All of the candy is homemade and handmade on the premises and sold in a small, but well-stocked retail store where you can buy chocolates by the piece or by the pound. From the top quality ingredients – premium chocolate, 40 percent cream, and just-roasted nuts – to the exceptional selection of more than 70 centers and seasonal novelties – Marie's sells nothing less than the best. Indeed, even the aroma of the chocolate is so rich and inviting that one woman we know likes to go into the store just to *inhale.*
311 Zanesfield Road; 513/465-3061. Mon-Sat 8-6. MC, V.

ACCESS – County Road 5 is one of the most scenic routes in Logan County. It veers to the northeast off State Route 68 at the north edge of West Liberty, then snakes toward Zanesfield along, between, and around the hills for more than twelve miles. All along the way, there are great views, blinds curves, unexpected bumps, brightly painted barns, tall silos, and the ever-present but chameleon-like cornfields – green in summer, golden in fall, snow-whitened in winter, and blackened by freshly turned soil in the spring.

MYEERAH'S INN/ZANESFIELD – Myeerah was a proud and powerful Indian princess, the product of the union between a French woman and Tarhe, Chief of the Wyandots. Her beauty was so extraordinary that the Indians gave her their name for the white crane, a rare and magnificent bird. When the White Crane grew up, she married the man whom the Wyandots called White Eagle. He was Issac Zane, who had been captured by the Indians when he was only nine years old and was raised along with Myeerah in Tarhe's village at the site of present-day Zanesfield. More than 200 years have passed since Myeerah and Issac lived along the banks of the Mad River, but when Joan Failor started her bed and breakfast, she gave it the name of the famous princess. The inn is a simple brick building that was once a stagecoach stop, and in a nod to Myeerah's heritage, Joan has given it comfortable French country furnishings and serves filling French country food at breakfast. Although Zanesfield is a quiet country village, it is located so close to the Piatt Castles, Ohio Caverns, and Mad River Mountain ski area that Joan provides bicycles so her guests can ride to these attractions. Just a few yards from the inn, a massive boulder serves as a monument to the pioneering efforts of both Simon Kenton and Issac Zane. But history-minded visitors need travel no farther than the backyard of the inn, where they will find memorials indicating the grave sites of the lovely Myeerah and her beloved Issac. *Corner of Columbus and Sandusky streets; 513/593-3746, 513/593-4793.*

ASIDE The last decades of the eighteenth century were a time of much trouble on the Ohio frontier as white settlement increasingly threatened the Indians' lands and way of life. Killing was commonplace, but the successful marriage of Issac Zane and Princess Myeerah was an uncommon example of harmony between the races fighting to control the land. At Zanesfield, Myeerah and Issac raised seven children, grew old together, and died within a few months of each other in 1816. The story of their early lives and romance is told in no better place than the biographical novel *Betty Zane*. While the book focuses on Betty Zane and her heroism during the siege of Fort Henry, West Virginia, which was the final battle of the American Revolution, it also tells much about the lives of Betty's famous brothers, Ebenezer and Issac. Ebenezer was the frontier trailblazer whom George Washington hired to cut the first National Road from Fort Henry to Maysville, Kentucky, and he also started the towns of Wheeling and Martin's Ferry in West Virginia as well as Bridgeport and Zanesville in Ohio. As a young man, Issac was torn between Myeerah's affection and his loyalty to his own people. During one of his attempts to return to white civilization, he was captured by a hostile Seneca chief and was about to be burned at the stake when

Princess Myeerah rescued him. Theirs was a wonderful and adventurous love story, and it is beautifully told on the pages of *Betty Zane* by author Zane Grey. Grey, of course, was a descendent of the Zane clan and had been born in Zanesville in 1872. He planned to be a dentist, but after writing and publishing *Betty Zane* at his own expense in the early 1900s, Grey abandoned dentistry and embarked on a remarkable writing career in which he became not only one of the nation's most prolific and best-selling authors but also the acknowledged "Father of the Adult Western."

DR. EARL S. SLOAN LIBRARY/ZANESFIELD — When Earl Sloan was a little boy in Zanesfield, his family was poor, and they lived in a house with a dirt floor. Young Earl loved to read, and he asked a man in town if he could borrow some books. The man took one look at the bedraggled boy and replied that he would never lend books to anyone who was so dirty. An Indian woman had given Sloan's father a recipe for a horse liniment, and after the Civil War Sloan went west to market the potion. He had no medical training but when he began advertising that "Dr." Sloan's liniment was as good for men as it was for beasts, sales zoomed. Sloan became a millionaire, and in 1914, he built a library for his hometown so that scruffy little boys in Zanesfield would never again be denied the chance to read. The library is a small, but lovely building with an architecture that fosters a certain old-fashioned respect for erudition. Fireplaces in the reading rooms practically invite folks to lose themselves in a book for an afternoon, and the trustees have kept the Sloan library so true to its origins that it is the only library in Ohio that does not have a telephone. The original oak library tables and chairs are still being used, and so is Sloan's enormous clock, which the librarian winds every week or so by standing on a ladder. An Italian piece with a solid gold face, the clock has garish gargoyles and sweet cherubs incongruously carved in the mahogany case. The library also serves as a small museum of local history. Glass display cases hold powder horns, Indian hatchets, an old-fashioned beaver hat, and, of course, bottles of Sloan's liniment, which smells vaguely like turpentine and is still being made by a major pharmaceutical company.
2817 Sandusky Street. Tu and Th 1-7, Wed and Fri 1-5, Sat 10-1. Closed last week of June and first week of July.

MAD RIVER MOUNTAIN SKI RESORT/VALLEY HI — Colorado it's not, but with a 300-foot vertical drop and runs as long as 3000 feet, Mad River Mountain is a convenient, accessible ski area for novices as well as seasoned skiers. As western Ohio's only downhill ski resort, it offers the only trail skiing in state, as well as bargain-priced, all-night "Midnight Madness" skiing on the weekends. Snowmaking machines keep the six slopes and trails white and ready all winter, and the chair lift affords a fine view of the surrounding valley. The facility includes a small motel, lounge, restaurant, and pro shop.
10 Snow Valley Road (five miles east of Bellefontaine off of U.S. 33); 513/599-1015. Motel open all year. Skiing Dec 1-Mar 31, Mon-Sun 9:30 a.m.-10 p.m. Midnight Madness skiing Fri-Sat 11 p.m.-4 a.m. AE, DC, Discover, MC, V.

Rollicking Hills

ROLLICKING HILLS FARM/DEGRAFF — Set on a picturesque wooded
bluff overlooking a lush valley carved by a river of glacial meltwater,
this historic farm is both a bed and breakfast and a peaceful, rustic
resort. Owned by retired schoolteachers Bob and Susie Smithers, the
farm has been in Susie's family since before the Civil War, and she was
born in the comfortable, rambling farmhouse. The original part of the
house was an Indian trading post in the late 1700s, but now the
primary visitors are overnight guests who stay in bedrooms furnished
with family antiques, quilts, and ruffled curtains. The clawfoot tub in
the bathroom dates back nearly a hundred years, and the huge
spinning wheel on the staircase was brought to Ohio in a covered
wagon. Three porches outfitted with rocking chairs entice guests to
just sit and watch the corn grow on this working farm, but Rollicking
Hills also offers plenty to do — horseback riding, hayrides, cross-
country skiing, swimming in the in-ground pool, hiking the hills along
miles of wooded trails, and canoeing and fishing for 22-inch bass in the
five-acre lake. In addition to the horses, the animals in residence
include a pair of friendly Great Danes, assorted barn cats, cows,
chickens, goats, and llamas. Yes, llamas. The Smithers discovered
these gentle South American animals during a trip to Holland — Bob
can tell you *that* story — several years ago, and they have since become
one of the state's more successful llama breeders. Susie spins the
llamas' fine, soft wool into yarn that she uses to make sweaters, and
the small herd they keep in the barn includes pert-eared Myeerah, who
won a blue ribbon at the state fair a few years back. The llamas have
also become a favorite among local kindergartners learning the
alphabet. Teachers call the farm and say, "Mr. Smithers, we're on the
letter "L," do you think you could bring over a llama?"
2 Rollicking Hills Lane (off of County Road 11 east of DeGraff); 513/
585-5161. Children welcome. No smoking or use of alcohol.

WHITMORE HOUSE/BELLEFONTAINE – At Whitmore House, you can have everything from tea in the English gazebo to a wedding reception...and the staff will even design and make the bride's gown. Sandra Musser operates a catering business, banquet and meeting facility, by-reservation-only restaurant, and a bed and breakfast in a grand old country house with lovely grounds and formal gardens about four miles west of Bellefontaine. Built in the 1870s by a Southern family that originally came to Ohio because they did not believe in slavery, the house was a local showplace for years, and folks used to drive for miles just to look at the colored lights decorating the house at Christmas time. Sandra and her husband Carey have completely renovated the house and appointed it with Country French and Victorian furnishings that provide a tasteful setting for business, social, or family events. The extensive and imaginative food selections are changed every three months, and Sandra provides pre-arranged breakfasts, lunches, and dinners that are custom-made from the appetizers to the dessert tray. Bed and breakfast guests not only are greeted with a complimentary fruit basket, but also get to choose their own evening snack from the Whitmore House catering booklet. *3985 State Route 47 West; 513/592-4290. Dining by reservation only. Moderate-expensive. Closed Easter Sunday, Mother's Day, Thanksgiving Day, and Christmas Day.*

BELLEFONTAINE BESTS – Though it has a population of only 12,000, Bellefontaine is blessed with several unusual points of interests that would be the envy of even far larger and more cosmopolitan places. The **world's shortest street,** for example, is McKinley Street, a 30-foot long piece of pavement located between Columbus Avenue and Garfield Avenue on the western edge of downtown Bellefontaine. The street was named for William McKinley, who is said to have campaigned for President from the caboose of a train stopped on the nearby railroad tracks. Court Street on the south side of the Logan County Courthouse was – and still is – the **first concrete street in America.** It was poured in 1893, by George Bartholomew, a mustachioed traveling hardware salesman who purchased a marl pit north of town and experimented with limestone and clay in a makeshift laboratory in a Bellefontaine drug store until he found the "wet" method for making Portland cement. Court Street is no longer open to traffic, having been turned into a city park complete with a statue of Mr. Bartholomew, and picnic tables and benches made of – what else? – concrete. The **highest point in Ohio** is Campbell Hill, which is 1550 feet above sea level and is located on the grounds of the aptly-named Hi-Point Joint Vocational School. The school is located about one mile east of Bellefontaine on State Route 540. Turn south onto the entrance of the school grounds and follow the signs to Ohio's top spot, a modest-looking knoll located just past the carpentry and animal care buildings. Campbell Hill used to be the location of a military radar station, and the installation's old buildings are still there, along with a flag pole and plaque that explains the significance of the site. Campbell Hill is an end moraine that was formed more than 20,000 years ago, when till and gravel left behind by the Wisconsinan glacier accumulated against an expanse of high bedrock known as the Bellefontaine Outlier.

ASIDE In 1891, George Bartholomew convinced the Bellefontaine town council to let him put an experimental, eight-foot wide strip of his "artificial stone" — the word "concrete" was not yet in use — on a Main Street crosswalk. The skeptical council members agreed only after Bartholomew posted a $5,000 bond and guaranteed that his Portland cement would last five years. In order to prove the practicality of using concrete on roads, Bartholomew two years later donated the Portland cement needed to pave the four streets surrounding the Logan County Courthouse. Court Street was the first one completed, and the project was such a success that engineers and city officials from all over the world came to Bellefontaine to look at the concrete streets. A piece of Bartholomew's eight-foot crosswalk was exhibited at the World's Fair in Chicago, where it received a gold medal for advancing paving technology. Bartholomew's streets in Bellefontaine not only proved that concrete paving was superior to cobblestones, bricks, and even macadam, but also ultimately changed the way the nation got around.

THE LOGAN COUNTY HISTORICAL MUSEUM/BELLEFONTAINE – In the early 1900s, William Orr used to enjoy sitting in a swing on his mansion's grand front porch. That mansion is now the focal point of the Logan County Historical Museum, and it's worth a visit there just to see Mr. Orr's lovely, curvilinear porch with its white Grecian columns. Since he was in the lumber business, the woodwork throughout the house – especially in the foyer – is superb, and many items that belonged to Mr. Orr and his wife – his desk in the upstairs den; her collection of Limoges plates in the dining room – are on display. The remainder of this unusually large local museum serves as a kind of attic for the entire county. Various theme rooms – Indian, Physician's Office, Schoolroom, Military – contain interesting memorabilia that have been donated by area residents. The museum also houses an extensive genealogy collection; significant archives of local history, newspapers, and photographs; and a very good gift shop that features a fine selection of books on Logan County history as well as the complete works of Allen Eckert, a well-respected local historical novelist.
521 East Columbus Avenue; 513/593-7557. Open May 1-Nov. 1. Wed, Fri, Sat, Sun 1-5. Free, but donations are welcome. Group tours by appointment.

ZANE CAVERNS AND BLUEJACKET CAMPGROUND/ BELLEFONTAINE – The entrance to these very rough and craggy caverns is situated, ironically, in sublime rural isolation atop a beautifully scenic wooded bluff. Although the caverns are between seven and ten million years old, they weren't discovered until 1892, when a hunter watched his dog disappear down a hole in the ground. The often-narrow nooks and crannies in these limestone caverns delight serious spelunkers, but most visitors are happy to simply follow behind the tour guides along the well-lighted pathways that drop about 132 feet below the ground. While the extremely rare white "cave pearls" formed by dripping water have made Zane Caverns famous, flowstone is common throughout the caverns. The fancifully-named formations — "beehives" and "Niagara Falls" — have been capturing people's imagination since the 1920s, when visitors were lowered into the caves in large baskets with only a single candle to light their way through the pitch-dark passages. But folks who prefer to enjoy the wonders of nature *above* the ground will find plenty of trees and green grass at the Bluejacket Campground, which is located above the caverns. The campground boasts great views; acres of woods and hiking trails; ponds for swimming and fishing; and an unusual variety of camping experiences. If you're a conventional camper, you can bunk in an RV with lights and running water, or you could pitch a tent in a remote area that has no roads or electricity. But for something different, try sleeping in the covered wagon or in any of the screened-in "nests" — eagle's, owl's, and hawk's — that are perched among the treetops.

7092 State Route 540 east; 513/592-0891. Apr 1-30 Fri-Sun 10-5; May 1-Sept 30 Mon-Sun 10-5; Oct 1-31 Fri-Sun 10-5. Admission fee. Group tours by appointment. Bluejacket Campground is open the same dates and days as the caverns.

COUNTRY VARIETY STORE AND COUNTRY BAKED GOODS/ BELLEFONTAINE — In the quiet Amish countryside about four miles north of Bellefontaine, Marion Schrock's general store has a hitching post as well as a parking lot; smoked hams hanging outside on the porch; seemingly endless stacks of bulk candies, spices, and staples; and assorted signs that exhort customers to turn off the TV and read the Bible. His polite and pretty daughters produce absolutely marvelous breads and pastries in an small, adjacent bakery that is illuminated by gas lights. Lattice-topped fruit pies made from family recipes are set out to cool on racks in the salesroom, and the truly heavenly angel food cakes have the consistency of velvet. Luscious cinnamon and pecan rolls are available anytime, but the young ladies only bake cream pies and dinner rolls on Saturday.

6263 State Route 68 north; 513/464-7093. Variety store is open Mon-Sat 8-6. Bakery is open Wed-Sat 8-6.

INDIAN LAKE — About eight miles northwest of Bellefontaine, Mother Nature once created a series of small kettle lakes from glacial melt water. In the 1850s, a bulkhead was built at the source of the Great Miami River, and those several lakes became one large reservoir that served as a feeder lake to keep the Miami and Erie Canal at constant depth of four feet. After the canal was abandoned, the State of Ohio took control of the reservoir, and the Indian Lake recreation area was born in the early 1900s. By World War II, amusement parks and dance halls that attracted the big bands of Glenn Miller, Guy Lombardo, Stan Kenton, and Sammy Kay made Indian Lake an enormously popular summer resort known as the "Midwest's Million Dollar Playground." Today, only the bridge that once connected the amusement parks in the lakeside village of Russells Point remains from the heyday when excursion boats plied the lake and tourists arrived by the trainload. Instead, ski boats now speed across the water, and families and retirees arrive in station wagons or campers. All manner of cottages, campgrounds, motels, marinas, taverns, eateries, and souvenir shops rim this fairly shallow (the depth varies between three and fifteen feet), 5800-acre lake, and the McDonald's restaurant in Russells Point is one of only two in the state that you can get to by boat. Indian Lake State Park is unique in Ohio because the facilities are not concentrated in one area, but rather spread out over various parts of the lake, thus offering the public a variety of year-round recreation opportunities — scenic campsites for tents and trailers, hiking trails, swimming beaches, picnic shelters, boat ramps, docks, and snowmobiling. One of the top five lakes in Ohio for bass fishing, Indian Lake is also excellent for crappie and saugeye. Located along a primary migration route, Indian Lake is a major resting and nesting area for Canada geese, swans, ducks, egrets, and other birds, and the 60-nest blue heron rookery on Big Walnut Isle is especially easy to spot in the fall and winter. A fine 1.5 mile biking and walking path skirts State Route 366 along the southwest side of the lake, where the flat shoreline offers irresistible opportunities for impromptu picnicking and fishing, as well as cool cross breezes on warm days and expansive, uninterrupted views of the water. A well-channeled game preserve area at the northeast corner of the lake near Pony Island affords the most scenic boating, but some of the prettiest land areas — and nicest homes — on Indian Lake are located on Shawnee, Seminole, and the other islands accessed from the Buckeye Drive causeway. All of the islands offer wonderful views of the lake, but the best of all is from the trail that circles Pew Island. Although the lighted buoys at Indian Lake glow prettily every night, the lake is at its brightest on the Fourth of July, when colorful fireworks boom out over the water and every inch of the lake is covered with boaters eyeing the display.

State park visitor center is located at 12774 State Route 235 north, Lakeview; call 513/843-2717 for the park office or 513/843-3553 for the campground. Tourist information is available from the Indian Lake Chamber of Commerce, 126 Orchard Island Road, Russells Point; 513/843-5392.

BICKHAM AND McCOLLY COVERED BRIDGES — Two Howe truss covered bridges built in the 1870s are located in the countryside near Indian Lake, both attended by herds of rather indifferent cows that just go right on grazing and ignore motorists who disturb the rural tranquility by tooting their horns to make the bridges echo as they drive through. Located about six miles south of the lake, the McColly Covered Bridge spans the Great Miami River and is about 125 feet long. The Bickham Covered Bridge is about one mile east of Indian Lake. Less than 100 feet long, it crosses the south fork of the Great Miami River.

McColly Covered Bridge is on County Road 13 west off State Route 235. Bickham Covered Bridge is on County Road 38 north of State Route 366.

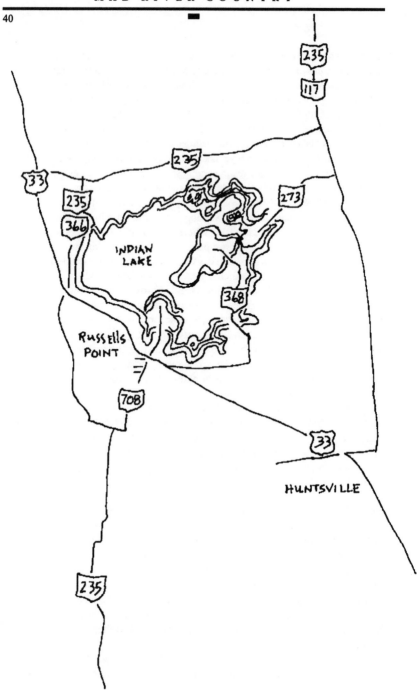

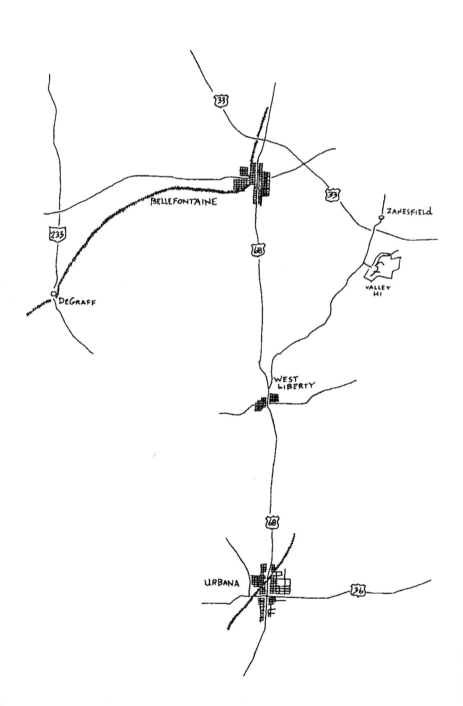

The Miami County Court House
The South Facade

The Great Miami River Tour, Part 1: Tipp City & Troy

It has been written that every river is the cradle of its own civilization, and in west central Ohio, the Great Miami River has nurtured the four pleasant and historic towns of Tipp City, Troy, Piqua, and Sidney. Each is located only a few miles from the other, and each was started in the first decades of the nineteenth century by pioneers and entrepreneurs in search of land, fortune, opportunity, and, often, destiny. Troy and Sidney became county seats, and their citizens built grand courthouses as a public display of community pride and prosperity. Piqua was platted on land that had once been an Indian village, and Tipp City, the youngest of the four towns, was founded in 1840 on the pure imagination of John Clark, a land speculator who thought that the intersection of State Route 571 and the Miami and Erie Canal had wonderful possibilities. ¶ For centuries, it had been the Great Miami that brought a succession of people – the Adena; the Miami; the Shawnee; French and English explorers, soldiers and traders; and finally American settlers – to the fertile till plains left behind by the glaciers, but in the nineteenth century, that changed when the new canals and railroads brought population and prosperity to the entire state. With their location along the Miami and Erie Canal and railroad lines, the four towns boomed. The canal brought German immigrants, the railroad brought the Irish, and both brought new industry and commerce that resulted in the towns producing some of America's most "American" products. Troy had WACO airplanes and KitchenAid appliances; Piqua, the "Underwear Capital of the World," was the home of the union suit; and Benjamin Slusser invented and manufactured the steel road scraper in Sidney. The towns became proud, hardworking, enterprising places, where people built fine homes on shady streets and the wealthy displayed a splendidly civic sense of noblesse oblige in the form of cultural and recreational facilities and community foundations. ¶ Today, of course, the role of the river is recreational, for the economic importance of that liquid thread has been eclipsed by the concrete thread of the interstate that now skirts all of the towns. Tipp City considers its location near the intersection of I-70 and 75 so fortuitous that it calls itself the "Crossroads of America," and fittingly, the radar detector dubbed the "Fuzz Buster" was invented there in the 1960s by Dale Smith. The interstate has brought the towns shopping centers and fast food franchises at the interchanges, but it also has attracted new, light industries such as BFGoodrich, which makes the brakes for the space shuttle in Troy, and a new set of immigrants — the Japanese, who have a Honda distribution facility and Panasonic picture tube plant near Troy. ¶ Although it is the interstate that now connects the towns to the world at large, it is still the Great Miami that gives them character, grace, and style. The four are far enough from any sizable city to escape the suburban sprawl that highways often bring. Thus, they still have real downtowns — attractive, commercially viable places where folks can park, shop, stroll the sidewalks, and greet their neighbors — and a real sense of their heritage as communities whose roots lie with the river. They now celebrate their past and create historic districts to preserve their best buildings and nineteenth century storefronts. Tipp City's quaint downtown enjoys a growing reputation as a mecca for antique lovers and dealers; Troy, with its good restaurants, recreational facilities, and cultural events, is a gem of a town; Piqua has a top-notch historical area; and Sidney's square is an architectural treasure chest. Given their geography, it might be tempting to call them sister cities, but that would be a mistake, for each town fiercely guards its own identity. Their townspeople are not merely Upper Miami Valley residents, they are first Tipp Citians, Piquads (pronounced Pick-wads), Trojans, and Sidneyites. ¶ And should there be any lingering doubt about their individuality, consider the matter of the location of the Miami County Courthouse. For more than seventy years, Piqua and Troy battled over where to put the courthouse. Piqua argued that it had the advantage of a larger population, and Troy countered that it was more centrally located. Some say their political rivalry grew so fierce that citizens from each town met at a bridge, exchanged epithets, and nearly came to blows. The Court House War finally had to be settled by the Ohio General Assembly, which in 1884, sent representatives to both towns to determine their suitablity as a county seat. When the lawmakers decided in favor of Troy, Piqua charged that the Trojans had bought their influence with "wine, whiskey, and even champagne." Troy, however, got not only the courthouse, but also what would seem to be the last laugh: the large statute of Justice that stands atop the courthouse dome was placed – some say purposely – with her back turned toward Piqua.

SAM AND ETHEL'S/TIPP CITY — The Moore family has been defining good taste in Tipp City for almost 40 years with home style cooking that has become as much a town landmark as the 150-year old building – it's on the National Register of Historic Places – where this warm and friendly little restaurant is located. Although the pork tenderloin and pan-fried chicken have given Sam and Ethel's a tall reputation, lots of folks claim the place has the best breakfast in the county, with old-fashioned favorites such as biscuits and gravy, fried mush, corned beef hash, and cinnamon toast. The buckwheat pancakes are superb and so huge that they hug the edge of an entire dinner plate. Before digging in, you might want to consult the instructions posted on the wall for pointers on how to properly tackle a Sam and Ethel's pancake. *34 East Main Street; 513/667-3435. Mon-Fri 6:30 a.m.-8 p.m., Sat 6:30 a.m.-11 a.m., Sun 7:30 a.m.-12:30 p.m. Inexpensive.*

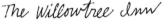

The Willowtree Inn

WILLOW TREE INN/TIPP CITY — A few years ago, Tom and Peggy Nordquist were celebrating their anniversary at this lovely bed and breakfast when they found out that it was for sale. They liked the inn so much that they bought it – pond, ducks, and willow tree – and have been welcoming guests ever since. The main part of this country mansion was completed in 1830 by Samuel Pearson, a Quaker settler who copied its Federalist styling from his old home in North Carolina. Mr. Pearson's original plank floors and bookcases still grace the front parlor, and the pretty spring house he designed and built with his own hands still stands in the backyard. Colonial furnishings, a country breakfast, and cozy bathrobes make guests feel welcome. Brides and grooms especially like the second story Blue Room, which has an adjoining sitting room and a screened-in porch above the rose garden. *1900 West State Route 571; 513/667-2957. MC, V.*

THE POTTER'S HOUSE COFFEE SHOP/TIPP CITY — An intimate cafe located on the main floor of the Hotel Gallery, the Potter's House takes its name from proprietor Sally Watson's occupation as well as the Biblical admonition to "get up and make your way down to the potter's house." Plenty of people are following that advice, for while the fare here is light – soups, pastries, gourmet coffees and teas – the ambiance is heavy with conversation and conviviality. Guitarists and piano players provide lively entertainment on the weekends, and since a fiddle and mandolin are standard fixtures in The Potter's House, customers have been known to grab an instrument and spontaneously start to play after the paid musicians have gone home. *107 East Main Street; 513/667-3696. Tu-Th 10-5, Fri 10-10, Sat 10-6, Sun 12-5. Inexpensive. MC, V.*

PADDY'S TIPPECANOE INN/TIPP CITY — Many years ago when proprietor Patrick Phelan was in real estate, he couldn't sell this restaurant, so he ended up buying the place himself and turning it into one of Tipp City's favorite gathering spots. But what else would you

expect from a man who reads cookbooks for fun and collects them by the dozen? Located in an historic downtown building, Paddy's is a friendly, pleasant pub know for fresh fish, good steaks, and excellent shrimp cocktail cooked in a special blend of spices. The beautiful inlaid wood bar dates to the 1940s, and Mr. Phelan's considerable collection of mirrored liquor signs decorates the walls. On St. Patrick's Day, Paddy's always hosts a properly Irish celebration complete with brass bands, but every Friday and Saturday night, a honky tonk piano player entertains the crowd with the hundreds of songs he knows by heart.
102 East Main Street; 513/667-9980. Mon-Sat 11-11, Sun 3-9. Moderate. D, MC, V.

THE NEW WEST MILTON INN/WEST MILTON — As befits a better restaurant in a rural village, the inn has a comfortable, country formal atmosphere with lace curtains and shutters on the windows and bright, floral linens on the tables. The inn has been a favorite destination for diners since 1927, and the current menu features traditional American favorites such as prime rib, filet mignon, rainbow trout, and baked pork chops. Although homemade cakes rank high on the dessert list, the best way to end a meal here is to stroll outside for a look at the beautiful 30-foot waterfall that cascades through a narrow gorge behind the inn.
136 North Miami Street (corner of State Routes 571 and 48); 513/ 698-4744. Mon-Th, Sun 11 a.m.-9 p.m., Fri-Sat 11 a.m.-11 p.m. AE, Discover, MC, V. Moderate-Expensive

PEARSON HOUSE/WEST MILTON — The former lobby of an old West Milton hotel is now one of the dining rooms where Bob and Beth Bianco serve some of the best home cooking in Miami County. Although furnishings may be humble, the made-from-scratch breads, buns, pastries, pies, and muffins are first class. Entrees lean toward old-fashioned comfort foods like ham loaf or chicken pot pie, but every cup of coffee comes served with the Biancos' own special touch: a tiny Italian cookie called biscotti.
28 North Miami Street; 513/698-6665. Mon-Sun 7 a.m.-9 p.m. MC, V. Inexpensive.

ASIDE Tipp City was originally named Tippecanoe because of the snappy slogan used in a presidential campaign. In 1811, General William Henry Harrison successfully defeated the Indians at the Battle of Tippecanoe in Indiana. The battle made him a national hero, but it was the last hurrah for the native Americans, whose defeat marked the end of the Indian confederacy that Tecumseh had organized to stop the whites' territorial and cultural encroachment. Harrison later capitalized on his famous victory when he became the Whig candidate for President with John Tyler as his running mate in 1840. Their patriotic campaign slogan "Tippecanoe and Tyler, too" not only handily helped to usher Harrison into the White House, but was also John Clark's inspiration for the name of his new town in Ohio. The Whigs had also used what was supposed to be a disparaging newspaper article about Harrison's lowly log cabin ambitions to give their candidate a common touch. Harrison had actually been born on a Virginia plantation, but the campaign's public relations magic made him the nation's first — but certainly not last — presidential candidate to make political hay out of log cabin origins. Ironically, when Clark named Tippecanoe in honor of Harrison's candidacy, he banned log structures from the new town. Frame and brick were used instead, which is one of the reasons so many of the early buildings still stand today. The name Tippecanoe served the town for nearly a hundred years, before it was officially shortened to Tipp City in 1938.

SHOPPING IN THE TIPPECANOE HISTORICAL DISTRICT/TIPP CITY

The Old Tippecanoe City Restoration Area is one mile east and, happily, a century or so removed from I-75 and the monotonous shopping centers that such expressways spawn. Building after building along Main Street is on the National Register of Historic Places, and the 1839 Roller Mill adjacent to the remnant of the old canal lock near Main and First streets was actually the place where Tipp City began. During the canal's heyday, there were so many saloons and pool halls along the north side of Main Street that respectable ladies never set foot there, but instead navigated the town via the south side. Today, the original wood floors and tin ceilings of those same buildings provide charming settings for the wonderful array of specialty shops concentrated on Main Street and North Second Street. Antique malls abound, while various boutiques feature the work of local artisans and craft persons. You'll find interesting and unusual items from primitive and Victorian furniture to a weaving studio/artists' gallery where soft shawls in vibrant colors are displayed along side stained glass and oil paintings. Some of the more notable shops are featured in this chapter, but since you can park your car along the street and easily walk anywhere you want to go, you'll want to stroll the historic district and explore the many unique shops on your own.

THE HOTEL GALLERY/TIPP CITY — Steve Watson is such an enthusiastic and unabashed promoter of Tipp City that he even named his son "Tyler" after the motto that gave the town its name. Several years ago, he rescued a downtown hotel built in 1850 from the wrecking ball by restoring it and filling the former sleeping rooms with specialty shops, art galleries, and artisans' workshops. The hotel is now the retail hub of Tipp City's historic district, with modern day shoppers instead of nineteenth century canal workers climbing the original spiral staircase to canvass three floors of diverse arts and antiques. The shops range from the Tin Peddler, which specializes in handcrafted reproductions, to The Moccasin Corner, a fascinating collection of American Indian art and artifacts that is almost a mini-museum of beautifully beaded, antique garments made by various tribes. In the summertime, Steve's wife Sally often sets her potter's wheel – and young children – on the sidewalk in front of the hotel, where she is joined by other artists working at their easels and sketch pads. And in the open area behind the hotel known as The Commons, Steve has even installed a reproduction of an Indian teepee that sets the stage for all manner of fair-weather, community-oriented events – bluegrass music concerts, craft demonstrations, horse-drawn carriage

rides, hot dog roasts, and soup pot suppers.
*107 East Main Street; 513/667-3696. Tu-Th 10-6, Fri 10-9, Sat 10-6,
Sun noon-5. MC, V.*

BENKIN ANTIQUE GALLERY/TIPP CITY — Ben Staub says that since
he works along with many of his kin, "Benkin" was a logical name for
this 10,000 square-foot antique mall with more than 40 dealers. In the
1900s, the building belonged to a funeral director, and there are still a
couple of old coffins – empty, of course – lurking in the basement.
While the entire gallery offers a wide variety of antiques, Ben has put
his personal stamp on the selections by offering an unusually large
number of vintage sporting goods geared toward men – old hunting
vests, canvas minnow baskets, fishing reels and lures from the 1930s
and 1940s, and beautifully preserved wickerwork creels. An antique
car buff and former tool maker, Ben makes and sells reproductions of
Visi Bowl Gas Pumps and has installed a replica of an old-fashioned
filling station in his sales area. He also stocks a wealth of automotive
memorabilia – traffic lights, glass gas pump globes, Cleveland clocks,
and old drive-in movie speakers.
*14 East Main Street; 513/667-5975. Mon-Sat 10-5, Sun 1-5. Closed
holidays. MC, V.*

TIPPECANOE FRONTIER TRADING COMPANY/TIPP CITY —
Twenty years ago, Mara and Ernie Back sold their handmade leather
goods by traveling to malls and craft shows. Today, their general store
is a singular establishment devoted to early American and frontier
items for history buffs and sportsmen, and the Backs cater to an
international clientele via a hefty mail order catalog. Specializing in the
era from 1740 to 1840, the trading company has thousands of hard-to-
find and unusual items – tinder boxes, powder horns, tomahawks,
blacksmith tools, reproduction swords and bayonets, sport bags for
powder shooters, and real coonskin caps. A mecca for people involved
in historical reenactments, the trading company even sells authentic
patterns for breeches, waistcoats, bustle ball gowns, and other
garments worn in days gone by. Ernie restores antique rifles in the
back room, but the trading company also sells everything needed –
the locks, stocks, and barrels – to fashion a firearm.
*114 East Main Street; 513/667-1816. Tu-Th 10-6, Fri 10-8, Sat 10-5.
Discover, MC, V.*

BROWSE AWHILE BOOKS/TIPP CITY — With 77,000 used, rare, and
antiquarian books in stock, browsing through this very complete –
and neat – store's warren of shelf-filled rooms does indeed take a
while. An entire room is devoted solely to histories and biographies;
another holds nothing but mystery, crime, and men's adventure books.
There are three different sections of titles just for children, and the
rows of western and historical novels go on and on. If you can't find
the book you're looking for, just ask Sue Cantrell, the genial clerk who
is so knowledgeable that you'll think she has the entire inventory
memorized.
*118 East Main Street; 513/667-7200. Mon-Th 10-6, Fri 10-8, Sat 10-4.
Discover, MC, V.*

BUCKEYE BOUNTY/TIPP CITY — The fancy pecans come from Oakwood; the honey mustard from Urbana; the apple butter from Wilmot; and the barbecue sauce from Springboro. Buckeye Bounty specializes in gift baskets packed with made-in-Ohio products, and their imaginative offerings include options from a complete Buckeye breakfast to a tailgate party. Or, use your own imagination to customize a basket for a friend with everything from bean soup (from Boswell Beanery) to peanuts (from Dayton Nut). The baskets themselves, of course, are also all the handiwork of Ohio artisans, which explains why you can even order one shaped exactly like the Buckeye State. *40 West Main Street; 513/667-8864; 800/446-8864. Mon-Fri, noon-4. MC, V.*

TROPHY NUT STORE/TIPP CITY — Located in an historic building that was once a wheelwright's shop, this factory outlet for Ohio's largest nut processor offers an incredible variety of nuts, dried fruits, chocolates, and old-fashioned candies. Customers help themselves from the long rows of bins that line the walls, and you can easily spend a half hour just trying to decide which kind of peanuts – there are more than a dozen varieties plus peanut butter and peanut candies – you want to buy. *320 North Second Street; 513/667-4448. Mon-Fri 9-5, Sat 9-2. MC, V.*

SPRING HILL NURSERIES AND GARDEN CENTER/TIPP CITY — Spring Hill has been in Tipp City since 1849 when it was founded by a German immigrant who started taking orders for plants by mail. It has since evolved into one of the largest mail order nurseries in the nation, and the annual catalog has put Tipp City, Ohio, on the map for many an armchair gardener. Spring Hill's immense garden center has almost ten acres of greenhouses that produce more than 25 million plants a year, including the exclusive Audrey Hepburn and Eternity roses. *110 West Elm Street; 513/667-4079. Mon-Fri 9-7, Sat 8-6, Sun 10-5. AE, Discover, MC, V.*

HERITAGE VINEYARDS/WEST MILTON — Ed and Sandy Stefanko's two-story tasting room is in a remodeled, hundred-year old barn with high windows that afford sweeping views of the surrounding farm fields and countryside. Ed makes the wine – their semi-dry Heritage White and semi-sweet Catawba are popular choices – from their own grapes, while Sandy serves up bargain-priced sample trays of six different wines. In the summer time, customers like to sit outside at the picnic tables on the lawn, and when the Dayton Air Show is going on at the nearby airport in Vandalia, they get a unique treat – a perfect view of the aerial acrobatics while they imbibe their favorite wine. *6020 South Wheelock Road (five miles east of Tipp City off of State Route 571); 513/698-5369. Fri 5-10, Sat 1-10.*

CHARLESTON FALLS PRESERVE/TIPP CITY — The centerpiece of this 169-acre nature preserve is a showy, 37-foot waterfall that naturalists call a "Miniature Niagara." The cascade has a long geologic history that includes two primordial oceans and a glacier, but most visitors are content to ignore the ancient earth and concentrate instead on the beauty of the falls and the rare plants such as wild columbine and rock honeysuckle that cling to its limestone gorge. The hike from

the parking lot – look for the self-guided tour brochures as you enter –
to the falls is only a half mile or so, but those who venture the trails
beyond it will be rewarded with such natural wonders as a limestone
cave and a tall grass prairie.
*On Ross Road, west off of State Route 202 about five miles south of
Tipp City; 513/667-1086. Dawn to dusk daily. Picnic area, but no
cooking fires are permitted.*

THE MUM FESTIVAL/TIPP CITY — Although most of the activities are
held in City Park, the streets and sidewalks of Tipp City's old downtown have been permanently painted with colorful mums in tribute to
the annual festival that has been a local tradition since 1959. Supposedly the inspiration of a Tipp City man who witnessed a Mum Festival
in a European town during World War II, the event features a classic
car cruise-in, a fun run, dances, live music, and two parades – one for
people and one for their pets.
Fourth weekend in September; 513/667-8300.

THE W.H. ALLEN VILLA/TROY — Located among the many splendid
old homes in Troy's charming Southwest Historic District, the Villa
was built in 1874 by W.H. Allen, owner of the largest factory in town,
the Troy Spring and Wagon Company. The three-story house has been
impeccably restored and furnished in Victorian style by proprietor
June Smith, a quiet woman of many antiques, who provides guests
with well-appointed rooms and their own self-serve snack bar.
434 South Market Street; 513/335-1181. AE, MC, V.

LA PIAZZA PASTA AND GRILL/TROY — In Italian, "La Piazza" means
"the Square," which perfectly describes this festive restaurant's
location in the heart of downtown Troy. Owned by the Anticoli family
that has operated one of Dayton's favorite restaurants for more than 60
years, La Piazza combines a traditional Italian menu with a very
untraditional, engaging decor of faux granite, broken walls, and a
purely decorative "staircase." Although your eye may be fooled, your
stomach won't be – the food is wonderfully prepared, portions are
plentiful, and the crusty Italian bread served with garlicky herb butter
and olive oil is almost a meal in itself. You might want to start with
Bruschetta Margherita, the authentic Italian appetizer of toast topped
with fresh tomatoes and basil, but do finish with a cup of the excellent
– and very frothy – cappuccino.
*2 North Market Street; 513/339-5553, 800/572-2330. Mon-Th 11:30
a.m.-2 p.m., 4:30 p.m.-11 p.m. Fri 11:30 a.m.-2 p.m., 4:30 p.m.-12 p.m.
Sat 4:30 p.m.-12 p.m. Sun 11:30 a.m.-9 p.m. Moderate-expensive. MC, V.*

TAGGART'S/TROY — Folks should probably only go to Taggart's in
pairs. That's because the best seats in the house are commodious wing
chairs, and they're found only at the tables for two. Located on the
town square, Taggart's is the latest establishment to occupy the
historic Dye Building, which previously housed a bank, a ballroom,
and a dime store. Richly decorated with wainscoting and traditional
burgundy-and-hunter green furnishings, Taggart's has an extensive
menu of updated American favorites and a comfortable ambiance.
*7 South Market Street; 513/39-8911. Mon-Fri 11-9, Sat 11-2 and 5-10.
Moderate-expensive. AE, Discover, DC, MC, V.*

K'S/TROY — Paul and Doris Klein have been feeding hamburgers, grilled cheese sandwiches, and gelatin salads to folks in Troy since 1935. In 1992, they were the Grand Marshals of the town's Strawberry Festival parade, which was an altogether fitting honor since their restaurant has probably served more people than any other establishment in Troy. For several generations, K's has been such a favorite haunt of high school students that a local newspaper once opined, "Who can call himself a Trojan if he hasn't been to K's?". The diner is *the* gathering spot in Troy, the place where people go to talk politics, trade goings-on and gossip, and find out who is running for office and who has had gall bladder surgery. Although Vice-President Quayle dropped in – for a milkshake and two cheeseburgers to go – during the 1992 election campaign, Mr. Klein is more likely to tell about the time years ago that a drunken man kept talking to a nicely dressed woman sitting next to him at the counter. Mr. Klein inquired if the drunk was bothering her, and when she said yes, he told the man to leave. After he was gone, Mr. Klein asked the woman, "Did you know that man?" "Yes," she replied. "He's my husband."
117 East Main Street; 513/339-3902. Mon-Sat 6 a.m.-10 p.m. Inexpensive.

CJ'S HIGH MARKS/TROY — Dining here is like going back to school, except that school was never this much fun and the cafeteria never served food this good. High Marks gets high marks for both its varied menu – the choices range from grilled chicken salad to Alaskan king crab – and its smart school house theme. In the lobby, the front half of a cheery yellow school bus greets diners, who have their choice of three cleverly decorated dining areas: the Study Hall, which has oversized pencils and crayons; the Locker Room, with its bar and mini basketball court; and the Library, where shelves of books separate the booths. In fair weather, they can also go to Recess, an outside dining deck. Although High Marks is famous for all of its appetizers, the one that rates an A+ is the Paul Bunyon Onion, an onion so artfully cut and breaded that it looks like a giant flower when it arrives at your table.
1750 West Main Street (Interstate 75 at State Route 41); 513/335-6569. Mon-Th 11-10:30, Fri-Sat 11 a.m.-11:30 p.m., Sun 10:30 a.m.-10 p.m. Moderate-Expensive. MC, V.

ASIDE Troy got its name because some of its first settlers brought copies of Homer's *Iliad* and *Odyssey* with them to Ohio. Since many of them had staved off the British in George Washington's Continental Army, they no doubt had a ready appreciation for how well ancient Troy withstood the attacks of the Greeks.

MIAMI COUNTY COURTHOUSE/TROY — Ever since it opened in 1888, this magnificent courthouse has been called "Miami's Pride." Architect J.W. Yost modeled the central dome after the dome of the U.S. Capitol, and he added four ancillary domes, a 160-foot clock tower, Corinthian columns, and rows of classic arches to produce what is arguably the handsomest courthouse in the state. With its inlaid tile floors and fine frescoes, the beautifully maintained interior is as impressive as the exterior. Especially notable are the figures of faces

in the third floor rotunda that represent the races of people that populate the nation.
West Main and Plum streets; Mon-Fri 9-5.

ASIDE The heart of Troy's historic downtown is a wide Public Square with a lovely illuminated fountain at its center. The square is formed by the meeting of Main and Market Steets, which the town's founding fathers supposedly made broad enough so that a farm wagon and team of horses could turn around. Modern drivers, however, have not always fared so well in the negotiating the square, for the traffic circle formed by the fountain is legendary for confusing drivers and snarling automobiles. The best way to get through unscathed is to remember this rule of the road: drivers in the inside lane have to yield at all times.

TROY CITY PARK/TROY — Bordered by a golf course on the south and the Miami County Fairgrounds to the north, this superb park stretches more than a mile along the Great Miami River in the heart of Troy. The park boasts picnic facilities, a swimming pool, a stadium, and the river levee, which in itself serves as a fine recreational spot. In winter, the levee is the town's favorite spot for sledding; in summer, it's the site of Troy's famed Strawberry Festival; and all year long, runners and walkers alike enjoy a unique fitness trail with specific exercise instructions laid out along the top of the levee. The jewel of this pretty park, however, is Hobart Arena, an outstanding ice rink and entertainment facility. The arena not only is the scene of concerts, circuses, trade shows, ice hockey games, and figure skating competitions, but also offers year-round public skating and serves as a training ground for Olympic judges.
Access the park from Adams Street between Staunton Road and Water Street. Hobart Arena is at 255 Adams Street; 513/339-5145. Public skating Fri 7:30 p.m.-10 p.m., Sat-Sun 2:30 p.m.-4:45 p.m. and 7:30 p.m.-10 p.m.

HOBART WELDED SCULPTURE PARK/TROY — The Hobart Institute of Welding Technology is the Harvard of welding schools, an esteemed training program that teaches advanced and specialized welding skills. The institute's Welded Sculpture Workshop once attracted students and artists from around the world, and they have created an unusual and intriguing collection of more than a dozen metal sculptures, which are displayed on the lawn of the school. Created in 1967, George Tsutakawa's *Unity of Man* is one of the nation's largest welded bronze fountains. Its tall, totem-like column symbolizes the past, present, and future of the family, while the water expresses the continuity of life. *The Sound Chamber* designed by Michael Bashaw is the latest – and perhaps most innovative – of the sculptures. Inspired by the musical ceremonial structures used by Pacific islanders, the steel and aluminum work incorporates thump pianos that actually allow visitors to "play" the sculpture.
400 Trade Square East; 513/332-5000. Dawn to dusk daily.

TROY-HAYNER CULTURAL CENTER/TROY — On the National Register of Historic Places, the Cultural Center was once the grand home of Mary Jane Hayner, an ardent prohibitionist who liked to lead temperance marches in spite of the fact that her husband made his fortune selling whiskey. Mrs. Hayner was a stellar hostess, and her home was the scene of frequent parties, receptions, and musicales. She would be pleased that it is once again filled with people, laughter, music, art, and applause, for the beautiful manse now functions as the local focal point for community events, cultural programs, and the visual and performing arts. The Center is also the home of the Troy Historical and Genealogical Library, whose extensive collection of research materials — some family records date back to the 1700s — is housed in Mrs. Hayner's former dining room.

301 West Main Street; 513/339-0457. Cultural Center is open Mon 7 p.m.-9 p.m., Tu-Th 9 a.m.-5 p.m. and 7 p.m.-9 p.m., Fri-Sat 9-5, Sun 1-5. Closed holidays. Historical and Genealogical Library is open Tu-Wed 10 a.m.-4 p.m. and 7 p.m.-9 p.m., Th-Sat 10-4, Sun 1-4. Closed holidays.

The Tavern of Benjamin Overfield

OVERFIELD TAVERN/TROY — A beautifully restored and authentically furnished hewed-log building, the tavern was built as an inn by Troy pioneer Benjamin Overfield in 1808. It was Troy's first tavern, school, hotel, and courthouse. Visitors are greeted by guides in frontier costumes, who explain the "noggin" on the bar, the antique kitchen implements hanging on the working fireplace, and where the judge and lawyers sat in the upstairs "courtroom." They also proudly point out treasures such a drum used in the War of 1812, a one-of-a-kind powder horn bearing a hand-carved map of western Ohio, and a circa 1804 leather cartridge pouch that is only one of three in existence. In spite of the tavern's importance to early Troy history, its exact location was forgotten for many years, for the logs had been covered with siding and the building was used as a residence. The tavern might still be in disguise had it not been for Edward Hobart, a local captain of industry and history buff who literally uncovered it in 1948. The story goes that his historical research led Mr. Hobart to the tavern's probable location, and late one night when the family who lived there was away, he quietly went down to East Water Street. Mr. Hobart drilled under the siding, and — *voila!* — the venerable lost logs

were found.
201 East Water Street; 513/339-6206. Open Mar 1-Nov 30. Th and Sun 2-5. Closed Thanksgiving, Christmas, New Year's, July 4. Free. Group tours by appointment.

MUSEUM OF TROY HISTORY/TROY — Focusing on life in Troy in particular and in the Midwest in general from the Antebellum through Post World War II periods, the museum serves as a fine historical companion to the pioneer-era Overfield Tavern across the street. It is located in a house built by a local tailor, John Kitchen, in 1847, and the stone lintels installed over the doors and windows are characteristic of that time. The parlor has been furnished to reflect the period from 1870-1880, and museum's wonderful collection of vintage clothing features a veritable timeline of wedding dresses.
124 East Water Street; 513/339-6206. Open Mar 1-Nov 30. Th and Sun 2-5. Closed Thanksgiving, Christmas, New Year's, July 4. Free. Group tours by appointment.

BRUKNER NATURE CENTER/TROY — From the stand of 55,000 mature pines to the forest of hardwoods, hepaticas, and ferns that covers the high hillsides above the pretty Stillwater River, the Brukner Nature Center is a 165-acre natural wonder amid the cultivated fields of Miami County. This internationally known nature preserve and wildlife rehabilitation facility began in the 1930s, when Clayton Brukner, the successful Troy aircraft manufacturer who built the famous pre-World War WACO airplanes, bought most of the center's present property and turned it into a wildlife refuge. The center is remarkable for its diversity of habitats as well as the network of ten hiking trails that crisscross the preserve. The trails are at their scenic best in the spring, when thousands of gorgeous wildflowers on the hills and ravines are in full bloom. Educational programs are held in both the modern Interpretive Center and the restored Iddings Log House, which dates to 1804 and is on the National Register of Historic Places as Miami County's oldest log structure still on its original site. The center's wildlife rehabilitation program started years ago when someone left a box of baby bunnies on the doorstep, and many of the permanently disabled animals – including foxes, raccoons, a bald eagle from Alaska, and a blind barn owl – that cannot be returned to the wild are kept at the interpretive building for educational purposes. The building's viewing rooms are the preserve's best place for watching wildlife. The second floor viewing room is a glass-walled area cantilevered into the treetops for a truly bird's eye view of the avian population, while the ground floor viewing room has one-way glass so that animals feeding only inches away won't be disturbed by human observations. Though the sights and sounds of the Nature Center are a wonderful experience, you might cap off your visit by driving a short distance west on Horseshoe Bend Road until you come to the bend – a hairpin turn on a steep hillside that provides not only an exciting, grip-the-steering wheel ride but also a sparkling vista of the Stillwater River.
5995 Horseshoe Bend Road, off of State Route 55 about 5 miles west of Troy; 513/698-6493. Interpretive Center is open Mon-Sat 9-5, Sun 12:30-5. Closed holidays. Nominal admission on Sundays. Trails are open dawn to dusk daily.

LITTLE PROFESSOR BOOK CENTER/TROY — Location may be everything in real estate, but for bibliophiles, it's selection, and with more than 20,000 titles in stock, Jay and Mary Vernau offer one of the deeper inventories around. They also have one of the top-grossing Little Professor stores in the nation, thanks in no small part to their outstanding children's book section. Not only is the store famous for hosting little people's literary events such as American Girls tea parties, but Clifford the Dog, the Berenstain bears, and other popular characters have also come to visit.
1849 West Main Street in the Troy Towne Center; 513/335-1167. Mon-Sat 10-9, Sun noon-5. AE, Discover, MC, V.

THE TIN MAN/TROY — Once the president of a well-known Troy corporation, James Hastings turned his hobby into a business when he retired and became the Tin Man. He makes brass, copper, and tin reproductions of lamps, lanterns, chandeliers, and wall sconces patterned after original Colonial and museum pieces. All of his wares are hand-formed using hand tools, and they are so authentic that he has done work for Colonial Williamsburg. Since Mr. Hastings makes each piece individually, no two are alike, and visitors can watch him working in his shop through a large window in the showroom.
537 North Elm Street; 513/339-2315. Mon-Sat 9-5, Evenings by appointment. MC, V.

STILLWATER WINERY/TROY — Allen and Peggy Jones operate the only underground winery in the state. The entire facilities – wine press, cellar, and multi-window tasting room – are buried beneath several feet of soil. The subterranean design is perfect for storing their wine at a constant 52 degrees Fahrenheit. It's also perfect for their customers, thanks to two cozy stone fireplaces in the tasting room that take the chill out of the air, but not out of the wine.
2311 West State Route 55; 513/698-6165. Fri 4:30-11, Sat 1-11.

TROY STRAWBERRY FESTIVAL/TROY — Strawberries are the first fruit of the summer in Ohio, and every June, Troy gets the season off to a tasty start with a tribute to the strawberry that has become one of the state's best-known and best-loved community festivals. More than 150,000 people consume some 10,000 quarts of berries during the two-day event, where they are treated to strawberry shortcake, strawberry ice cream, strawberry yogurt, and the all-time festival favorite, strawberry doughnuts. Hundreds of food and craft booths dot the lovely banks of the river levee, where folks can view a hot air balloon rally and canoe races on the Great Miami. The food is great, the crafts are all handmade, and the fun – pie eating contests, classic car and baseball card shows, bed races, and a Saturday morning Main Street parade with farm tractors pulling floats – is all homegrown. So are most of the berries, for much of the festival's fruit and inspiration comes from Bill and Joyce Fulton, whose Fulton Farms just south of Troy on State Route 202 is one of the largest strawberry producers east of the Mississippi River. Troy fancies itself "The Strawberry Capital of the Midwest," and just to prove the point, the water in the fountain on the town square runs pink throughout the festival.
First full weekend in June; 513/339-7714, 800/348-8993.

THE LIGHTS AT LUDLOW FALLS — Every December, the local Fire Department strings tens of thousands of colored lights over the broad gorge at spectacular Ludlow Falls. Since this village has only about 300 people, that averages out to several hundred lights per capita, which is a wonderfully telling ratio for one of Ohio's best holiday displays of grassroots good cheer. The tradition began in the late 1940s, when a local boy scout troop hung twenty lights over the falls at Ludlow Creek. Then the Ludlow Falls Fire Department took over, and the firefighters have since spent thousands of hours stringing miles of wire every Christmas. The event attracts more than 100,000 people every year, and the firefighters keep a running tally on a blackboard posted in the station.

About six miles southwest of Troy at the bridge just north of the intersection of State Route 55 and State Route 48; 513/698-3318.

ELDEAN COVERED BRIDGE/TROY — One of only about 70 covered bridges in Ohio that still carry traffic, this two-span structure was built over the Great Miami River in 1860 and is on the National Bridge Register. At 223-feet, it is also the second-longest covered bridge in the state. As you drive through it, notice the multiple wooden triangular trusses that are typical of Ohio's "Long truss" bridges.

On Eldean Road east of County Road 25-A, about three miles north of Troy

---

ASIDE Born and raised near present Tipp City, Robert W. Smith was trained as a carpenter, and his formal education consisted only of a six-week course in geometry; yet he invented one of the most significant of all covered bridge designs, the "double truss bridge." Smith was working as a house carpenter and barn builder in old Tippecanoe City when he patented his famous design in 1867. It had two sets of posts and braces, and the truss was built with two vertical posts at the ends and center, providing for a lightweight, but strong bridge that was relatively inexpensive to build. The double truss soon became one of the most popular covered bridge designs in the Midwest, and between 1867 and 1869 alone, the Smith Bridge Company built more than a hundred bridges. Soon after receiving his patent, Smith relocated his bridge company in Toledo, where he developed another innovation that anticipated today's pre-fabricated houses: pre-framed bridges that were built in Toledo, disassembled, shipped, and then reassembled on site.

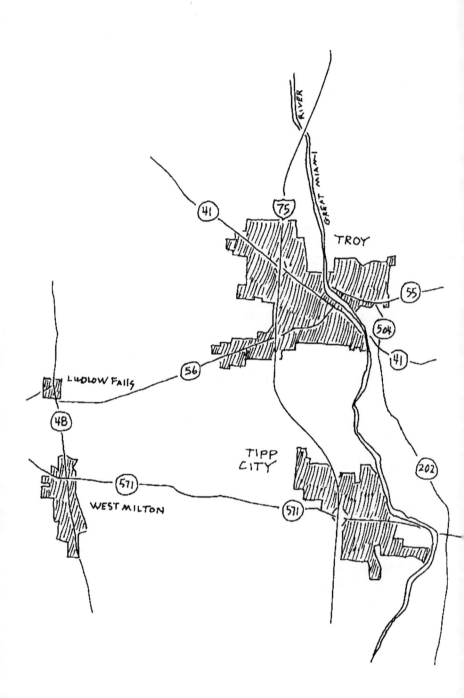

:THE :PEOPLES: FEDERAL : SAVINGS :&: LOAN: ASSN:

THRIFT

Bank Building · Louis H. Sullivan

The Great Miami River Tour, Part 2: Piqua & Sidney

The canal and railroads not only spurred new
industry in nineteenth century Piqua and Sidney,
they also sparked a building boom that resulted
in an architectural bonanza for both towns.
Happily, many beautiful and historic buildings
have been preserved both in a 23-block area of
Piqua, as well as in downtown Sidney, where
almost every edifice is on the National Register of
Historic Places. Bounded by Riverside Drive,
North Main Street, West High Street, and

Caldwell Street, the Piqua-Caldwell Historic
District encompasses private residences,
churches, and commercial structures that display
an exceptional diversity of architectural styles
ranging from 1820s Federal to 1930s Art Deco. ¶
The Hotel Fort Piqua at West High and North
Main streets was built a hundred years ago and
although it has been closed to guests for years,
the Richardson Romanesque stonework and
towers give this landmark building the formidable appearance of a medieval fortress still
guarding the heart of the town. The most famous
house in Piqua was built in 1907 at 650 North
Downing Street by Leo Flesh, one of the town's
underwear manufacturing kings. At the turn of
the century, it was the fashion among wealthy
industrialists to build grand houses as a testament
to their success, and Mr. Flesh spared no expense. The only Chateauesque style residence
town, his mansion imitates the enormous country
houses of sixteenth century France, and its
matching carriage house is a copy of a villa given
to Marie Antoinette by Louis XVI. ¶ On the east
side of Courthouse Square in Sidney, the commercial buildings along Main Street present a
pristine High Italianate streetscape that has not
been significantly altered since 1900. Defined by
Poplar Street, Main Avenue, Court Street, and
Ohio Avenue, the square constitutes the hub of
Sidney's historic district, but the most architecturally remarkable place in town is the intersection of Ohio Avenue and Court Street. ¶ The
northeast corner is the site of Sidney's most
prominent building, the Shelby County Courthouse. Built in 1881, this very decorative French

Second Empire courthouse has a mansard roof, symmetrical sides, and projecting pavilions at the entries. It is a fine example of the nineteenth century civic chauvinism that inspired communities to fund elaborate public buildings. ¶ On the northwest corner, the Monumental Building is an imposing Victorian Gothic structure and a Civil War memorial that once housed every municipal service from the library to the fire department. Today, a bronze statue, "Soldier in Blue," still proudly surveys downtown Sidney from a high niche in the center pediment of the front facade. ¶ The southwest and southeast corners have landmark buildings that are individually profiled later in this chapter – The Spot restaurant and the Louis Sullivan bank building. Sullivan's edifice, especially, is a true work of art, for it is not only the most architecturally significant structure in Sidney, but also one of the most important in the state. Walking through the streets of Piqua and Sidney truly is stepping back in time, and maps and additional information about both towns' architectural trove are available from the Piqua Historical Society *(124 West Greene Street; 513/773-2307)* and the Sidney-Shelby County Chamber of Commerce *(100 South Main Street, Suite 201; 513/492-9122).*

ALLISTEN MANOR/PIQUA — From the moment you use the telephone intalled in the the driveway to open the electronic gate and summon a valet to park your car, it's obvious that Allisten Manor is an extraordinary dining experience. The setting is a 160-year old country manse elegantly restored and operated by Sue and Don Smith, the well-known Piqua caterers who inadvertently got into the business by catering their own wedding. Their guests were so impressed that one week after their nuptials, the Smiths were catering another couple's wedding and launching their business. With its romantic fireplaces, luxurious furnishings, and custom menus, their lovely manor house is

Allisten Manor

today the scene of weddings, parties, receptions, and other celebrations. Allisten Manor is also open for leisurely lunches and pre-arranged dinners. The imaginative, perfectly prepared selections change every two months, except for the Smiths' famous Chateaubriand, a perennial favorite that is always on the dinner menu. *858 Garbry Road; 513/778-0848. Lunch, Mon-Fri 11-1. Dinner by reservation only. Moderate-expensive.*

OLDE CANAL COFFEE SHOP/PIQUA — The canal used to be located just outside the back door, but it probably never had as much traffic then as this coffee shop does now. The place is crowded, noisy, and friendly. The women who work behind the counter are in constant motion, and everybody is on a first-name basis with everybody else. You can get breakfast here anytime, and the freshly baked biscuits are a fine accompaniment to "Molly's mess," a savory concoction of eggs, sausage, and hash browns all mixed together to a single plate. *213 North Main Street; 513/773-7101. Mon-Fri 5 a.m.-4 p.m., Sat 5 a.m.-2 p.m. Inexpensive.*

GRANDMA'S KITCHEN/COVINGTON — The cooks at this family restaurant are local women who use made-from-scratch Dunkard recipes to make some of the best chicken and noodle dinners in the state. From the morning's sausage gravy and biscuits to the evening's meatloaf and bread pudding, everything here is homemade. The bakery turns out giant pecan tea rings, super pies and cakes, and wonderful breads that people can also purchase to take home. *8262 West State Route 41; 513/473-3031. Mon-Sat 7 a.m.-9 p.m., Sun 8 a.m.-9 p.m. Inexpensive-Moderate. MC, V*

BUFFALO JACK'S/COVINGTON — This tavern has been a Covington landmark and neighborhood bar since the doors opened in 1886, but it wasn't until Jack Maier acquired the place several years ago that eating here became an adventure. The rattlesnake on the menu comes from the Gulf shore, the alligator from Louisiana, and the buffalo from Montana. Wild and exotic game dinners are the specialty at Buffalo Jack's, where a buffalo head hung above the bar and assorted other mounted animals — squirrels, foxes, deer, raccoons — are displayed along the walls. An avid sportsman, Jack uses recipes obtained from his American Indian friends to prepare elk chops, antelope sausages, and delicious deep-fried alligator meat. But folks with timid palates will also find chicken, steak, and all-you-can-eat walleye specials on the menu. For side orders, try the tangy coleslaw and crusty potato wedges. And top everything off with a tame-but tasty-apple dumpling. *137 South High Street, Covington; 513/473-2524. Mon-Th 6 a.m.-10 p.m., Fri-Sat, 6 a.m.-11 p.m., Sun 7 a.m.-1 p.m. Inexpensive-expensive.*

ASIDE The name of Piqua comes from an ancient Shawnee legend. A warrior rose from the ashes of a burning fire, causing the Indians to exclaim, "Otath-he-waugh-Pe-Qua," which means "man formed from the ashes."

PIQUA HISTORICAL MUSEUM/PIQUA — Although the building itself was constructed in the 1830s and first used as a grocery store, the museum's remarkable Romanesque facade of red sandstone was designed later by J.W. Yost, who also masterminded the Miami County courthouse and the museum's architectural big brother, the grand Hotel Plaza (a.k.a. Hotel Fort Piqua) on Piqua's town square. The exhibits constitute a veritable timeline of Piqua and the Upper Miami Valley from prehistoric people to fast food artifacts and features items manufactured in Piqua, such as the Favorite brand stoves once popular in the United States, Europe, and Asia. A humorous mural in the second floor gallery of local artists depicts the Troy-Piqua feud over the courthouse and the cannon on the courthouse lawn in Troy that some disgruntled Piqua boys allegedly sank into a lake. The underwear exhibit has tiny salesmen's samples fit more for dolls than humans and what well may be the world's biggest-size 66-briefs. *509 North Main Street; 513/773-2307. Open Apr-Nov. Tu, Th, Sat, Sun 12:30-4:30. Free. Group tours by appointment.*

ASIDE The oldest ongoing high school football rivalry in Ohio is the Battle of Miami, which has been fought every year since 1899 between the Troy Trojans and the Piqua Indians. Apparently, the latent hostility between the two towns over the matter of the Miami County Courthouse location has been transferred to the football fields of the Trojans and the Indians. Both teams are football titans in Miami County, and their followers routinely swell the teams' respective stadiums to witness their annual contest. It is said that school officials have even threatened to fire coaches if they fail to win the game. Over the years, the Trojans and Indians have been surprisingly evenly matched, and when they met in

PIQUA HISTORICAL AREA/

PIQUA — Plan on taking at least two to three hours in order to properly tour this outstanding, multi-attraction museum and historical restoration site. Operated by the Ohio Historical Society, this beautifully maintained, 174-acre complex encompasses the Piqua area's history from the time of the ancient Indians to the mid-1800s, when it was the farmland of John Johnston, an Irish immigrant who became the last Indian agent in Ohio. The area is the also site of the **Piqua Heritage Festival**, an annual Labor Day weekend event that recreates the foods, crafts, and entertainments of the 1800s. Attractions include a French and Indian Encampment, a Mountain Men Rendezvous, a square dance, and canoe races.

The **Historic Indian Museum** is an especially fascinating place for children. Its diorama and displays of original artifacts-snowshoes, powder horns, a splendid birch bark canoe, and a pipe tomahawk used by Tecumseh-portray the daily life and culture of American Indians from the seventeenth through nineteenth centuries.

The **Prehistoric Earthwork** is a relic of the first known residents of the area, Indians of the ancient Adena culture. They built this ring-shaped mound for what may have been ceremonial purposes about the time that Christ was born.

The **Johnston Farm** was the home of John Johnston, a veritable Renaissance man of the Ohio frontier whose varied talents, interests, and successes-Indian agent, peacemaker, diplomat and friend; agricultural expert, educator, university founder and trustee, political activist, part-time physician, and canal commissioner-were

extremely significant to the settlement of western Ohio. The Johnston house and outbuildings have been restored to their appearance in 1829, which was Johnston's last year as an Indian agent. The barn is the biggest early nineteenth century log barn left in the state, and its beams are so massive that there aren't even any trees left in Ohio large enough to replace them.

The **General Harrison** is an authentic reproduction of a canal cargo boat from the 1840-1850 period, when Johnston was using the Miami and Erie canal that ran beside his property to ship apples and pork from his farm. The craft carries passengers on a mule-drawn ride along a restored, mile-long stretch of the old canal.

The **Site of Fort Piqua**, which is located just a few hundred yards from the Johnston Farm, is the place where a supply post was built in 1794 for General "Mad" Anthony Wayne's war to suppress the Indians and open Ohio to white settlement. Johnston had a job driving a supply wagon for Wayne's army when he first came to the area and saw the lovely site that would become his home.

The **Johnston Cemetery** has the graves of John Johnston, his family members, and other pioneers, including many of those who died during the siege of Fort Wayne, Indiana. *9845 North Hardin Road; 513/773-2522. Memorial Day Weekend-Labor Day, Wed-Sat 9:30-5, Sun and holidays noon-5; after Labor Day-Oct 31, Sat 9:30-5, Sun noon-5. Nominal admission. Group tours by appointment.*

regular season play in October, 1992, the series was tied at 50 wins, 50 losses, and 6 ties. The Trojans got the edge with a 22-7 win over the Indians, only to have Piqua settle the score with a 20-7 victory a few weeks later when they met for Ohio's Division I, Region 2 championship. Thus, the series was again balanced 51-51-6. Although Troy can claim the longest winning streak with six consecutive games between 1976 and 1981, Piqua has enjoyed five-game winning streaks four times: 1900-1903, 1924-1927, 1934-1938, and 1964-69. From 1969 through 1972, Troy trounced Piqua every year, thanks largely to the services of Gordon Bell, a talented running back who routinely rushed for hundreds of yards and scored touchdowns on the first play of scrimmage. Bell, of course, later found fame playing for the University of Michigan and the New York Giants, and the Piqua coach was so happy to see Bell depart from Troy's high school that he publicly offered to present him with his diploma.

THE ROSSVILLE MUSEUM AND CULTURAL CENTER/PIQUA —
Helen Gilmore operates a modest museum but she is a powerful storyteller, and she has a gripping tale to tell. In 1846, 383 slaves left Charlotte County, Virginia, for a new life in Ohio. They had been freed in accordance with the will of John Randolph, a powerful politician and plantation owner who not only took the extraordinary step of manumitting the slaves he inherited from his father but also provided money to buy more than 3,000 acres of land that they could farm in Mercer County, Ohio. When the group reached their property, however, they were driven away by whites who claimed the rich, fertile farmland for themselves. The Randolph slaves retreated to Piqua, where they built houses out of scrap wood and started the community known as Rossville, on the banks of the Great Miami River. In 1907, the families of the Randolph slaves filed suit to regain their promised land. The case went to the Supreme Court of Ohio, which ruled against them because the statute of limitations had expired. Mrs. Gilmore is a descendant of those slaves, and she is making their remarkable struggle immortal in the virtual one-woman museum that she maintains in a house built in 1873 by York Rial, her great-great uncle. Now on the National Register of Historic Places, the Rial house was copied after a Virginia slave cabin, and Mrs. Gilmore has painstakingly filled it with memorabilia and documentation that traces the fascinating, two-century sojourn of her ancestors from their African homeland to present-day Ohio. Many of the Randolph slaves-who were York Rial's kith and kin-are buried in nearby **Jackson Cemetery**, which is also on the National Register of Historic Places.
8250 McFarland Street; 513/773-6789. Mon-Fri 1-7, Sat and Sun by appointment. Free. Group tours by appointment. Jackson Cemetery is located at the corner of McFarland Street and Zimmerlin Road.

ASIDE When they made their first recording in 1928, the oldest of the four brothers was 18 and the youngest only 14. Two years later they had their first hit-"Tiger Rag," which was the first record by a vocal group to achieve seven-figure sales-and two years after that, they were appearing in the Hollywood musical, *The Big Broadcast*, with the likes of

Kate Smith, George Burns, Gracie Allen, Cab Calloway, and Bing Crosby. They were the Mills Brothers-John, Jr., Herbert, Harry, and Donald, who were taught to sing by their father, a barber in their hometown of Piqua, Ohio. When John, Jr. died in the mid-1930s, their father-John, Sr.-took his place in the quartet and sang with his three remaining sons until he died in 1957 at age 85. The Mills Brothers made more than 2200 recordings on the Brunswick and Decca labels, and their hits included such standards as "Bye, Bye, Blackbird," "You Always Hurt the One the Love," "Glow Worm," and "Paper Doll," the 1943 release that became their biggest hit and signature song. Although the Mills Brothers' pop music career peaked in the 1940s and 1950s, the popularity of their rich, mellow sound endured into the 1970s, when the surviving siblings still sang as a trio. In 1990, Piqua held a party for its most musical native sons, honoring them as "musical ambassadors" with a granite monument in the town square.

Flesh Public Library

FLESH PUBLIC LIBRARY/PIQUA — The library building was originally an opulent, exclusive club for Leo Flesh and other rich men in Piqua. Built in the early 1900s, the club featured a bowling alley and billiard room, and it is said that the reason Mr. Flesh did not put a ballroom in his mansion on North Downing Street was that he liked to do his large scale entertaining here. This once-private building now serves as a public library, and the Piqua History Room is a wonderful repository of books, photos, and research materials on Ohio, Miami County, and Piqua. The seventeenth through nineteenth century books collected by local newspaper editor Jerome Smiley provide a comprehensive study of the Northwest Territory, while a 1795 copy of Morse's *American Geography* is one of the room's rarest titles.

Women of course are no longer banned from the building as they were in Mr. Flesh's day, when they were permitted by invitation only on the second floor and had to use a separate entrance to avoid the men in the smoking room.

124 West Greene Street; 513/773-6753. Mon-Th 9 a.m.-8:30 p.m., Fri-Sat 9-5:30.

ASIDE Leo Flesh's chief business-and personal-rival was John Spiker, another eminent Piquad upon whom the nation relied for its foundations. Mr. Spiker built his Superior Underwear Company just beyond Mr. Flesh's Atlas Underwear Company on North Downing Street. After Mr. Flesh built his mansion, Mr. Spiker retaliated by building one of his own on the next block to the east. Mr. Flesh was associated with one Piqua bank; Mr. Spiker was with the other. Mr. Fresh was a Republican; Mr. Spiker was a Democrat. Death, of course, claimed both men equally, but if a winner of their feud were to be declared, it would have to be Mr. Flesh. His underwear factory outlasted all the others in Piqua, and was still doing business in the early 1990's.

CAROL EISERT DOLLS AND DESIGNS/PIQUA — One of the reasons that Carol Eisert's award-winning dolls look so realistic is that the glass eyes she uses are hand blown in Germany. Combined with her considerable artistic and creativity, that kind of painstaking attention to detail has made Ms. Eisert's handcrafted porcelain dolls known around the world. Working from a studio and salesroom in her home, she does everything from sculpting the molds used to make the dolls' faces to designing and sewing unique clothing fashioned from antique fabrics for each doll. Ms. Eisert makes the porcelain with a process used in Germany at the turn of the century, and it took her two years to develop the paints that give her dolls the natural skin tones for which they are famous. Not only is she one of the few people anywhere who repairs and restores dolls, but Ms. Eisert also will custom design dolls to look like actual people, especially children. One of her favorite projects was a doll she made to look like someone's grandfather when he was a young boy. She used his childhood saddle blanket to make the doll's jacket and one of his own shirts to make the doll's shirt.

515 Spring Street; 513/773-1230. By appointment.

WINANS' CARRIAGE HOUSE CANDIES/PIQUA — For more than thirty years, the Winans family has been selling homemade candy in a restored carriage house. Their fine chocolates are so popular-the mint chews, for example, are made from a classic candy maker's recipe-that the Winans routinely ship boxes of it to displaced Piquads who may be gone, but have not forgotten the candy they grew up with.

308 West Water Street; 513/773-1981. Mon, Tu, Wed, Th, Sat 9-6; Fri 9 a.m.-9 p.m. Discover, MC, V.

BIG WOODS RESERVE/PIQUA — For more than a century, much of the wooded area in this verdant reserve was maintained by the Garbry family of Piqua. Garbry's Big Woods Sanctuary consists of an almost virgin beech-maple forest that affords visitors the rare opportunity of experiencing what Ohio's natural plant and animal habitats were like before the state was settled. Now set aside for observation and nature study, the sanctuary is the biggest stand of upland woods in Miami County. It's most colorful in the spring, when the wildflowers are in full bloom and can be enjoyed via the boardwalk through the trees. *On Statler Road, east of its intersection with Union-Shelby Road, which is off of U.S. Route 36 about four miles east of Piqua; 513/667-1086. Dawn to dusk daily. Picnic area, but no cooking fires are permitted.*

STILLWATER PRAIRIE RESERVE/PIQUA — The extensive board-walk that snakes through this 215-acre reserve takes visitors on a journey through time, topography, and natural history via diverse areas of fields, marshes, woodlands, shrub lands, and a rare native Ohio prairie. Watch for the resident populations of deer and turkey vultures, and since the trail through the prairie takes you across the shallows of the Stillwater River, be prepared to do some wading. The river has several deep spots that harbor smallmouth bass, and two ponds are also available for fishing.
About seven miles west of Piqua on State Route 185, one-half mile from its intersection with State Route 48; 513/667-1086. Dawn to dusk daily. Picnic area with grills.

PIQUA-LOCKINGTON SCENIC AND HISTORIC ROUTE — One of the prettiest and most historically significant drives in the Piqua area is the loop formed by Piqua-Lockington, Landman Mill, and Hardin roads. To reach Piqua-Lockington Road, take County Road 25-A north out of Piqua, and turn left when the county road crosses the Great Miami River. Piqua-Lockington Road twists and winds through farm fields as it approaches the tiny village of Lockington. Once the highest point on the Miami and Erie Canal, Lockington still has the remains of several locks and the stone aquaduct via which the canal crossed Loramie Creek. To view the locks, turn left at the first stop sign in Lockington, go one block, and turn left again. Then follow Piqua-Lockington Road back to Landman Mill Road and turn west on to Landman Mill, which will take you past a privately owned, but virtually intact nineteenth century mill that is quite visible from the road. Take Landman Mill Road to Hardin Road, and turn left on Hardin, a pleasant rural route that goes past the Piqua Historical Area and will return you to Piqua proper.

GREAT OUTDOOR UNDERWEAR FESTIVAL/PIQUA — Piqua was once the proud home of eight underwear manufacturers, one of whom even hired Olympic gold medalist Johnny Weismuller to model long johns before he became famous as Tarzan in the movies. Billed as "a revealing peek at our foundations," the festival is a light-hearted look at the town's heritage and claim to fame as the place where the first practical drop-seat union suit was invented. For an entire weekend in October, underwear unabashedly comes out of the closet and on to the streets of Piqua. The festival's chili cook-off, square dancing, and "Undy 500" Malibu race car competition are mere sideshows to the main event-Sunday's "Made in Piqua" parade on Main Street, when majorettes march in granny gowns, two teens squeeze

into a single pair of oversized boxer shorts, and city officials appear in red union suits with the front flaps discreetly sewed shut. Everything, of course, is all in good fun . . . and good taste.
Second weekend in October; 513/773-3333, 800/348-8993.

THE SPOT/SIDNEY — Homemade hamburgers have been this restaurant's trademark since it opened on this-ahem-very spot in 1913, but architecture has been its hallmark only since 1941, when the place was rebuilt in the latest, Art Moderne style. Eating here is like entering a time warp: pre-World War II "streamlining" is everywhere from the white porcelain tile walls, to the curved corner entrance, to the round neon sign that declares this is "The Spot to Eat." Do have one of the burgers, preferably topped with The Spot's special "everything sauce." Then find a seat on one the chrome stools below the windows facing Court Street and enjoy a fine view of downtown Sidney and the goings-on on courthouse square.
201 South Ohio Avenue; 216/492-9181. Mon-Th 7 a.m.-10 p.m., Fri-Sat 7 a.m.-11 p.m., Sun 8 a.m.-10 p.m. Inexpensive.

SIDNEY DAIRY/SIDNEY — Tucked away in one corner of an actual dairy plant, this pleasant ice cream parlor offers the premium handmade ice cream that has been a favorite with locals for decades. The scoops of ice cream are generously oversized, and the crisp waffle cones are made on the premises. If you can't decide which of the more than 60 flavors of ice cream and yogurt you want, don't worry-the dairy offers free sample tastings.
507 North Miami Avenue; 513/492-4300. Open mid-March to mid-October. Mon-Sun, 11 a.m.-10 p.m. Inexpensive.

HUSSEY'S/PORT JEFFERSON — Dozens of ducks and a gaggle of geese greet customers at this beautifully situated restaurant on the banks of the Great Miami River. The dining room overlooks the water, and the splendid view across the white-barked birches is almost as celebrated as the deep-fried chicken that the Hussey family has been serving since 1933.
8770 South Broad Street; 513/492-0038. Tu-Sat 3:30-10, Sun 11-8:30. Inexpensive-Expensive. AE, MC, V.

ASIDE Sidney is supposedly named for Sir Philip Sidney because the landscape reminded settlers of the English poet's "Acadia." However, some say it was because the middle name of the farmer who donated 50 acres of land for the county seat — Charles Starrett — was Sidney.

THE LOUIS SULLIVAN BANK BUILDING (PEOPLES FEDERAL SAVINGS AND LOAN ASSOCIATION)/SIDNEY — Architecture classes from Ohio State often travel to Sidney just to see this building. So have people from Europe, Africa, and Japan. One architect from Connecticut even opened an account with the building's financial institution – Peoples Federal Savings and Loan – merely to be doing business in the splendid structure designed by Louis Sullivan. Known as the "Father of the Modern Skyscraper," Sullivan was the founder of

the "Chicago School" of modern architecture and the proponent of the principle, "Form follows function." He had designed the first true skyscraper-St. Louis's Wainwright Building-and helped to redefine much of the Chicago skyline in the wake of the Great Fire of 1871, but when his career declined after the turn of the century, Sullivan took on the design of eight banks in small Midwestern towns that included Sidney, Ohio. Sullivan dubbed his banks "jewel boxes," because he designed the buildings to represent safety, security, strength, and a place for storing valuables. Now a National Historic Landmark, the Sidney building was built in 1917, and it is considered to be Sullivan's best-and favorite-bank. He designed everything from the door knobs and drinking fountain-which is itself a small work of art-to the exquisite blue glass mosaic Syria arch over the entry. An intricate terra cotta cornice frames the flat roof; slabs of black marble hug the sidewalks at the base of the exterior brick walls; and decorative gargoyles double as drain spouts. Sullivan even made the interior of the bank symmetrical to purposely draw people's attention directly to the vault, and thus indirectly to the soundness of the financial institution itself.
101 East Court Street; 513/492-6129. Open during bank hours. Mon-Wed, 9-4, Th 9-noon, Fri 9-6, Sat 9-noon.

THE TITANIC MEMORIAL MUSEUM/SIDNEY — Museum founder and curator John Whitman estimates that he has collected so many souvenirs, artifacts, and items from and about the *Titanic* that in order to properly display them all, he would have to live to be 256 years old. When the ill-fated ocean liner sank in the North Atlantic in 1912, the disaster captured the attention of the world. Forty-one years later, it permanently captured the imagination of the then ten-year-old Whitman, when he saw the 1950s movie *Titanic* and started to "eat, sleep, and drink" the ship. He began reading-and collecting-everything he could about the *Titanic*, checking one *Titanic* book out of the Sidney public library so many times, that the librarian eventually just *gave* it to him. In 1987, Whitman opened the world's only museum dedicated to the *Titanic* in the unlikely location of a farm field just north of landlocked Sidney, Ohio. Nonetheless, some 60,000 people a year – including one man from Columbus who has been there 67 times – visit the museum to view Whitman's incomparable displays of more than 3,000 items, including the original interior blueprints of the ship, a launch ticket dated May 31, 1912, and the clothing worn by Mrs. Theodous Goodwin when she was put into one of the lifeboats. A recognized expert on the disaster, Whitman regales visitors with *Titanic* stories and delights in debunking *Titanic* myths: the band was *not* playing "Nearer My God to Thee;" and the ship did *not* hit the iceberg, the iceberg hit the ship. He also requires the guides who conduct tours of the museum to take a three-month training course and achieve a perfect score on a 785-item test that covers such arcane, but apparently often-asked *Titanic* questions as the number of survivors (719); the number of fatalities (1551); the weight of the rudder (100 tons); the number of rivets (3 million); and how many gallons of paint it took to coat the exterior (43,757).
10741 Russell Road; 513/492-7762. Mon-Wed 10-4:30, Sat 9-4:30, Sun 1-5. Closed holidays. Admission fee. Group tours by appointment.

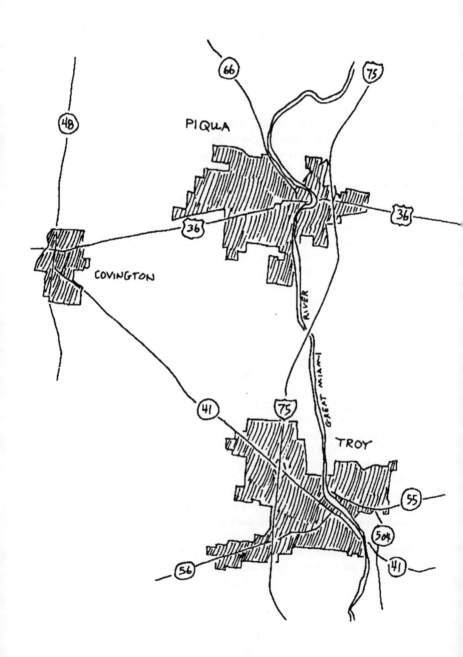

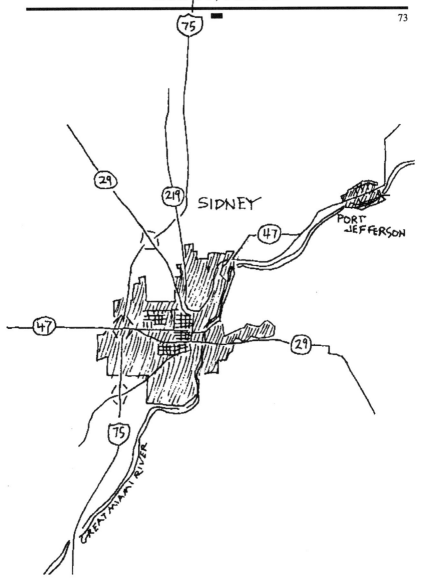

Fort Meigs

Maumee River Valley

Local historians like to say that the Maumee River was the first Ohio Turnpike. A short portage from the southward-flowing rivers across the divide, it carried the Indians, the French, the British and, finally, the Americans through that big sponge called the Black Swamp to Lake Erie and the St. Lawrence. It was a hotly-contested piece of real estate, a 150-mile freeway for our frontier forebearers that the Americans finally won from the Indians and the British. If it weren't for the local battles, the Treaty of Greenville would have never been signed and there would be no Rocky Mountain high or California dreamin'. Americans would be crammed on top of one another east from here to the Atlantic Coast and we'd have a national anthem that wouldn't rhyme. But we won it for ourselves, made a canal and built bridges, used it to dump stuff into and take fish out of. We drained the land around it, cut down the trees, built railroads and highways. Then, because we weren't really careful what we'd wished for, the river lost its usefulness, grew older, was ignored and would have liked to have retired to Florida, which it tried several times by way of Grand Rapids. As of late, though, it has noticed signs of appreciation. While travel agents aren't flying tourists into Toledo Express Airport for Maumee River vacations, natives know a good thing when they see it, even when it's up to their waists. Water doesn't need to be useful. Sometimes it just needs to be. ¶ The Maumee River snakes from Fort Wayne, Indiana, to Defiance, where it fattens and takes an honest course to Toledo and Lake Erie. Its smalltown flavor is carried upstream, at its midsection, from Perrysburg to Defiance. Across from the scattered sprawl of suburban Maumee, Perrysburg sits more peacefully than during the battle at Fort Meigs, though three years ago, there were Indian drums heard in Hood Park. One hundred American Indians and their supporters protested the removal of bones disinterred by excavators redesigning the park at Louisiana Avenue. ¶ "If we came to Perrysburg and dug up graves, we'd be arrested in a minute," said an Indian affairs activist. There was dissent and anger, but after the ceremony, everyone went for coffee at the First United Methodist Church. The

Maumee River Valley is more enlightened these days, but not too refined. In spring, thousands of anglers leap into the Maumee like lemmings; in summer, tourists descend on Grand Rapids like kamikaze pilots; in fall, college students war whoop their way to Defiance; in winter, visitors snort Campbell's creamy chicken in Napoleon. Energized by the economic current, they dance a limbo, tied to history not by bloodlines, but by a similarity of style, General "Mad" Anthony Wayne having danced a similar step two centuries ago.

LODGING — Choosing to launch a Maumee River tour in Perrysburg and not Maumee, or even Toledo, means suggesting you get a good night's sleep *before* you wander into town. David Hawley, who built the first frame house in 1817, having brought the lumber with him on the schooner *Blacksnake*, abandoned it after the death of his wife, thus leaving the first room vacancy in the area. Today, the only openings are in the two chain motels, unfortunate for a town with three historic districts listed on the prestigious National Register.

ACCESS — Any Ohioan living north of the Maumee River knows how to get to Perrysburg. They live but a stone's throw away. But travelers arriving from the south on I-75 or from the east on I-90 should watch for the minarets. Not only do they guide you to Perrysburg, the onion-top towers beckon Moslems to the **Islamic Center of Greater Toledo**, the first traditional Islamic mosque west of the nation's capital and a breathtaking vision rising out of the cornfields. If you wish to have a peek, you may (take the first exit going north or south on I-75 within full view of the mosque), though not during services. You will come away better educated and, having just exited the crowded highways, you may reflect as one Ohio writer did, that, "We are all one...fellow travelers in the human condition, rushing through the landscape of the moment, bound for a common end." Harken...Perrysburg.

THE COMMODORE CAFE/PERRYSBURG — Towns erect statues and monuments to celebrate famous people and events, thus allowing pigeons a more noble stance. Perrysburg followed suit with the logical figure of Oliver Hazard Perry, victor at the Battle of Lake Erie and the fellow for whom the town was named. (The marble statue in Hood park, at the foot of Louisiana Avenue, was the one that stood in Cleveland's Public Square for 69 years. It was replaced by a bronze one.) A more functional testament to his win now stands-a restaurant. Too bad Oliver only gets an outside view. The now-extinct Citizens Bank with drive-thru window, mezzanine offices and safety deposit box vault is now a gourmet cafe that sports a handmade California

The Commodore Cafe / Perrysburg

back bar with drive-thru window, mezzanine and first floor seating for
105, as well as a 15-paper newsstand deposit box vault. This one-time
financial citadel turned eye-popping restoration trichotomized in the
last 90 days of 1992. It was to open quietly on New Year's Eve and
instead served a full house, the liquor license arriving by messenger
that very day. Scott Parry, Rob Whitner and Chef Tim Beatty wanted it
to be a casual place. Well, it is and it isn't. How casual is a place from
which one can call and order, perhaps by mobile phone, an Acropolis
salad with kalmata, olives and pepperocini, prawns in prosciutto
served with rice pilaf and spinach tagliatelli a side order of pot stickers
Shanghi with plums, ginger or honey sauces, a swartswald torte and an
espresso macchiato to go and...pick it up at a drive-though window?
But how serious is a place where, from within, it feels like the inside
of a Maurice Sendak book, kind of an **Oliver Perry In The Night
Kitchen** tale? Fathers and daughters come in to get a sundae, local
artists stop by for their daily cappuccino, feminist Toledo professors
arrive to discuss Betsy Ross's garb (or lack of it), old bank customers
try to turn their keys in their old safety deposit boxes and everyone
wants to try the homemade breads and pastries. Don't miss it.
*114 Louisiana Ave; 419/874-1441. Mon-Th 7 a.m.-10 p.m.; Fri 7 a.m.-
11 p.m.; Sat 8 a.m.-11 p.m., Sun 8 a.m.-9 p.m. MC/V. Moderate*

SID & DIANE'S/PERRYSBURG — Had William Henry Harrison had the Roger sisters running food service at Fort Meigs, most losses would have been from gorging and the noisiest battles would have been inside. Daughters of Long Island restaurateurs, Sid and Diane turned a successful catering business into a restaurant into an upscale specialty food shop into a deli with jazz. Belying the "early cowboy" exterior, which would have attracted, perhaps, Harrison's horse, the inside is warm and cozy with the bonus of walking through the kitchen to be seated, an aromatic preview of what's to come. The visible, audible chef is Diane, a masterful cook and bakeress who claims no particular cooking style but is inventive enough to change the entire menu every few days to include whatever's fresh in season. Suppliers stop by with soft shell crabs, sorrels from Michigan, lots of pasta or rack of lamb. And, she makes over one ton of her secret recipe cranberry sauce each year. Sid, who's in charge of the wines, the specialty food shop and the customers, works the same way. There's no wine list, there's variety to the specialty foods and the customers are as diverse as the sisters themselves. "We don't like to commit," says Diane, and we believe her. "Pretty soon we'll be forty. Then our ticket outta here is either Prince Charming or my cranberry sauce." Better try this place soon.
105 W. 5th Street; 419/874-2293. Open Tue & Wed 10 a.m.-8 p.m., Th & Fri 10 a.m.-11 p.m., Sat 11 a.m.-11 p.m. Dinner is served on Th, Fri & Sat only. "Jazz in the Deli" on Fri nights 9 p.m.-Midnight. Closed the week of July 4th, the week of Labor Day, the first week in January. MC, V. Moderate.

LAMPLIGHT CAFE & BAKERY/PERRYSBURG — Six days a week, the wishful fisherman, Jim Haas, makes the best breakfasts in town. He begins serving his famous two and three-egg omelettes at 6:30 a.m., continues on with waffles and ends with egg, ham, bacon, and cheese sandwiches at 11 a.m. Meanwhile, Kathy Flick bakes and serves her hot pecan and cinnamon rolls. Around 11:30 a.m. the lunch crowd arrives. Hot sandwiches like turkey, cheese, sauerkraut and horserad-ish on a croissant with sides of fresh fruit and salad plates feed 58 people at a sitting. The fare attracts the diet conscious who, in spite of their healthy inclinations, find it nearly impossible to leave the bakery by 2:30's closing without Kathy's famous cookies, brownies, pies or cheesecake. Then, Lucy sweeps up and Jim takes out the trash. By the time the details are finished another good fishing day is gone. Maybe someday, Jim.
121 Indiana Avenue in Perry's Landing; 419/874-0125. Mon-Fri 6:30 a.m.-2:30 p.m., Sat 7 a.m.-2 p.m. Closed Sun & Major holidays. Moderate.

RIBBONRY/PERRYSBURG — Camela Nitschke travels to France once a year to study 17th and 18th century ribbons at the Bibliothéque Nationale. Choosing her favorite designs, she takes copies of the patterns and has ribbons made from them at the St. Etienne where jacquard looms weave ribbons that sell, in downtown Perrysburg, for $7-$65 a yard. Customers arrive or place orders from across the United States and buy these authentic reproductions to adorn wedding dresses, dolls and historical costumes. Some people just collect them. Jackie Onassis bought ribbons from Camela after they met at the

Louvre. Ribbonry also sells hats made by a milliner in Virginia. After arriving at the store, they're decorated...with ribbons. These are priced from $65-$350. It sounds like an elite sort of place but it caters well to the locals who love to come in for beautiful hair bows and headbands, too.
119 Louisiana Avenue; 419/872-0073. Mon-Sat 10 a.m.-5 p.m.

ASIDE Antiquing is good in Perrysburg. Try Jones & Jones Limited, or Perrysburg Antique Market, 116 Louisiana Avenue; 419/872-0231 or restorer Peter Jay Hoffman, 316 W. Front Street; 419/874-5157.

SANTA FE WAY/PERRYSBURG — Tourists run rampant in Sante Fe, New Mexico, but for the local traveler, with less time and tolerance, there's Santa Fe Way where Tina Mather Bothe imports museum quality folk art by well-established southwesterners. Consider woodcarver Paul Lutonsky's snakes and fish. Or David Alveraz's eight-inch-long to five-foot-long porcupines, coyotes, zebras, cats or bears. There are hand- painted pine trasteros (art-as-furniture) made by a collection of six artists. Perhaps the most unique pieces are by Michael Ives from Tucson who paints folk art memories of his Perrysburg childhood. Check out the one of Oliver Hazard Perry wearing a "Go Perrysburg" button.
113 Louisiana Avenue; 419/874-0707. Mon-Sat. 10 a.m.-5 p.m.

577 FOUNDATION/PERRYSBURG — Not long ago, a Dayton lady made national television when she chose to celebrate her 90th birthday with a parachute jump at the local airport. She told reporters she was worried a bit about her plastic hip and knee but the actual jump was less exciting than she'd anticipated and now wonders what to do to at 95. Perhaps she should visit Virginia Stranahan. At 86, Mrs. Stranahan is firmly grounded but no less adventuresome. She lives on a 14-acre estate that rises gracefully up from the southern bank of the Maumee. Recently divorced, she gifted the land to the city of Perrysburg so anyone could come over anytime to enjoy the grounds, experiment with plantings, learn about nature or just have fun. From that modest beginning is now a 14-acre microcosm of the ecologically correct world. A stable, dairy, cow barn, carriage room, cottage and surrounding grounds are now a concentrated oasis of organic, community theme gardens (name your theme and Mrs. S. will furnish the seeds, dirt, fertilizer, tools), a 22-foot-high geodesic biodome (a local world-traveler grows sixty varieties of hot peppers here), experimental compost heaps, nine bee hives (with personal bee-keeper), a pottery barn (locals dig their own Wood County clay from a pit), a used book store (with an experimental corn cob, oat, wood pellet and rice hull-burning stove), a cottage (for Yoga class, painting class, bird feeder building), and a river hiking trail through orchards (mind the fox den). Where everything is free to all, the energetic Mrs. Stranahan remains a strong presence, her favorite project reflecting her own free spirit-she makes a good beer from the hops she grows, but she has better dreams from the effect of sleeping on pillows stuffed with its dried catkins. Now that could make a nice 95th

birthday present...
*577 East Front Street; 419/872-0305. Daily 9-5. Group tours
available.*

FORT MEIGS STATE MEMORIAL/PERRYSBURG — Built on the edge
of the great Black Swamp by William Henry Harrison, the commander
of the Northwestern Army, this fort and its signal battles in 1813
helped push Harrison's worthy Indian adversary, Tecumseh, farther
north and to his ultimate demise. On the first of May, the British and
their Indian allies, set up across the Maumee, established six batteries,
and opened fire on the outmanned and outgunned Americans.
Harrison, short on ammunition, offered a gill of whiskey-a quarter of a
pint-for every British cannonball that fit his swivels and his men
crawled off into the night looking for them. By the time the siege was
over, Harrison owed his men over sixty gallons. Tecumseh, impatient
with the white man's ability at digging in and waiting, called Harrison
a "groundhog," and asked him and his men to come out and meet his
braves, hand-to-hand. The old general declined, and the attack was
staved off as much by prudence as by valor. (Later that year, Harrison's
men killed Tecumseh in the war's final battle of consequence, the
Battle of the Thames; Harrison went on to become the president, but
Tecumseh became a legend.) The fort has been carefully reconstructed, including its seven blockhouses and stockade wall. Exhibits
give an overview of the War of 1812, and explain the fort's various
intricacies. On summer weekends, re-enactment groups camp here,
lending some air of authenticity but barely compensating for the
encroachment of housing developments almost resting on the fort's
walls. (Note: As of this writing, $68,000 must be generated locally to
keep Fort Meigs operating until June, 1993. So far, $30,000 has been
contributed. Donations should be sent to the Ohio Historical Society in
Columbus.)
*State Route 65, west of intersection with State Route 25; 419/874-
4121. June-August, Wed-Sat 9:30 a.m.-5 p.m., Sun 12 p.m.-5 p.m.
September-October, Sat 9:30 a.m.-5 p.m., Sun 12 p.m.-5 p.m. Small
fee.*

ACCESS — Begin the pretty drive on Route 65 going west. It'll take a
few minutes to get beyond a heavy growth of new homes and to the
lush growth of old trees. The Maumee, of course, is more visible in the
winter, but the ride is prettier during spring, summer and fall.

WALL-TO-WALL WALLEYE — Like lemmings leaping to the sea,
anglers bounding into the Maumee mark the arrival of spring, thus
changing the best-kept fishing secret into a massive baptism. From a
hilltop perch or a nice bend on SR65, from mid-March to mid-May,
there have been spotted up to 12,000 fishermen in a four-or-five-mile
stretch. In 1990 more than 92,000 walleye were hooked, snagged
(illegally) or tangled by anglers from 30 states and Canada. One of the
best places to get a scaled down view of this phenomenon is at
Schroeder Farm's Campground about two miles west of Perrysburg
where Tom Steinwand is the on-site tackle vendor selling lures,
waders, fishing licenses and "more". Here, among the furored human
species, you can ponder the notion of 27 million frenzied walleye
swimming madly upriver to spawn. In the end, the fisherman get what

they came for (five-a-day limit), the fish leave what they came for (no limit) and the majority of both get home safely.

26997 W. River Road; 419/833-9411. March 10-May 15. 5:30 a.m.- dark. Fishing parking $3, Camping $8, Boat launch $2. Viewing free.

Columbian House

THE COLUMBIAN HOUSE/WATERVILLE — Anyone who's heard of or eaten at the Golden Lamb in Lebanon will easily identify with its cousin, The Columbian House. This very yellow, three-story spectacular sample of Colonial architecture was built in 1828 by John Pray, a Rhode Islander, who founded Waterville in 1831. It opened as a tavern, but became useful as an Indian trading post, hold-over jail and partying place. Restored about 45 years ago and used as a summer tearoom and an antique storage, it once again began serving travelers in 1971. It's owned by George and Jacqueline Arnold who serve 100 guests on the first floor, display four antique-filled bedrooms on the second floor and store what's left in the ballroom on the third floor. Known for their baked chicken with stuffing and soup romaine, their signature side dish is a smooth, rich, red tomato pudding, a mixture of tomatoes, sugar and torn bread. The Columbian House has been likened to an eating and drinking museum with the added attraction of a ghost that haunts the ladies' restroom on the second floor.

3 North River Road; 419/878-3006. Lunch: Tue-Sat, 11:30 a.m.-2 p.m. Dinner: Tue-Thu, 6-9 p.m.; Fri, 6-10 p.m.; Sat, 5:30-10 p.m. Reservations suggested. MC/V/AE. Moderate-Expensive.

ROCHE DE BOEUF (BUFFALO ROCK)/WATERVILLE — What this rock needs is a good marketing agent. Granted, Plymouth Rock had the Pilgrims, but the size and the colorful events surrounding Roche de Boeuf deserve more attention and care. Consider: it was on this rock that ancient Indians gathered for tribal councils; it was here that a French settler recorded the earliest incident of domestic violence as a young Indian chief pushed his wife off the precipice for the accidental drowning of their son; it was here that General "Mad" Anthony Wayne was supposed to have marched his army across the rapids; and it is here that lie the remnants of the Lima and Toledo Traction Co.'s longest steel reinforced, concrete, earthen-filled railroad bridge in the world. (Builders promised worried local citizens that the rock wouldn't be harmed-they'd stay at least six feet away. They lied, not only by putting the bridge on top of the rock, but by blasting one-third of it away.) Like Plymouth Rock, it's now a rock with papers. It's on the National Register of Historic Places. But unlike the merely famous rock on the Atlantic shore, this one serves a purpose-it helps break up the ice flows during spring thaw.

Artists and photographers love this rock. They get to it by following US24 to River Road. Follow River Road upstream. There's a pull-off directly opposite the rock. Another nice view of the rock and the bridge is from the Roche de Boeuf Area of Farnsworth Metropark on US24. Follow the path from the parking lot to the river.

ASIDE On July 22, 1830, close to Roche de Boeuf, the kind but drunken carpenter, George Porter, shot and killed the rich but mean innkeeper, Isaac Richardson. Years of Richardson's verbal and physical abuse had many thinking justice had been served. But upon sobering up, the remorseful Mr. Porter turned himself in and asked for a swift trial. The defense pleaded insanity, which might have worked had the attorney not claimed that the defendant must be insane to have requested trial in this court rather than waiting for a higher court that met in the fall. The judge took offense and sentenced Porter to be hanged in Perrysburg three months later. While jailed, the gentle Mr. Porter and his caretaker, the Perrysburg sheriff, became close friends, making it particularly hard for the latter to carry out his other duty as executioner. On Judgment Day, it took three swings of the ax to break the rope and as pioneer mentality gave way to an uproarious applause from an event-starved crowd, George Porter became the first man to be legally executed in northwest Ohio.

OSTEGO SHELTER HOUSE/OSTEGO — Voted the handsomest roadside stop along the Maumee, this piece of handiwork, the stately 1938 stone shelterhouse and popular picnic and reunion spot, is near an overlook with a sweeping view of the Maumee. Nice restrooms, too.

NAZARETH HALL — Be careful. Slooooow down. First-time travelers on SR65 can wrench their necks wondering what lies within those mansion walls. Since 1928, Narareth Hall was a piece of God's Kingdom, the Catholic part, and served as a nationally-known military school run by Ursuline nuns. About ten years ago it closed down and remained empty until Bob and Barb Bettinger, from Perrysburg, paid the nuns $37,000 for the building and 37 acres. Stealing from nuns, you say? Nah. In two years they've spent over $500,000 on new systems and interior designs and have opened the hall as a gathering place for weddings, receptions and events-kind of a dry-docked Maumee River *Love Boat*. This rent-a-palace has a chapel on the second floor with stained glass windows and oak pews that can seat 200. The 14 stained glass windows, ten chandeliers and marble floor in the original dining room is a reception hall. The nun's lunchroom is a ladies' room. The gym and stage now has a mezzanine, is carpeted and can seat 100. Classrooms can be booked for children's parties. Rehearsal dinners can be held in the library. For an outdoor ceremony, the grotto has a replica of the grotto in Lourdes, France. Chef Chuck Welker prepares the ice sculptures, the vegetable bouquets and all the delicious meals. Stop in and look around. Rentals must be done well in advance.

21211 West River Road; 419/832-2900. Office hours: Mon-Fri, 10-2. Rental fees: chapel or grotto $275, either reception room $450, rehearsal dinners and receptions, per person.

The Mill House

THE MILL HOUSE BED & BREAKFAST/GRAND RAPIDS — One day in Europe, the English sailor, John, met the Ohio wanderer, Nancy. "I'm in love with you, stay with me, but what was your name?" he asked. An inauspicious beginning? Not so. He nicknamed her "Bootz", which stuck, as did she, and together they sailed a 100-year-old square rigger, had the wee girl, Leah (who, now at age eight, has been to nine countries), and most closely resemble, through adventurous tales, the early French settlers of this valley. Their bed and breakfast, a mill that was once one of the working, steam-driven flour mills on the Maumee is, by far, the most charming place to stay during a trip along the river. Three well-appointed, air-conditioned, comfortable downstairs bedrooms with private baths serve the guests. John, Bootz and Leah live upstairs and in the morning John cooks a delicious gourmet breakfast that Bootz carries down the stairs and serves. The view from the breakfast room and deck overlooks the Gilead Side-Cut Canal, Bluebell Island and the Maumee. The Delvins are a wonderfully energetic and eclectic pair-John started a pottery in the basement and Bootz co-owns and manages **The Front Door**, a stylish women's clothing store down the street-whom you occasionally see gazing wistfully eastward as if the smell of salt air has traveled the St. Lawrence, Lake Erie and the Maumee just to give them a tease. *24070 Front Street; 419/832-MILL. No smoking, no pets or children under 8 years old. Room rates: $55-$85.*

■

SEVEN EAGLES HISTORICAL EDUCATION CENTER/GRAND RAPIDS — If you wander around Grand Rapids long enough, you're bound to see Naaman Thomas, the most visible host of the primitive Bed (as in on-the-ground) & Breakfast (as in over-the-fire) spot. He'll be the ruggedly well-built bearded fellow wearing the *capote* (that's French, for cape) and driving a brown and orange open (regardless of the weather) Jeep truck. While the groups of Grand Rapids preserve the history of the town, Naamam (and a Director and a Board of Trustees) protect the memories of those who were here first, the Ottawas and the Miamis, the French trappers and the Buckskinners. Seven Eagles-40 acres of woods, trails, clearings, tepees, a hermit's hut and pond, as well as a tomahawk, knife-throwing and archery range-represents this region's life from the early 1700's to the 1840's. Naaman's pragmatic function as physical caretaker and his spiritual function as educational enlightener have elevated him to mythical status with the locals. And he's only been there a year. During the six coldest months of 1992/93 Naaman slept on the ground around the periphery of the clearing, adjusting locations with the change of the winds. It was his one-man primitive experience just to get in the mood. His only belongings were corduroy pants, boots, a couple of military shelter halves and a poncho. He caught fish from the pond. As families and groups came for their own primitive encounters (meaning no electricity or hot running water) Naaman watched them light propane stoves and cook their food, and, when spotted while trying to get comfortable on a bed of sticks, he added an element of excitement and mystery to their stay. Naaman is a wonderful guide. And this is a notable place. Call for information and advance reservations. *16486 Wapakoneta Road, one mile south of Grand Rapids, 419/832-0114. Seven Eagles will provide tepee or tent with ground cover, canoe paddle and life vests, fire irons, firewood, survival skills equipment for supervised activities, candle lantern and candles, fresh water, and sanitary facilities. No modern camping equipment or modern fishing equipment permitted. Group and school tours available. Advance reservations required. Ask about dates for their festivals: Beginner's Rendezvous and Pre-1840 Garage Sale, Lost Arts Festival, Seven Eagles National Tomahawk Challenge. Primitive camping family nightly rates: Over 18, $15, 6-18, $10, Under 6, free. Primitive camping group nightly rates: Over 11 to adult, $12.50, under 11, $8. Special rates for groups over 75 people.*

 LAROE'S RESTAURANT/GRAND RAPIDS — The youthful, diplomatic Dave LaRoe is the unofficial ambassador of Grand Rapids. He arrived in town as a wet-behind-the-ears college graduate who meshed well with a wet-up-to-your-knees kind of town. With the help of friends, he renovated a building, opened The Village Ice Cream Parlor, lived in the apartment behind it through which he dragged the store's daily trash, and began a life. Youth and energy inspired him to buy the Rapids Tavern Bar across the street. Another nice Victorian renovation later, he moved to a second-floor apartment and began a restaurant that now serves 100 people downstairs and has banquet facilities for 150 on the second floor. (LaRoe's Backstage Dinner Theatre has shows during the Christmas season.) The husky, bearded brother, Tom LaRoe, is the unofficial chef of Grand Rapids. He bakes the great

LaRoe's of Grand Rapids

country chicken and cooks the BBQ country ribs, steak and seafood that tour buses stop for. The homemade cream pies have their own reputation, especially the chocolate mousse, which, like the *Northern Exposure* counterpart, is often seen wandering home through town, but in styrofoam containers.
24170 Front Street; 419/832-3082. Mon-Fri 11-11, Sat 8-11, Sun 8-8. Moderate.

ASIDE LaRoe's Restaurant is the repository for a distinguished art gallery. The walls are covered with the handsome, private collection of Grand Rapids artist, Bill Kuhlman. Mr. Kuhlman worked as a commercial artist, but began painting charcoal portraits of the local citizens for his own pleasure from memory and photographs. Dave LaRoe began hanging the portraits in 1981. There are about forty local citizens, mostly deceased, perpetually hanging about the town gathering place. Mr. Kuhlman was urged to do a self-portrait but hesitated because it seemed to encroach upon his own mortality. He agreed when it became clear that if he waited too long, he may not get up there at all. On the other hand, local mortals still eating and breathing, like their four-term mayor, Jim Carter, are holding out. "We'd like wall of our own," he said modestly.

FLORENCE'S ENGLISH GARDEN/GRAND RAPIDS — Every so often there's a place you want to keep to yourself. A secret garden sort of spot. Unfortunately, in the travel writing business, that's grounds for having your tires removed. So, hesitantly, we introduce Florence Oberle and her English garden and tearoom, perhaps the loveliest place in all of Ohiodom. Here, Florence has lived and waved her magic wand (handed down from four generations of gardeners and dipped in oodles of horse manure) around the yard of her California bungalow, producing decades of prizewinning blooms. In warm weather, guests are served in the garden and tea is served in china and on linen, with crystal and silver. She bakes delicious scones served with homemade jams, and varieties of outstanding cakes with her homemade ice cream. In flowered dresses to match her blooms, she serves tea from 2-5:30 or, by appointment. There is no sign, because this is not a restaurant. In fact, she doesn't charge, but accepts donations. Florence serves only three parties a week so you'll do well to make reservations a year in advance, because, now that you know, so does everyone else. *23811 River Road; 419/832-5833. Try for June, the garden's most spectacular display.*

SHOPPING/GRAND RAPIDS — Wandering through the Grand Rapids business district will take up the better part of a day. The shopkeepers have a propensity for covering every square inch of space, which must result in an entire town of migraines during their January inventories. This town, with under 1000 citizens, has 20 antique and specialty shops and you can have it all to yourself off-season. But come mid-spring and through late-fall, parking on Front Street will be hard to find and the locals, knowing better, will usually walk from home. Don't miss a store, but be especially aware that: **Dandy's Lane** sells superb homemade fudge, 40 flavors, that the owner makes in the second-floor kitchen; **Nan-tiques** is famous for its enormous and expensive line of dolls and bears plus trains, furniture, toys, decoys and santas; **Olde Gilead Country Store** is a wonderfully upscale general store with and old-fashioned candy counter (over 100 kinds of candy), a robust variety of imported and exotic beer (try the Wicked Ale), a second floor of unusual toys and a sea of greeting cards; **Old Fashioned Ice Cream Shoppe** is usually packed with tourists wanting their homemade soups or Nafziger's Ice Cream and customers often are dining on their sundaes by mid-morning; **Rapids Discount Pharmacy**, the oldest continually operated pharmacy in Grand Rapids, is owned by the affable Joe Boyle, who has maintained much of the original owner's apothecary bottles, paperwork and pharmaceuticals along the high shelves and in a small room to the back. Rapids Pharmacy houses the village fax machine, Xerox machine, Lotto machine, and a frozen ice cream case but consider its best seller-the antiseptic "Bag Balm", a soothing ointment for cow's udders and baby's bottoms.
Front Street. Shops usually open at 10am weekdays and Noon Sundays.

LABINO'S STUDIO GALLERY/GRAND RAPIDS — Dominick Labino was a world-famous glass artist, inventor, engineer and local citizen. When he died at age 76 his artwork was already in more than 100 museums, universities and public and private collections, including a 33-glass mural at the entrance of the Toledo Museum of Art's glass gallery. He left 60 glass-oriented patents in the U.S. and hundreds in other countries. His most notable invention was a furnace and new glass formula that permitted glass to melt at a lower temperature, allowing pieces of art to be created in a studio instead of a furnace. His development for glass fibers to insulate against extreme temperatures was used in the Apollo, Mercury and Gemini space capsules. In his lifetime, he only had one apprentice, Baker O'Brien, and the studio now is hers. O'Brien's glasswork is beautiful and expensive and this year, one piece will be auctioned off at the Applebutter Fest. The studio and gallery have the feel of the big city and if you sit across the street some evening at LaRoe's Restaurant, from a window seat you

can watch another local artist, Lucas Novotny, dance across the
second-floor studio painting his latest work.
Front Street. 419/832-4101.

ASIDE Nice as it is to wander through these shops on a fine summer
day, keep in mind another view. That is, under the frigid waters of the
Maumee where the business district has been more than once. Local
resident Steve Parsons once said, "Our determination to live here is
equal to the force of that river." Must be. Over the years, merchants
notched the high water marks in their stores, cleaned up and carried on.
Buildings might have a notch or two or three. In the pharmacy, a door
frame to the little museum room was cut at the level of the 1913 flood.
You have to stand on your tiptoes to reach the notch-level of that same
flood in the Olde Gilead Country Store. At LaRoe's Restaurant there's a
plaque on the bar, knee-level, commemorating the level of the 1959
flood. At the Mid-American Bank they raised the safety deposit boxes 30
inches off the floor. If you want to get the whole picture in one place,
there's a large board at one end of Front Street next to The Apple Tree
gift shop. Other towns have similar boards that measure campaign
money for the local YMCA. In Grand Rapids, it records the high water
level of each flood. Stand next to it and wonder it you would have the
courage to set up shop here.

THE TOWN HALL/GRAND RAPIDS — In 1898, Grand Rapids, in
existence for only 65 years (and having been called Gilead for the first
35), spent its wisest $5,500 ever. They purchased land near the end of
Front Street and built a Romanesque Town Hall. In continuous use for
almost one hundred years as the cradle of Grand Rapids' generations,
its second floor provides the mobile of focus-a mini-opera house with a
slanted stage (and a trap door), dressing rooms, balcony seating and
later, stage lighting made from large gutters and colored light bulbs.
Theatrical plays, graduations, recitals, reunions and even medicine
shows were held here. The hundred-year-old bell in the tower still
rings and has been used to announce town meetings, to warn of
floods, to celebrate the end of the Vietnam War and, more recently, to
signal the start of a town play or call the scattered canners together
during the apple butter season. The downstairs is shared by the
township trustees, the mayor, the city council, the police, the police
car and the Historical Society, all of whom have a key to the great
front double doors. A combination of form, function and charm means
it's definitely worth the climb up the stairs.

ASIDE Approximately 15 percent of Grand Rapids's population belongs
to the local Historical Society. That hefty percentage should make other
Ohio towns weep. The ongoing struggle to save Ohio's smalltown
identities from becoming a lobotomy of shoulder-to-shoulder fast food
strips and a monotony of highway-licking housing lots comes naturally in
Grand Rapids. Or at least appears to. A visionary Mayor Carter
encouraged a Historical Society to form in 1975. The trustees and
officers meet at LaRoe's. The members' programs are held in winter at

the Isaac Ludwig Mill where Ron Studer fires up the pot-bellied stove, and in summer at the Town Hall auditorium where the big windows are thrown open and programs compete with crickets in the night air. Town Hall Musicales and Apple Butter Festivals have made the Society the richest non-profit organization in town, and it plows the money back into the village on a regular basis.

The Kerr House

KERR HOUSE/GRAND RAPIDS — And speaking of riches...what's that black limousine doing driving through town? Well, there really *is* another place for guests to stay overnight in Grand Rapids. It's just that, well, it'll cost ya. Laurie Hostetler has welcomed hundreds of guests to her world-renowned holistic health retreat just two blocks up from Front Street. The immaculately restored 35-room Victorian, now in its 12th year of business, can accommodate six or seven guests who would like breakfast in bed at 7 a.m., mind/body exercises, massages, facials, manicures, pedicures, hand and feet waxings, reflexology, elegant candlelit dinners and peace and quiet all for the price of say, 1,275 jars of applebutter. (That's for a week in a private room. Knock off 200 jars for a double.) But most are from out-of-town and pay by check. These include the Dutchman who's built bridges all over the world, guests from Saudi Arabia, ranchers from Montana, and famous folk who wish to remain nameless. And because it's the way it should be, weary moms show up, too. Some from Texas, for the day. Others from Chicago, for the weekend. Doesn't matter. Laurie and her staff of 35 part-time housekeepers and specialists pamper men and women alike and do it so very well that most come back for more. Like the woman in her 80s who's returning for the 14th time. Now that's a lot of applebutter.

Corner of Beaver and Third Streets, 419/832-1733. Reservations are often booked a year in advance. Weekly rates $2,150 double, $2,550 single. Weekend rates $575 double, $675 single. Call for daytime program rates.

TOWN VIEWS/GRAND RAPIDS
— Forget the car. Try these:

By train: Weekends from May to November 1st and Tuesdays and Thursdays in July and August, walk to the depot near the grain elevators at Third and Main and board the coaches behind the 1946 turbo charged diesel for a ride on **The Bluebird Special**. It's a one-hour, 20-mile round trip from Grand Rapids to Waterville that includes spectacular views from the 900-foot-long bridge over the Maumee River and the old Miami & Erie Canal. Schedules are subject to change without notice, so call first. Autumn trips are the prettiest.
419/878-2177 or 419/832-4671. Round trip fares: Age 16-64 $7.50, Senior Citizens $6.75, Children 3-15 $4, 2 and under free. Ask about one-way fares.

By steamboat: From Providence Metropark across the river (1/2 mile west of the bridge) board **The Shawnee Princess**, one of the few, if not the only, steam engine-powered riverboats in the state. For $4, from Memorial Day through Labor Day, on Saturday and Sundays from 1-5, you can have an hour-long sail up and down the Maumee. For $120, you can have it all to yourself. Either way, the captain will let you take a turn at the 48"-steering wheel. *419/843-3882. Or write: 2608 Sequoia, Toledo, OH 43617. Adults $4, Children 12 & under, $2. One-hour charters, $120.*

By foot: Hike the riverside trails that lead from the **towpath** behind Front Street upriver to Mary Jane Thurston State Park, then go back downriver and across the bridge to the Isaac Ludwig Mill, a restored 1800's water-driven saw and grist mill. Wander among the rocky ruins of the old canal, under restoration. Hike about six miles to Bend View Metropark, only accessible by trail, and take in a dramatic view of the broad Maumee. If you do this in the dead of winter when the Maumee is frozen, you'll be entertained with the eerie creaking and groaning noises of the ice as it contracts and expands. If you want to do this in the spring, check with a local about the river level. Five is normal. Ten is think of something else to do. Fifteen is start swimming.

By canalboat: In the some-thing-to-look-forward-to category, is the **Canal Restoration Project**. A canal boat will be pulled by a team of mules from Providence Metropark to the Isaac Ludwig Mill, passing through a restored working canal lock of the Miami & Erie Canal. The boat is to be completed by the fall of 1993 and the entire project is due for completion by June of 1994. The steel-hulled boat will be 60 feet long and 14 feet wide, an authentic freight boat design with two small cabins and an open deck. Rides are likely Wednesday through Sunday, May to October. The Park District is launching a drive to help pay for the boat, so if you're eager to do this soon, send a lot of money now. *419/535-3050. Project information: Metropolitan Park District of the Toledo Area, 5100 W. Central Ave., Toledo, OH 43615.*

ASIDE In a village with only one doctor, one lawyer, one undertaker, one pharmacy, one hardware store, one grocery and one place to spend the night, Howard the policeman is the one means of law enforcement. Back when there were some rowdy bars in town, Howard came and cleaned them up. His formidable reputation still holds, causing a large decrease in his business, so his hours are sporadic. But that doesn't deter his call to duty. One night, he knocked on the door of the Mill House Bed & Breakfast at 2 a.m. to tell guests that the light was left on in their car.

APPLEBUTTER FEST/GRAND RAPIDS — "If you build it, they will come," the ball player said in *Field of Dreams.* "If you stir it, they will come," they say in Grand Rapids. So they did and they do, between 60,000 and 80,000 on the second Sunday in October. Three 50-gallon copper kettles are set up in the village park by the Town Hall. (The Historical Society makes four kettles in advance.) Included: two entertainment stages, pioneering demonstrations, the 18th Century Field Music Fife & Drum Corps drills, Canal Towpath craftsmen, soldiers and pioneer settlers, games, over one hundred juried crafts, a Labino studio glass auction and over 20 non-profit local specialty food booths. In one day the Ostego Athletic Boosters can sell enough soup and buffalo burgers to buy all the Little League team uniforms for the year. The town rents old-fashioned trolleys from Toledo to shuttle visitors from their cars in the cornfields into town. If you want to stay overnight at one of the three rooms at the local B&B, we suggest you call several decades in advance. A wait in line for a jar of applebutter can be two hours, which, we suppose is still shorter than making it yourself. A real sight is at the end of the day when the Youth Camp and their counselors begin The Big Sweep, literally, from one end of Grand Rapids to the other.
Second Sunday in October.

ACCESS — Several miles west of Grand Rapids, SR65 turns sharply south. Don't follow it. Continue west on SR110 following the smell of celery and chicken to the Campbell Soup factory. You are now in Napoleon, one of the few small towns in Ohio where the arrival of a Wal-Mart has been cause for celebration.

CAMPBELL SOUP COMPANY/NAPOLEON — The world's largest soup manufacturing facility makes 75 different kinds of soup and soup products 22 hours a day. A million cans a day are shipped to places between Nebraska and Philadelphia. The rest of the country is covered by plants in California, North Carolina and Texas. Over 50 of their 742 acres are under roof where visitors see ingredients like blue plastic bags of celery stacked two stories high, huge refrigerated storage rooms just for cheese, and dried chicken arriving by chute where it lands in boxes and ends up in gravy. Visitors see the process rather than the soup as well as lots of cans getting lids, getting labels, getting stamped, getting boxed. In 1957 tomato was the leading soup. Today it's cream of mushroom, except in winter, when colds and flu push chicken noodle to the top.

*East Maumee Avenue (Turn left at the Soup Can); 419/592-1010.
Nov 1-Apr 30, Tue & Thu, 10 a.m. & 1 p.m. Individuals and families
may join larger groups. Tours last 60-90 minutes, walk a mile and a
half, climb stairs. Must wear hair nets and earplugs and remove all
jewelry above the waist, including earrings and wedding rings,
which during the tour are left in a secure place with purses and
other bags. Call ahead.*

HENRY COUNTY COURTHOUSE/NAPOLEON — After crossing the
bridge to Napoleon, you will notice one noteworthy piece of architecture left standing. In 1879, a fire destroyed the Henry County courthouse and 22 buildings. In 1882, a new one of brick and sandstone,
with a 160-foot tower, a clock and two glassed circular windows, was
built and topped by a 15-foot Goddess of Justice. Imagine an elegantly
bedecked, buxom Victorian madam rising magnificently above a
crowd of, well, not much. That is the Henry County courthouse in
downtown Napoleon. God save the Queen. (The Henry County
Courthouse was the first building in the county on the National
Register of Historic Places. Now, one other, is the St. Augustine
Catholic Church on the corner of E. Clinton and Monroe. It's an
exquisite ecclesiastical High Victorian Gothic.)

ACCESS — Near the bridge, turn west onto scenic SR424. (Harley
Davidson, Inc. named SR424 between Napoleon and Defiance as one
of the ten best touring roads in the U.S.) A few blocks down, stop at
the Riverview Frosty Boy, a combination scenic overlook and old-
fashioned sandwich and ice cream drive-in. Swings and picnic tables
are at the top of a few steps. There's a lovely view of the Maumee and
Ritter Park. Try the barbecued beef.

GIRTY'S ISLAND/EAST OF FLORIDA — The island was named for
Simon Girty and his ruthless brothers, who supposedly had been
raised by Seneca Indians after their parents were killed in a raid. It's
said that in the early 1800's, they ran a trading post on Girty's,
swapping white man's scalps with the Indians. Another story of a brass
cannon lost off one end of the island during the War of 1812 has sent
decades of divers into the Maumee's waters. In 1899, Fred and
Maureen Voight opened an amusement park on the island. It was
destroyed by the 1913 flood. Years later, Voight started up a dance hall
that kept ferries going back and forth from the mainland on Friday and
Saturday nights. The ruins remain.

SILVER DOLLAR ANTIQUES/FLORIDA — Florida is an Ohio ghost
town. Presently a blip on SR424, it once supported a grist mill, 16
saloons, a slaughterhouse, a hoop mill, an ashery, and two hotels.
Thought to be on the site of Florida's first log cabin, Silver Dollar
Antiques was originally known as Hunter's Inn and later Ye Olde
Tavern and is filled to the rafters with an assortment of furniture, farm
equipment, collectibles and quilts. Better still, it has its own living
history in the form of its six owners, all local kids who grew up and
stayed put and developed a strong affection for their turf.
*Halfway between Napoleon and Defiance; 419/762-5333. Open Thu
& Fri 3-8, Sat 10-6, Sun 12-6.*

INDEPENDENCE DAM STATE PARK/INDEPENDENCE — During canal days, Independence rivaled Defiance as a shipping center on the Miami and Erie canal. But when the canal shut down so did Independence. Today, Defiance gets the business, but Independence has the fun. The 604-acre Independence Dam State Park is a skinny 604-acre oasis along six unbroken miles of the old canal. It's crowded in the summer when campers, boaters, water skiers, hikers, fishermen, picnickers, cyclists and sightseers descend on the spot. The three-mile main access road often looks like a Friday night cruise-in. One of the best things to do is walk the three-mile hiking trail through a dense hardwood forest to Florida. It begins on the east side of the campground and was once the canal towpath. In the winter, this is a great cross country ski trail. You're allowed to winter camp and if the conditions are right, there's ice skating on the canal and at the marina. *State Route 424, four miles east of Defiance; 419/784-3263. Open all year.*

FORT DEFIANCE/DEFIANCE — God made the world in six days, General "Mad" Anthony Wayne built Fort Defiance in eight. Said to be the strongest fort built during the Indian campaign, Wayne's confidence in his work was remembered by the words, "I defy the English, Indians, and all the devils in hell to take it." General Scott responded with, "Then call it Fort Defiance!" And they did. Abandoned in 1796, an exact replica was built for its 100th anniversary in 1894 with 533 donated logs. Vandals ruined it so it was later torn down. In 1904, Carnegie funds built another fortress on the spot, the handsome, red sandstone, Defiance Public Library. The most respected historical building in town, the library has a wonderful Ohioana room with artifacts from the fort, beautiful stained glass windows, and a tranquil reading room that overlooks the river. Outside, a granite boulder marks the location of the original fort's flagstaff, the surveying point for all land northward to Canada. It was from here that Wayne marched off to do battle at Fallen Timbers.
320 Fort Street; 419/782-1456. Mon-Thu 9:00 a.m.-8:30 p.m., Fri & Sat 9 a.m.-6 p.m., Sun 1 p.m.-5 p.m. July & August, Sat 9 a.m.-Noon, Sun Closed.

THE VALENTINE THEATRE/DEFIANCE — Across from Kissner's is one of the few remaining downtown movie theatres in Ohio and the only sign of life on Clinton Street on a Sunday afternoon. Originally the handsome Citizens Opera House built in 1892, it's gone through several remodelings, not all to its benefit. Buy some popcorn and ask the girl for a look at the wall of historic memorabilia. Then take a brief walk up to the balcony. Once your eyes get accustomed to the dark, you'll see some of its originality (this is the best place from which to watch a show), none of which comes from the movies on the screen.
602 Clinton Street; 419/782-5826. First-run movies. Call for times.

CHARLIE'S/DEFIANCE — Old Defiance College coeds will remember **Charlie's Down Under** as The Black Lantern, a dressy dinner spot and the place they were taken to if their date had any money left after buying beer. Old Defiance College males will remember **Charlie's Bakery and Deli** as the Tip Top, a 24-hour greasy spoon and the place they went to after leaving the coed they fed. Now that the face of downtown has changed from retail to service, Charlie's serves a more responsible crowd, the employed. Family-owned for over 40 years, two daughters have resurrected both eateries and the chef, Peter Lundberg, controls the grill. They bake healthy breads, pies, cheesecakes, and muffins that are sold in the bakery and served in the restaurant. They're best known for their "halves", a successful psychological dining tool allowing any customer on a diet to buy half of anything they serve – even a half a hamburger or half a salad-and still have room for, say, half a piece of cheesecake, thus going home with half the guilt.
200 Clinton Street; 419/782-2283. Charlie's Bakery & Deli, Mon-Fri &:30 a.m.-6:00 p.m., Sat 8:30 a.m.-3:00 p.m. Charlie's Down Under, Mon-Fri 11 p.m - 2 p.m.

ASIDE Architectural admirers should keep their heads down while in downtown Defiance lest they lose their lunch looking at the top of the county courthouse. Apparently, for need of space, the "powers that were" (in the 1950s) lopped of the head of the beautiful Victorian courthouse and attached a level that defies all description. Local embarrassment has spurred a grass roots effort towards restoration. Send money.

THE DEFIANCE COLLEGE — General Wayne chose to name his fort on the strength of his military convictions, and it's been heard that many a high school senior chose Defiance College by its name, that certainly. Founded in 1850, this four-year liberal arts college has a small, but eclectic enrollment. Though most students are from Ohio, recruiters have found students from 17 states and 15 foreign countries to study here and brave the landscape. The campus is flat, prone to mud from driving spring rains and to ice from windy winter storms. Most of the handsome, original buildings have burned giving rise to 1950ish, flat-roofed, boxy structures, except for the ultra modern, new library, (President Dwight D. Eisenhower arrived by train at 11:28 a.m. on October 15, 1953, to lay the cornerstone of the old Anthony Wayne Library. He was gone by 12.17 p.m.) rising worriedly from **below** ground level like a phoenix from the ashes. Yet what it lacks aesthetically is made up for by personal care. It's a one-on-one sort of school with faculty and administration available, practically, on 24-hour call. They deal with the worries and war whoops as well as offer classes in 55 major areas of study with a well-established program in education. They're one of a few small Ohio colleges now offering a master of arts in education.
701 North Clinton Street; 419/784-4010.

 JIGG'S DRIVE-IN/DEFIANCE — If the weather's nice and you're heading out towards Auglaize Village, stop at Jigg's, one of the few remaining 1950s root beer/carhop drive-ins in the state (Jolly's, in Tiffin, in another). The safety-orange, white-awninged root beer drive-in has 22 spaces for cars and inside seating for 12. Three car hops dressed in logo shirts and jackets still hook their trays to the car windows, work hard for their tips, and serve the best root beer and chili dogs in the area. Long before McDonald's, Burger King and shopping malls, Jigg's was where root beer was king and romance was, well, romance. Teenage boys worked in the kitchen, teenage girls worked as car hops. Liaisons were formed, many stuck, and now *their* kids are working here. Jiggs's daughter, Carol, runs the drive-in now, her own romantic past firmly parked in this lot. While she was a high school carhop, her sweetheart once peeled out, spitting gravel askew. Her mother forbid him to return. Unable to stay away, he gave her mom a rose bush as a peace offering. It worked; mom planted it in the yard; it still blooms. And the sweetheart? Well, he's Carol's husband, Roy, and now he *owns* the place.
111 Holgate Avenue; 419/782-4393. Open Mid April until last Saturday in August. Open 7 days 11 a.m.-9 p.m.

AUGLAIZE VILLAGE/DEFIANCE — Here's a nice place to end a
Maumee River Valley tour, a place to think from whence we
came...besides Perrysburg. Ohio and points west were settled because
we rousted the Indians who lived in tepees and grew vegetables and
had corn fields and apple orchards covering the landscape. Likely it
should have stayed that way. The white settlers had a different view,
drained the swamp, grew onions, and tenaciously survived. While
there ought to be a testament to the first residents (perhaps Seven
Eagles in Grand Rapids is a start), Auglaize Village reminds us of the
settlers who came after and lived here from 1860 to 1920. Forty acres
include a section of the Miami and Erie Canal, a pioneer cemetery,
doctor and dentist offices, a church, a school, a barbershop, a
blacksmith shop and two museums-a whole lot compared to the
Indians' needs. Today, the white man searches feverishly for ways to
clean up his land, eat more naturally, and live a calmer life. Someday,
perhaps from whence we came, will be to where we end.
*South of US24 on Krouse Road, 3 miles west of Defiance; 419/784-
0107 or 784-5730. Memorial Day-Labor Day, Weekends only, 10
a.m.-5 p.m. Admission: Adults $2; children & senior citizens, $1.*

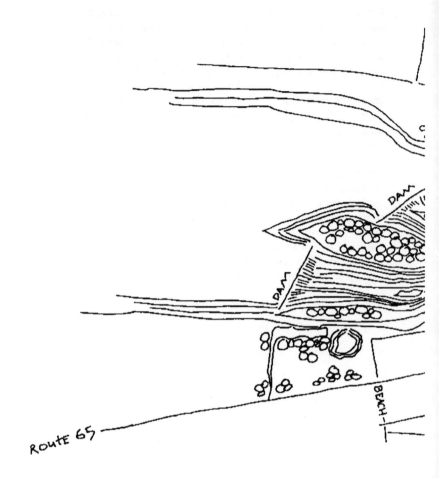

ROUTE 65

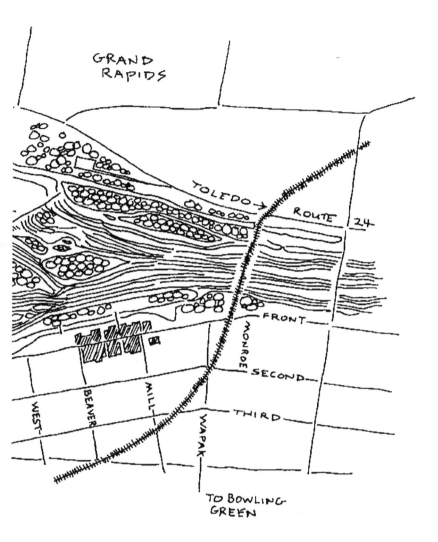

GRAND RAPIDS

TOLEDO →

ROUTE 24

FRONT

MONROE

SECOND

THIRD

WEST

BEAVER

MILL

WAPAK

TO BOWLING GREEN

Milan

First things first. This is *not* Milan, pronounced
"Muh-lawn", as in Italy, although in typical
nineteenth century fashion, the name was
grandly borrowed from the European city. No,
this Milan is "My-Lin" as in Ohio, and it is a
village neatly poised on a bluff above the Huron
River only a few miles south of Lake Erie. But if
the pronunciation seems deceiving, consider its
appearance: Milan looks far more like a New
England village than a Midwest one. Travelers
approaching via the Ohio Turnpike that cuts
across the state's northern coastal plain grow
accustomed to red barns, white farmhouses, and
green fields of corn and soybeans. Those who
leave the turnpike at Exit 7 and travel south on
U.S. 250 might rightfully expect to be greeted by
grain elevators when they turn east on State
Route 113 and enter Milan. Instead, they find a
pretty public square about which enterprise and
architecture are balanced in the best tradition of

Yankee town planning. The origins of that
square go all the way back to post Revolutionary
War Connecticut, which laid claim to some
3,000,000 acres of northern Ohio territory by
virtue of a colonial charter that gave it dibs on
land extending from sea to sea. The area was
known as the Connecticut Western Reserve, and
because many Connecticut families had lost
property when the British burned their towns
during the Revolution, 500,000 acres of it was
set aside specifically to compensate them. Now
located primarily in Erie and Huron counties, the
tract was dubbed "The Firelands," and the
people who settled it patterned their new towns
after the ones they had known in New England.
¶ In the middle of the Firelands in 1816,
Ebenezer Merry laid out a town around a public
square and christened it "Beatty" after the man
from whom he bought the land. The village
fathers later changed the name to Milan, apparently because they wanted to keep up with the
municipal Joneses after a neighboring burg took
the name Berlin. Merry built water-powered mills
along the Huron, and soon a lively commerce of
tradesmen and craftsmen developed around the
square. In the 1830s, some local entrepreneurs
caught the Canal Fever that was sweeping the
nation and decided to turn the village into a lake
port by digging a three-mile, deep-water ditch
that would connect Milan to Lake Erie via the
Huron River. It was an immediate success. Farmers from far and wide brought their grain to
Milan for shipment, and lake schooners soon
filled the canal. Teams and wagons jammed the
streets; a mile-long row of warehouses lined the

river bank; the population boomed; and ship-
building mushroomed into the newest village
industry. By the 1840s, the village was the second-largest wheat-shipping port in the world, its
exports exceeded only by those of Odessa,
Russia. Milan might have grown into a major
city, but the townspeople made an economically
fatal mistake by refusing to allow the new railroad companies access to the village. Thus, the
tracks went south through Norwalk, and when
rail transportation killed the canals, Milan's
prosperity died along with them. ¶ The family
of Samuel and Nancy Edison was one of the
many that had moved to Milan during the boom
years. Sam earned a living making roofing
shingles in Milan, and he and Nancy built a
house overlooking the canal, where in 1847,
their seventh and last child was born. They
named the baby Thomas Alva. It is said that
when Sam went out later that day to get medicine for his wife, he told everyone he met along
the square that he had a new son. None of the
villagers realized it at the time, of course, but
they were hearing the first announcement that
the world was about to change in ways that they
could hardly imagine and that the vehicle for
much of that change would be the baby who
would grow up in their midst in Milan. Young
Tom proved to be a somewhat difficult child: he
tried to hatch some eggs by building a nest and
sitting on them; he tripped into the canal and
had to be rescued; he fell into a grain bin near
the docks and nearly suffocated; he even set a
serious fire. Their neighbors probably breathed a
sigh of relief when the failing fortunes of the

canal made the Edisons move to Michigan in 1854. But who would have then anticipated that seemingly troublesome seven-year-old was a genius who would become the nation's foremost inventor? ¶ Thomas Edison's legacy to the world in general, of course, was a series of inventions – the phonograph, the first motion picture cameras and projectors, the alkaline storage battery, the first practical incandescent electric light bulb – that virtually defined modern life. Even more important than the now-ubiquitous light bulb, however, was Edison's development of a centralized power distribution system that delivered electricity from generators to families, farms, and factories, and thus truly transformed the way mankind lived and worked. But Edison's legacy to Milan in particular has been just as profound. He is his hometown's claim to fame, and the village has virtually become a cottage industry based on the happenstance of his being born there. Edison himself may have sealed that fate in 1906, when he bought back his birthplace and thus assured the village an historically important focal point. ¶ Today, Edison's influence on Milan is as subtle as "Edison Chargers" being the nickname of the local high school, and as obvious as the EDISON BIRTHPLACE sign at the turnpike exit, which diverts travelers from the nearby Lake Erie playgrounds to an historic sojourn on the village's quiet, tree-lined streets. With its pleasing public square and avenues of attractive old homes, Milan is a place of enormous charm. It present an antique patina that affords visitors an almost wistful re-creation of what the Good Old Days would have been – or perhaps more to the point – *should* have been like. Residents speak proudly of not having to lock their doors and say that a pot of impatiens put out on the lawn in May will still be unmolested in October. Much of its appeal is that Milan truly is the kind of place where visitors can without trepidation let their children walk freely on the street, as well as impart a history lesson or two. Milan's present is indeed past perfect. Quaint is one adjective that comes to mind. But that does quite not do the village justice. *Well-preserved* is far more like it.

GASTIER'S FARM BED AND BREAKFAST — Ted Gastier's roots run deep in Erie County; his land has been in the family since 1863, and he is the fourth generation of Gastiers to farm it. They raise corn, soybeans, melons, peas, beans, tomatoes, peppers, cabbage, and eggplant and sell much of it from a produce stand near the end of the driveway. Guests stay in the family homestead, a comfortable farmhouse kept spanking clean by Ted's wife, Donna. She cans her own peaches, makes her own pickles, and treats her guests to homemade blueberry pancakes in the morning. Breakfast is served in the kitchen at a lovely old ten-foot oak table that Donna bought for one dollar at an auction. One of the guest bedrooms has an adjacent room specially outfitted for children; it has an overflowing toy box, a well-stocked bookcase, and a doll house that one of the Gastier boys made from a melon crate one Christmas.
1902 Strecker Road; 419/499-2985. No pets, no smoking. MC, V.

BOOS FAMILY INN BED AND BREAKFAST — Their friends thought Don and Mary Boos were crazy to be leaving a modern home for a downtrodden house that dated to the 1860s and had a hole in the roof. But that was nearly two decades ago, and in the years since, Don and Mary have literally worked wonders with additions and improvements that transformed an old log cabin into a cozy country home. Don's mother made all the quilts, and Mary's mother provided the basic recipe for the sour cream kuchen she serves at breakfast. Mary assigns bridal and anniversary couples to a pretty room decorated in lace, chintz, and wicker, and then pampers them with a morning tray of muffins and strawberries. Guests can stroll out to the barn or follow shaded brick walkways through the lovingly landscaped front lawn. The grounds have so many plants that even the parking lot has flower beds.
5054 State Route 601, south of Milan; 419/668-6257. No pets, no small children, no smoking. MC, V.

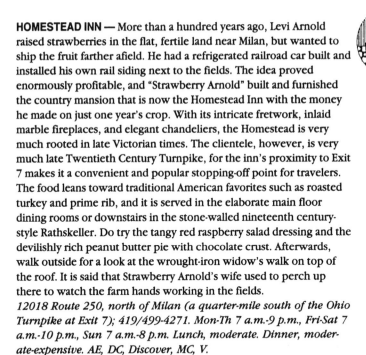

HOMESTEAD INN — More than a hundred years ago, Levi Arnold raised strawberries in the flat, fertile land near Milan, but wanted to ship the fruit farther afield. He had a refrigerated railroad car built and installed his own rail siding next to the fields. The idea proved enormously profitable, and "Strawberry Arnold" built and furnished the country mansion that is now the Homestead Inn with the money he made on just one year's crop. With its intricate fretwork, inlaid marble fireplaces, and elegant chandeliers, the Homestead is very much rooted in late Victorian times. The clientele, however, is very much late Twentieth Century Turnpike, for the inn's proximity to Exit 7 makes it a convenient and popular stopping-off point for travelers. The food leans toward traditional American favorites such as roasted turkey and prime rib, and it is served in the elaborate main floor dining rooms or downstairs in the stone-walled nineteenth century-style Rathskeller. Do try the tangy red raspberry salad dressing and the devilishly rich peanut butter pie with chocolate crust. Afterwards, walk outside for a look at the wrought-iron widow's walk on top of the roof. It is said that Strawberry Arnold's wife used to perch up there to watch the farm hands working in the fields.
12018 Route 250, north of Milan (a quarter-mile south of the Ohio Turnpike at Exit 7); 419/499-4271. Mon-Th 7 a.m.-9 p.m., Fri-Sat 7 a.m.-10 p.m., Sun 7 a.m.-8 p.m. Lunch, moderate. Dinner, moderate-expensive. AE, DC, Discover, MC, V.

MILAN INN — The best mini-history of Milan can be found on the walls of this restaurant in the form of nine murals that depict the life and times of the village. Painted in 1968 by Martha Hutchinson, nine panels surround the dining room with scenes depicting the first settlers on the Huron River, the heady canal era, Edison's inventions, and the sorry end of the proud schooner *Idaho*, which was left for more than 50 years to slowly rot away in the defunct Milan canal. Built in 1845 on the south side of the village square, the inn used to be a stagecoach stop, but it is now the province of Milan's mayor and most unabashed promoter, Robert Bickley. Known locally as "Mayor Bob," he is a stonemason by trade and says that whatever buildings in town he doesn't own, he has probably restored. One of his projects was the Hutchinson murals, which he began cleaning one night at 11 p.m. "in order to avoid the sidewalk superintendents." He used Ivory soap and a shop vac, and when he was done, the painter herself declared that the panels looked as good as the day she completed them. Look for the murals and Mayor Bob — he'll be the fellow with the ten-gallon hat — when you visit his restaurant. Then enjoy the inn's trademark salad and bread trays with the homemade sticky buns that have become a local legend.
29 East Church Street; 419/499-4606. Tu-Fri 11-9, Sat 8 a.m.-9 p.m., Sun 8-8. Breakfast is served all day on Sunday. Moderate. MC, V.

THE INVENTION — Since it's across the public square from Edison's statue and the menus have drawings of his light bulb on the cover, the inspiration for this restaurant's name is obvious. So are the customers: the Invention is where the locals go for fare such as chicken and biscuits, beef and noodles, meatloaf, and Swiss steak. Leo and Martha Smith have kept them coming back with a basic food philosophy: "Keep it simple and keep it good." Of course, their elderberry pie hasn't hurt business, either. Every summer, the Smiths go to a secret spot in Ohio's Amish country and pick enough wild elderberries to make between 400 and 500 pies. When they start serving them late in August, the word spreads, and people come from as far away as Cleveland.

15 North Main Street; 419/499-2661. Mon-Sat 5:30 a.m.-7 p.m. Sun 7 a.m.-7 p.m. Closed holidays. Inexpensive-Moderate. No credit cards.

HISTORICAL AND ARCHITECTURAL WALKING TOURS — The enterprising Yankees who built Milan left it both a rich heritage as a canal town and many fine homes that are still the obvious fruits of their labor. Among the most architecturally notable structures are three Greek Revival homes on Center Street built during Milan's heyday in the 1840s, but the village also has many splendid Federal, Gothic Revival, Italianate, and Queen Anne dwellings. The history and architecture of both the village's homes and its Public Square buildings has been meticulously documented by the Milan Historical Museum in self-guided tour brochures available at the museum's Visitors' Center/Gift Shop.

JIM'S PIZZA BOX — When Jim West tells you he can make you a calzone that you'll have dreams about, he's not kidding. His huge fresh spinach and tomato version comes encased in a garlicky, mouth-watering crust that makes you wish you could eat more. Jim comes from a close-knit family, and from his Italian mom's recipes to his sister's cooking, everyone lends a hand in the restaurant. Jim says that his pizza "speaks for itself," but it's the folks in Milan who speak for his spaghetti – so many of them come in for his Wednesday night special that finding a parking spot anywhere near the village square is almost impossible.

10 South Main Street; 419/499-4166. Tu-Th 11 a.m.-midnight, Fri-Sat 11 a.m.-1 a.m., Sun 3-10. Closed holidays. Inexpensive-moderate.

ASIDE "My recollections of Milan are somewhat scanty as I left the town when I was not quite seven years old. I remember the wheat elevators on the canal, and Gay shipyard; also the launching of new boats, on which occasion the piece of land called the Hogback would be filled with what seemed to me to be the entire population of the town who came to witness the launching. I also recall a public square filled at times with farmers' teams, and also what seemed to me to be an immense number of teams that came to town bringing oak staves for barrels."

— Thomas Edison

EDISON BIRTHPLACE — In 1947, Thomas Edison's second wife and daughter opened the small, red brick house where he was born as a museum to celebrate the centennial of his birth. Filled with Edison memorabilia — his automobile riding coat, slippers, derby hat, and

THE PUBLIC SQUARE — Milan's square is everything a town square should be. It has tall and sturdy oaks shading park benches; a flagpole from which the nation's banner proudly flies; a graceful gazebo with Corinthian columns; a Civil War monument honoring the local boys who served at Gettysburg and Lookout Mountain, and a statue of the local luminary, which in Milan's case happens to be the ultimate illuminary, Thomas Edison, who literally did light up not only his hometown, but also the entire world. Actually the Edison statue is something of a surprise, for it depicts not the mature and esteemed Inventor, but Young Edison, boy in a poignant pose with his mother, who cradles an open book on her lap. It was Nancy Edison, of course, who became Tom's teacher after a schoolmaster pronounced her son "addled." She had him reading Shakespeare by the time he was nine, and Edison later acknowledged, "My mother was the making of me. She understood me; she let me follow my bent."

The square is such a pretty and placid place today that it hard to imagine the raucous scene that it was during Edison's boyhood. With hundreds of farm wagons lined up waiting to get into town and big ships crowding the canal, Milan had plenty of hard working, hard drinking men coming into town. Taverns abounded, including the "pot houses," private homes where small amounts of liquor could be obtained. Horses were hitched in the public square, which was covered with dirt (there was no grass until after the Civil War), watering troughs, and manure. It was frequently the scene of fights and brawls.

When Edison visited Milan's public square in August of 1923, he brought along a couple of friends, Harvey Firestone and Henry Ford. Two thousand people jammed the square to hail the Triumvirate of American Industry and Invention that had graced the village with their presence. Looking out across the crowd, Edison quite probably recalled an earlier, far less pleasant day when people had once before come to the square to gawk at him. It was in 1853, when he was six years old and had set fire to his father's barn "just to see what it would do." The blaze destroyed the barn and could have taken all of Milan. Thus, Sam Edison devised a public punishment and proclaimed that he would give his son a whipping on the square. Tom took his licks in front of everyone, including many parents who brought their children to witness the instructional disgrace.

Though saved from Master Edison's fire, the buildings around the square were periodically ravaged by flames, beginning with an 1850 conflagration that started "in a wretched drinking establishment." As a result, the dates of the present downtown buildings range from 1821 to 1912. They harbor neat-as-a-pin shops that bespeak of civilized small town commerce — a bank, a florist, an art gallery, and an large concentration of antique shops and eateries. The Public Library has beautiful Moorish-looking terra cotta designs and was one of the first small town libraries funded by Andrew Carnegie. The villagers were so proud of having "one of the handsomest little libraries in the state," that when it opened in 1912, all the children in Milan were dismissed from school just so they could attend the dedication.

cane — as well as replicas of his inventions, the restored home now preserves many Edison family furnishings as well as household articles typical of the period. His mother's "disciplinary switch" hangs in its original spot in the basement kitchen, and her tea set is displayed in the parlor. But the most important room in the house is undoubtedly the little bedroom off the family sitting room where Edison first saw the light of day. When Edison paid his last visit to Milan in 1923, the inventor of the light bulb was astonished to discover that his old homestead was still being illuminated by lamplight and candles; it was an oversight that was soon corrected.

9 North Edison Drive; 419/499-2135. Closed Mondays, except holidays. Open Jan by appointment; Feb-May, Tu-Sun 1-5; Memorial Day-Labor Day, Tu-Sat 10-5, Sun 1-5; Labor Day-Nov, Tu-Sun 1-5. Group tours by appointment only. Nominal admission.

Milan Historical Museum

THE MILAN HISTORICAL MUSEUM — Local museums of this quality are rare, but to find such varied and beautifully displayed exhibits in a place as small as Milan is a surprise as well as a delight. Happily, the museum has benefited from the largesse of local folks who went on to bigger things, but had the generosity to share their good fortune with their hometown. As a result, the museum holds many hard-to-find treasures such as green opaque glassware and "Sandusky," a circa 1838 Staffordshire Willow Blue commemorative plate of which less than ten still exist. With some 80,000 artifacts from more than 1,000 donors, the museum is not limited to a single site, but consists of a complex of buildings, each of which features specialized collections and attractions. **The Visitors' Center/Gift Shop** offers an informative twelve-minute slide show that presents a fine overview of the museum and an introduction to the exhibits. Also available are here are books, brochures, maps, and self-guided tours of Milan. **The Galpin House**, also known as the Main Building, was built in 1840 by Dr. Leman Galpin, the physician who delivered Thomas Edison. It houses a collection of 75 mechanical banks (including a rare "Uncle Remus" who steals chicken) and one of the nation's finest doll collections. Cleveland's Mildred Coulton searched the world for more than 25 years to gather the 350 wax, wood, *papier-mâché, bisque,* and china dolls. The oldest, a primitive 1790 doll with a leather head and homespun body, came west in a covered wagon. The Robert Mowry Glass Collection occupies two rooms in the Galpin House. Considered one of the top ten American art glass collections in the nation, it consists of more than 1,500 pieces of pattern and pressed glass and English, Sandwich, Art Nouveau, Tiffany, Durand, Aurene, and Steuben glass. Dominick Labino, the renowned Toledo glass artist, did the lovely window panels and also donated several pieces. The Country Store, the Blacksmith Shop, and the Carriage Shed are located behind Galpin House. A replica of an old Milan general store, **The Country Store** features cracker barrels, a pot belly stove, and an old-fashioned post office. **The Blacksmith Shop** has the traditional – a bellows and anvil, plus the unexpected – a life-sized *papier-mâché* horse. **The Carriage Shed** houses buggies, farm implements, a working machine shop, and a potato digger invented by Milan's I.W. Hoover. **The Sayles House** was built during the town's boom years of the 1840s, and has been restored to depict a day in the life of canal-era Milan. Of special interest are the 1850 rosewood melodeon in the parlor and the weaving room's collection of spinning, flax, and wool wheels from pioneer Ohio and Pennsylvania. **The Newton Memorial Arts Building** is the jewel in the museum's crown. A lovely Early American structure, it was built by Gulf Oil executive Bert Newton as a loving tribute to his wife, Edna Roe Newton. Though the Newtons traveled the world during his career, they retired in the Milan area where both of them had been raised. After Mrs. Newton died in 1964, her husband gave the museum the eclectic and extensive collection of art, textiles, carvings, porcelains, and furniture that they had accumulated during their life together. Mrs. Newton was an expert at needlepoint and pettipoint, and her handiwork is on display everywhere from the seats of chairs to a magnificent 408-square afghan hanging on the wall. The set of exquisite lace placemats was presented to Mrs. Newton by the King of Belgium, the French porcelain coffee set dates to Napoleon, and the 50 intricately carved wood and ivory netsukes were used as buttons in sixteenth and seventeenth century Japan. In the upper gallery, the Anderson Dupree harpsichord not only splendidly displays scenes depicting the history of Milan, but also is often pressed into service for Sunday afternoon concerts. *Edison Drive between Church and Front Streets; 419/499-2968. Closed Mondays and Labor Day Weekend. Open Apr, May, Sept, Oct, Tu-Sun 1-5; June, July, Aug, Tu-Sun 10-5. Tours by prior arrangement. Admission by donation.*

ANNUAL MELON FESTIVAL — It started out years ago as Milan's homecoming celebration, but has since escalated to the biggest event in town with a parade, queen contest, family entertainment, and 100,000 people turning out to celebrate the musk melons and watermelons that thrive in the area's black loam soil. It's also the only time in the entire year that melon ice cream – in two varieties, no less – is made in Milan.
Labor Day Weekend, Town Square.

SETTLERS' DAY — Open house in the entire Milan Historical Museum complex is held in honor of the pioneer spirit with hot apple cider, popped corn, and working demonstrations of old-time arts, crafts, and games.
Third Sun in Oct, Edison Drive between Church and Front Streets.

CHRISTMAS TREE LANE — Every year, area organizations and individuals decorate some 100 Christmas trees that are put on display in the Town Hall by the Milan Garden Club. Many of the trees have themes (the local chapter of Habitat for Humanity uses tools as ornaments), and local orchestral and choral groups perform holiday music. In conjunction with the event, the Milan Historical Museum hosts a Holiday Open House with nostalgic seasonal displays and decorations.
Weekend after Thanksgiving Day, Town Hall on the Public Square

NATURALLY COUNTRY — Though it's down a country road, past a steep curve, and through stone gateposts at the end of a long driveway, this excellent and unique gift shop is well worth the trip. Outside, the setting is definitely bucolic: a golden retriever lounges lazily near the front door, and the barn-like building affords eye-popping views of the wooded ravine and creek out back. Inside, owner Tracy Lake has filled the two-story shop with beautifully crafted dried floral arrangements, bouquets, wreaths, gifts, and seasonal items. Since Tracy built the shop in her own backyard, it's not surprising that her flower garden contains many of the plants — yarrow, cockscomb, globe amaranth — she uses in her tasteful creations. The shop also boasts a freeze drying machine that turns roses, calla lillies, and peonies into "antiqued" flowers with muted shades that Tracy then fashions into custom-made bridal bouquets.
845 Lais Road; 419/668-4340. Daily 10-5.

THE HEN HOUSE — Joyce Ditz maintains a menagerie unlike any other. She has bears and sheep on rockers, pigs and cows used for footrests, and cats that serve as doorstops. In 1980, the Norwalk woman began cutting out patterns for animal puppets, and her one-woman cottage industry has since grown into Ohio's largest manufacturer of animal creations. Although Joyce employs more than a dozen sewers, she designs all of her — ahem — pet projects herself, constantly haunting the library for details like the long, curly eyelashes on a giraffe. Ideas such as putting large animals on wheels have even come to her in the middle of the night. You've seen Joyce's ivory brocade Decorator Duck and fully-jointed Teddy Bear in the Spiegel Christmas catalog, but only at the Hen House can you find all her creatures, great and small.
4888 U.S. Route 250, south of Milan; 419/663-3377. Mon-Sat 10-5, Sun noon-4. MC, V.

LAKE ERIE FACTORY OUTLET CENTER — This retail mecca just north of the Ohio Turnpike attracts the shopping faithful with 40 stores that offer discounts on name brand merchandise ranging from pots and pans to perfume. About 250 busloads of bargain hunters make the pilgrimage each year to the clean and attractively designed "village" complex, where a landscaped courtyard separates the storefronts. The center is not only Ohio's largest factory outlet, but also boasts factory stores for brands such as Mikasa, Bugle Boy, and Farberware.

11001 U.S. Route 250, north of Milan; 419/499-2528. Closed New Years Day, Easter, Thanksgiving, and Christmas. Open Jan 2-Mar 31 Mon-Th 10-6, Fri and Sat 10-9, Sun noon-6; Apr-Dec Mon-Sat 10-9, Sun 10-6. Food Court always opens one hour before retail stores. Senior Citizen discounts every Tu. Motor coaches and groups of 10 or more are encouraged to call ahead.

STATE ROUTE 113/EAST OF MILAN — When this road leaves Milan, it stretches past a variety of country markets selling a cornucopia of goods: antiques, lawn ornaments, rabbits, cider, and bountiful fruits and vegetables that are testament to the fat of the local lands. Just outside of Milan, **Miller's Melons** (which is easily spotted by the tank painted to look like a huge watermelon) sells fresh-picked produce from farm wagons, while **Mortensen's Greenhouse** offers an outstanding selection of not only premium plants, but also quality furnishings ranging from Windsor chairs to tea sets. But if you stay on Route 113 for about 15 of those country miles, you'll be rewarded with the opportunity to visit one of the most beautiful and least known gardens in Ohio. **Schoepfle Arboretum** is the remarkable result of the vision and work of one man, Otto Schoepfle, who described his 20-plus acres of Eden as "a garden that just grew." True enough, but it grew because of Mr. Schoepfle's knowledge and sense of the aesthetic into a meticulously manicured landscape that is as marvelous in the winter when conifers lend their particular character to grounds as in mid-summer when the 500-plant rose garden is in bloom. Mr. Schoepfle, who ran the Elyria newspaper for 40 years, began his garden in 1936 on property than had been in his family since the 1800s. He traveled to the fine gardens of the world for inspiration and ideas, and over the years, he acquired and planted more than 400 species of flora. Incredibly, every plant has been labeled with its botanical name. An avenue of hedges outlines the formal areas of the garden, while paths lead to smaller, informal spots with low stone walls, a pond surrounded by a sweep of hemlock, and the Harem of Holly, where a grove of female hollies service a single male tree. But it is the topiary garden that elicits oohs and aahs from folks and makes them wonder if Edward Scissorhands has paid a visit to northern Ohio. The walls of boxwood and mounds of taxus that have been sculptured into animals and geometric forms are, of course, the handiwork of Mr. Schoepfle, whose most popular piece is the Japanese yew that he shaped into a dog sitting in an overstuffed armchair.

To reach this Garden of Otto's Delights, take State Route 113 to its intersection with State Route 60 at Birmingham. Turn south on State Route 60, then take the first left hand turn off of Route 60, which is South Street. Follow South Street to Market Street and the arboretum. It is open daily during daylight hours. Admission is free, but visitors are reminded to respect the plants and property

NEIGHBORING NORWALK – Located just a couple of miles south of Milan on State Route 250, Norwalk has justifiably earned a reputation as one of the prettiest towns in northern Ohio. All of West Main Street from the public library to the 200 block a mile away has been designated as an Historic District, and many of its architecturally diverse homes — which date to as far back as 1826 and have 200-year old oaks on the lawns — are on the National Register of Historic Places. The beauty of the town began with the Connecticut "fire sufferers" who settled it in 1817. They had not only the foresight to have Norwalk designated the county seat, but also the insight to plant maple trees along Main Street soon after it was platted. Succeeding generations carried on that tradition, and the arboreous town became known as "Maple City." Norwalk has almost always enjoyed a certain prosperity, ensured before the Civil War by its being the site of prestigious academic academies that tutored the likes of Rutherford B. Hayes, then by the coming of the railroads and a succession of manufacturing industries. Today, Norwalk is blessed with a still-viable central business district that is largely free of national chain stores. The local merchants are so upbeat about holding their own against outlying shopping centers that they've taken to calling the downtown "uptown." Norwalk's Main Street is anchored by a genuine Ohio sandstone Courthouse (the fourth one to occupy the same site since 1818), and the Norwalk Public Library, an impressive domed building with a beautiful main reading room graced by a pair of fireplaces. The library was built in 1905 because a local barber happened to know Andrew Carnegie. The barber was a black man named Benjamin F. Stewart, who had once helped Carnegie settle a thorny Pennsylvania steel mill strike. Mr. Stewart appealed to Carnegie on behalf of the library, and the philanthropist responded by giving the folks in Norwalk much of the money they needed to build it.

MORGANS/NORWALK — Since Morgans owner Gloria Hart lives at Puckerbrush Farms, many of menu items — lamb, veal, even the berries baked into pies — are raised there. Gloria calls her cuisine "good home cooking," and that it is, from the made-from-scratch soups to the homemade breads and pastries. Be sure to try the Scottish eggs, which Gloria discovered in a pub in England. They're a novel and delicious appetizer — hard-boiled eggs encased in a sausage crust, then deep-fried and served with a dipping sauce.
2949 State Route 250, south of Norwalk; 419/663-2333. Tu-Sat 11-9, Sun 11-4. Moderate-expensive. MC, V

BERARDI'S/NORWALK — This family restaurant is new to Norwalk, although the Berardi family also operates well-known eateries in Huron and Sandusky. From the early 1940s to the late 1970s, Berardi meant French fries in northern Ohio, thanks to Al Berardi and his wife Roseanne, whose Cedar Point concession stands made their thick, oversized fries famous. Happily, Berardi's now offers the original recipe fries, plus an eclectic selection of entrees, their own specialty coffees, and a variety of to-die-for pies.
203 Cline Street; 419/668-2278. Mon-Th 6 a.m.-8 p.m., Fri-Sat 6 a.m.-9 a.m., Sun 7 a.m.-8 p.m. Inexpensive-moderate. D, MC, V.

ASIDE Though Norwalk can claim no native son as stellar as Milan's Edison (but then, what town can?), it nonetheless has had its share of people who made their mark in the world. Daniel Decatur Emmett, who wrote "Dixie", grew up there, as did George Kennan, the first Secretary of the National Geographic Society. Legendary football coach Paul Brown was born in Norwalk, and so was baseball's Alexander Bancroft "Ban" Johnson, who co-founded the American League and became its first president. Then there were the seven Fisher Brothers, who went to Detroit in the early 1900s and began building frames especially designed for automobiles instead of wagons. By the 1920s, they had made "Fisher Body" a permanent part of the American vocabulary and General Motors.

THE FIRELANDS MUSEUM/NORWALK — Before the Civil War, the Firelands Historical Society (which happens to be the second oldest in Ohio) started a "cabinet of curios" that expanded over the years into a whole house full of memorabilia. The museum's home is the Preston-Wickham House, built in 1835 by the Norwalk newspaper editor as a wedding present for his daughter. For years, he printed his newspaper on the upper floor of the house, and only the arrival of his thirteenth grandchild persuaded him to move elsewhere. The museum has the first printed map of the Firelands and an extensive gun collection that includes a Chinese hand cannon dating to 500 B.C. It is also the source for tours---guided, self-guided, and video---of Norwalk's West Main Street Historic District.
4 Case Avenue; 419/668-6038. Open Apr, May, Sept, Oct, Nov, Sat-Sun noon-4; June-Aug, Tu-Sun noon-5; Dec-Mar by appointment only. Tours by pre-arrangement. Nominal admission

AMISH OAK FURNITURE CO./NORWALK — Ten years ago, Chris Tuttle was a psychologist. Today he is the proprietor of the only company in the state that sells furniture made exclusively by the Ohio Amish. That unlikely transition occurred because he bought some land in Holmes County and found out about the high quality furniture that the Amish were building for themselves. Now, his line of 450 oak, cherry, and walnut items includes hutches, desks, chairs, chests, rockers, and a popular custom-made table that can be expanded from four to sixteen feet.
27 East Main Street; 419/663-0725. Mon-Th 9:30-8, Tu, Wed, Fri 9:30-5, Sat 9:30-4. Discover.

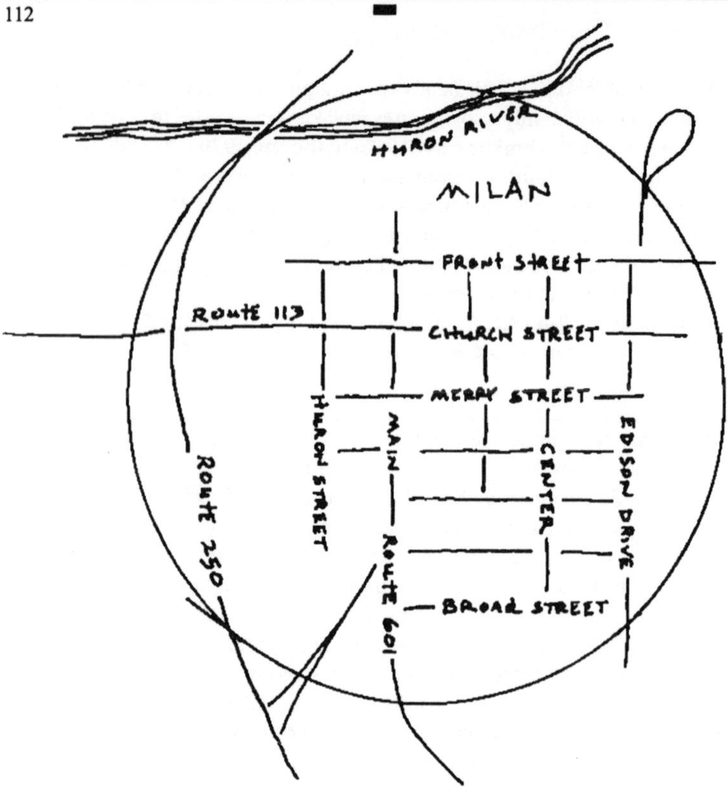

MILAN

HURON RIVER

FRONT STREET

ROUTE 113

CHURCH STREET

MERRY STREET

HURON STREET

MAIN

ROUTE 601

CENTER

EDISON DRIVE

BROAD STREET

ROUTE 250

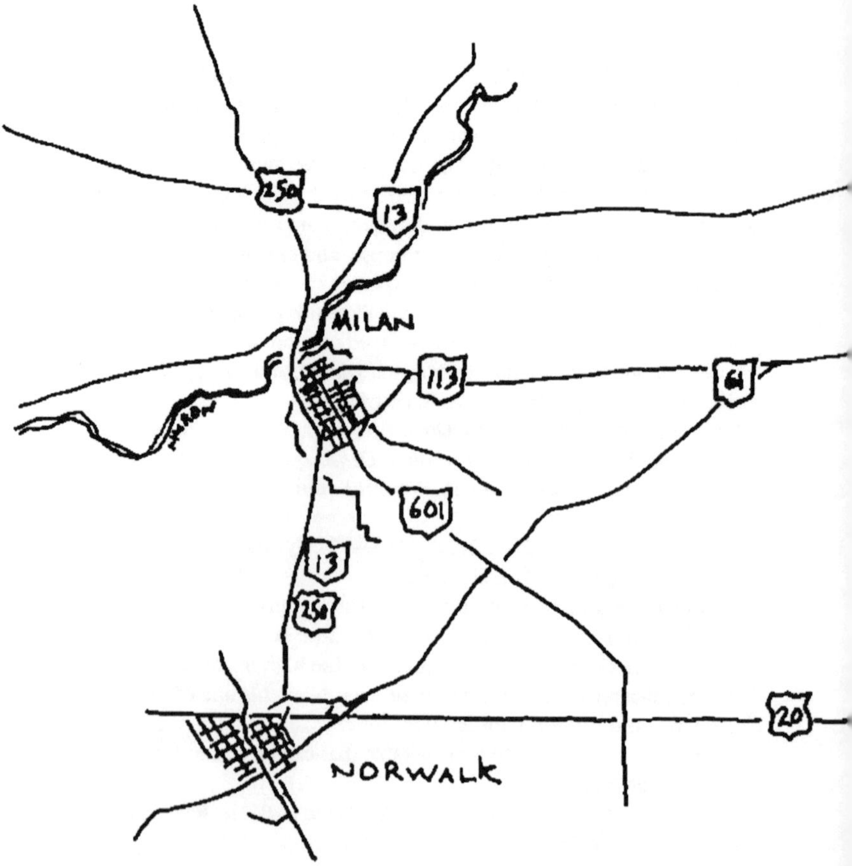

250

13

MILAN

113

61

HURON

601

13

250

NORWALK

20

Finney Chapel
oberlin College

Oberlin

Oberlin is the name of a town and a college in northeast Ohio, both founded in 1833 on the pure idealism of John Shipherd and Philo Stewart, two Christian evangelists hell-bent on changing the world through education. Inspired by John Frederick Oberlin, a French clergyman who devoted his life to educating impoverished people, they started Oberlin College to produce ministers and teachers for missionary work. The town was initially a religious colony, a moral toehold on the untamed Ohio frontier that was — and still is — the social, economic, and philo-sophical consort of the College. The co-mingling of town and gown was perhaps best illustrated a century ago by Charles Martin Hall, a piano-playing chemist who was both a resident and alumnus. In the woodshed behind his house in

Oberlin, he developed the first practical method for extracting pure aluminum from bauxite in 1886. His electrolytic process was the foundation for the Aluminum Company of America, and it made him a fortune, part of which still nicely feathers the nest of the College endowment.

¶ Shipherd and Stewart had purposely picked a remote site about thirty miles southwest of Cleveland in order to avoid interference from sinful city people. More than a century and a half has passed since then, and Oberlin is now linked to the rest of the world by telephones, computers, and the sound, straight pavement of State Route 58, but it is still very much a place apart. Physically and culturally, Oberlin remains off the beaten path — an island of ideals, art, and intellect tucked away in the flat countryside of Lorain County. Geoffrey Blodgett, the astute Professor of History at Oberlin College, once observed, "Oberlin often seems about ten miles from everywhere: ten miles from Elyria, ten miles from original sin, and ten miles from normal American society." ¶ That distance from the mainstream has been the primary reason that this small college town — the current population is only 8200 — has historically wielded a large influence over national issues and social problems. In the mid-1830s, Oberlin was the first college in the United States to enroll women, and one of the first to enroll blacks. The three women in the Class of 1841 were the first in the nation to receive bachelor's degrees, and by 1900, nearly half of all black college graduates in the United States were Oberlin alumni. The unheard-of mixing of the races as well as the sexes made Oberlin notorious. The town was considered a "hotbed of abolitionists," and as a primary stop on the Underground Railroad was "second only to Canada" as a haven for slaves. By 1860, the black population approached twenty percent, and Oberlin was probably the most integrated place in the nation. ¶ Its "radical" reputation was sealed on September 13, 1858, when a group of townspeople and students raided nearby Wellington and blatantly defied the Fugitive Slave Act by forcibly taking a young black man away from some slave-catchers. The Oberlin-Wellington Rescue became a *cause célèbre* that synthesized the nation's moral and Constitutional dilemma over slavery, sparking passions and debates that would soon be settled on the battlefield. When the Civil War began, humorist Petroleum V. Nasby declared, "Oberlin commenst this war. Oberlin wuz the prime cause uv all the trubble." Even as recently as 1990, the respected historian Nat Brandt titled his best-selling book about the Rescue, *The Town That Started The Civil War*. ¶ After Appomattox, town and gown alike took up the fresh cause of temperance, and in 1893, the Anti-Saloon League was founded in Oberlin. The crusading College alumnus Wayne B. Wheeler made the League a national force powerful enough to get Prohibition passed by Congress, and he often proclaimed, "Thank God for Oberlin, a town that gives a cheer, and not a sneer, for righteousness and decency." ¶ Today, the College has evolved into a private, liberal arts school with a tall reputation for academic excellence and innovation that disproportionately exceeds its small enrollment of 2800 students. It not only boasts one of the best under-graduate libraries and campus art museums in the country, but since 1920 has also produced three Nobel Prize-winning scientists and more Ph.D.s than any other undergraduate, liberal arts college in the country. Oberlin is progressive and proud of it. The campus has no fraternities or sororities, but it does have student-operated dining and residential co-ops, an AIDS political action group, an animal rights organization, a pacifist society, and, of course, the infamous co-ed dormitories that were so controversial when they opened in 1970 they put the College on the cover of *Life Magazine.* ¶ Oberlin students typically possess such a relentless spirit of inquiry and passion for pursuing ideas that the College has been dubbed "the Berkeley of Ohio." The town, on the other hand, is known as the "City of Music," thanks to the presence of the Conservatory of Music, a division of Oberlin College with an international reputation that vies with Julliard. The Conserva-tory has more Steinway pianos than any other place in the world except for the factory, and its outstanding performance facilities set the stage for so many orchestras, ensembles, operas, con-certs, recitals, and theatrical productions that the Conservatory has a 24-hour hot line (216/775 – 6933) for schedule information. The Cleveland Symphony comes to town every year to play in Finney Chapel, and residents often say that what they like best about living in Oberlin is being able to walk up the street and enjoy first-rate student and faculty performances, as well as world-class visiting artists and orchestras. ¶ Their only complaint is that it is virtually impossible to find a free evening when something wonderful is *not* happening. The international array of artists who come to Oberlin and the geographic, ethnic, and religious diversity of the students – they come from virtually every state and more than 40 foreign countries – have produced one of the most cosmopolitan campuses and small towns in the nation. Long before the Berlin Wall crumbled or the Japanese were building cars in Ohio cornfields, the College was combining the fine arts and the liberal arts with a global vision that satisfied the abiding Oberlin impulse to better the world. When the College celebrated its sesquicentennial in 1983, the *New York Times* commented, "In its century and a half, while Harvard worried about the classics and Yale about God, Oberlin worried about the state of America and the world beyond." ¶ That is a weighty responsibility for any place, but Oberlin continues to carry it well.

OBERLIN COLLEGE INN — Owned by Oberlin College, the inn has the best location in town – directly across from Tappan Square, practically next door to the Allen art museum, and within walking distance of most stores in town and all of the college's cultural attractions. Although most of the rooms are small and simply furnished, a handful of "classic" accommodations is available for those who want deluxe lodging. The bar is known for its wide selection of imported beer while the formal but comfortable dining room overlooks both the busy square and a meticulously landscaped garden...which is why everyone asks for a table by the windows. *7 North Main Street; 216/775-1111. Dining room is open Mon-Sun 7 a.m.-9 p.m. Moderate-Expensive. AE, DC, Discover, MC, V.*

THE IVY TREE INN AND GARDEN — A gracious, gabled home, the Ivy Tree sits on a hillside high above Plum Creek and has some of the best views in town. With its tall windows, pretty porches, and stylishly casual furnishings, this bed and breakfast has the look and feel of a rambling seaside cottage. That is altogether appropriate because a Great Lakes captain named Finney once lived here, and he scratched his name on one of the window panes, where the letters can still be seen. Owners Ron Kelly and Steve Coughlin offer their guests not only

"Irish" breakfasts of homemade bread pudding laced with peaches and nutmeg, but also expertly designed gardens with eye-popping beds of flowers. A professional landscaper, Steve has filled the rooms with greenery and often conducts gardening workshops on the grounds. One of the guest bedrooms – the Magnolia Room – was even named for the huge tree that flowers outside its windows.
195 South Professor Street; 216/774-4510. MC, V

PRESTI'S OF OBERLIN — When Sicilian immigrants John and Bess Presti arrived in Oberlin in the 1930s, they served spaghetti in a 25-seat truck stop with gas pumps out front. Today their grandchildren operate a fine, 250-seat restaurant with no gas pumps out front. The family, however, has remained true to Grandma's recipes, and the consistent goodness of Presti's ravioli, rigatoni, and veal parmigiana has kept folks from all over northeast Ohio coming back for years. Their wonderful homemade bread is deliciously crusty and just right for sopping up the pan juices of Presti's trademark sirloin tips cooked in lemon and garlic sauce.

580 West Lorain Street; 216/775-2511. Mon-Sat 11 a.m.-2:30 a.m.(kitchen closes Mon-Th at midnight and Fri-Sat at 1 a.m., but the bar remains open until closing). Moderate-expensive. AE, Discover, MC, V.

CAMPUS RESTAURANT — The Campus, says a regular customer, has been in town "forever," and it is one of Oberlin's favorite gathering spots. For years, students have steadfastly stuffed quarters into the chrome consolite juke boxes mounted beside each booth, and faculty members meet here almost every morning for traditional "mom and pop" restaurant fare such as bacon and eggs, hash browns, and melt-in-your-mouth blueberry pancakes.
9 South Main Street; 216/774-6214. Mon-Th 7 a.m.-8 p.m., Fri-Sat, 7 a.m.-2 a.m., Sun 8 a.m.-8 p.m. Inexpensive.

MAIN STREET MERCANTILE STORE AND TEA ROOM — Known to locals as "the Merc," this eatery is short on floor space but long on Euro-California style cuisine. The prodigious sandwich selection ranges from kosher hot dogs to hot shrimp, and imaginative salads offer combinations such as apples, apricots, and pears in an almond cream dressing. Pasta with a variety of sauces is a menu mainstay, but if you like your linguine and pesto with wine, you'll have to bring your own bottle. Since the hot fudge crepes are an absolutely decadent dessert, folks who are watching their weight might want to settle for a cup of the freshly ground coffee, which is also sold in the small gourmet food retail area near the front door.
18 South Main Street; 216/775-1017. Mon-Tu 8 a.m.-10 a.m., 11:30 a.m.-2 p.m.; Wed-Sat 8 a.m.-10 a.m., 11:30 a.m.-2 p.m., 6 p.m.-9 p.m.; Sun 8 a.m.-10 a.m., 11:30 a.m.-2 p.m., 6 p.m.-8 p.m. Moderate. MC, V.

ASIDE Expediency more than any sense of social justice prompted Oberlin's founding fathers to admit women to the College: they simply wanted to produce as many missionaries as possible. While men and women attended classes together at Oberlin from its beginning, many of the courses — sewing and French — in the "Female Department" were not as demanding as the college preparatory courses — Greek, Latin, and mathematics — required of the male students. It was not until 1837 that four female students applied to the school's Collegiate Department. When they were admitted to the freshman class and began taking the same course of study as the men, they made history. The four were not only the first women in the world to enroll in a standard college curriculum, but they also pioneered a revolutionary new concept: coeducation. Although one faculty member observed that "nothing acts as a better antidote for romance than young men and women doing geometry together at 8 o'clock every morning," the risque situation of purposely putting young members of the opposite sex together on the same campus required that the College take certain precautions and institute guidelines. The "seven-inch rule," for example, required that if a male and female were studying in the same room, the door had to be open at least seven inches, while the "three feet rule" mandated that at least three of any couple's four feet had to be on the floor at all times. Boardwalks across Tappan Square were purposely made narrow to discourage hand holding, and in class, men sat on one side of the room and women on the other. The same seating arrangement applied to religious services, and it was not until 1934 that Oberlin boys and girls got to sit together in the chapel.

TAPPAN SQUARE — This resplendent spot of green is Oberlin's oasis, the geographic, social, cultural, civic, commercial, and aesthetic pivot point about which both the town and campus revolve. It is also Oberlin's Plymouth Rock, for upon completing their journey to their new land, Shipherd and Stewart knelt here and prayed beneath an elm tree before starting a new school and society. The virgin trees on the square were promptly leveled to make way for the first College buildings, but the process was later reversed – thanks to Charles Martin Hall's money and affinity for green spaces – when the buildings were leveled to make way for landscaping designed by Boston's renowned Olmsted Brothers. With its 300 trees of 58 different species, pleasant brick walkways, and beds of fragrant flowers, the thirteen-acre square is today a fine park and arboretum, where children swing at baseballs beneath venerable oak trees and couples on picnic blankets can while away an afternoon. Named for Arthur and Lewis Tappan, two ardent and wealthy abolitionists who bankrolled the College in its early days, the square is punctuated by symbols of Oberlin's past, present, and future. A flagpole and circle of – what else? – aluminum mark the seminal spot where the Historic Elm witnessed the founding fathers' prayers; paint-slathered boulders bear the collected greetings and graffiti – "Oberlin Salutes Paul and Sally, 1942-92"; "Don't Do Drugs" – of citizens as well as students; and a whimsical bandstand built in the 1980s at the prompting of Oberlin President S. Frederick Starr literally puts the College, the Conservatory, and the community in concert. But the limestone and granite Memorial Arch is certainly the most meaningful – and moving – site on the square. A tribute to Oberlin missionaries massacred in China during the Boxer Rebellion, it represents the quintessence of the Oberlin outlook on improving mankind through individual sacrifice and personal involvement. Its neo-classic styling also provides the perfect

backdrop for the College's commencement exercises on Memorial Day
weekend, when an "OBERLIN" banner is stretched across the Arch
and a procession of graduating seniors passes underneath. Since
alumni traditionally return for reunions that weekend, Oberlin swells
in size, and everyone in town converges on graduation eve for what is
perhaps the College's best-loved tradition: the Illumination Night party
on Tappan Square. The entire square is hung with Japanese lanterns,
and for several hours, it truly shines with light, music, dancing,
laughter, and – with due respect to Shipherd and Stewart – a festival
of the brotherhood between town and gown, faculty and students,
and graduates old and new.

At the intersections of Lorain, Main, College, and Professor streets

---

ASIDE Notable Oberlin alumni: *John Mercer Langston*, Class of 1849,
first black man elected to public office in the United States (Clerk of
Brownhelm Township, Ohio, 1855); first black man elected a U.S.
Congressman (from Virginia, 1888). *Moses Fleetwood Walker*, Class of
1882, first black major league baseball player (from 1882-91 with the
Toledo Mudhens). *John Langalibalele Dube*, Class of 1890, first
president of the African National Congress. *Robert Millikan*, Class of
1891, winner of the 1923 Nobel Prize in physics for research on
photoelectric effects. *Jack Schaefer*, '29, author of Shane. *Roger
Sperry*, '35. winner of the 1981 Nobel Prize in medicine/physiology for
his work on right brain/left brain functions. *Stanley Cohen*, '45, co-
winner of the 1986 Nobel Prize in medicine/physiology for research on
the relationship between proteins and cell growth. *Carl Rowan*, '47,
syndicated Chicago Daily News columnist. *June Osborne*, '57, chairper-
son of the National Commission on AIDS. *William Goldman*, '52, best-
selling author (Marathon Man) and Academy Award-winning screenplay
writer (Butch Cassidy and the Sundance Kid; All the President's Men).
James Burrows, '62, television producer of Taxi and Cheers.

ON TOUR IN OBERLIN — The work of eminent architects such as
Howard Van Doren Shaw, Cass Gilbert, Frank Lloyd Wright, Minoru
Yamasaki, and Robert Venturi has produced a beautiful campus of
eclectic buildings so diversely designed that Professor Blodgett once
allowed that it was possible to survey the architectural history of the
Western world just by standing in the middle of Tappan Square. The
campus is anchored by imposing Richardson Romanesque buildings
that were largely built with blocks of sandstone taken from the huge
quarry in nearby Amherst and largely paid for with the money of rich
men who revered Oberlin's moral imperative. The single most
influential architect, however, was Cass Gilbert, who designed five
College buildings adapted from Romanesque and Renaissance designs
that impart warm Mediterranean elements to this northern Ohio
campus. Architecturally, the town has always been a poor cousin to
the College, primarily because it never developed an independent
economic base that would support grand buildings. Nonetheless, the
abundant historic structures in this "plain and thrifty" town act as a
fine supporting cast for such stellar college structures as "Moby Dick,"
the curving, post-Cubist, white marble building officially known as

Hall Auditorium. The beautifully preserved First Church (corner of Lorain and Main streets) was the Oberlin colony's first meetinghouse, and the Charles Martin Hall House (64 East College Street) had the famous shed where he experimented with aluminum on a cookstove. Maps and self-guided tours of both the town and the campus are available at the front desk of the Oberlin Inn, the College's Office of Admissions (on the first floor of the Carnegie building), and at the Chamber of Commerce (South Main Street across from the Apollo Theatre). But folks for whom touring is easier read than done should consult Professor Blodgett's superbly detailed book, *Oberlin Architecture, College and Town: A Guide to Its Social History.*

Allen Art Building, Oberlin College

ALLEN MEMORIAL ART MUSEUM — The Allen is one of Oberlin's prime cultural treasures. It is not only located in a splendid Cass Gilbert building but also widely considered to have one of the finest collegiate art collections in the nation. Founded in 1917, the Allen was the first college art museum west of the Alleghenies that was designed for a teaching collection. Today, its 14,000 items span the history of art from ancient Egypt to modern times and include works by Rubens, Monet, Cezanne, Rembrandt, Durer, and Picasso. Particularly notable are the collections of seventeenth century Dutch and Flemish paintings, Old Master and Japanese prints, and European art from the late nineteenth and early twentieth centuries. The Ellen Johnson Gallery of Modern and Contemporary Art was named for the influential Oberlin College art historian who acquired many important contemporary works for the museum and pioneered the teaching of modern art in the United States. Its permanent collection boasts Gorky's *The Plough and the Song* and *Laocoon*, the sculpture that Eva Hesse created especially for the Allen.
North Main and Lorain streets; 216/775-8048. Tu-Sat 10-5, Sun 1-5. Closed Mon and major holidays. Tours by appointment. Free.

OBERLIN HISTORICAL AND IMPROVEMENT ORGANIZATION —
Three of Oberlin's most significant structures have been restored and
preserved on a single site near the Conservatory of Music. The **Little
Red Schoolhouse** is both the oldest building in town and the only
one that still remains from Oberlin's founding years in the 1830s. With
a complete set of McGuffey Readers and a collection of antique lunch
pails, it recreates the era of America's one room schoolhouses. The
James Monroe House, a red brick Italianate dwelling built in 1866
and now furnished with period antiques, was once the home of the
abolitionist for whom it is named. Handsome and known for his
stirring oratory, Monroe knew the likes of Frederick Douglass and
Abraham Lincoln, and he had a multi-faceted career as an Oberlin
Professor of Rhetoric, a state legislator, a U.S. Congressman, and a
diplomat. Completed in 1884, the **Jewett House** exhibits elements of
both Italianate and Queen Anne architecture. Frank Fanning Jewett,
the beloved, bespectacled Oberlin professor who taught chemistry to
Charles Martin Hall, lived here with his family for many years, and he
frequently entertained students in its large and beautifully appointed
rooms.
*78 South Professor Street; 216/774-8003. Open by appointment
only. Free.*

GIBSON'S — Although the modern glass and aluminum facade of their
bake shop and food market dates to the 1950s, the Gibson family has
been in the business of satisfying Oberlin's sweet tooth with homemade candy and pastries since 1885. Everything at Gibson's is freshly
made – their bakery is on the second floor of the building, and the
candy factory is on the third – and so incredibly good that the only
problem you'll have is deciding what to select from the long glass
cases filled with cookies, cakes, chocolates, and their legendary whole
wheat doughnuts. The cream puffs are the size of softballs, and the
oversized "elephant ear" cookies have become a perennial favorite
with Oberlin students, who always try to pick the biggest one on the
tray.
23 West College Street; 216/774-2401. Mon-Sun 7 a.m.-11 p.m.

APOLLO THEATRE — At this little gem of an art deco style building, circa 1930s, black "marble" vitrolized glass still covers the ticket booth and lobby walls. The glass is no longer being made, but the Steel family is continuing its 50-plus year tradition of showing movies in the Apollo. Since all of the films are second-run, you may have already seen the feature, but go to the Apollo anyway for the sheer experience of standing in line underneath a vintage, triangle-shaped marquee with traveling yellow lights. Inside, there are chrome lobby chairs and lighted wall sconces from the 1940s, and the increasingly rare combination of a large auditorium – it seats 850 people – with a big screen. Adult tickets, by the way, are bargain-priced at $3, except on Tuesdays and Thursdays, when all seats only cost $2.
19 East College Street; 216/774-7091.

MIRANDA BOOKS — Bibliophiles Susan and David Hill keep their used, antiquarian, and out-of-print books impeccably organized and well displayed, and their bright, shelf-laden store is a pleasurable contrast to the dust and clutter that often typifies second-hand book stores. The Hills' "recycled reading" includes strong sections on the fine arts, literature, and history, as well as numerous children's books and regional titles focusing on Ohio in general and Oberlin in particular. They have one of the finest collections – some 700 titles – of music books in northeast Ohio, making the store a favorite haunt of scholars and musicians from the Conservatory.
19 South Main Street; 216/775-1296. Mon, Wed, Fri, Sat 10-6; Tu, Th 10-8; Sun 1-5. MC, V.

CO-OP BOOKSTORE — The Co-op is probably the only place in town – and one of the few places anywhere – where you can buy wool hats from Ecuador, have your pick of some 15,000 pieces of sheet music, and eavesdrop on conversations that begin, "I'm becoming increasingly disenchanted with MacLeish . . . " This uncommon emporium is the largest retailer in downtown Oberlin and has served both the College and community at-large for more than 50 years. The Co-op stocks the requisite college textbooks and emblematic clothing (we like the sweatshirt that says "HARVARD, THE OBERLIN OF THE EAST") of academe, but you will also find a fine selection of compact discs, games, puzzles, greeting cards, tarot cards, and unusual clothing and gift items from Third World countries. The eclectic general book department features literature, poetry, small press publications, and works by Oberlin College faculty members.
37 West College Street; 216/774-3741. Mon-Sat 9 a.m.-8 p.m., Sun 12-5. MC, V.

CAMCOTE HOUSE — Since *cote* is the Scottish word for an outbuilding, Don and Carol Campbell combined it with their surname to christen their Camcote House. However, Camcote House is no mere simple structure built beside their home, but rather a little bit of the British Isles so finely and faithfully detailed – the fireplace was copied from one in a sixteenth century painting – that visitors might think they had stepped into a Cotswold cottage instead of an Oberlin shop. Camcote House provides the perfect setting for the Campbells' "little business in retirement," which is based on the big idea of making bas relief castings that recreate architectural artifacts and ornamentations

found on their frequent trips to Europe. Their unique inventory offers more than 100 synthetic stone reproductions, including a planter with Romanesque figures copied from a French abbey, gargoyles from the Notre Dame cathedral in Paris, and a figure of Saint Nicolas taken from a Flemish cookie mold.
413 East College Street; 216/775-7032. By appointment.

OHIO SCOTTISH GAMES — Sponsored by the Scottish American Cultural Society of Ohio, this annual festival perpetuates Scottish customs and tradition by reenacting the historic gathering of the clans. On Friday evening, a parade through Oberlin is the prelude to a Highland concert featuring drummers, dancers, fiddlers, harpists, and, of course, bagpipers. The games on Saturday include musical and athletic competitions such as tossing the log *caber*, displays of Scottish arts and crafts, and a fairway filled with vendors selling imports from the British Isles. The day ends with a *ceilidh* (party) held in the college ice rink, but folks who yearn for more of the Highlands can stay for the Ohio Scottish Arts School, a week of classes in dancing, drumming, harping, and piping held on the Oberlin College campus.
Oberlin College athletic fields; 216/449-5373. Fourth weekend in June. Admission fee. For ticket information, contact The Scottish American Cultural Society of Ohio, Inc., P.O. Box 3, Lorain, OH 44052

ASIDE An Oberlin College professor once remarked, "if Oberlin should ever cease to produce graduates willing to go out on a limb . . . for new and risky causes on which the state of the world hangs balanced, then it would no longer be Oberlin." The cause for which alumna Katharine Wright went out on a limb did not initially affect the fate of the world, but it was new and it was risky, and she pursued it with all her heart. Katharine, Oberlin Class of 1898, was a high school Latin teacher in Dayton, Ohio, who might have lived a quiet, comfortable life as a middle class matron had she not been the loyal sister of two young men obsessed with building a flying machine. During all the years of Orville and Wilbur Wright's struggles and success in inventing the airplane, Katharine was their confidante, counselor, hostess, nurse, press agent, cook, official correspondent, greatest cheerleader, unfailing companion, and best friend. In 1909, in Pau, France, she took her first aeroplane ride, tying a rope around her legs to keep her skirts in place. The flight only lasted seven minutes, but her modesty was credited with starting the fad for hobble skirts. In 1926, at the advanced age of 52, Katharine decided she wanted a life of her own and announced her engagement to an old Oberlin classmate, Kansas City newspaperman Henry Haskell. Her surviving brother Orville couldn't believe that she would abandon him; he became so upset, Katharine was married in Oberlin rather than the family home in Dayton. She went to live with her husband in Kansas City, and Orville refused to speak to her until she was on her deathbed two years later. When she was brought back to Dayton for burial, planes from the air field that is now Wright-Patterson Air Force Base dropped flowers on her grave.

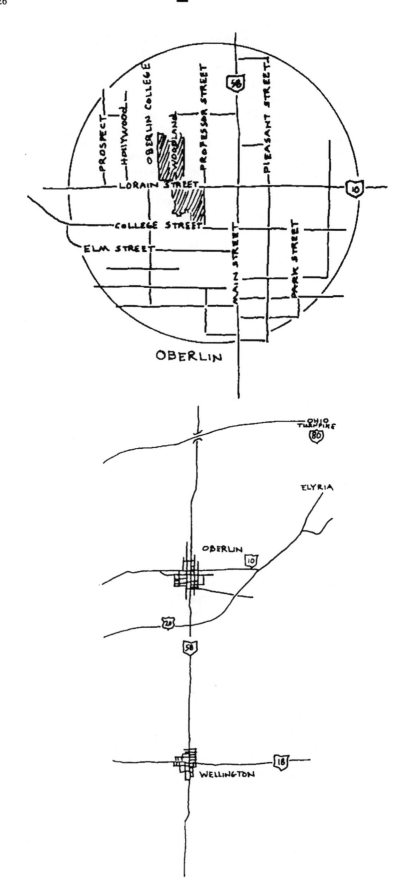

OBERLIN

Wellington, Ohio; Town Hall

Wellington

Visitors may find culture in the concerts and art of Oberlin, but when they want history, they go to Wellington, which is a mere eight miles to the south on State Route 58. Only about 4,000 people live in Wellington but a remarkable 113 of its buildings are on the National Register of Historic Places. Its fanciful Town Hall – an 1885 structure that combines elements of Byzantine, Greek, Gothic, and Spanish architecture and was once the largest opera house between Columbus and Cleveland – and grand old homes – especially those lining State Route 58 on the south side of the village – are an obvious attraction.

¶ They are also a vestige of the wealth that came to the village in the late 1800s, when it was the busy capital of the nation's cheese industry. Thanks to the prodigious productivity of the local Holsteins, as much as seven million pounds of cheese a year was shipped from Wellington, and at the corner of West Herrick and Depot, the flat iron building that was once the headquarters for 40 of the factories still bears a huge "CHEESE" sign. ¶ However, Wellington's quiet residential streets and cozy downtown — there is a hitching post behind the Town Hall to accommodate the local Amish farmers — can easily belie its importance as the place where two fateful events in American history occurred. One was significant: the Oberlin-Wellington Rescue of September 13, 1858; and the other was symbolic: the origin of the painting, *The Spirit of '76*. Wadsworth's Hotel where the Rescue occurred has been gone — and largely forgotten — for nearly a century, but *The Spirit of '76* has arguably become the most recognized and patriotic painting ever produced in the United States. ¶ It was the work of Archibald Willard, a local man of modest talent who drew his inspiration from the faces, fifes, and drums of his family and friends in Wellington. Willard gave the nation an immortal image, and he gave his hometown an incomparable claim to fame that has anchored it to the past. The village is a place of antique shops, well-preserved Victorian buildings, revered landmarks, and very prized Willard paintings. As much as Oberlin looks outward, Wellington looks backward in celebration of its proud history and the lasting impression made by *The Spirit of '76*.

albert Grimm home

THE DEACON EDWARD WEST HOME/WELLINGTON — Albert
Grimm started accumulating his vast and varied collection of international antiques when he was in high school. Now retired, he has found
the ideal place to showcase them in the 1872 Italianate house that he
operates as a bed and breakfast. Once occupied by Edward West, a
well-to-do farmer during Wellington's late nineteenth century boom
years, the home is on the National Register of Historic Places and has
splendid Victorian details that are original to the house — rare chestnut
woodwork; a lavish, hand-carved cherry staircase; marble fireplaces;
leaded windows; and cranberry glass light fixtures. The concave wall
niche near the top of the stairs now displays a lovely vase, but it was
originally designed as a "casket turn," a recess purposely placed in the
wall to allow enough room for a coffin to be rotated and carried down
the stairs without having to tip its contents. Mr. Grimm serves his
guests their morning juice in Waterford crystal goblets and their
breakfast on English bone china. Those who stay for more than one
night will also discover that he sets the table with a different pattern of
china every day. And since Mr. Grimm is also the curator of
Wellington's Spirit of '76 Museum, visitors will find him as delightfully
knowledgeable about local lore, legends, and history as he is about
antiques.
303 Courtland Street; 216/647-5703. Open May-Oct.

THE WATSON R. WEAN HOME/WELLINGTON — From the time he
first laid eyes on this grand Italianate house, Arthur Petro wanted to
buy and restore it. He had to wait almost a decade, but now he and his
wife Terri delight in sharing its beautiful staircase, stained glass
windows, elaborate plasterwork, and Victorian decor with their bed

and breakfast guests. Built after the Civil War by a Wellington businessman, the home is on National Register of Historic Places, and the Petros have furnished it with antiques. Although he supervised the restoration work, she has "the fun" of playing hostess for overnight guests as well as for teas and tour groups. Breakfasts include home-made breads and muffins, and guests get to choose where they would like to eat – by candlelight in the spacious dining room, on the romantic wraparound verandah, or in the great outdoors of the backyard terrace.

380 South Main Street; 216/647-6219. Open May-Oct. Children welcome.

THE VILLAGE DINER/WELLINGTON — A Wellington landmark for years, the diner is located in a converted railroad car and can only seat 32 people. It may be small, but the daily specials such as potato and cheese pierogi, homemade ravioli, and six-inch-thick slices of lasagna are mighty. They serve breakfast – try the sausage gravy and biscuits – all day every day, and since the kitchen is tucked across from the lunch counter, you get to view before you chew your food.

105 Depot Street; 216/647-5693. Mon-Fri 5:30 a.m.-7 p.m., Sat 6 a.m.-2 p.m., Sun 8 a.m.-1 p.m. Inexpensive.

ASIDE Marvelous Molly Baun was the making of many men in Wellington. She was a foreigner, an import from Holland, where she had caught the eye of some up-and-coming fellows from Wellington's Horr-Warner cheese factory. They brought her back home with them, and she not only became the most popular girl in town but also the most famous employee of the factory. Molly, you see, was a cow, and a most distinguished one at that. She was a Holstein-Friesian, one of the first purebred cattle in Ohio, and thus quite superior to the local girls who gave at most 5,000 pounds of milk per year. Molly produced a record-setting 17,000 pounds, an accomplishment so astounding that she became the mother of cattle-breeding in Ohio.

GOODIE BARN OF OHIO/WELLINGTON — This sprawling general store surprises shoppers with all manner of oddities and curiosities – a mounted buffalo head, a classic wooden Indian, and an original, fire engine-red Elgin coffee grinder as tall as a man. You could spend an entire day exploring the Goodie Barn's amazing, floor-to-ceiling inventory of antiques, old-fashioned cast iron banks, toys, toiletries, crafts, candles, and flat lace, not to mention the brooms and furniture made by the Amish in Holmes County.

105 East Herrick Avenue; 216/647-4101. Mon-Sat 10-6, Sun 12-5. MC, V.

A GUIDE TO WELLINGTON'S ARCHIBALD WILLARD COUNTRY —
Archibald Willard began his artistic career by painting decorative motifs and scenes on wagons, carriages, and furniture manufactured by factories in Wellington. Largely an untrained artist, Willard found fame in 1876 when his life-sized oil painting of three Revolutionary

War soldiers heroically playing a fife and drums through the smoke of battle debuted at the nation's 100th birthday celebration, the Centennial Exhibition in Philadelphia. Though the critics largely turned up their professional noses – one called the painting "ludicrous" – at *The Spirit of '76*, the public loved it. Many in the crowds who flocked to see the work were moved to tears, and President Grant reportedly was so affected that he requested a private viewing to "commune" alone with the painting. Willard, of course, found immediate fame, and he capitalized upon the painting's success by turning its patriotic appeal into a one-man industry. Varying the colors and subject's clothing, he painted at least fourteen more versions of *The Spirit of '76*, and ten of these "original copies" are known to still exist. Willard's concept tugged so hard at the nation's heartstrings that *The Spirit of '76* has probably become the most frequently copied image in the United State – from the thousands of lithographic and photographic reproductions sold at the Philadelphia Exposition to its subsequent use and reuse on cups, saucers, music boxes, and thousands of other products. It has been patriotically recreated in Fourth of July parades and fireworks displays; it has been altered for political purposes on the cover of *TIME* and the pages of *PLAYBOY*; and it was copied on the first U.S. postage stamps commemorating the nation's bicentennial. *The Spirit of '76* is timeless, and it is everywhere. Which is exactly what Mr. Willard intended. His work, he said, "was not painted in commemoration of 1776 or 1876, or any special period in the life of our nation, but as an expression of the vital and ever-living spirit of American patriotism."

THE PLACES:
121 UNION STREET/WELLINGTON — Now privately owned, this was once Willard's home. He was descended from proud New England stock, a lineage that began in 1634 when his ancestors first arrived at the Massachusetts Bay Colony. Willard's grandfather, who lived with the family in Wellington, fought with the Green Mountain Boys of Vermont during the American Revolution, and it is said that Willard used his war stories as an inspiration while executing *The Spirit of '76*. Willard was seventeen when the family moved into this house and his father Samuel, a minister at the local Church of Christ, became the subject of one of his early works. He decorated the door of the family outhouse with a picture of the Reverend Willard in a sitting position with his trousers down. Reportedly, Samuel Willard was the only man in town who had absolutely no appreciation for the young man's creativity.

WILLARD MEMORIAL SQUARE/WELLINGTON — The Stars and Stripes fly high over the this place and well they should, for it was here in front of Wellington's Town Hall that Willard conceived the idea for his landmark painting. In the summer of 1875, Willard looked out a second story window on East Herrick Avenue and on the square below, he noticed a fife and drum corps practicing for the Fourth of July festivities. Three clowning marchers caught his eye, and he dashed off a comic sketch of two drummers and a fifer. At the suggestion of a Cleveland art dealer, Willard changed his concept to a serious, patriotic painting. Working in a Cleveland studio through the winter of 1875-76, the artist used his own father as the model for the granite-jawed, white-haired older drummer. Hugh Mosher, a strapping Wellington farmer who was both Willard's friend and Civil War comrade, posed for the plucky fifer, and sixteen-year-old Henry Devereaux, the son of a Cleveland railroad magnate, was the young drummer. The Reverend Willard, incidentally, died before the canvas was completed, so he never knew how his resolute visage stirred the crowds in Philadelphia. But after the centennial celebration, Henry Devereaux's father bought *The Spirit of '76*, sent it on a national tour, and then gave the painting to his hometown of Marblehead, Massachusetts, where the famed work still hangs today.

Spirit of '76 Museum
Wellington

THE SPIRIT OF '76 MUSEUM/WELLINGTON — Located in one of Wellington's old cheese warehouses, this museum features a gallery of sixteen paintings and murals done by Willard, a bedroom set that he decorated when he worked for a village furniture company, and an incredible collection of objects — including bathroom tissue — that have displayed the *The Spirit of '76* motif. But two of its most-treasured items are the fife and drum used as models by Willard when he painted his 1876 version of *The Spirit of '76*. As he painted, Willard told Hugh Mosher to actually play that fife in order to properly capture his expression. Although the original drum exhibited in the museum is red, Willard sometimes made it blue in his later versions of the painting.
201 North Main Street; 216/647-4531. Open Apr-Oct. Sat-Sun 2:30-5. Group tours by appointment. Free

HERRICK MEMORIAL LIBRARY/WELLINGTON — It is said that when Myron Herrick was a boy, he told his mother that if he ever had enough money, he would give his hometown of Wellington a library. Herrick not only grew up to become a millionaire banker, Governor of Ohio, and Ambassador to France, he also kept his promise to his mother. In 1902, Herrick bought the old hotel where the famed Oberlin-Wellington Rescue took place, had it torn down, and built this small, but beautifully designed library. Now on the National Register of Historic Places, the building is both a working library and an art gallery that features many of Archibald Willard's works. His preliminary sketches for *The Spirit of '76* are on display, as well as his last oil "original copy," which Willard did in 1916, when he was 80 years old. For the humorous paintings *Pluck One, Pluck Two,* and *Bees,* Willard used his own children and the family dog as models. *Pluck One* was Willard's first commercial success, and only after several thousand lithographs of it were sold, could he afford to go to New York for a few weeks in 1873 for his first and only art lessons.
101 Public Square; 216/647-2120. Mon-Th 10-8:30, Fri-Sat 10-5.

GREENWOOD CEMETERY/WELLINGTON — Archibald Willard, along with several family members, is buried here. The grave is marked by an American flag and a plaque bearing the replica of – what else? – *The Spirit of '76.* Willard, by the way, is in good company in the cemetery, since many of Wellington's former – ahem – "big cheeses" such as Deacon Edward West have been interred there. While you're looking for their graves, you might also want to find the very tall monument surrounded by several smaller headstones near the turn to the Willard plot. It marks the resting place of a Cleveland madam who wanted to be buried with her extended family of "girls" around her.
Cemetery Road off of State Route 58 south of Wellington.

ASIDE *Places in Ohio that have versions of The Spirit of '76 painted by Archibald Willard:* The Western Reserve Historical Society, Cleveland City Hall, Cleveland; Herrick Memorial Library, Wellington; Ohio Historical Center, Columbus.

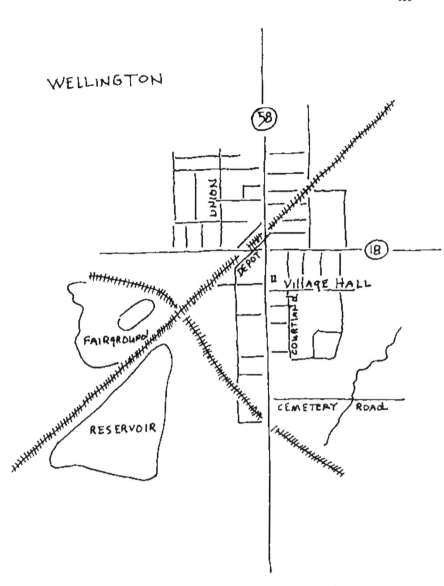

The Old Tavern

Lake Erie's Eastern Shore

Summer at the Lake Erie shore was something Ohioans did as a matter of seasonal ritual. Rich people owned their cottages; the rest just rented, by the week or the month. There was a certain protocol involved in these summertime decisions, and your cottage neighbors came to be as familiar as your "back home" neighbors. But vacation styles changed in the Sixties. A polluted Lake Erie was less inviting. Faraway resorts beckoned. Youngsters whined for Disneyland. And so it came to pass that virtually an entire generation grew up without knowing the sand-on-the-floor, bugs-in-the-bathroom, wet-towels-on-the-furniture thrills of the summer cottage on Lake Erie.   ¶ It is for such culturally deprived folks that we propose an updated version of the shoreline vacation that reflects the changes of the last few decades. Much has been lost, but much more has been gained. The cottage communities have virtually disappeared, replaced by bed and breakfasts and the more substantial marina/condominium settlements that now grace the shoreline. Gone too is the sprawl of chemical plants that once crowded the bluffs above Fairport Harbor, and the coal-shipping that darkened the waters at Conneaut and Ashtabula. Fortunately, the fragile wetlands at Mentor Marsh have been saved, as have the sand dunes at Headlands Beach State Park. The state has improved many beaches, and some shore towns have embraced tourism eagerly and lured many folks back up to the lake.

¶ Although the shore area east of Cleveland has been slower to develop its tourist potential than the busy vacation meccas to the west*, there is real beauty in the lesser known ports of Lake and Ashtabula counties. In places like Fairport, Grand River, and the muted honky-tonk town of Geneva-on-the-Lake, families are re-establishing the Ohio tradition of summers at the shore. A charter-fishing captain who operates in these waters says that his greatest pleasure is showing folks how wonderful it can be when the winds are fresh, the waves are white-capped, and the blue-green lake extends as far as the eye can see. He likes to keep them out late so they can witness that magical moment when the setting sun slips beneath the water. "One sunset on Lake Erie and they are hooked for life," he says. ¶ Indeed. There are some experiences that can happen only on the water.

* *To learn about traveling the Lake Erie shore west of Cleveland, please consult Particular Places, volume I.*

Rider's Inn
Bed 'n Breakfast

RIDER'S INN/PAINESVILLE — Painesville's oldest hostelry — and Lake County's first bed and breakfast — is a good place to park your suitcase before heading for the attractions on Lake Erie. The guest rooms are spacious and comfortable, and the charming downstairs parlors and dining room have antique pieces that belonged to the Rider family, who built the original log stagecoach stop here in 1812. Overnight guests can have their breakfast served in bed, and the chef custom designs the pastries to suit their personalities. Thus, joggers are apt to get oat-bran muffins, while sybarites might find cream-filled Napoleons on their trays. Most of the dining room's entrees are based on recipes from the mid-1800s, including an interesting "pioneer" salad that has an egg-based dressing. The bar is open again — local "dry" forces had tried to prevent it — and so the tradition of liquid hospitality continues. Early travelers *needed* their whiskey to dull the pain of the bumpy roads; modern tourists merely enjoy the peace of the cool, dark tavern.
792 Mentor Avenue; 216/354-8200. Lunch Mon-Sat 11:30-5. Dinner Sun-Th 5-9, Fri-Sat 5-10. Sun Stagecoach Breakfast 9-12:30. Sun Supper 12:30-5. Moderate-expensive. Discover, MC, V.

HELLRIEGEL'S INN/PAINESVILLE — One of Painesville's best-loved restaurants has scarcely changed in 40 years — it has the slightly frayed gentility of an old-fashioned country club — and the kitchen's best efforts continue to be the prime rib and flaky little dinner rolls made sweet and gooey with butter, brown sugar and cinnamon. If the place ever dared to change its ways, all of Lake County would rise up in protest.
1840 Mentor Avenue; 216/354-9530. Mon-Sat 11:30 a.m.-10 p.m., Sun noon-7:30, Holidays noon-6. Moderate-expensive. AE, MC, V.

ASIDE Old Painesville reveals its Connecticut heritage in the orientation of its Main Street (which begins as a long village green) and in the post-Colonial homes that survive on U.S. 20, the first wilderness road. One of the early settlers was Jonathan Goldsmith, a carpenter/builder who fashioned extremely fine homes and made liberal use of the *American Builders Handbook*, a how-to manual of fashionable Eastern

LAKE COUNTY — Some of Ohio's most beautiful lakefront scenery lies in this county, where the Grand River empties into Lake Erie. Here, at Headlands Beach State Park, are two little-known treasures: Ohio's longest natural beach, and Ohio's only state-protected sand dunes. There is also a wonderfully secluded pocket beach, tucked into the protecting embrace of the Grand River break wall, and, as a bonus, two pretty little port towns: Fairport Harbor on the river's east bank and Grand River on the west. Curiously, Lake County's waterfront assets appear to excite primarily local interest, and local people seem to prefer it that way and are satisfied to keep their beautiful secrets to themselves.

It is difficult to imagine the village of **Grand River** as it was when Thomas Richmond owned it lock, stock, and schoolhouse. It was called Richmond then, and the founder ran it like a lakeside utopia, where wholesome thoughts were encouraged and whiskey was banned (not too successfully when the sailors were in port). Richmond was a high-minded fellow with a short fuse. When the canal builders double-crossed him, he tore down everything he had built and quit the place entirely.

The present village, which was renamed Grand River in the 1940s, never approached the size and sophistication of the earlier town. It remained a sleepy fishing village with a population that never rose much beyond 400. Grand River is locally famous for its two good fish houses: **Brennans** (*102 River Street; 216/354-9785. Mar-Oct Mon-Th 11-10, Fri-Sat 11-10:30, Sun 1-9. Nov-Feb Mon-Th, 11-9, Fri-Sat 11-10. Moderate. Discover, MC, V),* and **Pickle Bill's** (*101 River Street; 216/352-6343. Tu-Th 11:30-10, Fri 11:30-11, Sat noon-11, Sun 1-9. Moderate. MC, V).* Both have outdoor dining and long lines on sunny weekends; Brennans faces the lake, while Pickle Bill's faces the river. Most of the rest of the river front is controlled by Mary Ann Rutherford, a widow who reigns as Grand River's entrepreneurial grande dame, with a marina, excursion cruisers (including one sternwheeler), bait shop, and the best view of the harbor.

Fairport Harbor is also a town of untapped tourist potential. For most of the twentieth century, the village prospered, with plentiful jobs at the Diamond Alkali chemical plants. Then Diamond pulled out in the 1970s, leaving Fairport stunned. Many of the stores and restaurants on High Street are closed, but the beach, which lies at the foot of the High Street hill, remains Fairport's ace in the hole. It is one of the finest anywhere on the lake, kept immaculate by a zealous parks department.

With its grid of wide brick streets and well-kept houses, Fairport Harbor is a pleasant town for walking. It wakes up once a year for a multi-day **Mardi Gras** celebration in early July that draws 60,000 or more for Lake County's biggest parade and beach party. Local church groups provide staggering amounts of cabbage rolls, kolachke, and strudel, to compete with the candied apples and corn dogs on the lakefront midway.

styles. As a result, Painesville's first families lived quite elegantly, while the rest of Ohio was still building homes out of logs. One of the best Goldsmith houses, the Mathews House, can be seen on the campus of Lake Erie College on Mentor Avenue (U.S. 20) at Washington Street.

ACCESS — Except for some covered bridges and the Victorian Perambulator Museum, the towns and attractions on this tour are all located north of Interstate 90, which cuts across the northern third of both Lake and Ashtabula counties. To begin the tour, exit Interstate 90 at U.S. 44, and follow it north toward Painesville, Fairport Harbor, Grand River, and Mentor. After you have visited those towns, follow U.S. 20 east toward Geneva, and then take State Route 534 north to Geneva-on-the-Lake. From Geneva-on-the-Lake, State Route 531 skirts the Lake Erie shoreline for a truly scenic drive as you go east into Ashtabula and finally Conneaut.

FAIRPORT MARINE MUSEUM/FAIRPORT HARBOR — When mechanization threatened Fairport Harbor's lighthouse in 1945, the people saved it and made it into a museum, the first lighthouse museum in the United States. The artifacts they saved – navigation instruments, marine charts, photographs, ship carpenters' tools – form an enduring expression of a lost way of life on the lakes. For a view beyond the breakwater, you can climb the circular steps to the top of the lighthouse, where on a clear day, you can see Canada. *129 Second Street; 216/354-4825. Open Sat before Memorial Day-Labor Day. Wed, Sat, Sun, and legal holidays 1 to 6. Nominal admission fee.*

ASIDE Ohio's nursery industry was born in the 1850s on Fairport-Nursery Road, where Storrs & Harrison had 300,000 plants growing on 1,200 acres of Lake County's superior sandy loam. From this single root sprang dozens of "pocket nurseries," so called because they were started with the seedlings that Storrs & Harrison employees sneaked home in their pockets. Storrs & Harrison is gone, but the county is still a major wholesale supplier of nursery stock for the landscape trade, and there are dozens of family-owned fruit farms and farm markets. Depending on the season, you can pick your own berries, cherries, apples, and grapes. Watch for the roadside signs, or check the advertisements in local newspapers.

HEADLANDS BEACH STATE PARK/MENTOR — There is a wonderful contrast between Headlands Beach State Parks and Headlands Dunes State Nature Preserve just east of it. The swimming beach is constantly being tidied up by the park crews, who sweep it clear of litter and rake the sand so the switchgrass can't take root. At the dunes, however, nature is allowed to take her course. The beach grasses sink their roots, trapping the wind-blown sand and causing it to drift, and the billowing sand forms lovely hillocks tufted with tall, sharp grasses that sigh in the wind.

Headlands Beach is best seen at sunrise, when the enormous parking lot is empty, except for the cars of a few fishermen who park here to fish from the break wall. Follow the "fishing access" sign at the east end of the beach. The trail takes you into the cool shade of wild cherry and swamp willow trees. Soon the deep sand begins to feel firmer underfoot. You are on the break wall, although the huge stones are not yet visible beneath the wind-blown sand. The water on your right is mirror smooth, no matter how rough the waves at the beach on the windward side of the wall. Timid bathers favor this secluded beach, and boaters drop anchor here when they crave tranquillity. Sandpipers and killdeer skitter among the driftwood, looking for breakfast. In spring and fall, birders take up positions on the beach to admire the variety of migrating species traveling the Great Lakes Flyway.

You can walk the sweeping curve of the break wall all the way out to the end, on the enormous flat-topped sandstones that have been breaking these waves for more than 170 years. Fairport Harbor, the first working port in the Western Reserve, was also the first to protect its interests with a break wall and lighthouse.

By mid-morning, the break wall attracts a few sunbathers. A young painter arrives, carrying sketch pad and charcoal. He sketches the scene: the secluded beach in the foreground, Fairport Harbor in the middle distance, with the lighthouse rising from the top of Lighthouse Hill. From this placid scene he omits the twin towers of the Perry Nuclear Power plant, although they are clearly visible in the distance, preferring to sketch in a few pretty clouds instead.

At the northern terminus of State Route 44 at Headlands Road; 216/ 257-1330.

MENTOR MARSH STATE NATURE PRESERVE/MENTOR — Follow Headlands Road west from the Headlands Beach State Park, and you'll reach the grass-filled lagoons of Mentor Marsh, which were formed when the Grand River changed its course centuries ago. There is an observation tower and an elevated walkway that takes you well out onto the marsh, a place of deep silence broken only by bird songs . . . and the ferocious whine of giant mosquitoes.

For additional information, contact the Ohio Department of Natural Resources; 614/265-6453. Mon-Sun dawn to dusk.

JAMES A. GARFIELD NATIONAL HISTORIC SITE/MENTOR — Among Lake County's most notable buildings is "Lawnfield", the thirty-room Victorian manse that was once the home of James Garfield. Thousands of people came here by train to hear him campaign for the U.S. presidency from the front porch. Now they come to see the family possessions, including Garfield's Congressional desk, his Presidential china, and the waxed funeral wreath Queen Victoria sent after he was assassinated. Lawnfield is also the home of the first presidential library, established here in 1885.

8095 Mentor Avenue (U.S. 20, north of Interstate 90 via State Route 306); 216/255-8722. Tu-Sat 10-5, Sun noon-5. Admission fee.

MENTOR SKATELAND/MENTOR-ON-THE-LAKE — The town's
cottages are gone, either washed away, or, in protected areas,
converted into year-round houses to accommodate the suburban
overflow from Cleveland. This relic of summers past, however,
remains intact. Mentor Skateland is an old roller rink, where a few
dollars plus the price of skate rental buys you the chance to test your
circle-waltz skills, or stagger around the edge of the floor clutching the
rail, if that's your style. There is live organ music on Wednesdays from
10 a.m. to noon.
*5615 Andrews Road; 216/257-3631. Hours for adult and children's
session vary; call for specific times.*

*chalet Debonne
Vineyards*

VINES AND WINES — Thanks to the area's beneficent soil and long
growing season (the warmer lake air delays the first frost), more than
half of Ohio's grapes are grown in Ashtabula and Lake counties. The
town of Geneva hosts a **Grape JAMboree** *(216/466-JAMB)* festival
every fall that celebrates the lush fruits of the local vines, and within a
45-minute drive of Geneva-on-the-Lake, there are several wineries
where you'll find music, meals, tours, lodging, and, of course,
libations. **Chalet Debonné Vineyards/Madison** – The Debevc
family has been making wine for four generations, and you can enjoy
their award-winning Chardonnays, Reislings, and Vidal Blancs at steak
cookouts and other special events – classic car shows, hot air balloon
races, jazz concerts – held throughout the summer. *7743 Doty Road;
216/466-3485.* **Ferrante Winery & Ristorante/Geneva** – Here
you'll find Italian cuisine, weekend entertainment, a spacious tasting
room, and fine views of the vineyards. *5585 State Route 307; 216/
466-8466.* **Buccia Vineyards/Conneaut** – Fred and Joanna Bucci
provide the comforts of wine and home with a tasting room, picnic
tables under the grape arbors, and two air-conditioned bedrooms that
– along with a hot tub and continental breakfast – accommodate
overnight guests. *518 Gore Road; 216/593-5976. MC, V.* **Markko
Vineyard/Conneaut** – This small, but distinguished winery had the
first vinifera wines in Ohio, and you can sip the Chardonnay, Reisling,
and Cabernet Sauvignon in a tasting room that takes full advantage of
the scenery. *South Ridge Road; 216/593-3197.* For maps and detailed
information about these and other wineries, contact the **Ohio Wine
Producers Association** *(822 North Tote Road, Austinburg; 216/466-
4417, 800-227-6972 in Ohio only. Mon-Fri 9-5).*

WARNER-CONCORD FARMS BED & BREAKFAST/NEAR
UNIONVILLE – Jerry and Kay LeFevre's commercial vineyard includes
a bed and breakfast located in a remodeled 150-year-old barn with high
– up to 35-feet – ceilings and open spaces. One of the guest rooms has
its own fireplace and balcony, and Kay makes elaborate gourmet
breakfasts such as four-grain pancakes or an omelette with crabmeat
and cheese. Your morning juice, of course, is made from their own
grapes.
*6585 South Ridge Road West (State Route 84, just west of State Route
534); 216/428-4485. No children. No pets. No smoking.*

THE OLD TAVERN/UNIONVILLE — The old Indian trail that ran from
Pittsburgh to Cleveland brought the first settlers into Lake County, and
the log cabin where they rested is still there. It was built in 1798,
improved in 1803 and enlarged again in 1818. In 1820, the owners
added the wooden pillars to give the inn a patriotic Mount Vernon
look. The Old Tavern is notable for its authenticity (it's on the National
Register of Historic Places), and its old-fashioned dinners – roast pork
with raisin dressing; grilled smoked Virginia ham; Swiss steak – and
homey desserts such as deep-dish apple cobbler and bread pudding
with vanilla rum sauce. Corn fritters have been the signature dish here
for more than a century. They come with every meal, or, you can buy
a single fritter, a la carte
*7935 South Ridge Road (State Route 84, just west of State Route
534); 216/428-2091. Tu-Sat 11:30-8, Sun 9-6. Moderate. Discover,
MC, V.*

Charlma Bed & Breakfast

CHARLMA BED & BREAKFAST/GENEVA — This bed and breakfast
whispers class and refinement. Everything is elegant at Charlma, from
the good antiques to the new art pieces gathered during the world
travels of innkeepers Charlene and Bob Schaeffer. The guest suites are
in a two-story tower addition that is beautifully designed with
abundant skylights, and the strategically placed windows provide
incomparable lake views. Besides the private beach a few steps from
the door, there is also a sauna on the deck. At sunset, when guests
gather for a glass of wine, Charlene slips a recording of the *1812
Overture* into the CD player, and Tchaikovsky provides the perfect
accompaniment to Lake Erie's molten red and gold sunsets.
6739 Lake Road West; 216/466-3646. No smoking. No Pets

**THE OTTO COURT LAKEFRONT BED AND BREAKFAST/GENEVA-
ON-THE-LAKE** — In the early 1980s, Joyce Otto converted her tourist
home to a bed and breakfast, without changing much but the name
and the fact that she now cooks hearty meals. The Otto Court is not

fancy. The furniture is summer-cottage indestructible. Summertime guests pitch horseshoes and sun themselves on the private beach when not enjoying the pleasures of The Strip. If someone shows up for breakfast in a bathrobe, no one blinks an eye. Two ladies from Pittsburgh used to appear in black lace Merry Widow corsets, which they considered more becoming than bathing suits.
5653 Lake Road; 216/466-8668. MC, V.

ASIDE The Otto Court is internationally known because it is the site of the annual Spencerian Saga, a combination calligraphy workshop and history lesson celebrating the life and times of America's foremost penman, Platt Spencer. Spencer was a local teacher, poet, and commercial college pioneer who developed the graceful handwriting style that bears his name in the early 1800s. Participants in the Saga come from all over the United States and Canada every September to practice their Spencerian loops under the tutelage of The Master's present-day apostles. When they're not working on their penmanship, they can be seen at the Geneva Cemetery making rubbings of their hero's monument, which features a three-foot-high quill pen in bas relief.

 WESTLAKE HOUSE/GENEVA-ON-THE-LAKE — Innkeepers Grace and Earle Haffa, who are handy with hammer and paintbrush, have created a cozy getaway in this large Colonial on the quiet end of the town's commercial strip. The hand-crafted porch swing is a perfect place for people watching, and you can see the lake from the guest room windows. It's only a two-minute walk to the pretty little beach at Geneva Township Park, or a seven-minute car ride to the much larger beach, marina, and fishing pier at Geneva State Park.
5162 Old Lake Road; 216/466-8013.

GENEVA-ON-THE-LAKE — In the beginning, Geneva-on-the-Lake was a popular blue-collar vacation land, attracting families from the steel towns of Youngstown and Pittsburgh who came to swim in the blue waters and stayed in rooming houses and tourist hotels. Today, it is the last of the Lake Erie honky-tonk resorts. Unlike Cedar Point, which grew huge and corporate, Geneva-on-the-Lake stayed small and funky with a carnival-type midway – **The Strip** – surrounded by cottages and small motels.

Not everyone appreciates a place like this. One who does, however, calls it "a county fair, without all that wholesome 4-H stuff." By day, Geneva-on-the-Lake is quiet. At night, it's all neon and noise, as the mile-long Strip along Lake Road (State Route 531) simmers in a haze of carnival smells: cotton candy, hot dogs, and pizza by the slice. Kids cruise; grown-ups do too, some in 1950s Chevies and Thunderbirds, which seem just right in this time-warped resort.

Most of The Strip is owned by the Woodward-Pera family, descendants of the man who built the first casino and dance hall in the early 1900s. The family keeps adding new attractions, and their electronic arcade, **Woody's World** *(5483 Lake Road; 216/466-8650. Open May 1-Oct 1. Mon-Sun 11 a.m.-midnight)*, is one of the largest in the country. There are several other vintage penny arcades on The Strip, a fine miniature golf course that is said to be the oldest in the state, and enough local characters to keep life interesting. One proprietor still talks about the burlesque headliner who was known, for obvious reasons, as "Busty Russell and her B-52s." Each afternoon, before show time, she'd stroll The Strip in a tight T-shirt with the number "52" on the front, a walking advertisement.

Geneva-on-the-Lake is so centrally located, you can swim at a different beach every day without driving more than 30 minutes east or west. Only five miles east of The Strip, **Geneva State Park** *(Padanaram Road; 216/466-8400)* has an excellent swimming beach, free boat-launching ramps, a long fishing pier, campgrounds, and fully-equipped cabins on the lakeshore. For additional information and a list of cottage rentals close to The Strip, contact the **Geneva-on-the-Lake Convention & Visitors Bureau** *(5536 Lake Road; 216/466-8600. Open June-Sept, Mon-Sun 10-5. Limited hours during the rest of the year).*

The Old Firehouse Winery

EATING YOUR WAY DOWN THE STRIP/GENEVA-ON-THE-LAKE —

At the **Old Firehouse Winery,** you can have your picture taken behind the wheel of Old Betsy, the 1924 Dodge that was Geneva-on-the-Lake's first fire truck, or in front of the original firehouse, which was Emery Tyler's barn (he was the first fire chief because he had the only barn big enough to house the fire truck). The grapes are pressed on the premises, so you can also sample the award-winning house wines while you relax on the brick patio or its adjacent gazebo. Since the winery is built on a bluff above the lake, the view is splendid, and the food — burgers, steak, barbecued chicken and ribs — is tasty. For the most refreshing dessert on The Strip, try the sherbet swimming in the winery's own fresh grape juice. *5499 Lake Road; 216/466-9300. Memorial Day to Labor Day, Mon-Sat 11 a.m.-1 a.m., Sun 1 p.m.-1 a.m. Labor Day to Memorial Day, Sat 11 a.m.-1 a.m., Sun 1 p.m.-1 a.m. Moderate. MC, V.* **Mary's Kitchen** — A huge lighted sign on The Strip points the way, and there is almost always a line of people waiting to get in. Tucked among the summer cottages, Mary's Kitchen doesn't look like much, but its reputation for an honest supper at an honest price is secure. This is the place to get hearty, home-cooked meals — stuffed peppers, lasagna, Swiss steak, cabbage rolls — when you tire of midway fare. *5023 New Street; 216/466-8606. Open Mother's Day-Sept. Mon-Sun 7 a.m.-9 p.m. Inexpensive-moderate.* **Eddie's Grill** — Located in the heart of The Strip, this restaurant is so clean it *shines*. Eddie Sezon and his family scrub down every square inch of it every night, whether it needs it or not. The menu is basic: burgers, chili dogs, fried fish sandwiches, with better-than-average slaw. The jukebox music is the innocent rock of the Fifties and Sixties, and the grill is a favorite hangout for cottagers . . . and the nostalgic. *5377 Lake Road; 216/466-8720. Mother's Day-Memorial Day, Sat-Sun 11 a.m.-midnight. Memorial Day-Labor Day, Mon-Sun 11 a.m.-midnight. Inexpensive.*

MICHAEL CAHILL BED AND BREAKFAST/ASHTABULA — Built in 1887 on the prettiest street in town, this enormous house is inviting, inside and out. It is painted in its original Victorian colors — subtle shades of olive, chocolate and crimson — and boasts enough lace and antiques to be charming as well as comfortable. You can lean back in the wide oak chairs without fear of breaking something, and the second-floor sitting room is especially appealing, with a large bay window that looks down on Hulbert Street. The swing and rockers invite lazy hours on the front porch, from which you can hear the far-off murmur of the harbor traffic and the commotion signalling that the Bridge Street span is about to be lifted. The guest bedrooms are all air-conditioned, and owners Pat and Paul Goode include a full breakfast. Although Ashtabula's Walnut Beach, shops, and restaurants are only a few steps away, guests may do their own cooking, stocking the refrigerator with produce from nearby orchards and fruit farms and with wine from the local vintners.
1106 Walnut Boulevard; 216/964-8449.

EATING IN ASHTABULA HARBOR — The tourist's first stop should be **Hulbert's Restaurant**, a commanding building (Queen Anne, with a tower) known not only for the pleasant Victorian atmosphere, but also for the excellent food. As a service to local fishing charters, owners Kim and John Wright clean, cook, and serve the day's catch at post-fishing parties in the restaurant. Besides all this, they make some of the best pies in northeast Ohio. *1033 Bridge Street; 216/964-2594. Memorial Day-Labor Day Tu-Th 11-8, Fri 11-9, Sat-9-9, Sun 8-8. Labor Day-Memorial Day Tu-Th 11-7, Fri-Sat 11-9, Sun 9-6. Moderate. MC, V.* **Tom Cats on the River** — Located at the foot of the Bascule Bridge, this restaurant is so close to the passing boats, you can almost feel the spray. Open for lunch and dinner, it caters to big appetites with all-you-can-eat specials of seafood, steaks, and pasta. *610 East Sixth Street; 216/964-2193. Mon-Sun 11 a.m.-2:30 a.m. Inexpensive-expensive. MC, V.* **Stan's** — If you prefer your breakfast eggs in the form of cheesecake, this is the place. The coffee is good and strong, and there is the usual breakfast fare, plus soups and deli sandwiches for lunch. *1010 Bridge Street; 216/964-7588. Mon-Fri 6 a.m.-2 p.m. Inexpensive.* **Hil-Mak's Seafood Market** — You can buy fresh fish here or enjoy the sit-down restaurant, which specializes in local and exotic fishes. *449 Lake Avenue; 216/964-3222. Market open Mon-Th 9:30-6, Fri 9:30-7, Sat 9:30-6. Restaurant open Tu-Sat 11:30-2:30, 5-10. Moderate. MC, V.*

ASHTABULA HARBOR — With its busy harbor, beaches, lovely bed and breakfast, and impressive, gentrified downtown, Ashtabula has everything a vacationer requires. It resembles a New England seacoast village with strong Midwest industrial overtones, for the town was once the busiest coal-shipping port on the Great Lakes. Ashtabula Harbor is uncommonly hilly, which adds to its charm, and **Hulbert Street**, which connects Walnut Boulevard and Bridge Street, is the steepest and bumpiest street of all, its worn old bricks having pitched and heaved over the years to form a terrain that's roughly as turbulent as Lake Erie during a storm. Locals say the street can make you seasick if you drive it too fast. The finest homes are on **Walnut Boulevard**, a beautiful street where sea captains once lived along a bluff that overlooks the harbor. The harbor traffic is mostly pleasure craft and fishing charters now, although some lake freighters still come in to unload stone and pick up coal bound for power plants in Canada. The shops and restaurants are grouped together on **Bridge Street**, where every 30 minutes throughout the summer, the – what else? – Bascule Bridge is raised to let boats pass through. **Point Park**, at the east end of Walnut Boulevard, is the best place to watch the boat traffic and catch the bridge show. Regular as clockwork, bells ring and sirens wail, and the Bridge Street traffic comes to a halt. The bridge tender releases the 450-ton counterweight. As the stone sinks, the bridge rises. Then the waiting boats scoot through and the bridge descends once more into place. The bridge operates on schedule, but everything else seems to run at half speed in Ashtabula Harbor. It is a pace well suited to the needs of sedentary, porch-sitting summer vacationers who are pleased to find themselves in a slow-moving harbor town that has a nautical, New England flavor.

THE GREAT LAKES MARINE & U.S. COAST GUARD MEMORIAL MUSEUM/ASHTABULA — The exhibits and photographs here explain the importance of Ashtabula's location – roughly halfway between the coal fields to the south and the iron ore fields to the north – when America's steel industry was the envy of the industrialized world. The museum is both instructive and whimsical; there's a knife "to be used cutting fog," but there is also a working model of the Hulett unloader (designed by Akron engineer George Hulett), which revolutionized Great Lakes shipping. The first Hulett was built at nearby Conneaut in 1898; it immediately put hundreds of laborers out of work – they used to unload the boats with shovel and wheelbarrow – and made Andrew Carnegie a happy man. Now that most freighters have self unloaders, the Hulett is also obsolete. The business end of a Hulett – the vertical beam with the clamshell bucket and the operator's cab just above it – is on display at across from the museum at Point Park, where there are old-timers about who will gladly explain how it worked.
1071 Walnut Boulevard; 216/964-6847. Open Memorial Day-October 31. Sat-Sun, holidays noon-6.

ASIDE Since Ashtabula's harbor is blessed with story tellers — retired fellows, mostly — who are experts on railroading, shipping and hell-raising (for which Ashtabula was also famous), someone will surely tell you how the town got — and kept — its name. Apparently, the Indians called the river that runs through it something that sounded like

Ashtabula, which meant there were a lot of fish. When frontiersman
Moses Cleaveland — yes, the metropolis on Lake Erie is named for him
— came through in 1789, he offered his survey party two gallons of
whiskey for the privilege of renaming the river after his daughter, Mary
Esther. That would have been an awful name for a tough town to live
down, and as subsequent historians have noted, the name Mary Esther
lasted about as long as the whiskey did.

HISTORIC BRIDGE STREET/ASHTABULA — The block between
Hulbert Street and the Ashtabula River was "modernized" in 1886,
when the old frame buildings were razed to make way for the
impressive brick structures. There were nine hotels and 52 saloons,
and only the notorious port of Singapore, it is said, had more. Some
structures were built on stilts over the water, with trapdoors in the
floor that could be tripped to remove rowdy drunks. Ashtabula also
had a madam with a heart of gold. When Kit Butler retired from the
harbor, in 1905, she established a home for unwed mothers in Dayton.
The Bridge Street buildings are mostly shops now (antiques, nautical
gifts, American Indian crafts), but you can match the present-day
businesses with their Victorian counterparts by consulting the maps
and walking tour brochures available through the **Ashtabula Area
Chamber of Commerce** (*4366 Main Street in the Second National
Bank building; 216/998-6998. Mon-Fri 9-4*).

COVERED BRIDGES — Ashtabula County is famous for its 14 covered
bridges – more than any other county in Ohio – and every October, it
pays homage to the quaint structures with a **Covered Bridge
Festival**. Although the main festival activities are located
at the county fairgrounds in Jefferson, there are
also excursions to each of the bridges, many
of which are decorated and feature
food or entertainment. Most
of the county's
covered bridges
date

from the mid-to-late 1880s, and you can still drive through them. One – built in 1862 – was dismantled, moved, and reincarnated in North Kingsville as the **Covered Bridge Pizza Parlor** *(6541 South Main Street; 216/224-0497)*, but the others, having survived both man and nature, are still where their builders intended them to be.

With a span of 234 feet, the **Harpersfield Bridge** over the Grand River on County Road 154 is the longest covered bridge in the state. Ashtabula County's other covered bridges are **Creek Road Bridge** on County Road 443F; **Middle Road Bridge** on County Road 425D; **State Road Bridge** on County Road 354; **Dewey Road Bridge** on County Road 334B; **Benetka Road Bridge** on County Road 350B; **Root Road Bridge** on County Road 414A; **Graham Road Bridge** on County Road 343A; **South Denmark Road Bridge** on County Road 291C; **Doyle Road Bridge** on County Road 287; **Mechanicsville Road Bridge** on County Road 9Z; **Riverdale Road Bridge** on County Road 69G; **Warner Hollow Bridge** on County Road 537C; **Caine Road Bridge** on Township Road 579.

You can get specific directions, maps, and detailed information about Ashtabula County's covered bridges and Covered Bridge Festival from the **Ashtabula County Convention & Visitors Bureau** *(36 West Walnut Street, Jefferson, OH 44047; 216/576-4707)*, or the **Ashtabula County Covered Bridge Festival Committee** *(25 West Jefferson Street, Jefferson, OH 44047; 216/576-3769)*.

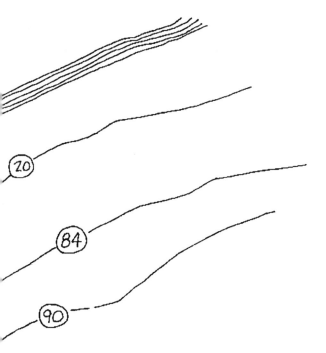

VICTORIAN PERAMBULATOR MUSEUM/JEFFERSON — More than twenty years ago, twin sisters Janet Pallo and Judith Kaminski inherited a baby carriage. They started collecting perambulators and now operate the nation's only baby carriage museum in an attractive 4000-square foot addition to Janet's home. Their international collection of more than 140 carriages includes many rare and ornate ones that are works of art in themselves, as well as several constructed in whimsical shapes such as swans, sea horses, and gondolas. There are also extensive displays of antique toys, games, books, and dolls, and every November and December, the entire museum is lavishly decorated for the holidays.

26 East Cedar Street (off State Route 46 south of Interstate 90); 216/576-9588. Open June 1-Sept 1. Wed and Sat, 11-5. Other hours and group tours by appointment. Call for holiday hours. Nominal admission fee.

ASIDE The northernmost point in Ohio is in far eastern Lake County near the town of Conneaut; its latitude is approximately 41 degrees, 51 minutes.

CONNEAUT — This harbor town is caught in an identity crisis: no longer much of an industrial port, it's not quite a tourist town either, although some residents are trying to make it so. On Park Avenue, more than half of the derelict buildings are in some state of restoration, and the splendid old bank building now houses a credit union.

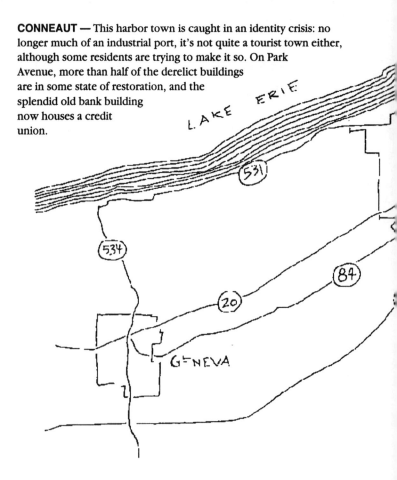

In the 1890s, Andrew Carnegie said he'd build a steel mill here. He didn't. Then, in the 1970s, U.S. Steel proposed a state-of-the-art rolling mill, but that didn't get built either. So, Conneaut seems disposed to give up its industrial pretensions and to develop its recreational assets. The waterfront possibilities are appealing. There is a vast natural harbor, although some areas are so silted that locals call it "the mud hole." Incomparable **Conneaut Township Park** *(480 Lake Road, Conneaut; 216/599-7071)* has unusually hilly and wooded picnic groves, superb recreational facilities, and one of the longest, finest beaches around. There is also excellent fishing in the deep waters off the harbor, as well as a sizable community of devoted summertime fans who snap up the spaces in the trailer parks and the hundreds of lakefront rental cottages. For more information, contact the **Conneaut Chamber of Commerce** *(289 Main Street; 216/5932402).*

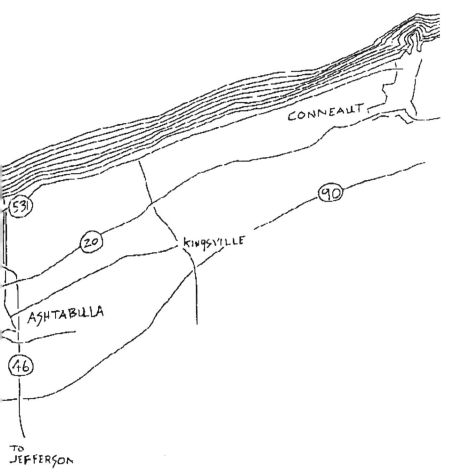

The Jonathan Hale House
at Hale Farm

Western Reserve Architectural Tour, Part 1: Peninsula, Hudson, Twinsburg, & Aurora

Although two centuries have passed since a large portion of northeast Ohio belonged to Connecticut, that New England state still has a strong cultural hold on the territory now known as the Western Reserve. When Connecticut was an English colony, King Charles II granted it a significant amount of land in Ohio. After the Revolutionary War, however, Connecticut relinquished its claim to everything except a 50-mile-wide swath of land between Lake Erie and the forty-first parallel. This "Western Reserve" stretched 120 miles westward from the Pennsylvania border, and in 1795, Connecticut sold three million acres of it to speculators from the Connecticut Land Company. The next summer, the company's first surveying party braved what one historian described as "vermin, varmint, nightmare, cramps, bears, wolves, snakes, germs, fever, disease, and dysentery," and hacked its way into Ohio. On July 22, they reached the mouth of what the Iroquois Indians called the "crooked" – *i.e.* Cuyahoga – river and established a settlement named for their intrepid leader, Moses Cleaveland. Although most of Cleaveland's name – except for an "a" – stuck to the city that today bears his name, he left after completing the survey and never returned to the Western Reserve. But he had opened the way for the thousands of Connecticut Yankees who followed, most of them courting the cheap land and a new start. They brought with them their Connecticut ways, which were reflected in the farms and towns they built. Many settlements started as models of places back home, complete with a village commons and copycat churches.

¶ Today, many parts of the Western Reserve still exhibit a delightful, if dignified New England air. Almost anywhere you journey, but particularly if you skirt the suburban sprawl that is flowing outward from Cleveland and Akron, you'll see innumerable proud "century homes" and other marvelous relics that you don't have to be an architectural expert to appreciate. You'll quickly begin to recognize a distinct look to many of the homes – two stories, a pediment facing the road, and, perhaps, a one-story wing – that is often described as the "Western Reserve" style of architecture. Experts say there is no such style *per se*, but that the buildings are actually examples of Early Federal and Greek Revival structures embellished with various elements the frontier builders borrowed from architectural handbooks they brought with them from back East. Of course, all manner of pleasing Victorian and later styles also abound, and you can tour, shop, eat, and sleep in many of the historical structures. Much of the architecture has been preserved with the same fierce determination of the settlers who created it, but rest assured that anyone touring the Western Reserve today can count on being considerably more comfortable than they were.

PENINSULA BED & BREAKFAST/PENINSULA — Although the rowdy hotels are long gone in this former Ohio and Erie Canal stop, Lily and Frank Fleder offer one suite of rooms – with a tiny bathroom – at the top of the steep stairway in their 1840 Greek Revival home. Five travelers once came all the way from Russia just to stay here, and the Fleders, who are the perfect eccentric innkeepers, will tell you that tale over a glass of wine in their living room. They'll probably even show you the inside of their closets so that you can see the bark that still clings to the beams. Just as in the old days, the water comes from a cistern and well, although the Fleders do have spring water for drinking. As for breakfast, Lily will fix one, large or small, that suits your taste.
5964 Center Street, south of State Route 303; 216/657-2284. No smoking. Because of the steep stairway, no children under 10.

STANFORD HOUSE/PENINSULA — For many folks, the Stanford House will be a different bed and breakfast experience: the bed is likely to be a bunk in the men's or women's dormitory rooms, and you'll have to cook breakfast yourself in the shared kitchen. Built in 1843 by George Stanford, this refurbished "Reserve style" farmhouse is now a hostel owned by the National Park Service and operated by the Northeast Ohio Council of American Youth Hostels. It's open to members of AYH, Hostelling International, and the general public. If

Stanford Farm Hostel

you've never hosteled before, you'll have to get used to a few rules —
no alcohol or smoking — and you also must have a sheet sleeping sack
and pillowcase, which can rent them at the hostel's travel "store". The
resident manager may even ask you to vacuum, clean sinks, or help
with some other light chores. But hostelling also means the rate is just
$10 a night and, even better, your bunkmates are likely to include
intriguing travelers from all over the world. Like all hostels, the
Stanford House gives priority to those who travel under their own
power, a locomotion that is easy and most pleasurable here because
the surrounding Cuyahoga Valley National Recreation Area encompasses miles of hiking and biking trails. You can walk out the back
door of the hostel and hike to Brandywine Falls on the 1.1-mile
Stanford Trail, which is part of the old Indian path that the Connecticut Yankees followed to get to their land in the late 1700s.
*6093 Stanford Road (it winds like a snake off of Brandywine Road
and also intersects Boston Mills Road near Riverview Road); 216/
467-8711. Check in Mon-Sun 5 p.m.-10 p.m. Reservations are
required for groups and recommended for most weekends. A few
private rooms are available for families and couples.*

FISHER'S CAFE & PUB/PENINSULA — You'll have to travel far to
find pie that is any crumbier than Barb Cecil's famed concoctions —
peach crumb, cherry crumb, etc. Her desserts, which include
marvelous cinnamon-glazed apple dumplings, may be the ultimate
destination for many diners, but getting there is delicious, too, thanks
to her home-style cooking. Rich Fisher keeps the original 1960s
vintage "Grandpa George" burger on the menu in honor of the
establishment's founder, his grandfather. The newer burgers are twice
as big, and their reputation has kept pace. Rounding out the menu is a
new shell bar featuring steamed Chesapeake Bay clams, mussels,
shrimp, and whatever else meets Rich's freshness standard that day. In
the adjacent pub, you could aim for an "oyster shooter," consisting of
a raw one swimming in vodka or Labatt's draft beer with a dollop of
cocktail sauce. In fine weather, sit outside on the patio facing the
Cuyahoga River; inside, you get historic views via the photos of

Peninsula that adorn the walls. Just hope you can find a spot to sit, period: Fisher's little building – one of the few relatively young ones in Peninsula's historic district – fills up quickly at meal times with local regulars, bicyclists using the nearby canal towpath trail, and, on Cleveland Cavaliers game nights, hungry basketball fans from nearby Richfield Coliseum. To assure yourself a piece of the sweet action, you may want to order a whole pie, which you can do if you give the restaurant a day's notice. Meanwhile, consider this ample notice if you plan on stopping for breakfast: the early birds get the muffins.
1607 Main Street (State Route 303 at the bridge over the Cuyahoga River); 216/657-2651. Mon-Th 7-10 (pub until midnight), Fri-Sat 7-midnight (pub until 2 a.m.), Sun 7-9. Breakfast and lunch, inexpensive. Dinner, moderate. AE, Discover, MC, V.

WINKING LIZARD TAVERN/PENINSULA — It used to be hard enough to find a parking space in the lot at Fisher's Cafe & Pub, but it got harder when this nightspot across the road began attracting overflow crowds. Now Fisher's employs a guard on weekends and other busy times, leaving Winking Lizard patrons, once the spaces along the railroad tracks fill up, to park where they can. The competition is obviously over more than just parking, because the food is very good here too. Besides salads, burgers, and charbroiled chicken breast, the house specialties include broiled walleye fillets and ribs slathered in their prize-winning sauce. Gastronomically, your best bet is to eat at both places, which will easily determine the winner – you. Architecturally, the Winking Lizard wins out – it's set in the former Peninsula Nite Club, a rambling, circa 1850 building whose old neon still winks away out front. Inside, the atmosphere is that of a rustic resort bar, with fish and game trophies and the tools used to bag them cluttering the log walls. The club's tradition of peanuts-in-the-shell is maintained – along with some of the original chairs – in the basement bar. There are even a couple of real live lounge lizards: two mascot iguanas who lead a fishbowl existence at the entrance to the Ballroom, which was renowned for its big band dances in the 1940s. These days, small bands play there on Wednesday, Friday, and Saturday nights. The dance floor is said to be haunted by a lady ghost, but co-owner Walt Callam says he doesn't believe in such things – "Only when I'm here alone at night and I hear a noise."
1615 Main Street (State Route 303); 216/657-2770; from Cleveland, 216/467-1002. Mon-Th 11-1 a.m., Fri-Sat 11-2:30 a.m.; Apr-Nov, Sun 12-9. Lunch, inexpensive-moderate. Dinner, moderate-expensive. AE, Discover, MC, V.

ACCESS — Despite its faraway feel, Peninsula is quite near several major highways, including Interstates 271 and 80, which is also known as the Ohio Turnpike. From Interstate 271, you can exit at Richfield Coliseum and follow State Route 303 east into town; from the Ohio Turnpike, get off at Exit 12, head south on State Route 8, and then follow State Route 303 west.

WALKING TOUR OF PENINSULA — If your interest is architecture, a good place to start is the **Peninsula Library and Historical Society** (*6105 Riverview Road; 216/657-2291. Mon-Th 9-8, Fri-Sat 9-5; Sept-May, Sun 1-5*), where you can obtain information on various walking

PENINSULA — You're welcome to view all the historic buildings that make up this exceptionally quaint canal town, just don't try to take any away. Back in the 1950s, when officials from Hale Farm and Village came to remove the Bronson Memorial Church for their collection, they were greeted by angry residents, including one woman holding a shotgun. The church stayed, and the people of Peninsula organized to begin saving the rest of their village as well.

Another local tale tells how a woman (possibly the same one) fended off bulldozers by sitting — this time with a baby instead of a gun in her arms — on the steps of the old Woods Store, the village's first permanent structure. Today, thanks to the efforts of many residents — but especially Robert Hunker, who restored the church, store, and several other structures — the entire "downtown" along Main Street (State Route 303) is on the National Register of Historic Places.

Peninsula got its name because it was built on a peninsula formed by the Cuyahoga River. When the railroad came through, however, the river was diverted, and the loop was lopped. If you look up river from the State Route 303 bridge, you can see what's left of the old mill and the aqueduct that once bridged the canal over the Cuyahoga, which snakes southwest from its source near Claridon and then takes a U-turn at Akron before heading back through Peninsula on its way to Lake Erie.

Should you go bushwhacking among the ruins, watch out for the Peninsula Python, sort of a local version of the Loch Ness Monster. The python reportedly escaped from a circus wagon 50 years ago, and the tall tail, er, tale has been slithering around since.

Historically speaking, the main thoroughfare was once the Ohio and Erie Canal, which cut through town along the Cuyahoga River in the 1820s. Since Peninsula was the halfway point on the two-day canal boat trip between Akron and Cleveland, it soon boomed into a hotbed of stone quarrying and boat building as well as drinking, gambling, and prostitution. At its peak, this "inland seaport" had five hotels and fourteen taverns, making it quite a challenge for the Methodist circuit preachers who rode through trying to float religion.

These days, the village isn't dry, but the canal mostly is, and so things usually are quieter. Peninsula's lack of "city water" — it relies on cisterns and wells — and secluded location in the midst of the Cuyahoga Valley National Recreation Area have helped keep the village beautiful and small in spite of its proximity to Akron and Cleveland.

Pizza delivery and cable television have only just arrived in Peninsula, but city folks come by the thousands on weekends, using it as a base for adventures in the wilds of the Cuyahoga Valley National Recreation Area, or, not unlike the early canal travelers, as a convenient place for eating, drinking, and shopping.

tours, complete with maps, sketches, and brief descriptions of important structures. With any of the tours as your guide, you'll be well prepared to amble over the limestone sidewalks of the village and learn something about its architecture and history. One pamphlet, for example, explains that the unique, four-spire **Bronson Memorial Church** *(1712 Main Street)* was built in 1835 by Harmon Bronson, the settler from Connecticut who built the first saw and grist mills here. It also tells how the community effort to restore the Episcopal church ended just in time for a wedding, but only after the future bride and groom had helped to paint the exterior. Most of the beautiful homes along Main Street are frame examples of Greek Revival style, but many other styles are evident, including Gothic, Eastlake, Italianate, and "Vernacular," a fancy term meaning whatever the locals happened to build. Besides the train station and G.A.R. Hall (both circa 1880s), there is also the huge, Stick Style Peninsula High School, which the Historical Society aims to fix up and turn into a community center.

ASIDE Since the early Western Reserve architects consulted the books of Asher Benjamin and others, it might not be a bad idea for the architectural site-seer to do a little technical research too. Probably the best source of useful information and photographs is *Architecture of the Western Reserve*, by Chagrin Falls resident Richard N. Camper, who also penned *Ohio — An Architectural Portrait*. Another handy source, which is based on the records of the National Park Service's Historic Building Survey, is *Historic Buildings of Ohio*, by Walter C. Kidney of Pittsburgh.

SHOPPING IN PENINSULA — Many of the historic buildings in Peninsula are open to the public as antique stores, art galleries, jewelry stores, and other shops (but not on Mondays, when just about everything is closed). **Among Friends Gallery** — Among the most interesting shops is this gallery set in the Woods Store. It was built around 1820 as a general store and home that later overlooked the canal (although after the canal closed, the structure faced the road again when a porch was added to that side). The two shuttered, closed windows were purposely built that way to maintain the symmetry of the exterior. The interior is not as interesting architecturally as it is artistically. A space called "A Gathering of Ohio Artists & Craftsmen" is filled with jewelry, paintings, textiles, pottery, and many more wonderful crafts by nearly 80 Ohio artisans, many of whom live nearby. Chatting about Peninsula with the pony-tailed proprietor, Chris Hixson, is a delight. He describes this place where he grew up as "a cool town" with a mix of "artists, welfare mothers, millionaires, upper middle class, and lower class, all in the space of about 125 houses." Hixson had a corporate career and almost moved into a huge new tract house in Hudson, but he and his wife, C.J., moved back to the village instead, and now they live in a rented cabin with an outhouse. That, if anything, sums up what Peninsula is all about. *1663 Main Street; 216/657-2929. Tu-Sat 10-5:30, Sun noon-5:30; extended hours in summer. AE, Discover, MC, V.* **Seahawk Miniatures** – "For

Sale" signs are rare in Peninsula, and when homes are quietly put on the market, they have exorbitant prices. That just makes it more of a hoot to purchase your choice of grand Victorian mansions for the small sum of a few hundred dollars at Seahawk Miniatures. Called "Ohio's Biggest Store of Little Things," it's one of the nation's largest outlets for dollhouses and furnishings, Hummel figurines, and other collectibles. Owner Lee Hawkins, who has been a "miniaturist" for more than 30 years, sells houses in a wide array of styles, although she says, "Most people seem to have a romance with the Victorian period." You can buy entire suites of furniture featuring tiny ceramic sinks with handles that turn, grandfather clocks that keep time, lamps that light, and other little goodies such as Jell-O rings – they're actually squishy – and wine bottles. The corker is, you can even buy minuscule corkscrews. "Of course," says Mrs. Hawkins. "How else are you going to get the wine open?" *1770 Main Street; 800/847-1803, 216/657-2716. Tu-Sat 10-5, Sun 1-5. Discover, MC, V.*

ASIDE Peninsula people will tell you, or personally prove, that there are a lot of authentic characters in the area, and apparently that has always been so. One of the most colorful, however, was Jim Brown, who, at the start of the canal era, ran a hotel in nearby Boston that made money, literally. Working with his brother and son (who were both named Dan), he became infamous as the head of a counterfeiting ring. Their bid to go international — by sailing to the Far East and printing money along the way to buy goods they could then resell — was foiled the night they were to sail from New Orleans. Dan died in jail there, but Jim talked himself free. He continued to make a mint despite numerous arrests and was even elected justice of the peace of both Boston and Northampton townships. Finally arrested on a federal charge in 1846, he got ten years, but served less than three, earning a pardon from President Zachary Taylor for heroism during a cholera outbreak in prison. His luck ran out in 1865, when he fell into a canal boat and died. There are still tales of fake money being buried in the area, but Brown is buried in the old cemetery in Boston.

THE INN AT BRANDYWINE FALLS/SAGAMORE HILLS — The 140- year-old clapboard farmstead that George and Katie Hoy lease from the National Park Service sits prettily on the edge of the 33,000-acre Cuyahoga Valley National Recreation Area. Just a short amble across the fenced horse pasture is the 65-foot waterfall on Brandywine Creek that was both the reason and the means by which mill owner James Wallace built the house here between 1848 and 1852. With loving attention to detail, the Hoys completely renovated the Greek Revival dwelling – it now graces the National Register of Historic Places – and have made it a nationally admired bed and breakfast. The entire home is furnished elegantly and authentically, down to the hand-painted shades (by George), the all-cotton sheets and period coverlets on the sleigh and cannonball beds, and the carefully picked antiques, many of which are Ohio-made. The suite beneath the eaves is named "Anna Hale's Garrett" after the teenager who lived there in the 1930s. Beneath the floorboards, she hid a veritable time capsule of personal

The Inn at Brandywine Falls

memorabilia, including photographs of the house, which proved invaluable for properly completing the restoration (the Hoys are still looking for Anna to thank her). The Hoys did break with tradition by giving the accommodations in the main house private baths, but Katie hides the showers with quilts. Such whimsy just adds to the charm: one of the rougher-hewn loft suites in the barn out back is encircled by a ceiling-level model of a steam train; the other sports a wood stove and a double Jacuzzi, which make it the Hoys most popular lodging. Both suites also have small refrigerators, microwave ovens, radios, and televisions. The inn often fills up well in advance, especially on weekends. One reason must be the Hoys' incredible candlelit breakfasts, which always include George-baked breads and Katie's fruited oatmeal soup. It's hard to imagine not wanting to also savor the couple's good company, but for those who "vant to be alone" in the barn suites, the Hoys provide "Greta Garbo" breakfast delivery. On Sundays, they serve up a special brunch that fills a menu board in the cavernous kitchen before it fills the guests. George gives culinary credit to Ruth, Hazel, and the rest of the "girls" out back — the Ohio Beauties he buys from an Amish-country chicken farm that advertises "chicks you can trust." A portrait of James Wallace presides over the dining room, a perfectly wonderful place where you can smell the baking bread, enjoy the classical music, and listen to the crackling fire in winter or the distant cascading of the Falls in summer.
8230 Brandywine Road (George likes to bring people in from Exit 12 of the Ohio Turnpike, directing them to drive north on State Route 8, turn left on Twinsburg Road, and when it dead-ends at Brandywine Road, turn right, "count to 38 and you're there"); 216/ 650-4965; from Cleveland, 216/467-1812. No smoking. No pets. Children under 6 may be accommodated in the Loft and Granary suites (in the barn) only. Discover, MC, V.

ASIDE Picturesque though it may now be, Brandywine Falls once was a bustling industrial site started by James Wallace's father, George, who built a saw mill, grist mill, woolen factory, and a distillery that produced liquid "Brandywine currency." At its peak in the 1850s, the settlement consisted of a dozen homes and even had its own school. But Brandywine and almost all of its structures gradually were destroyed by flood, fire, progress, and the construction of Interstate 271, which cuts perilously close to the Falls themselves. Today you can park at a visitors' facility on the south side of Stanford Road, and then tramp down wooden walkways into the 120-foot-deep ravine, where from different observation decks you can closely experience the grandeur of the waters.

CARRIAGE TRADE, HORSE-DRAWN VEHICLES FOR HIRE/ NORTHFIELD — The fanciest way to "do" the Falls is to ride on an antique, horse-drawn surrey through a neighboring farm, then be chauffeured to Brandywine Creek in a vintage convertible and be provided with a picnic basket containing a gourmet lunch of Cornish hens and (non-alcoholic) champagne. That's one of the romantic packages offered by Carriage Trade, Horse-Drawn Vehicles for Hire, a livery service owned and operated by Wade Johnson. For safety's sake, the horses do not often travel on the roads, so to get to the Falls, you'll be transported in an old Chevrolet. But you can tour Johnson's 53-acre farm via a carriage pulled by one his Norwegian Fjords. Afterwards, visit the carriage and sleigh museum in the barn, where cappuccino and sweets are served beside the wood stove after winter sleigh rides. Just call at least two days ahead to reserve a two-hour picnic trip, or as late as that morning just to go for a ride.
8050 Brandywine Road (south of the Inn at Brandywine Falls); 216/650-6262; from Cleveland, 216/467-9000. Mon-Sun 11-dusk. Prices start at $40 per couple. MC, V.

CUYAHOGA VALLEY LINE — A really delightful way to see the Cuyahoga Valley National Recreation Area is to chug right through the middle of it on one of the vintage passenger coaches of the Cuyahoga Valley Line. A non-profit group operates the excursion railroad – billed as the longest and best in the Midwest — on 22 miles of track owned by the National Park Service. They offer special nature trains, bike trains, holiday trains, and regular trips, all pulled behind the big blue, gray, and yellow CVL diesels (the steam engine, alas, was abandoned in 1991). The trains run from late May to mid-December, between Independence (near Cleveland) and downtown Akron, with stops in between at the Recreation Area's Canal Visitor Center and Hale Farm and Village. You can get a timetable and tickets by phone or mail or at the quaint railroad office in Peninsula.
1664 West Main Street, Peninsula; 800/468-4070, 216/657-2000. Office open Mon-Fri 9-4:30. Trains operate late May-early Nov. Wed, Sat, Sun, and holidays. Nature trains run June-Sept, every second and fourth Th; Oct, every Th. "Polar Bear Limited" trains run late Nov-mid Dec, days vary. Ticket fee. Group rates and charters available. MC, V.

CUYAHOGA VALLEY NATIONAL RECREATION AREA

— A national park with a gorgeous rushing river, tranquil forests, and beaver marshes is unexpected in Ohio, especially when it sits — as this 33,000-acre spread does — between the burgeoning metropolises of Cleveland and Akron. Even more unexpectedly, this park fights back at modern encroachment, for the National Park Service continues to "retrieve" natural landscapes, often by buying properties and removing homes.

This reverse-aging process has been loathed as well as loved since 1974, when this "urban park" was created, but the result — besides giving local folks something to argue about — is a true treasure of a place where contemporary explorers can readily return to the natural world and even, sort of, go back in time.

Whatever the season, there is a bounty of things to see and do in this recreation area, which straddles 22 miles of the Cuyahoga River and the old Ohio and Erie Canal. The two best places to start are the **Canal Visitor Center** *(Canal Road at the park's northern end; 800/445-9667. Mon-Sun 8-5. Closed Christmas)*, or **Happy Days Visitor Center** *(at the park's southeastern edge just off State Route 303 between Peninsula and State Route 8; 800/257-9477. Mon-Sun 8-5. Closed Christmas)*. The freshly remodeled Canal Visitor Center is located at Twelve-Mile Lock. One of the lock's twin halves was built around 1827; the other in 1853. During the canal's heyday, the building was known as "Hell's Half Acre," since it was the site of a "house of ill-repute" and, variously, a store, hotel, and tavern for the captive audience that floated past.

These days, it is home to a great mini-museum of canal-era artifacts and displays, including a working lock model. You still can partake of a naked view here, but it's via cutaways of the original lathe and post-and-beam construction of the building's walls and floor. The Happy Days Visitor Center was named for President Franklin D. Roosevelt's campaign song, and it was built — out of blight-killed Ohio chestnut — by his Civilian Conservation Corps back in the 1930s.

Do get — at a visitor center or from other area travel and tourism information racks — a copy of the park's official, map and guide. That in hand, you easily can find your way around the Cuyahoga Valley National Recreation Area, which actually encompasses several municipal parks and other sites, such as **Blossom Music Center** (summer home of the Cleveland Orchestra), Kent State University's **Porthouse Theater**, various youth camps, and golf courses. It's all connected by miles and miles of skinny, scenic drives (on which, it's not a question of whether you'll see deer, but rather, whether you'll run into them), hiking trails (including exquisite short treks to Blue Hen Falls and Brandywine Falls), and biking/hiking trails (that include the extremely popular canal towpath and the surfaced **Bike and Hike Trail**, which runs along an abandoned railroad grade for the entire length of the park and beyond).

Other than floating the river or riding the rails of the park's **Cuyahoga Valley Line** excursion train (see the entry elsewhere in this chapter), the towpath is the only way to get

into the most secluded stretch of gorge, the **Pinery Narrows** between State Route 82 and Canal Road. Since this is an architectural tour, you'll want to seek out the interesting historic structures — many on the National Register of Historic Places — that the park preserves, including the **Inn at Brandywine Falls** and the **Stanford House** youth hostel (see the entries elsewhere in this chapter).

Just south of Alexander Road on Canal Road, **Wilson's Mill** was built in 1853 and is still an operating feed mill with its original water-powered machinery preserved inside. A tad further south on Canal Road, **Frazee House** is an eye-catching red brick Federal structure that was built with local clay in 1826, and is one of the oldest buildings in the valley. Once a tavern/hotel for road and canal travelers, it is scheduled to become a museum focusing on life in the Western Reserve. **Jaite**, a company town consisting of a store and look-alike yellow houses, was built around 1907 by Charles Jaite for workers in his paper mill. Located just south of the intersection of Riverview and Highland Roads, it now serves as Park Service headquarters.

At the south end of the park, **Everett Road Covered Bridge** is a 100-foot long, wooden-shingled red bridge. It is also a reproduction piece: flooded Furnace Run smashed the original bridge in 1975. The Park Service reconstructed it in 1986 and opened the bridge to foot traffic, including the contra dancers who gather here every summer. "Square dancing wouldn't work, but contra is *line* dancing," says John Reynolds, the cultural arts specialist who oversees the activities held in the park.

Just north of the bridge, **Everett Village** is a hodge-podge of dilapidated structures that was once a settlement at Lock 27 nicknamed "Johnnycake." An 1828 flood dumped so much gravel into the canal that it was impass-able, and long boats carrying passengers were stuck until it could be dug open. One carried bags of cornmeal, and so the stranded had their johnnycake and ate it too — for breakfast, lunch and dinner. *Park superintendent's office is located at 15610 Vaughn Road, Brecksville; 800/433-*

HALE FARM AND VILLAGE/BATH — The Western Reserve Historical Society's popular living history museum offers one-stop shopping for the architecture buff. Its centerpiece is the red brick Federal home built in 1826 by Jonathan Hale, who moved to Ohio from Glastonbury, Connecticut. Across the road, on land where Hale used to grow wheat, there has sprouted an entire **Western Reserve Village** – a dozen structures that the historical society has rescued and moved here from various towns. You can walk around the village green and tour them all, from the tiny 1825 Federal-style Wade Law Office (moved from Jefferson), to the 1830 saltbox house (moved from Richfield), to the 1852 Greek Revival meetinghouse (originally a Baptist church in Streetsboro).

The largest and most elegant of all is the 1832 Federal/Greek Revival **Goldsmith House** (moved in eight pieces from Willoughby). It is one of the few structures still in existence that was built by the celebrated Western Reserve architect Jonathan Goldsmith. As is the case with all the other buildings here, guides describe the details of the Goldsmith House in detail. For instance, because it was the room where guests were received, the parlor was painted yellow, a particularly expensive shade in those days. Children were never allowed in this room (unless they were dead), and the carved parlor doorways are larger than those in the rest of the house to accommodate coffins. The entire house is furnished as it would have been for its original well-to-do residents, with period curiosities such as screens strategically placed before fireplaces to prevent the ladies' paraffin-based makeup from melting. If you think that you can smelling food cooking on the cellar hearth, you're probably right. Guides give regular cooking demonstrations – and tastes – of food to visitors.

History not only is preserved but also lives at Hale Farm, for artisans there demonstrate various pioneer crafts. In an addition behind the Hale house, candle makers use fragrant bayberries – just as the original New Englanders did – plus beeswax, tallow, and spermaceti (synthetic, of course). You also can watch broom making (they use broom corn, a type of sorghum grown right on the farm), blacksmithing, spinning, weaving, and more. The exceptional hand-made goods – everything from salt-glazed pottery to maple syrup boiled down in the sugar house – can be purchased in the superb museum shop. It's located in the sprawling new **Gatehouse**, which includes a restaurant, snack bar, and orientation area where tours begin. From there, you can stroll at your own pace to the steam-powered sawmill and other working displays on this self-sufficient farm, which recreates what life was like when Jonathan Hale lived here. With their period costumes, the workers even look like real pioneers – except when you see one wearing a bonnet and a shawl and driving into the parking lot in a Toyota.

2686 Oak Hill Road (follow the signs from Interstate 271, State Route 303, and other major access points); 216/666-3711. Open late May-Oct. Wed-Sat 10-5, Sun noon-5. Additional hours for the holidays in Nov-Dec, for maple sugaring in Feb-Mar, and for programs held throughout the year. Admission fee. MC, V.

SKIING — Alpine skiing is something else that the Western Reserve shares with New England. The hills aren't as long or as steep, and the snow doesn't fall as deep, but with three resorts to choose from,

there's plenty of skiing here (see also **Alpine Valley Ski Area** in part
two of the Western Reserve tour). The vertical rise at each resort is
just 240 feet, but with a little imagination – and the magic of snowmaking equipment – you can have a mountainous good time, even
here in the so-called flat lands only a half hour or less from the big
cities. Consider some of the amenities offered by all of the resorts, and
you'll realize it's all downhill from there – lodges with restaurants, ski
shops, rental equipment, lessons, season passes, and discounts for
children, senior citizens, and groups. **Boston Mills Ski Resort/
Peninsula** – This and Brandywine resort – it's only three miles away
– are surrounded by the Cuyahoga Valley National Recreation Area
and operated by Dick and Erleen Ludwig. Thus, skiers can use a single
lift ticket or pass – and on weekends, a shuttle bus – to access some
75 acres of varied terrain at both resorts, all buried under up to 60
inches of high-tech, man-made white stuff. The combined staff of more
than 300 instructors is the largest in Ohio, and one of the largest
anywhere. As for slopes, there are eight at Boston Mills: the longest is
1,800 feet; the two highest have full moguls; and Tiger Hill is the
state's steepest. Six chair lifts and two handle tows will take you to the
top. Although you can wine, dine, and unwind in the lodge, there is
also a snack shop on the slopes. Thursday is race night. *7100
Riverview Road; 216/657-2334; from Cleveland, 216/467-2242. For
ski report, 216/655-6703; from Cleveland, 216/656-4489.*
Brandywine Ski Resort/Sagamore Hills – Ten more runs are
offered here – the longest is 1,850 feet – and all but one are open to
snowboarders, who can also roar down their own 650-foot halfpipe,
which is billed as the longest and most challenging in the Midwest.
Return trips are provided by five chair lifts and three handle tows. The
lodge also offers a cafeteria and lounge. Racing day is Sunday. *1146
West Highland Road; same telephone numbers as Boston Mills.*

ACCESS – When you're finished exploring Peninsula and the
Cuyahoga Valley National Recreation Area, head east on State Route
303. After about one mile, you'll see on the left **The Olde Players'
Barn**, which is now the home of more than a dozen antique dealers
*(1039 West Streetsboro Road; 216/657-2886. Wed-Sat. 11-5, Sun
noon-6)*. Continue on State Route 303 to the heart of Hudson, its
Village Green, which is located on your left (north) at the intersection
with State Route 91.

PARK PLACE INN/HUDSON – Frustratingly for the architecture buff,
the strict zoning laws that preserve picturesque towns such as Hudson
apparently also help discourage bed and breakfasts. Thus, you will
need to find alternative lodgings such as these brand-new quarters
above – of all things – a Colonial-style office building. The inn is just
off the Village Green, and the deluxe suite and five expansive rooms
are most comfortably appointed, from 12-foot ceilings down to
complimentary beverages in the under-the-counter refrigerators. The
building has no night staff, but you can get room service from
neighboring restaurants. As a bonus, you also get a pass to a nearby
health club.
*10 West Streetsboro Street (State Route 303); 216/650-2233, from
Cleveland, 216/656-3555. AE, V, MC.*

THE INN AT TURNER'S MILL/HUDSON — With a setting as intriguingly different as its "seasonal American cuisine," this is one of the Western Reserve's architectural as well as culinary landmarks. For such a gracious restaurant, it had a rather common beginning in 1852, as a steam-powered mill built by Edgar Birge Ellsworth and friends. In 1989, the Buchanan family, who had operated a country inn in Vermont, opened The Inn at Turner's Mill with its first floor dining rooms and the E.B. Ellsworth Tavern in the basement. "It's atmosphere you can't build," says Brad Buchanan, who runs the inn with his brother, Todd, and their father, Ralph. With bare brick walls and thick beams, the basic look of the interior is still industrial, but it's nicely fancied up with glinting hurricane lamps, antique furniture, quilts, and period artwork. The real art, however, is on the menu, which changes with the seasons. Autumn's offerings are especially colorful, beginning with a harvest of first course selections such as sautéed sweet potato pancakes accompanied by a mixture of mushrooms, leeks, and smoked duck wrapped in phyllo and served with roast garlic cream. Entrees, which come with a house salad and "appropriate vegetables," are just as creative – roasted farm-raised venison in a Cabernet Sauvignon natural reduction; a sautéed breast of pheasant in cranberry orange glaze; chargrilled breast of duck; and two dishes of "free-range" chicken. The emphasis on naturalness and freshness carries through to the desserts, the bread, and even the Bloody Mary mix, which are all freshly made daily. If you think the menu makes good reading, well, the award-winning wine list goes on for nearly 20 pages and tells short stories about the 200 selections. A special treat for patrons is the Winemaker Dinners, which are held on the last Wednesday and Thursday of every month and feature winemakers who host a tasting and six-course dinner.
36 East Streetsboro Street (State Route 303); 216/655-2949; from Cleveland, 216/656-2949. Lunch Mon-Fri 11:30-2:30, Sat 11:30-4. Dinner Mon-Th 5:30-9:30, Fri-Sat 5:30-10. Tavern is open 11:30-closing and serves food Mon-Fri 2:30-closing. Lunch, moderate. Dinner, expensive. AE, DC, Discover, MC, V.

BREWSTER'S CAFE/HUDSON — This coffeehouse facing the Village Green is located in a building known as the Brewster Mansion. You can't miss it: the imposing sandstone facade is ornamented by an even more imposing two-story entrance decorated with minarets and small onion domes. Obviously the architect – Frederick Bunnell from Waterbury, Connecticut – took seriously the adage that a man's home is his castle when he created this mansion for mover-and-shaker Anson Brewster in 1853. It is built, by the way, on the first homestead of Owen Brown, father of the notorious abolitionist John Brown. As one of the most interesting structures in a town that is full of interesting structures, the mansion is said to be the only stone Gothic Revival home still standing in the Western Reserve (actually, there is also a superb *cobble*stone specimen that you'll pass later on this tour, on State Route 82, just east of Aurora). Over the years the mansion was a hotel, a rooming house, and a nursing home before being renovated into office and retail space. In the lobby, you'll notice portraits of Brewster and his wife, the Hudson Heritage Association office, and a display of architectural artifacts before reaching the cafe entrance. It's an informal place, where the changing, made-from-scratch items on

the menu board are named for the staff and customers. "Bruno's Ham-Provolone" is the sandwich that a fellow known as Bruno ordered every single day, even though manager Jason ("Jason's Chicken Pasta") Fordu tried to talk him into getting something else. Besides the light cuisine, you can buy frozen yogurt, baked goods, and the Fordu family's own coffee blends.
9 Aurora Street; 216/650-0765. Mon-Sat 9-8:30, Sun 1-5. Extended hours in summer. Inexpensive to moderate.

HUDSON — Lily Fleder sums up the difference between her Peninsula and neighboring Hudson thusly: "Peninsula was the callous trade, and Hudson was the carriage trade." The phrase "carriage trade" aptly fits the neo-Colonial motif that this burgeoning bedroom community absolutely exudes from the moment you reach the surrounding housing developments, which have names such as "The Woods of Williamsburg." In a shopping plaza called "Cambridge Commons," even the McDonald's restaurant is in appropriate architectural costume. However, if you get to the heart of Hudson – the Village Green with its landmark clock tower and bandstand – the town really does have true New England charm, and Hudsonites are uncompromising about preserving their Federal, Greek Revival, and Victorian buildings. The locals are so passionate about the historic core of what they consider "the village" that when the population passed 5,000 and Hudson gained city status, they officially named it "The City of the Village of Hudson." Displayed on all the historic homes, you will see the distinctive – and not easy to obtain – double-H plaques of the Hudson Heritage Association, which works with the city's vigilant Architectural and Historic Board of Review to preserve all this fine architecture (and keep newcomers such as McDonald's consistent with it). One story tells how a couple had to get approval to simply open the shutters on an attic window. Explains one of the association's directors, William Danforth, "We feel we have the right to deprive or deny alterations or additions that would be offensive for everybody to look at." Most residents wouldn't have it any other way, and whether the shutters are open or closed, you will readily see why.

HUDSON'S HISTORY — In order to appreciate Hudson's rich architecture, you need to know something about its rich history. The short course requires you to remember three names: Hudson, Brown, and Ellsworth. **David Hudson** was the Goshen, Connecticut, man who with five other investors bought "Range Ten, Town Four" of the Western Reserve in 1795. On June 26, 1799, after following Brandywine Creek from the Cuyahoga River, he reached the southwestern corner of what is today Hudson Township and proceeded to lay out a civilization in the image of his New England – complete with the town commons – in the middle of nowhere. His first home, a log cabin, is long gone, but his second still stands at 318 North Main Street and is said to be the oldest frame structure on its original foundation in the state. The founding of a town was Hudson's first life goal. The second was to "raise an altar to God in the wilderness," which he achieved with a Congregational Church. His third goal was to start a college, and it took him 25 years, but he finally did that too in 1826, when the charter was signed for Western Reserve College, the Reserve's first institution of higher learning. **Owen Brown** was a

Connecticut tanner who settled here with his family in 1805. His son John grew up to lead the infamous 1859 raid on Harpers Ferry and was hanged for it. **James W. Ellsworth** was the native industrialist who pumped a lot of money into Hudson – its 1912 clock tower is one gift – in his quest to make it a model town in the early twentieth century. In a plan that got national attention, the forward-thinking eccentric encouraged townspeople to renovate and preserve their properties and agreed to help build the town's infrastructure (including underground wiring); in exchange, he asked the town to abolish alcohol and to cooperate with him. Folks went along so far, but when they elected an anti-Ellsworth mayor, Ellsworth aimed his money at the Western Reserve Academy.

ASIDE In winning the charter for Western Reserve College, Hudson beat out other nearby towns, including Aurora (where malaria was a problem) and Cleveland (which was jaundiced by the immorality of sailors). Soon after it opened in 1826, the "Yale of the West" had to add a preparatory division because, says librarian Nora Jones, "there weren't enough Ohio farm boys who knew Latin." In 1882, the college moved to Cleveland, where it evolved into Case Western Reserve University. The prep division that was left behind closed, but in 1916, James Ellsworth rechartered and reopened it as Western Reserve Academy, which it remains, looking much the same architecturally but with one scholarly difference: girls as well as boys can now attend.

SAYWELL'S DRUG STORE/HUDSON — Choosing which of the many Main Street shops you want to visit – Clothing? Books? Antiques? Model trains? Gourmet cooking tools? – is one thing. But the really difficult thing is deciding what to order in the Hudson institution that is Saywell's. An orange creme shake, perhaps? Or a maple-walnut sundae? How about a brown cow? Or a cherry phosphate? Yes, this downtown gathering place is an honest-to-goodness pharmaceutical soda fountain. Although the menu board says Saywell's offers ten flavors, one more permeates the place: old-fashioned. With padded stools and a black-and-rose marble counter, it hasn't changed much since Fred Saywell started the place back in 1909. He was the great uncle of the current proprietors, brothers Harvey "Rick" and John Hanna, who took it over when their father retired. Feel free to look around: the after-shave lotion and other toiletries are displayed in vintage pine-and-glass cases topped with old medicine bottles, and beneath the green neon Art Deco clock is a wood phone booth with a stained glass window.
160 North Main Street; 216/653-5411. Mon-Fri 9-9, Sat-Sun 9-5, holidays 9-noon.

ACCESS — Leave Hudson's Village Green on State Route 91 North and drive straight into Twinsburg.

WALKING TOUR OF HUDSON — The entire core of Hudson around the Village Green is on the National Register of Historic Places, and the best way to see it is literally foot by foot. That is the premise behind one of Hudson's biggest annual events, the **Home and Garden Pilgrimage**, which is usually held the third week of June. But if you're in Hudson at any other time, guiding yourself around town is easy, thanks to several readily available maps and walking tours that various groups publish.

Start by getting one or more of them from the **Hudson Area Chamber of Commerce** (*upstairs at 156 North Main Street; 216/650-0621. Mon-Fri 9-4*), or the **Hudson Heritage Association** office in the Brewster Mansion at the north end of the Green (*9 Aurora Street; 216/653-9817. Mon-Fri 1-3*). At the Heritage Association, you'll find a number of books, booklets, and pamphlets, including "A Walk Around the Green" and "A Walking Guide to Western Reserve Academy." Catty-corner from there, in the 1834 Frederick Baldwin House, is the **Hudson Library and Historical Society** (*22 Aurora Street; 216/653-6658. Mon-Th 10-9, Fri-Sat 10-5, Sun 1-5*). This very resourceful institution offers an entire series of publications about local people, history, and architecture, including "A Brief Walk in Hudson," which leads you to 28 different structures.

Although there are too many fine architectural sites to list individually, the Historical Society's knowledgeable Director, Tom Vince, has kindly suggested his favorite strolls. "I like the walk from the **Village Square to the Western Reserve Academy**, following Aurora Street to College Street," he says. "I think you get a nice sense of the village. Highlights include the 1865 First Congregational Church and the prettily landscaped 1910 Georgian Revival House on the corner of Aurora Street and College Street, which "relates well" to the former cheese factory that is now the Academy's Greek-columned Hayden Hall.

Mr Vince will, with advance notice, give tours (be sure to ask him about his Lincoln impersonations).

Librarian Nora Jones also will lead insightful group tours of the **Western Reserve Academy** campus, if you call ahead (*216/650-4400*). The tour highlight is the Chapel, which was built in 1836 and is the focal point of the Greek Revival "Brick Row." Many people come to view the campus's carefully preserved halls, dorms, and houses where students and faculty alike live.

Ms. Jones tells the story of a professor who awoke one morning to the sound of banging. He lived in the 1831 Rufus Nutting House on Hudson Street, and the noise turned out to be an architecture buff removing the screen door in order to take an unadulterated photograph of the professor's exquisitely carved doorway. You're welcome to look around anywhere on the campus, but please ask before removing any doors.

TWINSBURG — Developed in the early 1800s by identical twins Aaron and Moses Wilcox, this city is renowned for its annual Twins Days Festival – billed as the world's largest gathering of twins – during the first weekend of August. Architecturally, however, there isn't much to make you do a double-take on the town's Square, except perhaps for the Dairy Queen and the Mail Pouch Barn. The barn belongs to the **Twinsburg Historical Society**, which has a museum next door in the neat stone building that was built in 1860 by the Reverend Samuel Bissell *(8996 Darrow Road; 216/487-5565, 216/425-2571. Open May-Dec on the last Sun of the month. Tours by appointment).* That building and many others are described in the "Walking Tour of Historic Sites" pamphlet that you can obtain from the **Twinsburg Area Chamber of Commerce** *(10075 Ravenna Road, north of the Square in the new city hall; 216/425-7161. Mon-Fri 9-5).* Also on the Square – and the National Register of Historic Places – is the 1848 **First Congregational Church** *(9050 Church Street),* another New England-y masterpiece that, says the historical marker out front, "is notable for being a Classical Revival translation of the meeting house of the preceding Federal period." In two rooms of the Italianate century home next-door, you can shop for period antiques, reproduction lamps, jewelry, and other accessories and gifts in the quaint **Varner Shop**. Even the name is Victorian: Barbara Boyce says her sister and mother help run the shop, which they named for mom's grandmother, Sarah Jane Varner. *(9044 Church Street; 216/487-5108. Mon-Sat 10-6, except Wed when they close at 5:30. Discover, MC, V).*

ACCESS — Head east from the Square on State Route 82 and follow that to the heart of Aurora, where State Route 82 crosses State Route 306. Turn south (right) on State Route 306, and you'll drive right into the center of Aurora and its four-block Historic District, most of which is on the National Register of Historic Places.

THE AURORA INN/AURORA — Despite its period appearance, this is a big – 69 rooms – modern motel and restaurant. Its mission, however, is the same as the old "Inn of Aurora." That establishment was built at this intersection in 1927 in order "to provide a type of suburban inn of which there are all too few in this country, particularly in the Middle West – a place where good food may be had, in an atmosphere of dignity and homelike charm, and where clean, simply furnished rooms are available for over-night guests." It burned down in 1963, but can still be seen in some of the photographs hanging in the present Aurora Inn's antique-filled lobby, which, like the rest of the place, has a Colonial feel. The beams and other woodwork in the country-style dining room and tavern were salvaged from area barns, and the chandeliers in the ballroom checked out of the original Waldorf Astoria Hotel.
At the intersection of State Route 306 and State Route 82; 800/444-6121, 216/562-6121. Breakfast Mon-Th 7-11, Sun 7-10. Lunch Mon-Th 11:30-2:30. Dinner Mon-Th 5:30-9, Fri-Sat 5:30-10, Sun 2-8. Sun brunch 8:30-1. Breakfast and lunch, inexpensive to moderate. Dinner, expensive. AE, DC, Discover, MC.

MARIO'S INTERNATIONAL HOTEL AND SPA/AURORA — This
unique luxury complex offers much more than just bed and board —
foot rubs, seaweed scrubs, Dead Sea mud facials, and escapes into a
Habitat, where you can experience steam, sun, rain, and gentle
breezes. Most of the people running about in white terry cloth robes
are here to be pampered by the extensive spa treatments, but you can
simply dine and lodge here too. The spa building itself, the Aurora
House, started out across the road in 1842 as "The Grey Hotel," a
stagecoach stop famed for amenities such as its "moving" dance floor.
It was rolled across the road on logs, then used as a multi-family home
for many years. Not much looks as it originally did, but the place does
incorporate an artily Victorian motif, especially in the Victorian
Parlour, one of the three restaurants. Most dining takes place in the
rustic Cabin Lounge, which was built around an original maple sugar
shack. There, Chef Roberto Buttolo recreates the dishes of his native
Northern Italy, including "le pizze" baked in a wood-burning oven.
Luckily, drop-in diners don't have to follow the spa's low calorie meal
plan. The menu's most popular specialty is chateaubriand, and the
desserts — including treats such as chocolate ravioli — are enough to
keep the spa patrons *having* to come back. The fanciest, weekends-
only restaurant, the Waterford Room, is perched atop an adjacent
hotel/conference center building that has fourteen guest rooms and a
suite, each opulently furnished with European antiques, feather
pillows, whirlpool baths, and, of course, white terry cloth robes.
35 East Garfield Road (State Route 82 at State Route 306); 216/562-
9171. The Cabin Lounge is open Mon-Th, Sun 7 a.m.-10 p.m., Fri-Sat
7 a.m.-11 p.m. Victorian Parlour open Mon-Sat 11-3. Call for
Waterford Room hours. Breakfast, moderate-expensive; lunch and
dinner, expensive. AE, Discover, MC, V. Limousine service available.

AURORA — There is more to Aurora than its trio of famous, traffic-
jamming modern attractions: **Sea World of Ohio** *(State Route 43*
northwest of town; 800/63-SHAMU), **Geauga Lake** amusement park
(1060 State Route 43; 216/562-7131), and the 30 plus stores at
Aurora Farms Factory Outlets *(549 State Route 43; 216/562-2000)*.
Yes, there is history here and a wealth of historic architecture,
including more than 125 century homes. Photographs of many of the
buildings are on display in the **Aurora Historical Society** museum, in
the basement of Aurora Memorial Library *(115 East Pioneer Trail;*
216/562-6502. Mon-Th 9-8:30, Fri-Sat 9-5, Sun 1-5; weekend hours
curtailed in summer). The museum features all manner of local
artifacts, including Indian skulls and bones, cheese-making equipment
such as a curds-and-whey machine, and even a door from a long-gone
house. The museum doesn't have regular hours, but Historical Society
curator Barbara Cassidy, who also works at the library, will be happy
to show you through if you call ahead. When she leads bus groups on
architectural tours around Aurora, she explains that the town's
picturesque, but prevalent white-with-black-shutters color scheme is
the result of white once being the paint of the wealthy. "It's so
repetitious it's almost ghastly," she says somewhat heretically. A few
of her favorite buildings are **Harmon House**, a brick standout catty-
corner from the library across Pioneer Trail; the circa-1905 **Aurora**
Depot located just east of the center of town on State Route 82, and
that cobblestone triumph, the 1853 Gothic Revival **Chester Howard**

House, which is also on State Route 82 just before the Aurora branch of the Chagrin River. The latter's construction — cobblestones with iron window frames, door frames, and porch columns — is said to be unique in Ohio. The **Aurora Area Chamber of Commerce** (*173 South Chillicothe Road; 800/648-6342, 216/562-3355. Open mid-May-mid-Sept. Mon-Th 9-7, Fri 9-9, Sat 9:30-9, Sun 11-5*) also has a lot of maps and information about the area's more well-known attractions, but do take some time to browse through the several upscale home furnishings shops located in old buildings in the Historic District. The **French Country Shop** (*170 South Chillicothe Road at State Route 306; 216/562-4544. Mon-Sat 10-5. Discover, MC, V*) is actually six shops, offering pottery in the former kitchen, Limoges china in the dining room, chintz bed linens in the bedroom, and wicker furniture on the porch. And while you're in town listen — every 15 minutes — for the musical chiming coming from the grand Church of Aurora.

ASIDE At the turn of the century, cheese was a main industry in Aurora, which was the center of an area known as "Cheesedome." In 1904, a record four million tons of cheese was shipped from here. However, by 1921, the cheese had turned back to milk, since that is what people in the cities wanted. Thus ended an industry that had had an illicit beginning. Around 1819, two Aurora boys, Harvey Baldwin and Royal Taylor, were caught stealing apples. They skipped trial by skipping town and wound up in New Orleans. There, the boys learned that cheese was fetching the outrageous price of $1 a pound, and so they came back to Aurora, where they first made amends and then started making cheese.

ACCESS — From the center of Aurora, head north on State Route 306 until you pass under the new freeway that is Alternate U.S. 422. Immediately veer left, or northwest, on Chagrin Road, which will take you to Main Street in Chagrin Falls and part two of the Western Reserve Architectural Tour.

Geauga County Courthouse

Western Reserve Architectural Tour, Part 2: Chagrin Falls, Gates Mills, Kirtland, Chardon, Newbury, Mantua, Tallmadge, & Atwater

The most scenic drive in the entire Western Reserve is probably Chagrin River Road between Chagrin Falls and Gates Mills. Reputed to be the address of more millionaires per mile than any

other Buckeye byway, it more or less follows the
Chagrin River, which gracefully winds between
tree-veiled mansions, rolling horse pastures, and
polo fields. For part of the way, you'll skirt the
South Chagrin Reservation, which is part of the
Cleveland's "Emerald Necklace" of park lands.
The views are naturally beautiful, and even the
road signs are genteel.   ¶ Supernaturally, however, the Western Reserve countryside might not
be the most comfortable journey for those whose
baggage includes a guilty conscience. Every
village has at least one church – although not
every church has its own village – and you can
often see these straight-backed, New England-
looking structures from miles away. Their white
countenances are so bright and white that they
may seem a bit too penetrating for those with
shadowed souls. But if your own house is in
order, there are several of God's houses – especially the Kirtland Temple and old Congregational
Church in Tallmadge – that are well worth seeking out.   ¶ Two additional New England-y
aspects of this part of the Western Reserve are
the rigorous winters and the sugar maple trees,
both of which are encouraged by the high eleva-
tion. Geauga County, for example, leads the state
not only in maple syrup – Ohio is thus one of the
leading producers in the nation – but also in
snowfall. When people in Chardon tell you that it
is Ohio's snowiest town, take their word for it:
they get an average of 106 inches every winter. A
rewrite man from Cleveland's *Plain Dealer* once
doubted the report of a country correspondent
who got paid by the inch, as it were, to phone in
snow reports. One night, the correspondent was

piling it on especially deep, but there wasn't a single flake in Cleveland. When the rewrite man decided to drive to Chardon and catch the caller in a lie, he got caught in a blizzard and had to be rescued by a farmer with a team.

THE INN AT CHAGRIN FALLS AND GAMEKEEPER'S TAVERNE/ CHAGRIN FALLS — This attractive establishment has been famous ever since Clarence Arthur Crane – the inventor of Lifesavers candy and father of poet Hart Crane – joined two cottages together in 1927 and opened Crane's Canary Cottage restaurant. No less than Duncan Hines raved about the food, which now is served in the Gamekeeper's Taverne located in one of the cottages; the other cottage is home to some shopping boutiques, and it's "inn" between. Just off the lobby, the formal Gathering Room has English-style dark woods and an elegant green and burgundy color scheme. A bookcase surrounds the fireplace, and the reading materials include the works and a biography of Hart Crane, who is said to have composed some verse here. The Poet's Corner is one of fifteen guest suites and rooms; each has a private bath and three have Jacuzzis. All are finely furnished with Victorian antiques and reproductions, and most have gas fireplaces. Continental breakfast, which starts the day on a sour cream coffee cake note, is served in the adjacent, pine-paneled dining room. The rest of the rambling restaurant has a rich English hunt club feel with game on the walls . . . and on the menu. The changing quarry includes elk tenderloin slices sautéed with shitake mushrooms, and wild boar striploin chargrilled and served with a horseradish cream sauce. After your meal, you can stroll around the gardens or follow the steps down to the lovely Falls. But if you're too full to walk, innkeeper Mary Beth O'Donnell can arrange a carriage ride.
87 West Street; 216/247-1200. All rooms are non-smoking. Usually no children under 8. Limited wheelchair access. The Gamekeeper's Taverne (216/247-7744) is open Mon-Th 11:30-2:30 and 5:30-10, Fri 11:30-2:30 and 5:30-11, Sat 11:30-4 and 5:30-11, Sun 5-9:30. Lunch, moderate; dinner, expensive. AE, MC, V.

CHAGRIN FALLS — This is no run-of-the-mill town, even though that's how Noah Graves and other New England transplants envisioned it when they crowded mills all along the Chagrin River. At one time, local foundries here had more irons in the fire than any other town. Although Chagrin Falls has long since lost most of its industry, the village has managed to keep hundreds of its lovely Federal, Greek and Gothic Revival, and Victorian homes. About 50 of them are listed on the Ohio Historical Inventory, and the entire impressive inventory is what makes this place so picture perfect . . . and touristy.
The quaint business district – much of which is on the National Register of Historic Places – teems with shops and restaurants and surrounds the town square, which is actually a triangle. The distinctive bandstand on Triangle Park, as the area is known, sets the stage for the concerts that draw hundreds on Thursday nights in summer and for

Chagrain Falls' historic Village Hall House

special events such as the annual "Octubafest." Just to the north, the
Main Street bridge straddles the Chagrin River and the Falls themselves
at the entrance to peaceful Riverside Park. There, you can share the
brick walkways with the ducks and follow the steps down to the base
of the cascade.

Chagrin Falls has the kind of small town atmosphere you'd expect to
encounter on a stroll down Memory Lane, and strolling is precisely the
way to experience it. You don't have to find the exceptional structures here; they find you. But if you want some guidance in the form
of maps and such, you can stop at the **Chagrin Valley Chamber of
Commerce** *(13 1/2 North Franklin Street; 216/247-6607. Mon-Fri 9-
5)*, or the **Chagrin Falls Historical Society** *(21 Walnut Street; 216/
247-4695, 216/247-5209. Th 2-4, or by appointment)*, which is
tucked behind the Village Hall (a grand 1874 brick home) and has a
small museum. Still, with the entire village so well preserved, who
needs a museum?

EATING YOUR WAY DOWN THE MAIN STREET/CHAGRIN FALLS —
In the town that Crane's Canary Cottage made famous as a good place
to eat, you still have a number of excellent restaurant choices.
Hunter's Hollow Taverne – Located below ground (there's a steep
hill), it offers the deep, dark atmosphere of an English club and a
superb menu – featuring quail, duckling and veal specialties – that
perfectly matches the decor. *100 North Main Street; 216/247-5222.
Mon-Sat 11:30 a.m.-2 a.m. Live entertainment nightly. Lunch,
inexpensive-moderate. Dinner, moderate-expensive. AE, DC,
Discover, MC, V.* **Rick's Cafe** — You can't beat the Art Deco decor at
Rick's, where the ambitious menu offers homemade soups and
gourmet hamburgers. At lunch, sandwiches named for cast members
of *Casablanca* get star billing, while dinner entrees include fresh
sautéed vegetables over brown rice (a welcome nod to vegetarians), as
well as barbecued ribs and chicken, mesquite-grilled lamb chops, and

chargrilled swordfish. *86 Main Street; 216/247-7666. Lunch Mon-Fri 11:30-2:30, Sat noon-3. Dinner Mon-Sat 5:30-10, and from Memorial Day-Labor Day, Sun 5-9. Bar open until 2:30 a.m. Lunch, inexpensive. Dinner, moderate-expensive. MC, V.* **Dink's** — This short-order, family-style diner became nationally famous in 1992, when 82-year-old William Cruxton, a twice-a-day customer, died and willed most of his $500,000 estate to Cara Michelle Wood, a 17-year-old waitress there. *16 North Main Street; 216/247-5679. Daily 6:30 a.m.-9 p.m. Inexpensive.* **Rosey's Place** — Located on the outskirts of town, Rosey's features homemade Italian specialties that you can be sweetly polish off with White Diamonds, a tasty, puff pastry covered with powdered sugar. *540 East Washington Street (U.S. 422 East); 216/247-3364. Mon-Th 11-10, Fri. 11 a.m.-midnight, Sat 4-midnight, Sun noon-9. Inexpensive-moderate. AE, MC, V.* **Suzy's Back Yard** — Go another mile or so on U.S. 422, and you'll run into Rosey's sister restaurant, Suzy's. It has been wowing customers not only with its clean, white California decor but also with big 10-ounce burgers and other American specialties. *8370 East Washington Street; 216/543-7899. Mon-Th 11-10, Fri. 11 a.m.-midnight, Sat 11 a.m.-1 a.m., Sun 4-9. AE, MC, V.*

SNACKING YOUR WAY DOWN MAIN STREET/CHAGRIN FALLS — There may or may not be something about this town that will make you hungry, but there certainly is enough food here to make you full. Besides the restaurants, there are several places to snack. **Cambridge Candy Popcorn Shop** — This awning-fronted landmark is perched on the Main Street bridge, right over the Falls. You'll find all kinds of locally made candies here, plus popcorn and frozen custard. *53 North Main Street; 216/247-7430. Daily 10-7, extended hours in summer.* **The Bavarian Pastry Shop** — The proprietress has not only an authentic costume but also an authentic name: Hanna Von Carlowitz. She and her husband, Carl, fled East Germany in 1957 and settled in the Cleveland area. Carl eventually opened the Bavarian Pastry Shop in Lakewood, which is where this satellite shop gets all of its goodies — Weisbadener tarts, fresh blueberry muffins, poppy seed rolls, and eclairs, to name a few. Everything here is very, very special; there are no pre-mixes or preservatives, and the only "additives" are things such as fresh apples. "We peel our own," says Hannah, who describes the place as "almost a health food bakery." Her husband is one of the few bakers in the country who uses amaranth, which is one of the five grains in their most popular bread. *On the ground level at 100 North Main Street; 216/247-4086. Mon-Fri 9-7, Sat 9-6.*

ASIDE The most fun to be had with food on Chagrin Falls's Main Street has to be the great pumpkin roll. Every year, in the dark wee hours of a morning around Halloween, local high school seniors assemble on Grove Hill and let 'em roll — hundreds and hundreds of what is, after all, squash. The police set up barricades at the bottom of the hill, but no one tries to stop the pumpkins or the tradition.

CHAGRIN HARDWARE AND SUPPLY CO./CHAGRIN FALLS —

There's a lot of shopping – especially during the August sidewalk sale – to be done in Chagrin Falls, and thousands of people come to do it. But whether or not you're the type who enjoys boutiques, be sure to pay a visit to Chagrin Hardware and Supply Co., which has been the village's one-stop shop since 1857. The third oldest hardware store in Ohio, it remains family-operated and is overseen by 73-year-old Ken Shutts, who has worked here since 1938 and bought the place from his uncle in 1964. The store spans two brick storefronts, and some of the inventory dates back to the water-powered mill days. This store sells EVERYTHING. When Shutts points out the pump washers, bull rings, hog scrapers, and horse blanket pins, he is not even standing on the side of the store where antiques are sold. Do walk through; none of the Shutts family – three sons, a daughter, a son-in-law, and an "adopted son" – will mind. Says their cigar-puffing patriarch, "A lot of people come in and say, 'I'm just reminiscing. . . ' "
82 North Main Street; 216/247-7514. Mon-Sat 8-5:30. MC, V.

DUFFY'S CARRIAGE/CHAGRIN FALLS — By riding in Robin Wallis's

"vis-a-vis" carriage, you can see both the Chagrin Falls business and historic districts face-to-face. He gives hour-long rides any time of the year by appointment, but only in the summer does he regularly drive his horse-drawn, four-seat wagon from Riverside Park on Main Street. Beginning in May, rides are available on a walk-up basis for as little as 20 minutes or as long as one hour (for which Robin will even pick you up at local restaurants).
216/729-3714; Wed-Sun 6 to midnight; Sat-Sun 1-5, 6 to midnight. Fee starts at $20 for four passengers.

ASIDE One of the characters who left his mark on Chagrin Falls was the eccentric blacksmith-turned-even-more-eccentric artist **Henry Church, Jr.** Actually, the mark that he left — the likeness of an Indian maiden — is on Squaw Rock beside the Aurora Branch of the Chagrin River south of town (you can find it by following the trail from the Squaw Rock Picnic Area in the South Chagrin Reservation). He carved his own elaborate headstone too, which is in Evergreen Cemetery not because the town fathers wanted it there, but because Henry placed it in his front yard at Franklin and Washington streets until they relented. He also planned a surprise for his friends at his funeral, which he urged them to attend because he wished to have a few last words with them. Indeed, when the day arrived in April, 1908, they gathered around the departed in his home and heard his familiar baritone utter, "I have passed the valley of the shadow of death. Life goes out as sweetly as in a refreshing sleep. Good-bye at present." Only then did Mr. Church's friend, George Flohrs, removed the wax cylinder from the gramophone.

ACCESS — Head west out of Chagrin Falls on old U.S. 422 and, just over the river, turn north (right) on Chagrin River Road, which takes you to Gates Mills.

GATES MILLS — This isn't a place you go to *do* anything, just a particularly special place to *see*, especially the Village District on Old Mill Road (it's entirely on the National Register of Historic Places). Stand among the impeccable white frame buildings and picket-fences, and it's like being transported to another place. That is exactly the effect most residents want. "It's just a quiet little New England town," says Richard Seymour, who lives in the village's oldest house, which was built in 1826 by its founder, **Holsey Gates**. Across Old Mill Road from the Gates house stood the old Eagle Tavern, which has since become the exclusive **Chagrin Valley Hunt Club**. The club's doorway is one of the few parts of the building that survived a 1935 fire, and you could try to slip through for a peek at the wealthy retreat inside. Be sure, however, to walk around the club and see the hounds and horses boarded out back.

Directly across from the club is Gates Mills' architectural pièce de résistance, **St. Christopher's-by-the-River** Episcopal Church (7601 Old Mill Road), which Holsey Gates built in 1853 according to his recollection of architecture "back home in Connecticut." With its steeple piercing the trees, the church is pure New England charm. If anyone is there, you can enter via the side door and peek at the straight-backed pews, some of which still have the doors that originally reserved them for certain families. You also can tour the 1834 Southwick House, which was moved beside the mill race at Old Mill and Epping roads to be the home of the **Gates Mills Library and Historical Society** *(7580 Old Mill Road; 216/423-4808. Mon-Tu and Th-Fri 9-5, Wed 1-9, Sat 9-1)*. Two rooms on the first floor and three on the second are restored and furnished with period pieces, and Holsey Gates's portrait hangs here too. In the basement — watch your head, because the ceiling is awfully low — are displays of toys and tools for cooking, farming, and smithing. If the flag is flying outside, it's open, and one of the librarians will be glad to show you around. When you're finished, continue to stroll around this well-to-do village, crossing over the old Cleveland and Eastern interurban bridge to the other side of the Chagrin River, where there are only a handful of businesses, including **Cahill's The Village Door** *(River Road; 216/423-1819. Mon-Sat 10-6)*. Proprietress Deborah DeMarco offers gourmet and not-so-gourmet foods and beverages, which you can eat right in the outside tables.

ASIDE Perhaps the most evocatively English spectacle in the Western Reserve is the annual Blessing of the Hounds at the opening of hunting season, which is usually the last Saturday in September. The hunters, horses, and hounds all assemble on the lawn of St. Christopher's-by-the-River, where a priest recites the traditional service: "Bless, O Lord, rider and horse and the hounds that run in their running/ Bless and shield these riders from danger to life and limb ..."

ACCESS — Head north out of Gates Mills along Chagrin River Road (State Route 174), which remains superbly scenic. As you pass through Cleveland Metroparks' North Chagrin Reservation, watch for Squires Castle, an elaborate gate house for a never-completed estate where you can now picnic. At the intersection of State Route 174 and U.S. 6, go east on U.S. 6.

THE MAILBOX FACTORY/KIRTLAND — When Wayne Burwell worked for the nearby suburb of Highland Heights, he used to drive a snow plow, and sometimes he knocked down mailboxes. His supervisor made him replace them, and Burwell did such a good job that when someone got one of his mailboxes, everybody else on the street wanted one too. Although his business is based on the sturdiness of his early models, it has since taken a decidedly lighter turn, for Burwell now produces mailboxes shaped like cows, trucks, pelicans, even flamingos. "People come in with an idea and we build from there," says Burwell, who employs several men as what can best be described as mailbox artists. They custom make just about everything from pay phones and to replicas of houses complete with brass porch lights. The biggest seller is a cow – with a cowbell – mailbox in which you get the mail by opening the head. Tacky? Perhaps, but untouchable: even the most architecturally staid municipality can't regulate a mail box because, says Burwell with a big grin, "It's federal." Although some of his mailboxes sell for several hundred dollars, he says customers usually don't have trouble with theirs getting bashed. He has had to repair one cow several times for a lady in Gates Mills, who suspects it's being hit by her snooty neighbors, not adolescent vandals. The last time, she fixed the neighbors by having Burwell fix the mailbox with its rear end facing the road.
7857 Chardon Road (U.S. 6); 216/256-MAIL. Mon-Fri 10-6, Sat 9-5.

ACCESS — Continue east on U.S. 6, and then turn north on State Route 306 to reach the Kirtland Temple.

KIRTLAND TEMPLE/KIRTLAND — One of the most remarkable structures in the Western Reserve, this was the first house of worship for the followers of Joseph Smith, Jr., who founded the Latter-Day Saint movement in New York in 1830. After being invited to Kirtland by one of his converts, Smith decided the village should be the site for the "house of the Lord" described in his church's latter-day scripture. The cornerstones were cut from nearby quarries and laid in July, 1833. For nearly three years, everyone in the congregation – including Smith – pitched in to erect the rest of the building, all the while fighting persecution from local rabble-rousers. The story is told by the floor: some boards were roughly hand-hewn by frontier farmers; others were smoothly sliced by skilled craftsmen; and the irregular gaps caused by shrinking occurred because the builders had to use green wood after enemies burned their seasoned timber. The congregation wanted a stone exterior, but since the local stone wasn't suitable, they covered the rubblework with gray stucco and painted on lines. The exterior remains a sight to behold with rows of Gothic windows along the sides and great Federal windows at each end. Through all of this glass streams the light that so beautifully illuminates the Temple's upper court (used for education) and lower court (used for worship). Both levels are connected by twin staircases that curve through a shared light well, and they have box pews in seven sections that could be divided by curtains draped from ropes on the ceiling. Each court also features unique elevated pulpits at both ends, and the details – hand

Kirtland Temple

carving on the fluted Ionic columns, moldings in "egg and dart" and "everlasting circle of life" designs – are extraordinary. Tours begin with a brief film at the welcome center next door and end on the Temple's top floor, where Smith created his "New Translation" of the Bible in a sacred room. While the guides aren't pushy about the religion, they do maintain that visitors – believers and unbelievers alike – can feel a higher presence here. As for Smith, he and his followers eventually were driven out of Ohio and wound up in Illinois. The church split into factions, one of which is the Reorganized Church of Jesus Christ of Latter-Day Saints, which won legal title to the temple in 1880 and still runs it today. The Reorganized church has its differences with the other factions, including the much larger Mormon church now based in Salt Lake City, Utah. However, all the Latter-Day Saint churches share the same roots, which were planted in this National Historic Landmark.

9020 Chillicothe Road (State Route 306), just south of Interstate 90; 216/256-3318. Memorial Day-Labor Day, Mon-Sat 9-7, Sun 1-7. Labor Day-Memorial Day, Mon-Sat 9-noon and 1-5, Sun 1-5. Free.

NEWEL K. WHITNEY STORE AND MUSEUM/KIRTLAND — For an additional perspective on Mormon history, continue on to this historic site operated by the Church of Jesus Christ of Latter-Day Saints. The hour-long tour begins with a film in a visitors' center across the street and concludes in the resorted country store and post office where Joseph Smith, Jr. and his family lived for a time. Here, the Lord is said to have revealed to Smith many important things, including a health code called the Word of Wisdom that specified abstinence from tobacco, tea, coffee, and alcohol.

8876 Chillicothe Road (State Route 306); 216/256-9805. Mon-Sun 9-dusk. Closed Thanksgiving and Christmas. Free.

ACCESS - Head south on State Route 306 and return to U.S. 6. Turn east (left) on U.S. 6 to Lake Farmpark.

LAKE FARMPARK/KIRTLAND — Part of the Lake (County) Metroparks system, this "science and cultural center devoted to farming" shows urbanites the sources of food and other agricultural products. You can see and often participate in the full range of farm life, from planting and harvesting crops to milking cows and making ice cream. Of course, many of the activities are seasonal on this 235-acre working farm, but with multiple breeds of sheep, swine, dairy cows, beef cattle, draft horses, and poultry, there is always something see and do. Attractions range from interactive computers to antique farm machinery, and by following the agricultural process to its logical conclusion, you can sit down to a home-cooked meal at the farm's cafeteria, the "Calf-A."
8800 Chardon Road (U.S. 6, just east of State Route 306); 216/256-2122. Daily 9-5. Admission fee. Discover, MC, V.

ACCESS — Continue east on U.S. 6 and follow it toward Chardon. As you enter the town, ignore the shopping plaza, motel, and such. Instead, look at the proud century homes on either side of Water Street until you're "Squared" away.

DEEP SPRINGS MINERAL WATER/CHARDON — Only members of the Deep Springs Trout Club may fish these waters, but the public is welcome to drink them. Gushing from eight copper pipes on a fountain topped by the figure of a boy riding a fish, the water only looks as if it's coming from the adjacent pond. Actually, both are fed by an artesian well, 320 feet down, that keeps the water at a constant 48 degrees. Many local folks swear by it; others, well, wouldn't. But the water tastes just fine, and it tests fine, too, four times a year per the State of Ohio. You can fill up your own gallon container for 20 cents, payable at the clubhouse, where owner Tom Montagna and his family will cook any of the members a meal of rainbow trout, regardless of whether or not they catch any.
11069 Chardon Road (U.S. 6); 216/286-3185; from Cleveland, 216/946-0630. April 1-Thanksgiving Mon-Sun 8-dusk. Thanksgiving-Mar 31 Sun 9-5.

SAGES APPLES/CHARDON — You could walk into this place blindfolded and know from the fragrance what it's all about: apples, apples and more apples. On the 100-acre family farm, brothers Bob and John Sage grow more than 50 varieties, including the Melrose, the state apple of Ohio. The Sages even offer a sort of greeting apple, which has various phrases – "Happy Birthday," "For Teacher" – ripened right into the skin. Locals say their "big red apple barn" is the best farm market around, and they also have cider and treats such as apple butter, preserves, local maple syrup, candy, popcorn, and much, much more. And if you can't come to the Sages, they'll ship apples and gift boxes to you between October and April.
11355 Chardon Road (U.S. 6, on the south side, about 1 1/2 miles west of Chardon); 216/286-3416. July-Oct, Mon-Sat 9-6, Sun noon-6. Nov-May, Mon-Sat 9-5:30, Sun noon-5:30.

RICHARDS MAPLE PRODUCTS/CHARDON — Debbie Richards manages one of the sweetest family businesses around in a cabin-like landmark that her grandparent built in 1937. The interior is a veritable rustic museum, with mounted deer and bear heads on the walls, hundreds of arrowheads, old photographs, and maple syrup artifacts that include antique cans, candy molds, and syrup-making equipment. Also displayed are rows of blue ribbons won at the Ohio State Fair and gold medals from the first Geauga County Maple Festival in the 1920s. The family sells three grades of maple syrup, and they transform some of the sweet stuff into a spread and a maple sugar that tastes divine sprinkled on oatmeal. They also make maple syrup-coated popcorn and their own maple sugar and maple cream candies, including a huge confection some folks call a "maple cow pie." Spring is probably the best time to visit them, but if you need something in the dead of winter, you can always take advantage of their mail order catalog. *545 Water Street (U.S. 6, just inside Chardon proper); 216/286-4160. Mon-Sat 9-6, Sun noon-6. MC, V.*

CHARDON — It's not an insult to say that downtown Chardon looks so pretty because it once burned down. On July 25, 1868, a disastrous fire erased the white clapboard business district. During the next five years, the townspeople raised money and then re-raised the entire Square in High Victorian Italianate, a then-cutting edge architectural style that wouldn't become popular until the 1880s. Today, the pleasingly matched brick storefronts along Main Street anchor many buildings on the National Register of Historic Places, and from the Square, Chardon appears much the way it did 100 years ago. Its architectural centerpiece is the **Geauga County Courthouse**, which towers magnificently over the entire town from the north end of the Square. The beautifully landscaped Square has a white bandstand and sugar maple trees that sprout buckets as soon as the sap begins to run. Every spring on the weekend after Easter, it's the site of the hugely popular **Geauga County Maple Festival** *(216/286-3007, 216/285-9050)*. A sugar shack is put up on Square, where you can not only watch the maple sap being boiled down to syrup but also help make maple candy.

The best way to experience Chardon is to simply park somewhere around the Square, then stroll the brick sidewalks as you go in and out of the shops. The Courthouse is open on weekdays (be forewarned: the interior has suffered unjust "improvements"), and you can pick up maps and information on the front porch of the **Chardon Area Chamber of Commerce** *(across from the Square at 112 East Park Street; 216/285-9050. Mon-Fri 8-11:30)*. Those stubbornly seeking the old over the new are in luck, for Chardon has several well-stocked, realistically priced antique stores. The best is **Antiques on the Square** *(101 Main Street; 216/286-1912. Mon-Sat 10-5, Sun noon-5. MC, V)*, where twenty dealers now occupy a former music company. The cubicles in the basement that originally were practice rooms are filled with clocks and other old-time items, including a large selection of photos, prints, postcards, and "Victorian scrap." **Steeplechase Antiques** *(111 Main Street; 216/286-7473. Mon-Sat 10-5, Sun noon-5. MC, V)* has eleven dealers, while **Tea Rose Antiques** *(109 Main Street; 216/285-7088. Mon-Tu 11-4, Th-Sat 11-4, Sun 1-5. MC, V)* specializes in "Victoriana, jewelry and fine smalls."

141 MAIN STREET CAFE/CHARDON — A sign at the center of town proclaims "Chardon's Square and Proud of It." But with two very good restaurants – this cafe and Just For the Fun of It – being located on the Square, it's a wonder that the residents aren't all round. Although the cafe is a rather nondescript dining room with a little bar in the back, it makes a big impression at the door with a chalkboard that lists as many as 20 desserts a day. From the Chardon Square Sundae to the gingerbread, they're all homemade, as is most everything else on the menu. The mashed potatoes are made from scratch, a condition so rare that manager Lisa Knazek once got in an argument over their authenticity with a customer, whom she figures plain forgot what real ones taste like.
141 Main Street; 216/286-2211. Mon-Wed 8-3, Th-Sat 8 a.m.-9 p.m. Breakfast and lunch, inexpensive. Dinner, moderate. AE, Discover, MC, V.

JUST FOR THE FUN OF IT/CHARDON — Tucked behind the Geauga County Courthouse, Just For the Fun of It not only gives its top-quality desserts chalkboard billing but also displays them like jewelry in lighted cases. "The idea is to let you see them when you come in, so you make sure and save room," says baker Lisa Willis, who every day makes eight kinds of perfectly wonderful pies. Lisa's mom, Shaina Klaar, used to have a restaurant in Cleveland's old Terminal Tower, but lost her lease when it was renovated. She bought this place in Chardon, explains Lisa, "just for the hell of it, but you can't really name a restaurant *that*." Since their goal at Just For the Fun of It is "to make food people really like to eat," the menu includes homemade soups and, yes, real mashed spuds. They also create hearty weekly specials such as chicken schnitzel and meat loaf, and like their friendly rival cafe on Main Street, serve real Geauga County maple syrup at breakfast.
105 North Hambden Street; 216/285-0725. Mon 6:30 a.m.-3 p.m., Tu-Sat 6:30 a.m.-9 p.m. Breakfast and lunch, inexpensive. Dinner, inexpensive-moderate. AE, MC, V.

ACCESS — Going south on South Street (State Route 44), you'll pass more lovely century homes on your way downhill to the outskirts of Chardon, where you'll see the Bass Lake Inn. Then continue on to the intersection of U.S. 322.

BASS LAKE INN AND TAVERNE/CHARDON — This newish but comfy motel and restaurant is owned by the same gentlemen who have the Inn at Chagrin Falls and Gamekeeper's Taverne, and the menu here is accordingly similar (if you're – ahem – game, try the sliced rabbit loin in sherry-lemon cream sauce). A dozen guest rooms have gas fireplaces, hot tubs, televisions, kitchenettes, and views of the lake and surrounding eighteen-hole golf course. The stagecoach decor is a nod to the stage stop that once stood on this spot.

400 South Street (State Route 44, just south of Chardon); 216/285-3100; from Cleveland, 216/338-5550. The inn does not accommodate children under 5. Lunch Mon-Sat 11:30-2:30. Dinner Mon-Th 5-10, Fri-Sat 5-11, Sun 5-9. Lunch, moderate. Dinner, expensive. AE, MC, V.

FARLEY'S COUNTRY STORE/CHARDON — Although this store is more than 100 years old, it doesn't look a day over 125. Florence Farley's grandparents took it over in 1924, and sold, as the vintage photos show, "Groceries, Cigars, Cigarettes & Tobacco, Soft Drinks and Auto Supplies." Florence has expanded the product line, without diminishing the impression that you're going back in time whenever you jingle the sleigh bells on the door by stepping inside. The structure itself is delightfully decrepit, but you can't see much of it because the store is so full of old-fashioned items such as muscadine and dandelion jelly, maple pickles, pickled fiddleheads, bags of whey, stone-ground flours, bath salts, soaps for the relief of sundry skin conditions, and odd spices that include cardamon pods and juniper berries. "I kind of go for the things you can't find – the weirder the better," says Florence. Many of the goodies – egg noodles, baked goods, meats, cheeses, and butter – hail from the Amish country to the east, but Florence herself makes the velvety goat's milk fudge using only milk from local 4-H clubs, butter, sugar, sea salt, and pure flavorings. All that, and she ships parcels, too. Now *this* is a corner store.
State Route 44 at U.S. 322; 216/286-3765. Mon-Sat 9-9, Sun 9-8. Closed Christmas.

ACCESS — From this intersection State Route 44 at U.S. 322, you have the option of taking two side trips. By going a couple of miles east on U.S. 322, you can take in the finely detailed, 1831 Greco-Gothic First Congregational Church at Claridon, which according to the township hall next door, is also known as "Land of Steady Habits." Or, continue west on U.S. 322 until, before State Route 306, you grind to a halt at Fowler's Mill.

FOWLER'S MILL — This little settlement, at the intersection of U.S. 322 and Fowler's Mill Road, takes its name from the gristmill built in 1834 by Milo and Hiram Fowler. In 1985, Columbusites Rick and Billie Erickson bought the old mill, which they restored and reopened as a wholesale/retail milling company. The mill is no longer water-powered, but everything is still stone-ground. On weekends, visitors are welcome to explore the three-story mill, which was built with pegs and hand-hewn beams. Rick can point out the 160-year-old saw marks, but he'll literally leave you in the dust as he dumps grain into the noisy system of blowers, cleaners, and sifters. A much more peaceful part of the operation is the rustic **Fowler's Mill Store** *(12500 Fowler's Mill Road, just north of U.S. 322; 800/321-2024. Mon-Sun 10-5. Closed holidays).* There, you can purchase more than 30 different milled products, including the Ericksons' own pancake and cookie mixes, Ohio jams and jellies, pickles, relishes, pottery, and baskets that you can fill with the edibles.
At that same intersection are a number of other attractions, architectural and otherwise. You can't miss the perfectly restored Greek Revival cottages, built and lived in by the Fowler brothers, that cluster around the mill. An adjacent shopping complex, the **Village of Shops** *(U.S. 322 at Fowler's Mill Road),* includes the **Fowler's Mill Restaurant and Tavern** *(10700 U.S. 322; 216/286-3111. Lunch Mon-Sat 11:30-2. Dinner Mon-Th 5-10, Fri-Sat 5-11, Sun 1-7. Sun brunch 10-2. Lunch, moderate-expensive. Dinner, expensive. AE, DC, Discover, MC,*

V); it offers fine lunches and dinners in an historic, antique-filled setting. One of the most interesting shops is **The Brown Barn** (*U.S. 322 at Fowler's Mill Road; 216/286-3511. Tu-Wed 10-5:30, Th 10-8, Fri-Sat 10-5:30, Sun 11-5:30. MC, V*), a furniture showroom located in a converted barn that was once part of a dairy farm. The old pasture out back is now the Alpine Valley Ski Area.

ALPINE VALLEY SKI AREA/CHESTERLAND — This small, park-like resort offers six slopes that range from gentle for beginners to steep for experts. The longest run is 2,025 feet. Two chair lifts, three rope tows, and a J-bar take you to the top. At the bottom, the lodge offers a cafeteria and lounge. There is open racing on Thursday nights and Sunday afternoons (see also SKIING in part one of the Western Reserve tour).
10620 Mayfield Road (U.S. 322), at Fowler's Mill; 216/285-2211; for snow conditions, 216/729-9775).

ACCESS — Go back to State Route 44 and continue south through the gently rolling Western Reserve countryside, which, via signs along the road, offers you its bounty of eggs, honey, pumpkins, rainbow trout, and more.

GILDAY GALLERY/NEWBURY — Although it looks like just a typical, white Western Reserve barn on the outside, the inside of this gallery "for those who appreciate something different" is filled with fine sculpture, carvings, paintings, pottery, furniture, stained glass, jewelry, and other quality items. "This isn't the kind of gallery that has straw figures," says Tom Gilday, who runs it with his wife, Barb. They're both artists; her ceramic studio is beside the gallery, while his woodworking studio is elsewhere on the 50-acre site. The Gildays' creations grace the gallery, along with works by other local artists and curiosities that they import from the Far East.
13860 Ravenna Road (State Route 44, one mile north of State Route 87); 216/564-7559. Th-Sat 10-5, Sun noon-5.

REDLING'S FARM SAUSAGE/NEWBURY — Frank Redling prepares meats just the way he learned to do it 40 years ago in his native Hungary. That explains the paprika-powdered bacon and garlic-stuffed kielbasa hanging from racks in this little cinder block building. His Hungarian-born wife, Theresa, notes that the ribs, bratwurst, ham hocks, and other locally raised meats are prepared "just like they did it in the old days," with much of it being slow cured over wild cherry and other hardwoods. The most popular item here is the homemade "smokies," which you can buy in sticks up to three-feet long.
14174 Ravenna Road (State Route 44, just north of State Route 87); 216/564-5729. Mon-Sun 8-6 ("We live here," notes Mrs. Redling. "Whenever we're not out front, just knock on the door of the house.").

ACCESS — Continuing south on State Route 44, turn west (right) at State Route 87 to get to Punderson Manor at Punderson State Park.

PUNDERSON MANOR/NEWBURY — In the beginning, or at least not too long after that, was the lake, which was created about 12,000 years ago when the great glaciers receded. One large chunk of ice broke off and created a depression that filled with meltwater, and the resulting kettle lake is the largest — 90 acres — and deepest — at least 65 feet — of its kind in Ohio. It was a natural place to settle for Lemuel Punderson, who came from Connecticut to establish a gristmill — and his name — here in 1808. Those who followed also found this to be a pleasant spot, and after the turn of the century, people had resorted to turning it into, well, a resort. The huge English Tudor manse that is now Punderson Manor was meant to be a summer home for Karl Long, a wealthy Detroit man. But the Depression crimped his plans for 29 rooms and 14 baths, and after spending $250,000, he abandoned the property. The State of Ohio later acquired it, and amid the natural beauty of the 1,000-acre Punderson State Park, the public can now enjoy dining — the menu has something for just about every taste, from poached salmon to prime rib — and staying in the mansion, as well as 26 two-bedroom cottages. The park's recreational amenities include golf, camping, boating, swimming, and fishing; in winter, there is sledding (on a lighted run), cross-country skiing, and snowmobiling. You might say people are dying to stay here, for "Murder Mystery Weekends" are among the manor's most popular overnight packages (see also the entry on Punderson Manor in the Mesopotamia tour).

11755 Kinsman Road (park entrance is 1.3 miles west of State Route 44 on the south side of State Route 87); 800/AT-A-PARK, 216/564-9144. Breakfast Mon-Sat 7:30-11, Sun 7:30-10. Lunch Mon-Sat 11-2:30. Dinner Mon-Th 5-8, Fri-Sat 5-9:30, Sun 4-8. Sun brunch 10-2:30. Breakfast and lunch, inexpensive-moderate. Dinner, moderate-expensive. AE, Discover, MC, V.

ACCESS — For a quick architectural detour, go west on State Route 87 past Punderson State Park and look for Materials Park on the south side of the road.

MATERIALS PARK/RUSSELL TOWNSHIP — The headquarters of ASM International (the Materials Information Society) is canopied by an awesome, aluminum-tube geodesic dome that is the distinctive creation of architectural visionary R. Buckminster Fuller. Inside the 103-feet-high, 272-feet-in-diameter structure is a mineral garden of 80 specimens, including gold and silver ore, from all over the world. *9639 Kinsman Road (State Route 87); 216/338-5151. Grounds open 8:30 a.m.-10 p.m.*

ACCESS — Go east on State Route 87 to State Route 44, then head south on State Route 44 toward South Newbury.

UNION CHAPEL/SOUTH NEWBURY — The best architecture pleases more than just the eye and embodies more than just rooms. That is definitely true of the Union Chapel, a diminutive one-room, white frame building that isn't really a chapel and isn't owned by anybody. Its story dates back to 1856, when the Old Brick Congregational Church stood across the road. The trustees retracted an invitation to one of the best known speakers in the nation, a young teacher at

nearby Hiram College. "The church is reserved for sermons," they explained, but the talk around the township was that the church fathers feared the speaker would advocate total immersion baptism, which the Congregationalists didn't practice. The area's free thinkers decided the village needed a "Chapel for Free Speech," and they banded together to quickly erect this one on land donated by Anson Matthews. Asked to dedicate the little building was the speaker they had been denied the right to hear: James A. Garfield, who, of course, accepted, then went on to become President of the United States. Others followed to speak their minds here, including Susan B. Anthony, Louisa M. Alcott, Lucy Stone, and Theodore Parker. The building also was the birthplace, in 1870, of a chapter of the Northern Ohio Women's Dress Reform Movement, and in 1874, of the Newbury Women's Suffrage Political Club, the second of its kind in the state and one of the first in the nation. After serving as a community center for most of a century, the building is no longer regularly used, but Anson Matthews's original lease allows it to stand here as long as God allows it. If you stop to read the historic markers or peer in the windows, you may attract the attention of Beverly Ash, a neighbor who is one of the "friends of the chapel" who quietly helps maintain this historic and inspirational building. She might be willing to take you into the chapel's spare, untouched-by-time interior, where you'll see Garfield's portrait and framed embroidery with hoary slogans such as "Suffrage Is A Human Right" and "Judge Not Lest Ye Be Judged."
State Route 44, on the east side of the road, just south of State Route 87.

ASIDE One historian notes that the first attempt by Newbury women to vote was unsuccessful in 1871. Their illegal votes for Ohio's governor were "lost" between Chardon and Columbus. The next year, they tried to vote again, but politicians hired boys to smoke up the polling place. The men apologized, and the women finally did get to vote in the municipal election of 1874.

ACCESS — From State Route 44 turn east (left) on to Pioneer Trail Road, a scenic byway that intersects State Route 44 just south of State Route 82. Follow the signs to the John Johnson Farm Home.

JOHN JOHNSON FARM HOME/HIRAM — Architecturally, this is a well-preserved 1829 Western Reserve farmhouse with period furnishings that is open to the public for tours. Religiously, it's an important historic site for The Church of Jesus Christ of Latter-Day Saints, which owns and operates it (see also the entry above on the Kirtland Temple). The pleasant church "missionaries" who serve as resident guides will explain the area's significance to the Mormon movement. In the 1830s, the much-persecuted Mormon leader Joseph Smith and his family lived on this farm with John and Elsa Johnson for about a year. During that stay, Smith and his scribe, Stanley Rigdon of Kirtland, are said to have had more than 130 divine revelations in the sacred upstairs bedroom. Fifteen are accepted as scripture in the Church's "Doctrine and Covenants," including the section that describes the Latter-Day Saints' view of life after death. That was the high point; the low point came on the cold night of March 24, 1832, when a mob dragged Smith from his rope trundle bed, beat him, and then tarred and feathered him. It's believed that they intended to kill him, which is exactly what an Illinois mob did 12 years later. These days, the farm is a far more peaceful place where you can picnic and – since it's also a working church "welfare farm" – buy strawberries and apples in season.

6203 Pioneer Trail, about a mile southwest of Hiram; 216/569-3170. Mon-Sun 9-dusk. Closed Christmas and Thanksgiving. Free.

ACCESS — Return to State Route 44 and continue south into Mantua, which was named in honor of Napoleon's victory over that Italian city fourteen years before the township was organized in 1810. Pronounced "Man-o-way," the hilly village is home to the annual September Potato Festival, which features such earthy delicacies as potato ice cream and mashed potato wrestling. Turn west (right) on Prospect Street, and go up the hill, where you'll see Mantua Manor Antiques on your left.

MANTUA MANOR ANTIQUES/MANTUA — The sleepy town of Mantua consists of many fine homes of different styles. Owner Gail Shuss describes this, the biggest one, as a "grudge house." As she tells it, Mantua bank president H.L. Hine initially had his eye on the mansard-roofed brick beauty across the street (notice its National Register of Historic Places marker and the stone carriage step at the curb). When he couldn't buy it, he decided to outdo it. Beginning in 1892, Hine put ten men to work seven days a week for three years to erect this porch-and-balcony-surrounded, Shingle Style beauty. The interior has only the finest hand-picked woods (Hine owned the lumber company too), and every room features a different wood – oak in the foyer, birch in the first parlor, beech in the second parlor, and so on. All in all, there are 26 rooms, and you can see ten of them because they're furnished with the antiques and collectibles (glassware collectors, head for the dining room) that are for sale. Ms. Shuss is only the third owner, and she can tell you all about the house's old glories, including the original carbide lighting system, which is said to have been installed by none other than Thomas Edison, who also ate some apple strudel in the kitchen.

4624 West Prospect Street; 216/274-8722. Tu and Th-Sun 1-5. Additional hours when Ms. Shuss is available (her motto is "If I'm home, I'm open.").

ACCESS — Head west out of town on Prospect Street to where it dead ends at High Street. Turn west (left) on High Street, which becomes Mennonite Road. Just outside of town, make the first right turn (you're at a gravel pit) and head north on Mantua Center Road. You'll pass several grand homes before stopping at the intersection with State Route 82, which is Mantua Center.

MANTUA CENTER — The long stone wall leading up to the village green is pure New England, as are the simple white structures gathered around it. Between the stone wall and an iron fence is ancient **Eastlawn Cemetery**, filled with stones for Ezekiels, Hesters,

Danforths, and Sabrinas, plus a granite boulder resting atop G.L. and
M.J. Merryfield. Beside the graveyard is the 1837 **Mantua Civic
Center**, with its Gothic shuttered windows, and beside that, the
steeple of "the oldest Disciples Church in Ohio," the **Mantua Center
Christian Church** (the congregation started in 1827; this building
dated to 1840). Beside that is the cupola-topped 1840s **Mantua
Center Town House**, which is home to the **Mantua Historical
Society** *(216/274-8128. Open Spring-Fall, Wed 1 to 4. Tours by
appointment)*. The Historical Society's museum is packed with
fascinating items, and if nothing else, you should make it a point to see
the incredible collection of arrowheads, stone tools, and other Indian
artifacts. "We were told, and we believe it to be true, that the
collection we have up here is the best in Ohio," says Mantua Historical
Society President Al Summerlin, who adds that Kent State University,
Ohio State University, and the Ohio Historical Society have all wanted
to buy it. He says nearly all of the thousands of pieces were found in
surrounding fields by the late Joe Warani of nearby Hiram Rapids.
Other rarities include several examples of beautiful Mantua Glass and a
rocker that belonged to Judge Amzi Atwater, who organized Mantua
Township and presided over its first wedding and first funeral. Be sure
to go outside and feast your eyes on what may be the architectural
highlight of the entire tour: the twelve-hole boys' outhouse. "We've
said it's the only one in the country," says Summerlin, "and nobody
has ever disputed the fact." Built in 1907 when the Town House was
serving as a school, the outhouse also has a long tin urinal that, as
Summerlin puts it, "probably let 'em all come out at recess."

ACCESS — State Route 82 will pleasantly return you to Aurora, where
you could backtrack to your starting point at Peninsula and end your
Western Reserve tour. But if you still want to see more of the area's
architecture, you can take side trips to either Tallmadge or Atwater by
going south on State Route 44. To reach **Tallmadge**, take State Route
44 south to its intersection with State Route 59 in Ravenna. Go west
on State Route 59 to State Route 261. Turn south (left) on State Route
261 and follow it into Tallmadge. To get to **Atwater**, go south on State
Route 44 until it intersects State Route 14. Follow State Route 14 south
to State Route 183. Follow State Route 183 south to the intersection
with U.S. 224.

TALLMADGE — At least eight roads – including State Route 261 –
lead to the gorgeous **Congregational Church**, a landmark on the
green inside Tallmadge Circle. The circle, which is actually shaped like
an oval, was laid out by the Reverend David Bacon in 1806. He hoped
to establish a church-centered community named after Benjamin
Tallmadge, a devout Congregationalist and one-time secret agent for
George Washington. Completed in August 1825, the church was the
work of one of Ohio's first architects, Colonel Lemuel Porter. He was a
native of Connecticut, which explains why the church is considered
to be the "most New England-like" one in Ohio. Now a state memorial,
the church can be rented for weddings but is no longer regularly used
for services, despite the historical marker that describes it as "the
oldest Ohio church to be continuously occupied as a place of
worship." That marker, which was planted by the Ohio Historical
Society and the Architects Society of Ohio, also notes that "the

Tallmadge

structure is considered to be a perfect example of the pure Connecti-
cut-type of Federal architecture." Sunday probably is the best day to
visit the church. Do admire its interesting details such as the wooden
shingles, but ignore the encircling siege of cars, fast-food restaurants,
and shopping places. You should also go across the green to the Olde
Towne Hall, built in 1859 as a combination town hall and academy.
It's now the home of the **Tallmadge Historical Society** *(216/633-
3852; call for tour hours)*, which has transformed the old government
offices into a blacksmith shop, a general store, and other period
displays around a village green. You can call to arrange a tour of the
museum, which is well-stocked with local artifacts. You also can get
inside "everybody's church" by calling ahead to the Congregational
Church's curator, Cliff Herholz (216/253-2079). Just outside Tallmadge
Circle, **Bumpas Emporium and Drugstore** *(10 Tallmadge Circle;
216/633-4911. Mon-Sat 9-9, Sun 10-8)*, looks old on the outside and
has its own early Victorian museum of pharmacy-related items on the
inside.

ACCESS — If your side trip to Tallmadge leaves you hungry, it's more
than worthwhile to drive a few miles to eat at The Zephyr in Kent.
Take State Route 261 to State Route 43, turn north (left) and follow
State Route 43 into downtown Kent, where you'll turn left again on
Main Street.

THE ZEPHYR/KENT — The Zephyr is the rarest of finds in rural Ohio – a vegetarian restaurant. You need not be a vegetarian, however, to appreciate the delectable food, which includes several types of homemade bread and "picture-frame eggs" prepared with home fries, spicy grilled peppers, onions, and melted cheese. Try the bread sampler plate or one of the restaurant's special "roll-ups" – various fillings wrapped in Middle Eastern lavash bread. There are soups, desserts, and other daily specials that come with a clientele that is, well, as natural and unconventional as the food.
106 West Main Street; 216/678-4848. Tu-Fri 8 a.m.-9 p.m., Sat 9-9, Sun 9-7. Breakfast, inexpensive. Lunch and dinner, inexpensive to moderate.

RIES' VILLAGE INN RESTAURANT/ATWATER — Set in a restored 1825 Federal farmhouse with a country decor, this restaurant has a menu featuring homemade soups and pies and, from Thursday through Saturday, charbroiled steaks. Upstairs is a gift shop where you can purchase photographs of vintage village scenes, crafts, quilts, and antique furniture.
1281 State Route 183 at Waterloo Road; 216/947-3005. Mon-Th and Sun 6-8, Fri-Sat 6-10. Breakfast and lunch, inexpensive. Dinner, moderate. Discover, MC, V.

CONGREGATIONAL CHURCH/ATWATER — Completed in 1841, this stately Greco-Gothic Revival edifice – it has Ionic columns on the front and pointed windows along the sides – not only is one of the Western Reserve's finest churches but also is on the National Register of Historic Places. The congregation, which is more than 175 years old, originally helped pay for its construction by purchasing slips, or pew rentals. That custom has long been discontinued, so don't be concerned about having a place to sit if you come for the United Church of Christ services on Sundays. You can't miss the towering, 112-foot-high cupola as you drive in on State Route 183. you make an advance call to the pastor, he'll be happy to come over and tell you about the community and his church.
1237 State Route 183; 216/821-1183.

THE BUCKEYE LADY/ATWATER — With its pink paint and multicolor trim in shades of olive, cream, plum, and carnation, you can't miss this bed and breakfast, which is located beside the Atwater United Methodist Church on the south side of Waterloo Road. Joyce Paolino picked the colors for this circa-1900 "painted lady" after she and her husband, Fritz, moved here from suburban Akron in 1989. Joyce says they didn't buy the home with the intent of opening a bed and breakfast, but "I just thought we should be doing something with all these rooms." Thus, they have three truly colorful rooms for guests – the Amethyst, the Emerald, and the Sapphire – and two shared baths. The Paolinos also share their authentically restored and furnished parlor and dining room – Joyce serves a big country breakfast – with guests, but if you choose, you can eat outside on the verandah near the buckeye tree.
6374 Waterloo Road (west off of State Route 183); 216/947-3932. No smoking. Well-behaved children welcome.

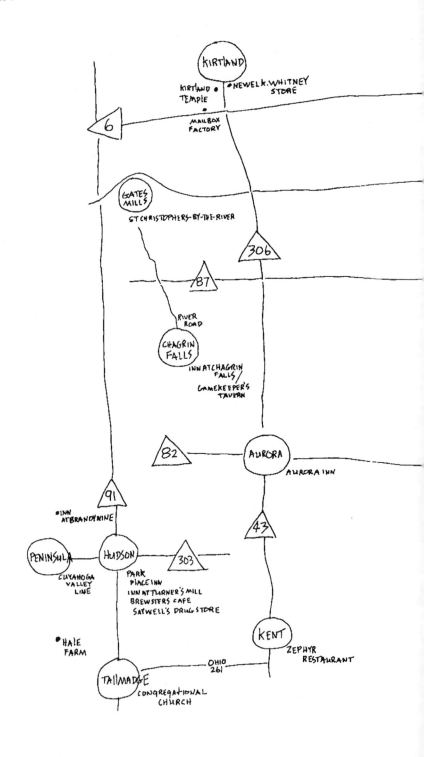

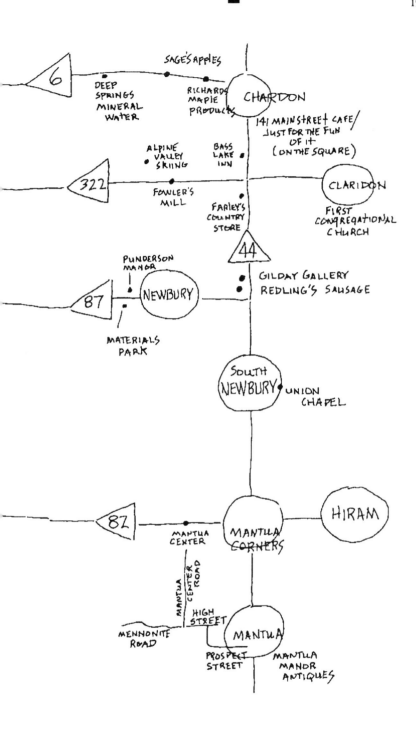

True Brook Inn

Mesopotamia

Mesopotamia is a nearly perfect place: an undersized village with an oversized green commons filled with sugar maple trees. Most of the 28 houses and other buildings around this commons date from before the Civil War, and they're still in use. Just ten miles west in Burton, the traveler can pay an admission charge to see the Geauga County Historical Society's Century Village, consisting of twenty nineteenth-century structures that have been moved in, restored, and furnished. It is a fine exhibit that 10,000 people tour every year. But then there's Mesopotamia, where you can't go traipsing into the houses, because they're still lived in. Mesopotamia is the real thing, free to see, and set around that lovely commons just as it was built. It's a miracle as much as a place. ¶ A tour of the area around Mesopotamia is a tour of places most of the world, even most of Ohio, has never heard of —

the forgotten recesses of the Western Reserve, the far corners of four counties. Here, Mesopotamia is only one (the best, perhaps, but still only one) of several New-England-like towns that sit contemplating their central greens. Many of these townships also have Amish residents, as the hitching rail near the Mesopotamia store attests. The Amish arrived in the 1880s and have stayed to thrive and multiply. Ironically, while the Amish cling to old-fashioned tools, clothing styles, and practices, their houses, which were built for a growing population, are more likely to be new than those of "Yankee" or "English" residents. Around here you will find Amish res-taurants — nowadays surely the only places in America where the waitress might admire the butter in which your sandwich was toasted — but at least so far, you won't find a lot of glittery, ersatz Swiss development for tourists. ¶ The 1,900 people living in Middlefield make it the most populous town around here, but in a sense, that's misleading, for most of this area is just 35 to 40 miles from Cleveland. It is a commuting fringe for urban escapists like Ken Schaden, who went from corporate management to a country store, or for Marge Townsend, who grew up in the Columbus suburb of Bexley and has been raising pigs near Windsor for twenty years. For almost all that time, her husband commuted to a Cleveland job. Organic farmer Ted Bartlett — he grew up in a Cleveland suburb — still commutes. He teaches part-time at Cleveland State. ¶ So this is no wilderness. It is farms, but it is also building supply businesses and auto repair shops and factories, especially rubber and plastics

factories (even Mesopotamia has a plastics factory
– a discreet one). It is pretty roads, with spectacular views of distant Pennsylvania hills from
around Parkman or from State Route 305 just east
of Nelson. It is black and dark blue clothes on
Amish clotheslines. It is following a buggy on the
highway (they do fifteen miles per hour, tops). It
is having an Amish clerk tell you to have a nice
day. It is the vestiges of the Western Reserve,
settled in the early 1800s with people from
Connecticut the principal developers; today
some of their descendants still live in their
houses. It is dozens and dozens of century-old
houses still used and still tended because, in this
limbo of far corners, they're at once near enough
and far enough.

TRUEBROOKE INN/MESOPOTAMIA — More than a bed and
breakfast, TrueBrooke Inn is a mini resort with a quiet ambiance. The
gray hilltop building is relatively new – it was built in 1979 – and the
guest rooms have creature comforts, private baths, and floor-to-ceiling
windows that afford a fine view of the surrounding countryside.
Breakfast is included, and for an additional charge, guests also have the
option of a four-course dinner, with a set but special menu. The inn's
property extends 320 acres, and amenities include a tennis court,
billiard table, swimming in a spring-fed lake, secluded picnic areas,
and wooded hiking trails with names such as Ridge, Grandparents, and
Raspberry. Guests can also walk to Mesopotamia, which is only about
a mile and a half down the road. The adjacent TrueBrooke Dairy Farm
is run by an Amish family. It's possible to reach the end of the
driveway in your car and see an unaccompanied horse walking up
State Route 534. Look toward the farm. Sure enough, a boy is running
up the road, chasing the horse, which perhaps intimidated by the
stopped cars and watching people, turns into a driveway and waits to
be recaptured.
9637 State Route 534; 216/693-4200. MC, V.

PUNDERSON MANOR/NEWBURY — This state park lodge started not
as an everyman hostel, but as a rich man's summer retreat, and it still
has the look of the Tudor-style mansion it was intended to be. Karl
Long chose the site overlooking Punderson Lake and started building
in 1929. He never quite finished, although he spent a quarter of a
million dollars before he ran out of money. Fortunately, the lodge is
still run with appropriate touches, such as fires in the Tudor fireplaces

in winter. The 90-acre Punderson Lake, a relic of the glaciers and one of the few natural lakes in Ohio, is a pretty setting, although if you want to see it from your window, you have to ask for a room at the back of the lodge. With tennis courts, an 18-hole golf course, an outdoor swimming pool, and a lighted toboggan run (this *is* snow country), the recreational facilities are among the best at any state park in Ohio. The manor also has a restaurant, where the quality may vary.

11755 Kinsman Road (park entrance is 1.3 miles west of State Route 44 on the south side of State Route 87); 216/564-9144, 800-AT-A-PARK. AE, Discover, MC, V.

WALKER JOHNSON INN/MIDDLEFIELD — After her daughters were grown, Judy McDowell assessed the advantages of her attractive Victorian house on Middlefield's main street, and decided to turn it into a bed and breakfast. By the next year, she was offering three rooms: two small ones with double beds and a shared bath, and a larger one with a queen-sized bed and its own bath. All the furnishings are antiques, except for the queen-sized bed, which wasn't an option in days gone by. Breakfasts are special — fresh-squeezed juices and homemade breads and muffins.

15038 South State Avenue; 216/632-5662. Reservations preferred.

Walker Johnson Inn

ACCESS — As befits far corners, access to the Mesopotamia region is indirect, since most of the towns are fifteen to twenty miles from such lordly thoroughfares as interstate highways. State Route 534, which

runs north-south and intersects Interstates 90 and 76, is one good way
to start. Another is U.S. 422, which is accessible from Interstate 271; it
is the most businesslike road that goes into the area and the most
efficient means of access from populous places such as Cleveland and
Columbus. In most of the Mesopotamia area, the map is a grid of roads
about five miles apart, with towns sprouting, more and less successfully, at intersections. This tour was laid out like a tiara with
Mesopotamia being the crown jewel in the middle, and other
communities being lesser jewels on either side. Since it forms a loop,
this tour can be picked up at any point, although Welshfield, because
of its good restaurant and location on U.S. 422, is a likely starting
place.

WELSHFIELD INN/WELSHFIELD — Welshfield is located at a
crossroads – U.S. 422 and State Route 700 – fortuitously enhanced
with an inn that was built for stagecoaches in the 1840s and continues
to have a good restaurant. The ambiance is early American, including
authentic touches such as sloping floors; the menu is American, well
and imaginatively prepared. The inn's modern future was secured in
1972, when Norman Simpson stopped by and recommended it in his
Country Inns and Back Roads guide book. Manager Susan Steffee says
that eventually (after a new kitchen is added, for instance) the inn will
once again have overnight accommodations.
14001 Main Market Road (U.S. 422); 216/834-4164, 800/882-1144.
Tu-Sat 11:30-2:30, Tu-Th 4:30-9, Fri-Sat 4:30-10, Sun noon-8.
Moderate. AE, MC, V.

GEAUGA FARMS COUNTRY MEATS/NEAR WELSHFIELD — Just
down and across the road from the Welshfield Inn is this small store,
which specializes in homemade sausages and has its own smokehouse
– the aroma will likely fill you with delight. If you're a long way from
your own refrigerator, at least try the home-made beef jerky, which is
meant to last but is so tasty that it doesn't last long.
14320 Main Market Road (U.S. 422); 216/834-8476.

NORA MILLER BAKERY/NEAR WELSHFIELD — The Jug Road
intersection with U.S. Route 422 is just east of Geauga Farms Country
Meats; on the right you'll see a black-and-white sign for Nora Miller's
home bakery, which is only a few doors down. Follow her driveway
around to the back of the house, where the bakery is located. Nora
Miller is an Amish woman who makes very good bread, pies, and rolls,
but she is open for business only on Friday and Saturday because she is
too busy to bake every day. On baking days, she gets up at 4 a.m. and
starts working; by 10 a.m., she has made about 40 pies and 30 loaves
of bread, with the last fifteen still baking in the kerosene-fired oven
located in the shop. She also has a refrigerator, but it has been
converted into a non-electric ice box. Even though Jug Road is an out-
of-the-way destination, Nora's bread is so good that she often sells out.
18071 Jug Road. Fri-Sat 10-6.

SILVER CREEK FARM/NEAR WELSHFIELD — Silver Creek Farm is a
certified organic farm that produces and sells berries, vegetables,
chicken, lamb, pottery, wool, and so on. Owners Molly and Ted
Bartlett are both from Cleveland, where as children they could hardly

have imagined that one day they would have 1,000 chickens and twelve acres in vegetables. Visitors are encouraged to walk around the farm, and a map is available. To find Silver Creek farm, take Jug Road south from Nora Miller's bakery to Allyn Road, just above the township line, and turn left (east).
7097 Allyn Road; 216/562-4381. Open Mother's Day to New Year's. Sat 10-4; other times too, but call first.

ACCESS — From Welshfield, this guide follows the tour circuit clockwise, which means that you should head north on State Route 700 toward Burton.

BURTON LOG CABIN/BURTON — The center of the town of Burton is the Square, a long, well-treed park with a very large water tower at one end and a Log Cabin at the other. The Log Cabin wasn't built by early settlers, but dates back to 1931, which is a long time for an institution run by a Chamber of Commerce. Indeed, for a town of only 1,300 people, Burton has a particularly lively Chamber of Commerce. Every March, it sponsors the making of maple syrup in the Log Cabin; then the rest of the year, visitors can watch maple sugar candy being made (pieces sell for a quarter). The biggest of the town's many events is the Great Geauga Antique Market at the fairgrounds. It's held on a Saturday in mid-September after the Geauga County Fair – the oldest county fair in the state – has packed up.
14590 East Park Street; 216/834-4204. Open Feb 15-Apr 15, Tu-Sun 10-5; Apr 16-Dec 23, Tu-Sun noon-5.

CENTURY VILLAGE/BURTON — Just as few chambers of commerce make candy, so do few county historical societies run restored villages. Century Village and the Geauga County Historical Society both began July 5, 1941, when the society was formed to accept a gift of the 1838 Hickox House and adjacent land at the southeast corner of Burton Square. Hickox House was never moved, and since 1941, nineteen other buildings – all gifts – have been brought in and set down near it. Dating from 1798 (a log cabin) to 1900 (a general store), and located originally in Burton and other parts of Geauga County, they've all been restored and furnished. The best known single exhibit is 9,000 lead soldiers, the gift of Lyle Thurburn, a Gates Mills man who has more at home. The 9,000 soldiers on display represent all the wars though World War II – that's ancient Egyptians through GIs.
14653 East Park Street; 216/834-1492. Open May 1-Oct 31. Two-hour guided tours Tu-Sat at 10, 1, and 3; Sun at 1 and 3. Admission fee; group rates available.

COUNTRY COURIER CARRIAGE SERVICE/BURTON — Barbara and Mark Titus run a horse-drawn carriage service that offers tours of Burton. No mere buggy, their carriage is modeled on the Queen of England's own conveyance and is pulled, usually, by a horse named Big Bill. Barbara drives; Mark is footman and narrator. The carriage seats parties of one to six people, and weather permitting, waits for customers in front of Burton's Log Cabin on weekend afternoons. Rates are $10 for a 10-minute tour; $20 for 25 minutes.
On Burton Square; 216/834-8770. Sat-Sun noon-5.

ACCESS — Go east to Middlefield on State Route 87; at the stoplight turn left (north) onto State Route 608 and go to Nauvoo Road. Take Nauvoo Road east for a mile and a half to State Route 528; turn left and drive north to Huntsburg and U.S. 322. Turn right on U.S. 322 and go east into Ashtabula County's Windsor Township. Along this route, most of the houses between Middlefield and Huntsburg are owned by the Amish.

MIDDLEFIELD — Not only is Middlefield the biggest place in this area, but it also feels the most Amish. The shopping center has a black-smith, and carriages flock into town for shopping, especially on Fridays. **Spectors,** just east of the traffic light on State Route 87, and **Kleinfelds,** just to the west, are among the stores that cater to Amish clientele with, respectively, dry goods and clothing. Middlefield has a number of factories making plastic, rubber, and wood products. Many of the blue collar workers are Amish, and when shifts change, you'll see Amish workers walking along the roads, carrying their lunch boxes.

ASIDE If you're interested in the products of Amish craftsmen, the back roads around Middlefield harbor many, not all of whom are easy to find. Peter Gail, a former Cleveland State professor, has been traipsing around this Amish country for years. His guide to Amish home shops — *Amish Craftsmen, Merchants, and Service Providers of Northeastern Ohio* — should be available at TrueBrooke Inn or Walker Johnson Inn. It will tell you how to navigate the back roads to find craftsmen who make and sell hickory rockers, quilts, rag rugs, cabinets, shoes, and so on. However, don't expect any Amish merchant to take a credit card or do business on Sunday.

MIDDLEFIELD CHEESE HOUSE/MIDDLEFIELD — A town landmark, Middlefield Cheese was founded by Amish and Yankee farmers who wanted a market for their milk. As you'll learn in the factory's museum, the venture was shaped mostly by a man who earned a diploma in cheese making in Switzerland. Factory tours were dropped years ago, but visitors can see a 20-minute movie about cheese making. The adjacent store sells a variety of specialty foods, but the best thing to buy is the cheese maker's pride: the sharp Swiss aged for up to eighteen months.
State Route 608 just below Nauvoo Road; 216/632-5228. Mon-Sat. Store 7-5:30; museum 9-5; movie every half hour 11-3. Museum and movie, free.

MARY YODER'S AMISH KITCHEN/MIDDLEFIELD — Amish cooking is like American food, before it was diversified with sushi and salsa. It's hearty, plain, and pre-cholesterol-awareness. Mary Yoder's is a good place to try it. If you order family style, your table will be inundated with fried chicken, roast beef, ham, mashed potatoes, and the like. In the unlikely event that you have room for dessert, the Amish date pudding is especially good. The restaurant also has a gift shop and a good bakery.

14743 North State Street (State Route 608); 216/632-1939. Mon-Sat 11-8; breakfast Fri, Sat, Mon 7-11. Lunch, inexpensive. Dinner, moderate.

AUCTIONS — There are two livestock auctions in the Mesopotamia area. The Geauga Livestock Commission auctions, held Mondays starting at 10, are near Middlefield on Nauvoo Road east of State Route 608. Bloomfield Livestock Auctions, on the south side of State Route 87 just west of State Route 45, are held Thursdays starting at 1. Both sales have flea markets, coffee shops, lots of farm animals, and Amish buyers and sellers.

SIR HENRY/WINDSOR MILLS — Even though Windsor Township was settled in 1799, the population is today only about 1600. An antique store and a restaurant have closed; the creamery's gone; and the basket factory burned down. But it does have a few exceptional sights for travelers. Take, for instance, Sir Henry, which you shouldn't miss as you approach from the west on U.S. 322. Sir Henry is a horse statue located in a front yard on the south side of the road 1.8 miles east of the county line. Carved in 1871 by Mesopotamia sculptor Howard Brigden, Sir Henry was a champion trick horse with the Hamilton Circus, which was based in the area at the time. The dog depicted in the statue was Sir Henry's constant companion.

CHRIST CHURCH EPISCOPAL/WINDSOR MILLS — A quarter mile east of Sir Henry, you'll find Christ Church Episcopal on the north side of U.S. 322 at Wiswell Road; it has a distinctive crown steeple, topped with five pointed spikes. Built in 1832, Christ Church is one of the oldest Episcopal churches in Ohio, though it hasn't had an active parish since the 1950s. It's now under the aegis of the Windsor Historical Society, which runs a museum in a room at the back. The interior, in browns and whites, is simple in design. The pulpit is centered and is so high that, at the occasional service held in the church, no one ever has the nerve to stand there, opting instead for the stairs at the side.
U.S. 322 at Wiswell Road; 216/272-5401 or 216/272-5174. Open Memorial Day-Oct. Sun 1-4. Tours at other times by appointment.

WINDSOR MILLS (A.K.A. WARNER HOLLOW) COVERED BRIDGE — Across the highway from Christ Church, Township Road 257 (Warner Hollow Road) leads the very short distance (less than a quarter mile) south to the Windsor Mills Covered Bridge, which must be one of the prettiest in Ohio. Though it's no longer open to road traffic, the bridge is still in its original setting and is open to pedestrians and bicycles. It has a town lattice type of truss and was built in 1867.

SCENIC DRIVE — Follow the road that leads to the bridge, Township Road 257 or Warner Hollow Road, east along the creek. For about a mile and a half, the view of the woods and ravine is spectacular. Turn left at the fork, onto Township Road 532 or Chub Road, and before you return to U.S. 322, you'll pass the house of boxing promoter Don King, on your left at 8083 Chub. As you pass, watch for the life-size, full-color statues of an elephant and a giraffe under the flag pole.

ASIDE A Windsor farmer who died not long ago was a faithful patron of Taylor's Pub at the northwest corner of U.S. 322 and State Route 534. He had his license taken away for driving home while under the influence. Then in his late 70s, the customer was not to be denied. He drove his tractor to the pub instead.

OLD ROMAN BRIDGE/WINDSOR — Rather than beautiful, the Old Roman Bridge is unusual and thus worth the short detour out of town. A concrete bridge named for its high, round arch, it is just one lane wide, and so high that you can't see if there is another car on the other side. Marge Townsend says many an argument at Taylor's Pub has debated whether two cars can pass on the Roman Bridge. They can't, but since the bridge crosses the Grand River at an angle, you can watch for traffic approaching on the other side. Around here, the once-navigable Grand River now seems more swamp than river, partly because of silty runoff.

From the intersection of U.S. 322 and State Route 534, head north. Though State Route 534 almost immediately forks to the left, keep going straight north on Noble Road. After about a mile, turn east on New Hudson Road; the Roman Bridge is within two miles.

OCTAGON HOUSE/WINDSOR — Just over a mile south of Windsor on State Route 534, you'll pass a large white Octagon House that is two stories high and surmounted by an octagonal cupola. When it was built in 1847, each floor had four square and four triangular rooms.

ACCESS — Go south on State Route 534, which is predominantly Amish from Windsor to State Route 88.

MESOPOTAMIA COMMONS — Mesopotamia, village and township, has an uncommon name, meaning "between two rivers" in Greek — the two rivers here being the Grand to the east and the Cuyahoga to the west. Ancient Mesopotamia, now part of Iraq, has been dubbed the Cradle of Civilization, which may not apply to this place, though once established, it did keep itself intact, which is more than we can say for most places. Mesopotamia (which everyone calls Mespo, a four-syllable saving) has an extraordinary Commons that is a quarter mile long and five-eighths of a mile around. It's surrounded by 28 buildings; 21 of them date from before the Civil War, and all but two are from the nineteenth century. Not surprisingly, the whole town center is on the National Register of Historic Places. Most of the houses are modest. The oldest, built in 1816, is a small white structure three doors north of the store on the southwest side. Originally the Commons gave villagers a grazing area for livestock, while yards were enclosed with picket fences to keep in the children. In the middle of the east side of the Commons are three church buildings. The Methodists still use their 1830 church; Congregationalists built and abandoned the one whose paint has weathered off; and the third, constructed in 1874 as a Spiritualist Church, is now the Mesopotamia Historical Society meeting place and museum.

END OF THE COMMONS GENERAL STORE/MESOPOTAMIA — Ken Schaden and his family – he and his wife Margaret have eleven children – moved from a Cleveland suburb to Mespo in 1975. A few years later, Schaden quit his Cleveland job and bought the End of the Commons General Store – he was already well acquainted with the place from stopping in with the kids to buy penny candy. Schaden likes to tell bus tours about his new life; then everyone from the bus comes into the store, which sells pottery and gifts in a section for tourists. The store also carries groceries such as cereal, grape jelly, and bulk foods for Amish customers. There's a hitching rail outside for buggies. Schaden gazes at the buggies parked there and sighs with contentment. "I love that sight," he says.
8719 Mesopotamia Historical District; 216/693-4295. Mon-Fri 8:30 a.m.-8:30 p.m., Sat 8:30-6.

ELI MILLER'S LEATHER SHOP & COUNTRY STORE/ MESOPOTAMIA — Just a few doors west of Mesopotamia Commons on State Route 87, Eli Miller has opened a leather shop and store for tourists. Where Yankees are concerned, Miller is an unusually accessible Amish man who organized Mespo's annual shindig – the Fourth of July ox roast and flea market, which lasts three or four days every year. By profession, he's a leather craftsman. If possible, you should watch him at work as he cuts leather and sews it with awls and needles.
4390 Kinsman Road (State Route 87); 216/693-4448. Mon-Sat 9-5.

FAIRVIEW CEMETERY/MESOPOTAMIA — Accessible from the east side of the Commons, the cemetery is known for sculptures by Howard Brigden. Look for the dog watching the dead boy's hat, just as the animal did in life. Brigden died in 1913. His own monument, presumably sculpted ahead of time, is surmounted by a smiling bear.

SHOPPING IN MESOPOTAMIA — Mesopotamia's small post-office building holds a minuscule T-shirt shop where you can buy sweatshirts decorated with a horse and buggy. Two Amish stores west of town on State Route 87 are relatively easy to find and worth looking for. **Bricker's Home Bakery** has very good cookies. *5162 Kinsman Road; Mon-Sat 8-5.* **Yoder's Country Store and Quilt Shop** has pans, quilts (you have to inspect them near a window because the store doesn't have electric lights), and toys. Look especially for the Amish dolls – their faces are blank, to keep them from becoming graven images. A soft fabric doll with black cap and coat costs $28.
19860 State Route 87; Mon-Th 8-5, Fri 8-9, Sat 8-5.

ACCESS — From State Route 534, go east on State Route 88 to Bristolville. (If you think things are quiet along this stretch of road, you're right. The state has bought up properties for the Grand River Wildlife Area.)

BRISTOLVILLE VILLAGE — Settled in 1805, Bristolville has an attractive New England-style square, in the middle of which is the nation's first **Civil War monument**. The marble post with a draped urn was erected in 1863, after the township lost more than a dozen men early in the war. Three large white buildings flank the square on

BACK ROADS AMISH TOUR
— Most of the Amish in this area are Old Order Amish. They prefer an agricultural way of life, don't use electricity, travel by horse and buggy, and work their fields with draft horses. Being photographed is against their beliefs. They shun ostentation, so their clothes are in somber colors, blacks and blues rather than red or plaids.

Among themselves they speak in a German dialect, for they are all descended from Swiss Anabaptists, from whose numbers came the Mennonites. In 1697, a Mennonite group led by Joseph Amman protested that church discipline was too lax and broke away; they became the Amish. Today, Mennonite and Amish sects represent all degrees of strictness, and Mennonites are often hard to distinguish from other conservative Protestant churches.

Mesopotamia Township has a total population of 2,500 and is nearly two-thirds Amish. The proportion is growing because the Amish believe in large families — seven to twelve children are the norm. Their high population growth also means that they may become crowded, or that they can't all practice farming, or that some of them have to move. Much of this information about the Amish comes from Linda Angstrom, a Yankee who lives in Mesopotamia Township and gives a wonderful back roads Amish tour. If you have a large or small bus, you can hire her to take your group around (**Mesopotamia Tours**, 216/693-4459), but if you are a very small group in a car, you can at least follow the same route that her tours take.

Start your tour of the Amish back roads by turning south from State Route 87 onto Bundysburg Road, on the Geauga-Trumbull County line. On the right, you'll come to an example of the only type of public building the Amish have: **Pine View School**. It's a white cement-block structure with two rooms and 40 to 60 students in grades one through eight. So that no child has to walk more than two miles to school, a school is built every four miles.

After traveling just over two miles, turn back with a sharp left to head northeast on Parkman Mesopotamia Road. Because Amish church services, weddings and funerals are all held in homes, there are no more than 25 families in a church district.

You can spot an Amish house, Angstrom says, by the curtains: there will be only one curtain per window, and it will be draped to the side. Look for the wires leading to phone booths in some yards. The wires aren't permitted inside the houses, but outside they're acceptable. Every half mile or so there's another phone booth, which everyone in that neighborhood can use. Amish business cards typically say "Let Ring" because someone has to run outside of the house to answer the phone.

At State Route 87, turn east and take the first right turn south on Girdle Road. Take the first left turn onto Gates East Road, which in a mile intersects State Route 534 just south of Mespo. Another school, **Gates Hills**, is on the right. According to Angstrom, although the Amish have 30 last names altogether, around here they have only fifteen. To avoid confusion, many children are given four names. Once, 50 of 57 children in a Geauga County School were named Miller.

the east. The one in the middle is the 1882 **Town Hall**, which is still used for meetings. To the south is a Methodist church whose congregation dates to the 1840s. To the north is the oldest of the three buildings, the **1846 Congregational Church**, which hasn't been used as a church since the turn of the century. Across the street to the south is an antique shop. The pioneer cemetery is immediately east, between the fire station and the post office. The **1912 Carnegie Library**, one of three built in Trumbull County, is on the other side of State Route 88. It has a community museum upstairs and is open daily except Sunday and Tuesday. All the square's surroundings are generally harmonious with it, except for the dozens of concrete boxes – about five-feet square – on the lot just to the north. Since some time in the 1970s, they've been there as a monument to a feud. The lot's owner, who is in the construction supply business, wanted to put up a nonconforming building, but the township denied his variance. Ever since, his company has been storing septic tanks there.

OLD HOUSE TOUR/BRISTOLVILLE — Wendell Lauth, president of the Bristol Historical Society, suggests an old-house tour around Bristolville, and provides interesting facts about the houses. The first two houses in this tour are on the west side of State Route 45 south of the square. The **Kagy House** was the boyhood home of abolitionist John Henri Kagi, who changed the spelling of his family name and was killed at Harpers Ferry. It is the white house with green shutters at number 6121. Two doors south is the **Corey House**, an Italianate home from the 1880s, light brown with dark trim and beautifully maintained. The Corey House has been perfectly preserved; according to local rumor, it has never been electrified and has no indoor plumbing. Then, turn around and head north of the square on State Route 45. Bristolville's oldest house, number 6292 State Route 45, is the green one with dark green trim. A sign makes it easy to spot the 1859 **Hubbard's House** at 6416 State Route 45. Notice the cottage in the side yard. For many decades, it was occupied by a bachelor. When the present owner went to repair the cottage basement, she stumbled on the bachelor's home savings bank: a cistern filled with jars of coins. Next, go north on State Route 45, and in the town of North Bristol, turn left on Oakfield Road. It's a beautiful road, lined with large trees, attractive older houses, and a white church built in 1868. On the right, just past a ravine is the 1828 **Norton House**, which was occupied by the same family for almost 200 years. Further north on State Route 45, just below Bloomfield and State Route 87, you'll come to **Brownwood**, a white house with dark green shutters on the east side of the road. It was built in 1819 by Ephraim Brown, a major early landowner in this township. In 1846, he also built the Gothic Cottage across the road as a home for his daughter.

MOSQUITO CREEK LAKE — Just seven miles to the east of Bristolville on State Route 88, Mosquito Creek Lake makes a wonderful detour. State Route 88 crosses the lake on a mile-long causeway, with an extra, quarter-mile-long lane on each side where fishermen can park. On a cool day, joggers on the causeway almost seem to be running on the water, which is a dazzling silver in the sun. At the south end of the lake, accessible from State Route 88 on Hoagland-Blackstub Road or via State Route 305, there are picnic grounds with a

fine view and a swimming beach.
The park office is located at 1439 State Route 305; 216/637-2856.

SOUTHINGTON (PRONOUNCED "SUTHINGTON") — When boxer
Mike Tyson gets out of jail, he'll return home to a house that you'll
pass on State Route 534, three quarters of a mile north of Southington.
You'll know it because his name is on the roadside gate. The most
notable landmark in Southington is the 1906 **Chalker High School**,
on State Route 305 just west of State Route 534. It is a grand two-story
building in buff brick with brown quoins. The front has a portico with
four fluted white columns, and two sculpted lions, at rest, flank the
entryway. The money for the building and the land was donated by
Newton Chalker, a native son who did very well as an Akron lawyer
and banker. The building now houses district offices for the school
superintendent, treasurer and others; but it also has three high school
classrooms, the computer lab, chemistry, and math. The rest of the
school system – 680 children in grades K-12 – is in a newer building
just to the east.

ACCESS — From Southington, head west about four miles on State
Route 305 to State Route 282; turn right (north) and go to Nelson-
Kennedy Ledges State Park, which has a parking lot on the east side of
the highway and hiking trails on the west side of the highway. Later,
you can take State Route 282 (which is only three miles long) north to
U.S. 422, which will – if you wish – reconnect you with the rest of the
world.

NELSON-KENNEDY LEDGES STATE PARK — The ledges are rock
outcrops. They're about the size of large houses and look as though
they were dropped randomly, some landing askew and tilted against
one another. Trails, ranging from difficult to easy, run through and
above them for 2.5 miles. The easy White Trail is in a flat, partly
wooded area. The more challenging Yellow and Red Trails wind
between (as at Fat Man's Peril) and under the rocks, through a tunnel,
and into a cave. You will need to watch the children, because some
sections could be treacherous. Otherwise, it's a wonderful walk. The
conglomerate rocks are uncommon examples of exposed bedrock
formed hundreds of millions of years ago, back when northern Ohio
was a sea. It's long ago enough for perspective on 1819 houses, on
European settlers in North America, and, for that matter, on North
America.
*State Route 282 north of State Route 305; 216/564-2279. Open year
round, with park staff on duty daily from mid May to mid Sept.*

THE PRESERVATION OF
MESPO — The founders called it Troy, but since there were already two Troys in Ohio, they were compelled to search for a more imaginative name. They retired to the Town House, where they thumbed through their Bibles until an inspired choice presented itself: Mesopotamia, the land between two rivers. The name suited, for the town lay between the Grand River to the east and the Cuyahoga to the west. Indeed, the location, between the rivers, would determine the town's future, or lack of it, as a succession of promoters advanced various schemes for damming the waters and putting Mesopotamia *under* the rivers.

The most persistent of these was Michael Kirwan, a New Deal Democrat with a third-grade education and a PhD in the art of pork barrel, a talent he exercised shamelessly as chairman of the spendthrift House Public Works subcommittee. Kirwan served from 1936 to 1970, when he died in office at age 83. Through all those years he sought to build a canal to connect Lake Erie with the Ohio River, to serve as a cheap water route for Youngstown steel-makers. Mike's Big Ditch, as it came to be known, called for damming the Grand River in Ashtabula County to create a 35-mile-long reservoir with Mesopotamia roughly at midpoint, under 50 feet of water.

Talk of Mike's Big Ditch put a damper on development for a third of a century. Under threat of water, Mesopotamia languished. Some of the stores on the Commons closed as the old shopkeepers died. The antebellum homes weathered with the seasons, many standing empty as the old families expired. The last of the industries, a cheese factory, closed. And the railroad elected to take its business elsewhere. The people, having grown accustomed to the quiet, decided it was a blessing.

"We have no high school, no manufactures, no commerce to draw a noisy rabble," one satisfied writer noted. "We don't *want* a rattling railroad belching through our quiet town."

So Mesopotamia drifted into a long sleep, in the shade of its sugar maples. And when it awoke, in the 1970s, and rubbed the sleep out of its eyes, it discovered it had accomplished a remarkable thing: it had *preserved* itself. For its old houses still stood, only slightly out of plumb beneath the peeling paint. The churches remained, although two had lost their steeples, and Mr. Cunningham was storing farm equipment in the sanctuary where the Congregationalists had once argued over where the pump organ should be placed. The National Register of Historic Places acclaimed Mesopotamia's preservation a remarkable achievement, although in fairness it should be allowed that it had less to do with the preservation movement than the do-nothing movement. — *Sue Gorisek*

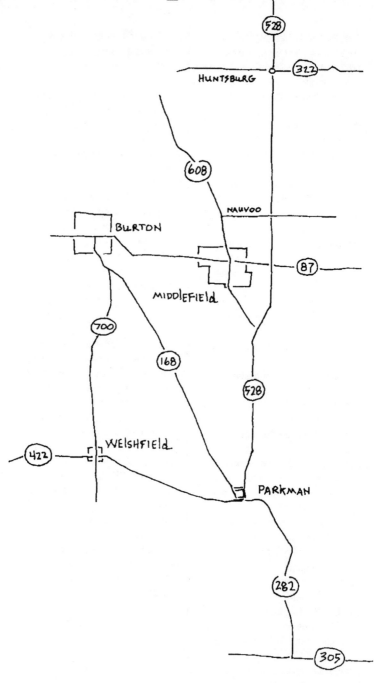

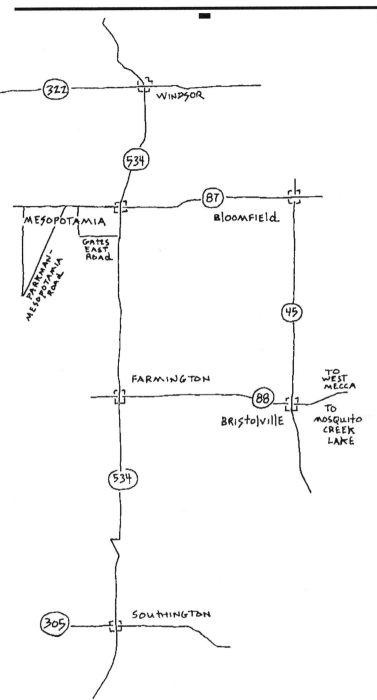

The Wooster Inn

Wooster and the Wayne County Amish

In summer, the rolling hills around Wooster are lush with crops and fat cattle. In early winter, when the stiff corn left in the fields has turned champagne-colored and the first halting wisps of smoke emerge from farmhouse chimneys, early snows dust the hilltops and make them seem sugar-coated. This is picturesque Wayne County, where the gentle valleys of the Killbuck, the Apple, the Sugar, and other colorfully-named creeks define the lovely landscape that in the early 1800s enticed a group of federal surveyors to purchase property and start a town themselves. The founding fathers named it in honor of the Revolutionary War hero, General David Wooster, and they supposedly selected the highlands where Killbuck and Apple creeks converge as their town's site because of the ready water supply and strategic location near main Indian trails. They chose well, for Wooster today is not only the Wayne County seat, but is also located near the main modern trail – Interstate 71 – that links Cleveland and Columbus. ¶ Wooster has many charming homes in fine, old neighborhoods and a busy downtown, where a raft of Victorian storefronts is anchored by an elaborate, Second Empire courthouse where ambitious sculptures of imposing ancient gods guard the halls of justice. Someone once said Wooster is so pretty it looks as if it belongs under a Christmas tree. That is a fair observation, aesthetically as well as historically, for Wooster happens to be the home of what almost certainly was Ohio's earliest Christmas tree. In 1847, the young German immigrant August Imgard introduced the town to his homeland's much-loved Christmas custom when he cut down a spruce and adorned it with popcorn, candles, and a tin star. His effort was such a success that for many years Wooster fancied itself the location of the nation's first Christmas tree, but when that distinction proved false, the town did not forget Herr Imgard. He is buried in the Wooster Cemetery, and every Christmas an evergreen near his tomb is adorned with decorations and colored lights. ¶ Trees in general are an important tradition in Wooster, where they are generally treated with veneration – if not adoration – by the citizens. Their esteemed status probably started in the early 1800s, when the legendary John "Johnny Appleseed" Chapman had one of his frontier nurseries in the area, but it is now propagated by the presence in Wooster of the widely respected Ohio Agricultural Research and Development Center and its magnificent arboretum. Wooster is routinely designated a Tree City by the National Arbor Foundation, and every year, local civic groups present a dogwood to every first grader as well as a sweetbay magnolia to every fifth grade student in town. A fast food restaurant once touched off a furor when the management cut down a 300-year old oak. That prompted Wooster's fierce defenders of the flora to lobby for the county tree registry and city laws that now protect historic trees.

¶ Wooster also has a strong agricultural tradition by virtue of its being both at the center of Ohio's dairyland and on the northern fringe of the world's largest Amish population, which is concentrated directly to the south in Holmes County.* Wayne County ranks first in the state in production of dairy products; second in calves and cattle; and third in total cash receipts from agriculture. Until 1990, in fact, Wayne County actually had more cows than it did people. The stalwart Amish, who are much admired for their farming skills, have contributed significantly to the agricultural success of Wayne County. They are a familiar sight in and around Wooster, and their peculiar presence – not to mention the absence of telephone poles and electric wires near their farms – has certainly helped spur the growing tourism that now complements the stable economy Wooster has typically enjoyed.

¶ As if it were not enough for one community to be both the county seat and twice-blessed as a college town – by the College of Wooster and the Ohio Agricultural Research and Development Center, which is affiliated with Ohio State – Wooster is also the home of one of the nation's

most highly regarded corporations, Rubbermaid
Incorporated. Given that the J. M. Smucker
Company is located in nearby Orrville, Wayne
County is in the highly unusual — and enviable —
position of having two corporate world headquarters in an area with only slightly more than
100,000 people. The colleges and corporations
have yielded an exceptionally high number of
PhDs and white collar workers among Wooster's
22,000 inhabitants. The combination of small
town values and a sizable proportion of profes-
sionals who expect certain social and cultural
amenities have made Wooster a community with
a somewhat oxymoronic character, described by
one resident as "conservative progressive."
Woosterians are conservative enough that George
Bush carried their town in the 1992 election, but
they're also liberal enough that a group concerned about radioactive waste succeeded in
passing a referendum that made Wooster one of
the few towns in the state that is a nuclear free
zone where transporting or producing nuclear
materials is prohibited.   ¶ Wooster is
unpretentious enough that its downtown traffic
easily accommodates hay wagons, but ambitious
enough to be the smallest municipality in Ohio
with its own transit system, which currently
consists of three big buses. Wooster is rustic
enough to host a first class county fair every
summer, yet sophisticated enough to have an arts
center, a light opera company, and the second-
oldest symphony orchestra in Ohio. Wooster also
has a homegrown department store that has been
a town fixture for decades; downtown stores that
still stay open on Friday and Saturday nights with

shoppers that still patronize them; extensive parks that boast an observatory as well as playgrounds custom-designed for Wooster's kids; and an exceptionally cordial town-gown relationship in which the community and the College of Wooster have cooperated on everything from the donation of the school's seminal land to residents taking free classes. ¶ Folks over 40 often comment that Wooster reminds them of the town where they grew up, and that perhaps is both its greatest strength and greatest attraction. Wooster is a *real* place, one of the increasingly rare towns that still survive as a self-contained, functioning community. Wooster works, and it does so splendidly, with an identity of its own quite separate from any urban or suburban sprawl. Wooster is a sterling example of the quintessential American hometown, the kind of place where everybody wishes they were from: proud, well-scrubbed, mostly mainstream, slightly cornball, somewhat collegiate, sufficiently cultured, and just contrary enough to vote Republican when the majority of the state is going Democrat.

To learn more about traveling in Holmes County, please see "Amish Country," Particular Places, Volume I.

THE WOOSTER INN — With only seventeen rooms for overnight guests, this lovely bed and breakfast inn is a cozy, quiet, and congenial hostelry with the top, literally, location in town. Perched on the crest of a hill adjacent to the college golf course, it overlooks all of Wooster, and the panoramic view from the big bowed window in the dining room is particularly pleasant in the evening, when the lights of the town come on and sparkle in the distance darkness. The inn's menu is as traditional as its elegantly understated decor, and the well-prepared, but tried and true entrees such as filet mignon and pork chops are topped off by home-baked cheesecake and warm bread pudding. Owned and operated by the College of Wooster, the inn was the gift of alumnus and trustee Robert Wilson, an oil company executive who modeled it after his own Georgian Colonial home in New York state.

The inn is open to the public, but since the rooms fill up quickly for college occasions such as Parents' Weekend and Commencement, reservations are strongly recommended. Guests at the inn also get the privilege of using many of the college's facilities — swimming pool, tennis courts, golf course, and bowling alley.

801 East Wayne Avenue; 216/264-2341. Dining room is open Mon-Sat 7 a.m.-2 p.m. and 5:30 p.m.-8, Sun 7 a.m.-11 a.m. and 11:30 a.m.-8 p.m. Moderate-expensive. AE, DC, MC, V.

Howey House

HOWEY HOUSE — The Gothic Revival home where Jo and James Howey operate their bed and breakfast was the brainchild of a local craftsman who endowed it with pretty peaked gables, foot-thick brick walls, inlaid wooden floors, and a superb curving walnut staircase. Though the house was built in 1849 and is on the National Register of Historic Places, the Howeys enjoy the good fortune of being only the third owners, having purchased it from Miss Charlotte Ames, who had not only been Mr. Howey's third grade teacher, but also had lived in the home for a remarkable 79 years. Miss Ames left behind the lovely Circassian walnut furniture in the dining room, where the Howeys treat guests to made-to-order breakfasts and a morning copy of the Cleveland *Plain Dealer*. While you're eating, do take note of the portraits hanging on the dining room walls. The subjects are Miss Ames's grandparents, whom the Howeys rescued from obscurity after finding the rolled up paintings in the barn behind the house.

340 North Bever Street; 216/264-8231. No smoking. No pets. Cash or personal check only.

T.J.'S — From the classical music playing subtlely in the background to the tasteful contemporary decor, owner Greg Tieche clearly sets big city standards for his small town restaurant. Great attention to detail is obvious everywhere at T.J.'s, but most conspicuously in the kitchen, which turns out perfectly prepared, wonderfully creative American cuisine with international accents. The house specialty is roast prime rib of beef, but T.J.'s also offers deliciously different entrees such as chicken amaretto sauteed with cranberries and walnuts or lemon fettuccine with shrimp and bay scallops. The service is prompt and attentive, and the staff seems as proud of the place as the owner, pointing out that Greg himself built the bar and put up the wallpaper. While T.J.'s is classy without being pretentious, **C.W. Burgerstein's**, a casual restaurant and bar located downstairs, is unpretentious with a touch of class. Popular with students from the College of Wooster, C.W. Burgerstein's serves gourmet sandwiches and finger foods. *359 West Liberty Street; 216/264-6263. T.J.'s is open Mon-Th 11-9:30, Fri 11-10:30, Sat, 4:30-10:30, Closed Sunday except Mother's Day and Easter. Moderate to expensive. AE, DC, Discover, MC, V. C.W. Burgerstein's is open Mon-Th 3-midnight, Fri 3 p.m.-1 a.m., Sat 11 a.m.-1 a.m. Closed Sundays. Moderate. AE, DC, Discover, MC, V.*

MATSOS — Many years ago, in a restaurant in Athens, Greece, the owner put up a precautionary sign for his customers: "Please do not step on the baby." The baby was Spiro Matsos, and the restaurateur was his grandfather. Spiro, of course, grew up in the restaurant business, learning what folks like to eat firsthand from his grandfather's customers, who were frequently pressed into service as his baby-sitter. Spiro found his way to Wooster after unexpectedly falling in love with the place – which he describes as "the perfect town that you see in the movies" – on a visit to his wife's home state of Ohio. He immediately sold the restaurant he had in Connecticut and moved to Wooster – lock, stock, and barrels of his famous white matsosauce. Trained as a professional singer as well as a cook, Spiro is an artist both on the stage and in the restaurant, which he regards as another form of theater. A tenor, he has sung with Wooster's Ohio Light Opera for eleven years, playing such parts as Ivan in *Die Fledermaus* and Toni in *The Student Prince*. When properly inspired, he also spontaneously breaks into song in the restaurant, which is appropriately decorated with posters and memorabilia from various Ohio Light Opera productions. The menu at Matsos features Greek dishes such as moussaka and dolmathes, as well as the Grinders, hot, hearty, French bread sandwiches that Spiro has named after friends and family members whom he wanted to immortalize. Spiro also created Spaghetti Pizza, a feast of hot pasta and cheeses atop a crispy crust. Our universe, Spiro points out, has been hit by meteors many times and in many places, but pizza spaghetti made an impact only once – on April 27, 1987, when he invented it in Wooster, Ohio. *154 West Liberty Street; 216/264-8800. Mon-Th 11 a.m.-11 p.m., Sun noon-11, Fri-Sat 11 a.m.-midnight. Inexpensive-Moderate. Cash or personal check.*

THE GRANARY AT THE PINE TREE BARN — This is quite possibly the only Christmas tree farm in the world where you can also enjoy lunch with gourmet wines. When Roger and Rita Dush started their

tree farm several years ago, they thought that the picturesque 1868 Dutch bank barn they had remodeled would be a place where they could sell a few Christmas ornaments and customers could warm themselves with cocoa in a small restaurant. That ornament shop has since evolved into a full-fledged home furnishings store, and the restaurant has become one of the area's all-time favorites. Open for lunch only, the Granary attracts folks from far and wide with freshly prepared foods that feature their signature quiches, crepes, muffins, and sour cream fruit pies. Though the menu is limited, the offerings are exceptional, as is the experience of lunching beneath the rafters of a barn while a guitarist or dulcimer players provide background music. While The Granary is located in what used to be the grain bin, the rest of the barn is crammed with upscale country and traditional furniture, fine gifts, and gourmet food items. With a staff that includes six interior designers, the Pine Tree Barn has everything from carpeting to Christmas decorations imported from Europe. From November to mid-December, visitors can also board horse-drawn wagons, ride out into the farm, and choose their own Christmas trees. Saws, incidentally, are available for sturdy souls who wish to fell their own trees.
4374 Shreve Road; 216/264-1014. Luncheon Tu-Sun 11:30-2. Moderate. Shops Tu-Sun 10-5. Extended hours Thanksgiving-Christmas. MC, V.

OHIO LIGHT OPERA — The Ohio Light Opera is the only professional repertory company in the United States devoted to the operetta. For nine intense weeks every summer, 32 actors and a full orchestra present 68 performances of seven different operettas in rotating repertory at the Freedlander Theatre on the College of Wooster campus. No show is ever done two times in a row, and during the first week alone, four new operettas debut. Now in its fifteenth season, the Ohio Light Opera company performs the entire Gilbert & Sullivan repertoire as well as lesser-known, but equally light-hearted works from the late nineteenth and early twentieth centuries. The Ohio Light Opera annually attracts some 25,000 patrons and has acquired an international reputation as a true festival of pure operetta, thanks largely to the efforts of James Stuart, its founder, artistic director, frequent performer, and a well-known tenor in his own right. The operetta is the forerunner of American musical comedy, and Dr. Stuart's fidelity to the genre has guided the Ohio Light Opera through an astonishing 170 productions of 47 different operettas by 22 composers. The Ohio Light Opera, by the way, is a resident company, and thus its entire crew – some 100 people including musicians, vocalists, technicians, costumes and set designers, and even the box office staff – moves into student housing at the College of Wooster every summer.
The Ohio Light Opera box office opens for the season in mid-January; 216/263/2345. Discover, MC, V.

THE COLLEGE OF WOOSTER — Nationally known for its Independent Study program, this small (enrollment is about 1800), private liberal arts college has graduated such a prodigious number of experts, executives, Ph.D.s, and all-around high achievers, that many regard it as a midwest version of the Ivy League. The College's roots are nineteenth century Presbyterian and its endowment is very healthy, two circumstances that have resulted in a spacious, gracious 320-acre campus where impressive Collegiate Gothic buildings stand shoulder to shoulder with masses of trees high on a hill above the town of Wooster. Trees have been a hallmark of the College ever since 1870, when it first opened its doors – to women, as well as men, by the way – on a 22-acre grove of oaks donated by Wooster banker Ephraim Quinby. The health and well-being of the 1,500 ashes, oaks, maples, sycamore, and elms currently on campus were recently assured by another donor, albeit anonymous, who started a most unusual endowment at the College – a fund for the conservation, maintenance, and replacement of its trees. The fund currently totals more than $300,000, which equates to a bank account of $204 for each tree on campus. Abundant landscaping everywhere lightens the loftiness of the battlement-laden architecture, and the effect is an exceedingly attractive campus that, fittingly, encourages contemplation as well as perambulation along the network of brick pathways linking the mostly buff and cream-colored buildings. Many maintain that the College's most picturesque spot is the seventh hole of the Boles Memorial Golf course, but visitors should not neglect the Notestein Room in the Andrews Library, which contains many rare and beautiful seventeenth century books from the personal collection of Wallace Notestein, a Wooster alumnus who became an eminent scholar of English history at Yale. Quinby Quadrangle, the square bounded by Wayne, Beall, University, and Bever streets was the original site of the College and is the location of two campus landmarks – Kauke Hall and The Rock. Built in 1902 as a gift from the people of Wooster and Wayne County, castle-like Kauke is the home of the Delmar Archway, a pleasing passage through the heart of the hall that is lined with various plaques providing a veritable history of the College and its generously loyal alumni. The enormous granite Rock, truly a sizable donation from the Class of 1874, is located just southeast of McGaw Chapel. The Rock has long been a gathering spot for students, and in those innocent days when freshman had to wear beanies, anyone caught hatless was required to climb The Rock and sing a song, presumably the *alma mater*.

Campus tours are available by appointment only through the Office of Admissions; 216/263-2270. Sept-May, Mon-Fri 9-4, Sat 9-noon; June-Aug, Sat 10 a.m.

ASIDE A key discovery in the development of modern physics was made in the 1920s by Arthur Holly Compton, a 1913 graduate of the College of Wooster. His observation of wavelength changes in diffused X-rays — the Compton Effect — was fundamental to the development of the quantum theory of energy and resulted in his being awarded the Nobel Prize for physics in 1927. Born in Wooster on September 10, 1892, Compton throughout his life held sincere humanitarian principles that were undoubtedly rooted in his upbringing as the son of the first dean of the College of Wooster, whose motto is "Science and Religion from One Source." In addition to numerous technical studies, he also published several books that espoused his convictions, including *The Human Meaning of Science* and *Atomic Quest*, an account of the Manhattan Project.

OHIO AGRICULTURAL RESEARCH AND DEVELOPMENT CENTER (OARDC) — The esteemed scientists at OARDC, which conducts agriculture research for The Ohio State University, have pioneered agricultural advances from crop dusting to adding vitamin D to milk. But among the schoolchildren of Ohio, the facility is known as the home of the dairy barn animal whose fame has reached legendary proportions: The Cow With the Window in Its Stomach. Actually, the cow in question does not possess a window per se, but a surgically implanted fissure via which researchers can literally reach the animal to study bovine nutrition and digestion.

While in the dairy barn, youngsters also get to watch the resident Jerseys and Holsteins being milked, an age-old process to which the OARDC scientists have given a computer-age twist: each cow wears a sensor on her collar that automatically records the milk she is giving, much the way a service station pump automatically tracks the amount of gasoline being dispensed.

The dairy barn, however, is merely the tip of the considerable OARDC iceberg. With a 2,000-acre campus in Wooster and another 5,000 acres of fields, facilities, and laboratories located at branches throughout Ohio, OARDC is not only one of the foremost agricultural experiment stations in the nation, but also a world famous center of science. For more than a hundred years, the "wizards of Wooster" have conducted basic and applied research on everything from insects to greenhouse insulation.

OARDC's scientists give new meaning to the old joke about the farmer: they are outstanding in their field, for the staff includes numerous experts with international reputations in areas ranging from honey bees to composting. While the laboratories, livestock, greenhouses, and general working farm facilities are an attraction anytime, the prettiest time to visit OARDC is perhaps in May, when the nearly 200 kinds of crabapple trees at its **Secrest Arboretum** bloom in spectacular shades of pink and red. With thousands of species and varieties of plants, the 85-acre arboretum is both a living horticultural laboratory and a place of great beauty.

Major areas within the arboretum include the Rhododendron Display Garden, where 282 different cultivars of rhododendrons and azaleas flower from mid-April to mid-July; the Roses of Legend and Romance Garden, a 2.7 acre plot with 500 fabled varieties of roses, some of which date back to the twelfth century; and the Chadwick Living Herbarium of Taxus, which has the distinction of being the world's largest collection of yews. None of the yews, by the way, has ever been trimmed, meaning that the specimens give browsers and botanists alike an accurate picture of the various species in a truly natural state.

1680 Madison Avenue; 216/ 263-3700. Guided tours of OARDC facilities by appointment. Secrest Arboretum is open daily dawn-dusk. Self-guided tour maps are available at the Visitors Center in the Research Services Building and in the box near the RHODODENDRON AND AZALEA GARDEN sign.

ASIDE In 1921, J. S. Houser, an entomologist at what is now the Ohio Agricultural Research and Development Center, recruited an aviator from Dayton's McCook Field to conduct the world's first crop dusting experiment. When Lt. J. A. Macready dropped lead arsenate from a modified Curtiss biplane onto a catalpa grove near Troy, sphinx moth caterpillars died by the millions. The *National Geographic* reported the successful "airplane dusting," and farmers had a new weapon for waging war on insects: aerial application of pesticides.

WAYNE COUNTY HISTORICAL SOCIETY MUSEUM — This museum consists of four buildings that were either constructed or moved onto the grounds of property that once belonged to Reasin Beall, a former General in the Continental Army who became locally important as a land commissioner, Congressman, and a founder of the Presbyterian Church in Wooster. The **Reasin Beall Homestead**, which was the grandest house in town when it was completed in 1817, now has the distinction of being the oldest. Once used as a girls' dormitory by the College of Wooster, it houses the historical society's fine collection of local historical, geographical, and genealogical materials, as well as some two dozen life-sized portraits of Wooster's founding fathers painted by the noted local artist, Michael S. Nachtrieb. General Beall's hand is still very much in evidence throughout the homestead. The original wood floors complete with handmade nails that he installed are still there, as are many family furnishings. It is said that the cypress trees along the west driveway were personally planted by the General as a pretty framework for the house whenever a carriage approached. The **Pioneer Log House** was built about the same time as the Beall Homestead, and this one room cabin is now filled with the accouterments of everyday living – kitchen pots, spinning wheels, and rudimentary tools – that vividly illustrate how common folks lived in early Ohio. Children especially like the rope bed. Every night, the roping that supports the straw mattress had to be pulled tight so that it would not sag during the night, whence came the bedtime expression still used by parents: "Good night, sleep tight." The **Kister Building** features a fine collection of horse-drawn carriages that range from sleighs to a sleek 1900 Landau to the celebrated surrey with fringe on top. It also houses various collections of tools, arrowheads and Indian artifacts, vintage farm equipment, and an entire blacksmith shop. In the basement, a taxidermy display of small mammals and birds features a remarkable squirrel orchestra. Each of the 15 mounted squirrels is positioned behind a music stand and "plays" a different instrument. Each squirrel, that is, except one – the conductor. The **Little Red Schoolhouse** was built in 1873 and served the students of Wooster Township until 1939. A classic one-room schoolhouse constructed of handmade bricks, it invokes plenty of nostalgia with its complete set of McGuffey Readers, pot-bellied stove, collections of old pencil cases and chalk boxes, and photographic displays of Wooster schoolchildren from days gone by. Visitors who pull on the thick rope hanging just inside the door can still ring the original school bell.
546 East Bowman Street; 216/264-8856. Tu-Sun 2-4:30. Closed holidays. Group tours by appointment. Nominal admission.

THE WAYNE CENTER FOR THE ARTS — Arts centers are rare in small towns, but Wooster has the good fortune to have an exceptionally ambitious one that supports the performing as well as visual arts. Begun two decades ago in borrowed space at the College of Wooster, the Wayne Center found a permanent home when Rubbermaid Incorporated rescued and beautifully renovated a dilapidated, turn-of-the-century elementary school. The center's mission is to bring the arts to everyone in the region, and it does just that with hundreds of classes in all manner of disciplines, traveling exhibits, and a chamber music series featuring such world-renowned musicians as the Emerson Quartet. The center's exhibits, which change monthly, have ranged from the Arts of Africa to Medieval Life, while the Gault Gallery features works by artists from across the state and nation. Unique pottery, jewelry, and fiber art made by local artisans is also available in the Gallery Shop.

37 South Walnut Street; 216/264-2787. Mon-Fri 9-5, Sat 9-noon. Closed holidays. Tours by appointment.

ASIDE Wooster's early years coincided with the increasing popularity of the romantic movement in Europe and the United States. Reviving and glorifying medieval Christianity, the movement emphasized self-fulfillment and the positive effect of nature on the human spirit. Romanticism significantly influenced early nineteenth century culture, manifesting itself in art with the landscapes of Cole and Durand; in literature with the novels of Sir Walter Scott; and in architecture with the Gothic Revival style. Gothic Revival was a favorite choice for church buildings, and understandably so, since its elements — pointed arches, towers, steeply gabled roofs, and lacy "gingerbread" barge boards — were very "Christian"; they not only physically reached toward heaven, but were also intended to inspire the mind as well as uplift the spirit. The style became popular for houses after the 1840s, when Andrew Jackson Downing published *Cottage Residences*, a pattern book for builders that contained plans for picturesque Gothic Revival houses and cottages. Although the Gothic Revival heyday is long gone, Wooster still has several buildings from that era, and art historian Scott C. Brown, a 1985 graduate of the College of Wooster, has identified six that are splendid examples of Gothic Revival architecture. **Charles Gasche House**, 439 Bever Street, was originally built as a residence by Charles Gasche in 1849, it has recently taken on a second life as the Howey House, a bed and breakfast. The brackets appearing in the eaves of the center gable were almost certainly copied from Downing's book when the house was built in the late 1840s. **John Jeffries House**, 745 Pittsburgh Avenue, was built about 1845 by attorney John Jeffries, and it is probably the finest example in Wooster of a Downing pattern house. **John Sloane House**, 429 North Market Street, was constructed around 1845 by Sloane, a colonel in the militia during the War of 1812, who later became a U.S. Congressman and Secretary of the Treasury under Millard Filmore. **John McSweeney House**, 531 North Market Street, was built in 1855. An attorney, McSweeney lived there for many years and entertained several famous guests, including Clarence Darrow, Wendell Wilkie, General George Marshall, and Presidents Cleveland, Hayes, McKinley, and Truman. **St. James Episcopal Church**, Market and North Streets, was begun in 1853. The building is notable for the towers on each of its front corners. **Trinity United Church of Christ**, North and Buckeye streets, dates to 1871 and has fine frescoes in the interior.

EVERYTHING RUBBERMAID — This "laboratory store" for Rubbermaid products is not a conventional factory outlet, but a retail store where the Wooster-based corporation can test new products and monitor consumer trends. While Rubbermaid Incorporated is perhaps best-known for its houseware products, Everything Rubbermaid sells not only dustpans and food storage containers, but also office and computer accessories, restaurant and industrial items, casual furniture, decorative coverings, Little Tikes toys, and lawn, garden, and recreational goods made by the far-flung divisions of the company. With an inventory of more than 2500 different products, this unique store has an unsurpassed variety of Rubbermaid merchandise that offers shoppers a value-priced, global selection.
115 South Market Street; 216/264-6464. Mon-Sat 10-9, Sun 11-5. Discover, MC, V.

QUAILCREST FARM — Tom and Libby Bruch left Cleveland nearly 40 years ago with four small children and the notion that they could make the change from the big city to rural living on a dairy farm in Wayne County. They succeeded, and one of the finer fruits of their bucolic labors is the expansive garden center-gift shop complex that Libby began years ago with only a few field-dug perennials. Today, Quailcrest has both herb and perennial nurseries, greenhouses, field-raised plants, and diverse gift shops selling lawn furniture, pottery, baskets, books, statuary, wreaths, potpourri, bird houses, sundials, and other garden-related items. The farm's twenty-five different display gardens – including formal herb, English border, shade, cottage, hosta, hillside, and round gardens – not only are beautiful to behold but also provide some truly down-to-earth ideas for folks with green thumbs. The Roses of History include varieties cultivated since the 1600s, and every year on the Saturday after Labor Day, Libby hosts an Herb Festival, when scores of highly-skilled artisans are invited to display their handiwork at the farm.
2810 Armstrong Road; 216/345-6722. Open mid-March-January 1. Tu-Sat 10-5, with extended hours Thanksgiving-Christmas, Sunday 1-5 during May and Thanksgiving-Christmas. Discover, MC, V.

CENTURY KOUNTRY BARN ANTIQUES — An eclectic selection of local crafts, vintage clothing, home furnishings, and, of course, numerous antiques share the space and the rustic ambiance of this historic 1870 barn. Look for the massive – it's eight feet in diameter and weighs 200 pounds – grape vine that is on permanent display, and then explore the circa 1800 pioneer cabin that was moved here from the next county and reconstructed log by log.
State Route 95 at Smyser Road; 216/264-9076. Apr-Dec Tu-Sat 10-5, Sun 1-5. Closed Sun in Jun, July, and Aug. MC, V.

BUCKEYE BOOK FAIR — The state's premier event for writers who are from Ohio or who write about Ohio brings nearly a hundred authors and thousands of bibliophiles to Wooster every November. It attracts nationally as well as regionally known novelists, journalists, historians, biographers, photographers, columnists, and cartoonists, much to the delight of the fair's growing legion of patrons, who spend the day stuffing bags, backpacks, and even baby buggies with books. Sponsored by Wooster's newspaper, *The Daily Record*, the book fair not only allows the public to meet authors and buy autographed books at a discount, but also raises thousands of dollars for Ohio literacy programs.
At Fisher Auditorium on the campus of the Ohio Agricultural Research and Development Center; 216/264-1125. First Sat in Nov, 9:30 a.m.-4 p.m. MC, V, Personal checks.

WAYNE COUNTY FAIR — Since Wayne County is one of Ohio's prime agricultural areas, this annual six-day fair is not only a prime local attraction – attendance consistently tops 105,000 – but also one of the most successful county fairs in the state. There's a midway, of course, as well as horse races, a demolition derby, and a tractor pull, but the Wayne County Fair is perhaps most famous for its three nights – Sunday, Monday, and Tuesday – of top notch country music entertain- ment, when stars such as George Jones, Johnny Cash, the Statler Brothers, the Oak Ridge Boys, and Ronnie Milsap pack the grandstand. Wayne County also boasts the largest Junior Fair in the state. Every year, about 2,000 Future Farmers of America and 4-H members garner more than $30,000 for entering nearly 4,000 projects, including cows, calves, horses, swine, rabbits, poultry, sheep, and goats. But many folks come to the fair just to eat in the Grange Dining Hall. The old- fashioned meals of chicken, meat loaf, mashed potatoes, and pie are obviously worth waiting for, since the line outside the hall forms as early as 10 a.m. and lasts all day.
Vanover and West Liberty Streets; 216/262-8001. The Fair begins the Sat after Labor Day and ends the following Th. Gates open at 8 a.m. and close at 9 p.m. Nominal gate and grandstand fees. Children under 12 free.

THE WAYNE COUNTY AMISH COUNTRY — Within a short driving distance of Wooster, enclaves of country stores, craft shops, auctions, antique malls, general stores, handmade-furniture shops, and small-town restaurants that truly do have local flavor can be found in the small communities of Apple Creek, Dalton, Kidron, Orrville, Shreve, and Smithville. These establishments are too numerous to mention, but we have featured some of the most notable ones below. Since many cater to the Amish and Mennonites of Wayne County, travelers will encounter stores that sell not only broadfall trousers and white prayer caps but also the stove-warmed sad irons used to press them. The food to be found in here is not for the faint of stomach – portions border on prodigious and the prevalence of made-from-scratch country cooking makes matters of calories and cholesterol quite beside the point. Driving through the area's gentle hills is always picturesque and pleasant, and the Wayne County Visitor and Convention Bureau (237 South Walnut Street, Wooster; 216/264-1800) can provide maps, directions, and specific information regarding particular destinations and the proper way to pass an Amish buggy on a narrow country road. Travelers should be aware, however, that in keeping with their conservative religious customs, many Amish establishments are closed on Sunday.

DES DUTCH ESSENHAUS/SHREVE — Shreve is so small that you can park your car in one spot and walk anyplace else you want to go. Which is fortuitous, because after downing one of the family style, all-you-can-eat chicken, beef, or ham dinners at Des Dutch Essenhaus, a walk is exactly what you'll need. One city couple we know thought that the cooks and waitresses wearing Amish garb were not really Amish at all, but just "English" dressed up for the tourists. Then they asked two of the girls in the gauzy prayer caps for directions. When the girls conferred in the "low German" dialect of the local Amish, the couple realized just how well Des Dutch Essenhaus lives up to its name, "the Dutch eating house." Not only are most of the employees Amish, but all of the food is also prepared from authentic Amish recipes. Tourists like to help themselves to soup from the kettle that hangs in the stone fireplace and browse through the restaurant's quilts and crafts, but local folks like to come for the traditional Thanksgiving Day feast or the Saturday morning Country Buffet with its rib-sticking cornmeal mush, corned beef hash, pancakes, and farm fresh eggs. *176 North Market Street; 216/567-2212. Mon-Th 7 a.m.-8 p.m., Fri-Sat 7 a.m.-9 p.m. Open Thanksgiving, Fourth of July, Labor and Memorial Days. Moderate. Discover, MC, V.*

FUNK COUNTRY MALL/FUNK — The Funk Country Mall isn't exactly a mall; it's more of a general store. And it isn't exactly country, either; it's more, well, funky. But to experience the place, you first have to get there, and getting there is half the fun, if you take State Route 95 west out of Wooster and toward Funk. State Route 95 is a scenic road that dips and turns and goes up and down past spanking white country churches and pretty Italianate farmhouses that are scattered like marbles across the hillsides. About all you have to do is enjoy the scenery and watch out for Amish buggies, until about ten miles later when you come to the Funk Country Mall at the intersection of State Route 95 and County Road 16. From that crossroads, you can view most of Funk, population more or less 68, depending on recent births, deaths, and the health of the real estate market. The state once tried to take Funk off of Ohio's official road map, but the proud residents fussed enough to get Funk back on the map the very next year. One of those protesters was Mary Austin, the matriarch of the mall, over which she presides with daughter Jane Bone and daughter-in-law Phyllis Austin. Mary is in charge of **Gram's Crafts**, which offers hand-made items from about 40 local artisans; Jane will sell you sandpaper or a sandwich in **Austin's Country Store**; and Mary manages **Antiques & Things**, her "things" encompassing miscellany from personalized Rockdale Union Pottery to fishing poles specifically intended for use in local ponds. There is nothing kitschy or contrived about the Funk Country Mall, and therein lies the very genuine appeal of the place, which is housed in an ancient school building (Jane will play you a tape recording that tells its 120-year history) with a working wood stove, creaky wooden screen doors, and a red gas pump out front that displays the hoary "Flying A" trademark. Farmers like the mall because it's the only place where they can shop without getting out of their dirty boots and overalls, and Phyllis says she can always tell when the farmers are in trouble at home, because they come in looking for gifts for their wives. Hunters come by to enter the annual Longest Squirrel Tail contest (the record is 16 inches), and locals stop in for fresh pastries and hot coffee in the morning, a game of checkers (the board and two benches are a permanent fixture), or to read the assortment of newspapers kept on a table near the stove. Be sure to look for the restored sleigh displayed above the front door that earned a blue ribbon at the Ohio State Fair for one of Mary's grandsons, and ask about the old-fashioned rope machine. Children can turn the handle and make their own jump ropes, custom-sized to just the right length.

10785 Blachleyville Road; 216/263-1288. Mon-Sat 6:30 a.m.-6:30 p.m., Sun 8-5. Closed major holidays. MC, V.

TROYER'S HOME PANTRY/APPLE CREEK — After Sarah Troyer started baking in her home kitchen in the 1960s, her pies and cakes got so popular that she and her husband Abe decided to build a bakery. The eating area at Troyer's Home Pantry is small, but the selection of goodies made from Sarah's recipes is mighty — cakes, cookies, noodles, breads, 28 kinds of pie, and seven different flavors of oversized angel food cakes. The Troyers even have regular customers from as far away as Michigan and West Virginia who come by for coffee and their enormous, made-from-scratch cinnamon rolls.

668 West Main Street; 216/698-4182. Christmas-Easter, Mon-Sat 6 a.m.-6 p.m.; Easter Monday-Dec.24 Mon-Sat 6 a.m.-8 p.m. Inexpensive.

LEHMAN'S HARDWARE/KIDRON — The Lehman family has an acre's worth of tools, non-electric appliances, pumps, gas lights, wood stoves, farm equipment, gadgets, and just plain hard-to-find items like sock darners that most folks assume aren't even being made anymore. Many of them, in fact, can no longer be found in the United States, so the Lehmans seek out vendors all over the world to obtain wooden hay forks and butane-fired irons for their Amish and Mennonite customers, who have eschewed electricity and other "conveniences" of modern life. Some things, like the gasoline engine washing machines and the "miracle of engineering" hand-cranked apple parer that peels an entire apple in twenty seconds, truly are one-of-a-kind items because the Lehmans are the only ones in the world who make them. Although the store is becoming increasingly popular with tourists, the 180-foot hitching rail outside is still crammed with black buggies every Thursday, when the Amish come to Kidron for the livestock auction.

4779 Kidron Road; 216/857-5441. Mon-Wed, Fri-Sat 7-5:30; Th 7 a.m.-8 p.m. Discover, MC, V.

THE KIDRON AUCTION/KIDRON — Started in the 1920s as a way for Wayne County farmers to exchange farm animals, the Kidron Auction is not only Ohio's oldest livestock sale, but also one of the largest. The bidding at this country event begins shortly after 10 a.m. with hay, straw, and grain, then at 11 a.m. comes the livestock — more than 3,000 cattle, calves, hogs, horses, feeder pigs, and other animals bought and sold. While the auction is the main attraction, a flea market, food booths, and produce stands are worthy sideshows. Three times a year, the local Amish as well as buyers from several states also crowd the bleachers for machinery auctions of horse-powered farm equipment.

4885 Kidron Road; 216/857-2641. Livestock auction every Th 10:15 a.m.-late afternoon. Machinery auction the first Sat in Mar and Apr and the third Sat in August, 9 a.m.-late afternoon. Closed holidays.

OHIO MENNONITE RELIEF SALE/KIDRON — Attracting nearly a half million people every year, this auction is one of Ohio's premier events. Members of more than a hundred Amish, Mennonite, and Brethren churches donate handmade, work-of-art quilts and wood items such as clocks, dollhouses, and furniture that attract knowing dealers and collectors from as far away as New York City. With live, "old-time" musical entertainment and quilting and craft demonstrations, the event raises hundreds of thousands of dollars to support good works around the world. But the only thing at the auction more nonstop than the bidding is the eating. Be prepared to indulge your stomach with a hog roast, country style pancake breakfast, apple fritters and dumplings, homemade ice cream, locally made cheeses and Trail bologna, and several thousand extraordinary pies, which are made by the ladies of the churches and usually all gone by mid-morning on Saturday.

On the Grounds of Central Christian High School, Kidron Road; 216/ 682-4843. First Fri and Sat in Aug. Fri stands open at 4 p.m. Sat breakfast begins at 6 a.m.; auction starts at 9 a.m.

SMITHVILLE BED AND BREAKFAST/SMITHVILLE — More than a hundred years old, this red brick house was once the home of the owner of the famous Smithville Inn next door. Today, it accommodates guests in comfortable bedrooms with understated country and colonial decor, as well as in a separate cottage offering suites of rooms. The entire home is graced by floors, banisters, and trims made of various woods, but the dining room with its cherry floor and walls is an especially charming setting in the morning when guests sit down to blueberry muffins.

171 West Main Street; 216/669-3333. MC, V.

SMITHVILLE INN/SMITHVILLE — Owners Rick and Kathie Hammond grew up smelling the baked chicken dinners that have made the inn famous. But then, so did everybody else in town, because the inn has been a Smithville landmark since 1818, when it opened as a hotel on the Old Portage Trail (now State Route 585) between Akron and Wooster. The inn exudes history: Presidents McKinley and Franklin Roosevelt both paid a visit; the rare wormy chestnut covering the dining room walls came from a stand of woods in Holmes County more than 50 years ago, and the fine collection of antiques and old dishes that elicits admiration from visitors dates back to the 1700s. But the good home cooking served family style is undoubtedly what keeps most folks coming back. Dinners are accompanied by bowl after bowl of coleslaw, mashed potatoes, celery stuffing, and the rich Inn Maid noodles that this establishment made popular. So, pass the homemade biscuits and apple butter, but save some room for a slice of the inn's signature eggnog pie.

109 West Main Street; 216/669-2641. Tu-Sun, 11:30-8. Inexpensive-Moderate. MC, V.

THE BARN/SMITHVILLE — The foyer has a corn crib and the dining room has a farm wagon that dates back to 1907. Welcome to The Barn, which was just what its name says it was until the early 1980s when Wayne County's Davenstrott family turned it into a restaurant. The Barn is huge – it can seat about 600 – and the portions are sized accordingly: simple, down-home dishes such as smoked pork chops, fried chicken, barbecued chicken, and apple dumplings for dessert. Waitresses wear ankle-length country dresses, and displays of quilts and assorted farm implements reinforce the rustic atmosphere. But the most popular place in The Barn seems to be that old farm wagon, which has found a new life as a huge, help-yourself salad bar.
877 West Main Street; 216/669-2555. Sun-Th 10:30-8, Fri-Sat 10:30-9. Inexpensive-moderate. Discover, MC, V.

THE SHOPS OF BUCHANAN PLACE/SMITHVILLE — Lloyd and Welma Mast have turned a local landmark – the elegant old house where Dr. James Buchanan practiced medicine a century ago – into the lovely centerpiece for a set of specialty shops located adjacent to The Barn restaurant. The Buchanan homestead is divided into theme areas such as Golf, Baby, Bath, and Music that offer suitably selected, quality gifts and accessories. Since the Masts are one of the world's largest dealers in the Cat's Meow Village collectibles, the Cat's Meow Room is a mecca for devotees of the popular series of architectural renditions produced by FJ Designs in Wooster. Their other shops are the **Oak Cupboard**, a gourmet country store, and the **Kids Collection**, which features innovative and unusual toys and games.
4642 Akron Road; 216/669-3911. Jan-Feb, Mon-Th 9-5:30, Fri-Sat 9-9, Sun 12:30-5:30. Mar-Dec, Mon-Th 9-8, Fri-Sat 9-9, Sun 12:30-5:30. Discover, MC, V.

THE SMUCKER RETAIL STORE/ORRVILLE — Having a name like Smucker's meaning that its products must be good is something most folks already know, thanks to the J. M. Smucker Company's advertising. But you may not know about the store that the company operates in Orrville on the premises of its very attractive flagship plant. It offers the entire line of Smucker products – jams, jellies, preserves (including the ever-popular strawberry), juices, peanut butters, ice cream toppings, apple butter, and even ketchup. In addition to gift boxes of Smucker items, the store stocks products such as Knudsen juices, Lost Acres mustards, and Elsenham lemon curd made by Smucker subsidiaries. Also for sale is an unrivaled assortment of souvenirs – sweatshirts, beach towels, umbrellas, watches, toys trucks, etc., etc – that bear the Smucker name and strawberry logo.
J.M. Smucker Company, Strawberry Lane; 216/682-3000. Jan-Nov, Mon-Fri 8-4:15; Dec, Mon-Fri 8-5, Sat 8:30-noon.

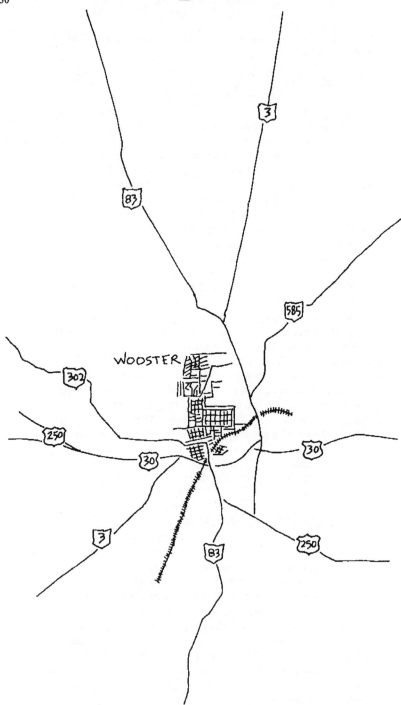

Morgan County Courthouse

Morgan County

The Muskingum River leaves Zanesville in a wide rush, flowing to Marietta and the Ohio River, 78 miles away. At first, its path meanders gently, but as it moves south into Morgan County, its turns are harder and more obscured by the steep and slanted valleys. In cool weather, they are traced by mist and fog that, sooner or later, lead to the river. As it always has been, the river is the footprint of the county – the landmark by which distances and spaces are marked. ¶ In 1817, Robert McConnel, a former brigadier general in the War of 1812 who knew the Muskingum countryside, decided that the area, fabled for game and lumber, needed a town. He drew up a petition and, after a month of lobbying in Marietta, had it accepted. It was three months before McConnel found any takers; he finally convinced a traveling Virginian to take plot one. When the third resident moved down from Zanesville later in the year, McConnel — flushed with entrepreneurial zeal — decided to form a new county around his small city of seven (four of whom were children). ¶ In the fall of 1817, eight months after petitioning his town, he wrote a state bill to annex 420 square miles into an area he proposed to name after Daniel Morgan, a Revolutionary War general. The legislature passed the bill but required that a panel of three commissioners determine where the new county would have its governmental seat, a noble idea that backfired in execution. The commissioners carped about each other's bad judgment until a disgusted legislature disbanded them and tabled the measure for a year. Senator McConnel, ever enterprising, encouraged the building of churches, then argued that the rising population of McConnelsville was now God-fearing. ¶ The ensuing election was bloody and factious, with so much disregard for due process that, when McConnel's candidates prevailed, the opposition rode to Columbus to lie about the results. It took days to confirm the truth but, in the end, Morgan County and its county seat were created as twins, even if breeched. ¶ The establishment of the county brought roads, the railroad, and greater boat traffic down the Muskingum. Little by little, the area was denuded of its hardwoods. Underneath the surface, coal was discovered and beneath the coal was salt. Some of the newly opened land and the farms were supported by small towns and factories that were, in turn, supplied by the river. For the entire length of the eighteenth century, when hill farming and boat commerce brought prosperity, Morgan County and its small towns grew and even flourished. ¶ In that era, steam excursions became common between Zanesville and Marietta. They stopped in McConnelsville for fuel and entertainment, and they stopped in Stockport, the county's other major river town, where men were reputed to spit on the street and fight on Sundays. But as the nineteenth century wore on, civility *did* touch Stockport and even embraced McConnelsville. From a collection of prominent factories that processed tobacco, salt, stoves, fertilizers and oil, wealthy owners built large brick homes with fanciful gardens. Civic pride was expressed in the 1890 construction of a town hall and opera house. In it, merchants and businessmen formed a Masonic lodge whose accomplishments were apocryphal. According to a former native of McConnelsville, the best example of the lodge's idiosyncratic behavior occurred in the winter of 1902, when the area was subjected to a series of blizzards that made commerce awkward, and travel even more so. Everyone suffered from the weather, but the Masons grew particularly ill-tempered, and the poker games they held each Saturday night reflected their sullenness. Halfway through the winter, the customary 1 a.m. curfew was lifted. In February, drinking was allowed on the premises. In March, a dentist from Malta wielding pliers attacked another player. The poker games became hurly-burly events with no restrictions. ¶ On a Saturday night in April, there was still ice on the Muskingum and a foot of snow on the streets. The sun had only shone once in sixteen days. A new snow was starting, and the poker game was more mean-spirited than ever. Whiskey was downed with abandon, and bets were steep and harsh. Fortunes scattered around the room until no one had the dexterity to shuffle a deck.

¶ At noon on Sunday, most of the Masons awakened to a brilliant, sunny sky. They had missed church, but even more seriously, they discovered that the entire town had changed hands. The druggist owned the hardware store, and the hardware store owner had title to two goats and a dairy cow. The harness maker owned a shipment of undelivered dry goods still up in Zanesville, and the mayor owned a portrait studio. ¶ Fearing a scandal of unrecoverable proportions, the high templar priest called a meeting to pray for forgiveness and fair exchange. Only one man, seeing the opportunity of a lifetime, refused to take back the wife he had given up to a lockkeeper for two ring hogs. By mid-afternoon he had reduced his bickering to a reluctant exchange, and at last, McConnelsville was whole again. The Masons, it is believed, never sponsored a poker game again. ¶ Today, the population of Morgan County rests at 14,500 people, which is about the population it had during the Civil War. McConnelsville is quaint and self-contained, without strip plazas or malls. Stockport — about 16 miles down the river — boasts two restaurants, a remarkable old mill and the best river fishing in the state. Winding country roads link Chesterhill to Pennsville to Mill Grove to Hackney. There are few other towns, but in their simplicity, all are places where a person is likely to invite you to supper if your car breaks down in front of his house.   ¶ In the meantime, its landscape remains largely undiscovered. Those who do visit often talk of its patchwork fields, its sudden rains and the traceries of fog that give it a sense of mystery. If it *is* haunted, it is only by its frontier heritage that still seems to lurk in the landscape. On quiet, blistering summer days when haze envelops everything, Morgan County has *mood*; that is its power and its connection to history.

THE OUTBACK INN BED & BREAKFAST/MCCONNELSVILLE —
Perhaps no other Bed & Breakfast in the state offers a choice of room *and* a choice of innkeeper. Guests staying on weekends have as their hostess Emily Matusek, a patient, demure schoolteacher and weaver who fulfilled a townhouse dream by renovating this 1880 banker's home, putting her loom in an upstairs bedroom, and hiring a meticulous housekeeper. During the week, she lives in her country house on a hill outside of town and her husband, Chuck Bosari, runs the Inn. *Run* being the operative word. Bosari, a bearded and effervescent artist, fulfilled *his* dream by leaving the big city for the slower pleasures of country and village living. He's still working on the slower part. It's a mutually beneficial arrangement to the ultimate advantage of the guests who usually get to meet both anyway, by way of Emily's coffee cake or Chuck's fresh fruit compote. Two bedrooms upstairs have private baths. One bedroom downstairs has a private bath and a private entrance. It's enormously comfortable and unpretentious, has the original stained woodwork throughout and is the first stop on a Morgan County tour of Bosari stained glass. Three beautiful windows – the front door, the landing and the upstairs bath – announce the beginning of Morgan County's future legacy. The Outback Inn, only two blocks from the village's 2000-person epicenter, is the only place McConnelsville visitors might spend the night. But *should* is the operative word.
171 East Union Avenue, 614/962-2158.

BOSARI STAINED GLASS/MCCONNELSVILLE — Four hundred
years ago an Italian named Bosari tried to win the favor of the Duchess
of Parma. To rid the earth of peasant effluvia, the duchess liked to
have servants sprinkle violet leaves on the ground in front of her as
she walked. So Bosari created fragrances for her. He made a name for
himself that apparently lived on because four centuries later, Chuck
Bosari, grandson of Italian immigrants, continues the tradition – of
winning women's favor, that is. Ridding the gray light from the Ohio
sky, Bosari's windows create color and reflection, and during his
fifteen years in Morgan County, he has replaced the skepticism of the
natives (a ponytail, beard, and earring are not the typical Morgan
County accouterment) with thousands of bevels, prisms, and colors.
Today, a tour of Morgan County stained glass is like a tour of the
county jewels, and no one likes to lead the way as much as Bosari
himself. **744 East Main Street** – Here's a stunning eyebrow window
of brown stained glass with a beveled cluster and Flemish glass. **507
East Main Street** – The antebellum mansion, now The Howard House
Restaurant, has an arched insignia window in the third story, a
handsome clear beveled window in the front door transom and several
other pieces on the interior. **137 South Kennebec Street** – Dr.
William Gables commissioned Bosari to do 19 pieces for his dental
operatories. Bosari sat in dental chairs, leaning back to get the proper
alignment for patients' line of vision. Most are 48" long and 6" high. He
also did a dental caduceus and, as Dr. Gables is an ardent Buckeye fan,
a scarlet and gray OSU piece. **The Opera House Theater/15 West
Main Street** – Here Bosari did three windows and a colorful Victorian
transom above the front door. **The Barn/CR4** – From McConnelsville
take SR78 west for 5.5 miles. Turn left on CR40, right on CR4. Follow
all signs that say *Stained Glass*. The Barn is Bosari's studio, a 1904
English Classic barn perched atop perhaps the most pastoral setting in
all of south-eastern Ohio. It took six years to restore, has 39 windows
and two floors and is a microcosm of Bosari's mind, too expansive for
self-containment anywhere. For Bosari, former newsman, lobbyist, and
speech writer traded his suits for seed catalogues in 1977, swapping
the whimsicality of politics for the fragility of glass. Bosari has sown
his seeds. Morgan County has reaped the harvest. *Call 614/962-4284.
Open Sun-Th, 1-6 p.m. Closed Fri & Sat. County Road 3* – In a private
home eight miles NW of town, Bosari created his largest single piece, a
20-square foot window that took him three months to complete. Made
for a young couple who wanted a nice view from their hot tub, it has a
peacock as its central figure, which, says the owner, is so lifelike, that
after a good soak of tub and wine, has the habit of moving. Bosari
personally choreographed the placement of four exterior soffit
spotlights with dimmers so that nightfall wouldn't inhibit the
peacock's, or anyone else's, dance. **Third & Jefferson** – Bosari, it can
be confirmed, doesn't miss much. He noticed this house was being
renovated, but that the front door was covered with a piece of
plywood. One day, he knocked on the front plywood and announced
to the owner, "Hi. I'm Chuck Bosari. You need me." The front door
now houses a handsome piece of wavy, clear Flemish glass. **Miller -
Huck Funeral Home/72 Seventh Street and Tatman Funeral
Home/165 North Kennebec Street** – Both have Bosari glass. When
the famous Morgan County-reared physicist, Dr. Roger Rusk, was 92,
he returned to his home, attended a party at Bosari's studio on a

Sunday, saw the piece Bosari was finishing for Tatman's, and commented on its beauty. On Tuesday, Rusk died. On Friday, he was the first to view, and be viewed, under Bosari's window. **Chesterhill Methodist Church** – There are eight ten-foot windows in this tiny village's church. Bosari has done three of them. All are memorial windows done in six sections. Bosari always speaks at the dedication ceremonies. **Ringgold** – High on a hill in Union Township sits a private residence once owned by the vice president in charge of an Indiana window manufacturing company. The entire south side of the house was three stories of windows, enough to make a stained glass artist weak in the soldering joints. Bosari was commissioned to put stained glass in the third-story level. Now, surrounding a magnificent stained glass abstract tree are ribs of glass with 60 bevels. When the sun shines through, 240 surfaces cast prisms of light. **McDonald's Restaurant** – The nation's smallest McDonald's is in Morgan County and its tiny 2000-square foot interior is graced with five large Bosari hanging lamps above the booths.

The Howard House

THE HOWARD HOUSE RESTAURANT/MCCONNELSVILLE — There was a time not long ago when one could get a estimable meal in Morgan County, but you'd have to catch and clean it yourself. Steve Hann has changed that. He saved the old 1850 Thompson antebellum mansion from demolition, transformed it into a fine restaurant known for its prime rib, hired a hearty Columbus chef, and has restored grace and appetite to the proud home that sits on a knoll overlooking Chatauqua Grove. The mansion seats 150, there's a handsome lounge in what was once the front parlor, dining rooms upstairs in what were once the bedrooms, and picturesque views from every window in the house. Now, in the heart of wild turkey and venison country, one may dine on Fettucini Gardeniera, Veal Benjamin and Medallions Russo. Diners are arriving from everywhere, for a look at the transformation, and a taste of the trade. The best perspective comes from a photo album they keep by the hostess desk. There's a great one of the kitchen when it still had a dirt floor.

507 East Main St., 614/962-5861. Sun 11 a.m.-3 p.m., Brunch Buffet only; Closed Mon. Tu-Th 4:30-10 p.m.; Fri 4:30-12 a.m.; Sat 4:30-11 p.m.. Reservations accepted. MC, V. Moderate to Expensive.

THE BUTTON HOUSE/MCCONNELSVILLE — When local schoolchildren take a tour of the labyrinth of rooms that now houses the history of Morgan County, they casually pass by the original founding documents, artist Howard Chandler Christie's honorary naval academy ring and waterproof watch (he loved to swim), the silver baseball given to the McConnelsville baseball team when they beat the Cincinnati Reds in 1867, and the wooden drum used by a local boy in the Civil War. "But where did she *die?*" they ask, which is really what they want to see. And then it's time to climb the steep stairs to the room in which Evelyn True Button spent the last moments of her hundred years. Actually, she spent most of her moments in this house. It had belonged to her father, the town doctor, who had built the home in 1836. His desk, medicine bottles, and most of the furniture in the place are Button originals. When Ms. Button died in 1975, her secretary, Bertha Blackburn, maintained the home and it was opened to the public several years before *she* died. So a historical repository is somewhat of a new concept to Morgan County. The good news is, the locals have opened their pasts and their attics to the Historical Society. The bad news is, the society doesn't know where to put it all. For a while, the little commercial building next door served as the Now & Then Shop. The society sold off people's collections and kept a commission. It's now an extension of the museum and the place to learn about McDonald Birch, the last of the big-time magicians who had the largest one-man touring show in America — it took 57 crates of equipment to do one performance. His home was called Birchwood and it stood on a hill in Malta, across the Muskingum. He built the equipment for his shows here, sold all the pieces when he retired and now lives in a local nursing home. Here, too, are pictures of Augusta True, Evelyn's sister, a famous Shakespearian actress. And tucked on an inconspicuous shelf next to Augusta's pictures is the gravestone of Tom McGee, the name 19th century locals gave to one of Morgan's Raiders, who died on July 23, 1863, and was buried in a shallow grave near Eaglesport crossing, along the Muskingum. It is the sort of place that makes a good historian break into a sweat, hopeful to live long enough to make sense of it all, protect it from harm, and enlighten the world to its existence. Potential curators ought to take a peak. *142 East Main Street, 614/962-4785. Open Mon, Wed, Fri 10-2p.m. Sat 10-12 p.m.*

who became the furnituremaker. At one time he was the oldest living funeral director in America. A perfect case of how one thing leads to another. His status rated having family portraits painted in oil by Sala Bosworth, an early Ohio portrait artist of gaining notoriety. These, along with a attic trunk filled with personal letters and business records have kept Andrews in a cloud of ancestral dust, which he is determined to safely put to rest. When he sent the five oil paintings to a restoration company in Washington, D. C., he had no clue as to their worth. The hint came when they were returned by special courier in an unmarked secured truck. Today, Andrews, the seeker, has become Andrews, the seekee, and a strong thread linking Morgan County's past to its present to its future.

Opera House, McConnelsville

THE OPERA HOUSE THEATER, INC./MCCONNELSVILLE — Gaylen Finley was keeper of the keys of McConnelsville's Opera House. He'd been in love with the place for half of its life, which was most of his, bought it several dozen years ago, set up housekeeping on its stage (he'd push his furniture into the wings when they needed it for high school graduations), and put his own money into renovating it. Now he lives in a magnificently restored home high above town with a view of the Opera House tower and a Board of Trustees runs the house. Their first-run movie format has been the same since 1936 with performance times Friday through Monday. No movies are shown the week of the Morgan County Fair. There are live events year round, from the Bellamy Brothers to local talent shows, but the one that's most vividly recalled happened in the summer of 1990 during the Opera House's 100th anniversary celebration. A sudden storm came up during Phil Dirt & The Dozer's concert held out in front of the theater to accommodate the huge crowd. They had closed two state highways and over 3000 people were sitting on blankets and folding chairs in the intersection when the winds picked up $8000 of speakers and equipment and dropped them nearby. The crowds ran for cover, the Dozers ran for their bus, but Gaylen and his volunteers ran for the equipment. Drenched, they headed for the Opera House. Gaylen took them to the costume department and started handing out dry clothes. They continued to work. Shepherds, angels, Civil War soldiers, southern belles. Gaylen, the last to find something, had on soldiers pants and a choir robe. The biggest guy was in drag. "Touch my skirt and I'll punch you," he said. Some towns have all the fun. *15 West Main Street, 614/962-3030.*

CITIZENS NATIONAL BANK/ART GUILD GALLERY/ MCCONNELSVILLE — Aside from being an agreeable place for financial transactions, the local bank has become the area repository for art. The Howard Chandler Christy Art Guild (Christie painted *The Signing of the Constitution of the United States*, which hangs over the grand staircase in the national capitol, *The Signing of the Treaty of Greenville*, was famous for his patriotic naval posters as well as the famous Christy Girls, and was born in a log cabin on Meigs Creek in Morgan County on January 10, 1873, where he lived until he moved to Muskingum County) has grown from a tiny group and $36 to a burgeoning collection of talented area artists with a $10,000 budget. There are so many good local artists that in the two years since the gallery opened, they haven't had enough days to show them all. But one of the best times to see what the county has to offer is during the Art Guild's summer Howard Chandler Christie Art Show. Last year, 28 professional artists came to McConnelsville, many from out of the county, to compete for a record amount of prize money. *100 East Main Street, 614/962-4565. Mon, Tu, Wed, 9-3; Th & Sat 9-12; Fri 9-6. Exhibitions change every three months. Major art show is held on the village commons the last weekend in July.*

THE MORGAN COUNTY COURTHOUSE/MCCONNELSVILLE — To lovers of classic American Colonial architecture, this courthouse is the most beautiful in the state. Built of brick in 1858 it has clean white lines and four regal pillars. It adds a certain elegance to this tiny teacup of a town, an aura of respect, and is a fine backdrop for the farmers' market held on its lawn every Friday from 10-noon all summer long. Years ago, a young Elmer Parsons would come to town every Saturday wearing his best green suit, remaining by the courthouse as if it were his best friend. He became the courthouse janitor, its protector and keeper of its flag – especially on Thursday, when he lowered it at noon for his own afternoon off.

STOCKPORT MILLING CO., INC./STOCKPORT — Head east on Main Street, turn right at the Kate Love Simpson Library, and take a pleasant ride south along the Muskingum Parkway (State Route 376) to Stockport. There, across the Muskingum River, rising above the dam and across from a set of the last hand-operated canal locks in the state, is the formidable 1907 Stockport Mill. It appears as a fortress and is in fact the working castle of Amy and Bob Groves, a handsome couple who reign over not just the only grain mill in town, but one of two Xerox machines in town as well. The Groves bought the mill in 1979 to custom grind corn and oats and sell farm supplies, garden seed and plants, but spent hundreds of hours assessing its use as a hydropower plant. That plan is now on a back burner. But the Groves are not short on ideas. "This is going to be a hotel and restaurant someday," says

Stockport Mill

Bob. Tourists already stop by. And Bob and Amy welcome them in for a step onto a narrow deck that hangs out from the mill thirty feet above the dam. But the best view is from a large round window Bob installed right by his desk. From here he can see his fiefdom, or damdom, as it may be, though as a county commissioner, a more suitable view is from the roof.
State Route 266. 614/559-3030.

BIG BOTTOM STATE MEMORIAL/SOUTH OF STOCKPORT — One mile south of the Stockport bridge on State Route 376 is a little grove of trees on the riverbank of the Muskingum. It is a quiet reminder that long ago it wasn't so quiet at all. One can hardly see the obelisk carved with the names of the three lonely survivors who escaped the Indian massacre that the traveling historian, Henry Howe, recorded in his 1888 historical collection. It was a lackadaisical group of 36 who came from Marietta to settle the area in 1790. They weren't much on the fine details of settlership, like using a sentry, a stockade, discipline, or organization. And one other oversight — the Indian War Path from Sandusky to the mouth of the Muskingum passed along on the opposite shore. The Indians arrived one evening at dinnertime — the dogs didn't even bark — killed twelve, let two run off because a good meal was still hot on the table, and, having gotten their fill, spared the young boy they later found hiding under a bed. It is the names of these three on the monument. But do read Henry Howe's version of the story. It's better than a TV western.
Historical Collections of Ohio by Henry Howe, Vol 2, pages 303-305.

STATE ROUTE 78 — Several years ago *Car and Driver* magazine rated the 105.3 miles of State Route 78 as one of the ten best roads in the country: "Just as the 78-rpm phonograph record was once the truest sound around, Ohio 78 plays a dancing tune that keeps your tires humming their best." And you can hum on 37 of those miles in Morgan County. The entire route begins at the Ohio River at Clarington in Monroe County and takes a gentle southwesterly turn until it ends in Nelsonville in Athens County. With a full tank of gas, good tires, no deadlines, and an empty stomach, State Route 78 mixes country charm with stimulation. If you want a third dimension, drive it after lunch.

BEST VIEW — Someday, scientists may have to create an "earthatarium" so future generations will know what a fine country landscape once looked like. If they do it right, it will appear as the 365-degree view from the Bosari-Matusek farm on CR4. The surrounding hills piggyback one another, as in an American Gothic painting — an apple orchard on this one, a pine grove on that one, a placid herd of Holsteins in between. It wasn't long ago that Mr. Bosari read in the city newspaper that in case of a nuclear attack, citizens of Columbus were to head for Morgan County. "Over my dead body," he said. For now, only the wind across the hills can reply.

WOLF CREEK WILDLIFE AREA — Thirty years ago they never told Frank Brown that the worst wildlife in the area to manage was the two-legged kind that drove. "Oh, I've worked with deer, wild turkey gobblers, woodcock, rabbit, crows, and coyote, but they're nothing compared to those people beating on your door all night to ask what kind of fish are in these ponds." New wildlife manager Dan Smith can confirm the sightings. "They stop for maps, information, accidents, lost cattle. Once my wife had to put out a van fire. They didn't even thank her." Well, this isn't Walden Pond, but then Thoreau wasn't responsible for the mourning dove surveys either. There are wild turkeys to move from one county to another, rabbit studies, brush-land, openland, and woodland to maintain and, in total, 3,800 acres to keep in shape for public hunting and fishing. Wolf Creek is only one of three sites in Ohio where you can hunt with primitive weapons (the last week in October). And if you really want to get a feel for 18th century Ohio, try one of the four primitive camping areas — no flush toilets, no electricity, just a little clearing that's bushhogged four times a year. Don't get too comfortable. There's a ten-day limit.
Call 614/962-2048.

BURR OAK STATE PARK — If you take State Route 78 to the far southwestern border of Morgan County you will find the one long-standing commercial tourist package the county has to offer. The park surrounds Burr Oak Lake, with swimming, boating, and camping facilities, year round events that include, with lodging, hoedowns, country dance bands, murder mystery weekends, and the like. Warm weather visitors make good use of the beach, golf course (not part of the park), and pontoon boats. The lodge has 60 rooms, 30 deluxe housekeeping cabins, and six meeting rooms. If you want to leave the hustle and bustle of city life, arrive at Burr Oak and find it's time to leave the hustle and bustle of state park life, try hiking some of the 29 miles of trail. Only then, will you have arrived, and it will be because you have left.
The Park: Call 800/ATA-PARK or 614/767-3570. The Lodge: Call 614/ 767-2112.

OHIO POWER RECREATION LAND — The northeastern portion of Morgan County, largely anywhere east of the Muskingum River, is Morgan County's "other side of the tracks." The mining industry has been here for decades, surface-mining coal to fuel generators along the Muskingum. By the grace of someone's good conscience, the parent company of Ohio Power, the American Electric Power Company, reforested the land and constructed ponds behind their work, even as long as 40 years ago. Today, 30,000 acres are open to the public with eleven park sites, nine available for camping. Ten miles of the Buckeye Trail cross the land and though it's not virgin territory – not much of Ohio is – it's a great eight-mile hike, the ponds are filled with lots of fish, the beaver are back, and in the fall, the foliage is brilliant. Permits and maps are a must. Write to the Ohio Department of Natural Resources Publication Center in Columbus. Then buy a copy of Ralph Ramey's book, *Fifty Hikes In Ohio.*
Call 614/962-4525. Open Mon-Fri, 8 a.m.-12 p.m.

CIVIL WAR ENCAMPMENT DAYS — If the saying, "Be careful who you pretend to be because that is who you are" holds true, then John B. Jett of Taylor Mill, Kentucky, *is* Brigadier General John H. Morgan of Morgan's Raiders fame. For 25 years, he's played the role as the leader of the 2nd Kentucky Cavalry and those who play host and hostess to him during the weekend re-enactment find the difference between John B. and John F. gets slimmer and slimmer every year. But, hey, what's a re-enactment all about? In Morgan County, it's about the time General Morgan led 2,460 mounted men on a wild raid through southern Ohio in the summer of 1863. They began north of Cincinnati and continued their manic pillaging eastward (Basil Duke, Morgan's second in command, said one man carried a bird cage with three canaries in it for two days while another rode with a chafing dish.) Seven hundred of his men were captured at Buffington Island; 300 more escaped across the Ohio 20 miles upriver; they headed north again into Morgan County where they crossed the Muskingum and got as far as Columbiana County where Morgan surrendered ten miles north of East Liverpool. This "I'll get you back for what you did to us" ride, unlike "The British are coming!" ride of Paul Revere holds great re-enactment possibilities. After all, how much fun is it to watch one man with a lantern riding down the street? So, one of the most exciting times to visit Morgan County is the third weekend in July. Last year about 200 re-enactors, including women and children, took part in the show. There were 70 Confederates and 50 Union soldiers. This year, recruiting speeches begin at 7 pm at the Malta Riverfront Park. A cannon skirmish across the Muskingum is at 9 p.m. Events run from 9 to 9 on Saturday, including a parade, a weeping and dying contest, a grand Civil War Officer's Ball at the Opera House, and a lantern tour of authentic Civil War camps in the Grove. The major battle is at 1:30 on Sunday at Springbrook Farm, three miles west of Malta and McConnelsville on State Route 37. Had the *real* General Morgan had a longer attention span and hung around for more than 24 hours the locals could carry this one on for a week.

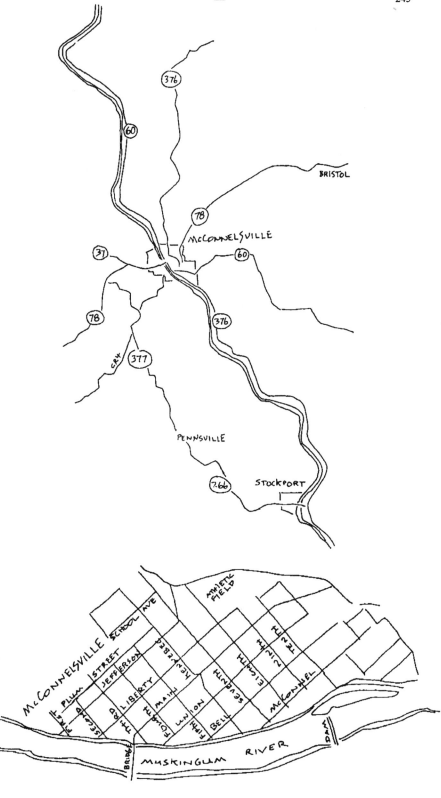

The Ohio Museum

Route 52

By mid-September of last year, the Mail Pouch tobacco barns that speckled the roadside along U.S. Route 52 between Portsmouth and New Richmond had tobacco hanging so thick it looked like giant bats had taken up residence in wooden caves. Not only was it an early harvest, there were more acres of chartreuse leaves still to be cut, and with the market for U.S. tobacco at an all-time high, the 80-mile roadway that played tag with the Ohio River seemed, for once, a highway of prosperity, a sinewy Atlas, holding up the economic decline of the state that rose above it. The truth, of course, was something else. But truth to the traveler is not statistics and data, it is how something *feels*. And a journey along U.S. 52 that fall felt very good indeed.　¶ In fact, if one were to drop in on U.S. 52 today, a good place to launch the tour would be in Portsmouth. (Unless, of course, you're from Cincinnati or Dayton, and then it would be silly. Those travelers should begin in New Richmond.) Bags should be left at

Shawnee State Park Lodge. *(Seven miles west of Portsmouth on U.S. 52, 614/439-4406. Double rooms, May 28-Oct 31, Sun-Th $72; Fri & Sat $78; Winter rates, $69. Ask about cabins. They're octagonal, have two bedrooms, a loft and a fireplace, are heated and air-conditioned.)* ¶ In the fall reservations must be made in advance. This guarantees a room furnished in handmade knotty pine and red cedar in a 50-room lodge on 62,000 pristine, forested acres (ask for a room facing the forest). Of course, there is the chance you never get to Portsmouth at all, for the temptation to hole up here is almost primordial and venturing into Portsmouth may take an act of will. A state park lodge with personality, charm, service, and amenities in a town named Friendship is enough to make a traveler weep. ¶ But there is much to see and the best place to start is in what was the "original" **Portsmouth**, when Portsmouth was a river port and hummed with industry. Follow the signs that say "Downtown" and you will find yourself on 2nd Street, the main street through the **Bonneyfiddle District**. In 1801, the original 2,024 acres became 542 sections that sold for $50 each. Here's where the first courthouse, jail, school, homes, warehouses, gristmill and taverns stood. Fifty years later it was larger than Toledo or Akron and a major manufacturing center for steel, shoes and cement. This commercial core remains, with a collection of handsome 19th century buildings that withstood the 1937 flood. The best are two bellwether hotels of the late Victorian era, **The Biggs House** and **The Washington Hotel**. Scheduled for demolition several years ago, the astute Scioto Memorial Hospital bought the buildings and, with funding from HUD, restored the exteriors and rebuilt the interiors to accommodate 110 marvelous apartments for the elderly and handicapped. A center section of The Biggs House had one part of its interior gutted leaving only the facade standing and giving it the appearance of a 19th Century Parthenon. ¶ The ballroom of the Washington Hotel is now a beautiful outside courtyard. *This* is the building that houses Portsmouth's dawn, for here, warmth, vigilance and order sustains not merely the old and infirmed, but also the largest and finest historical photograph collection of Portsmouth and Scioto County, the **Carl Ackerman Collection** *(The Washington Hotel, 500 Second Street, Portsmouth. By appointment. 614/354-4676).*

¶ Carl Ackerman, a retired commercial flower grower and now part-time groundskeeper for the Old Market Square community for the elderly, knows how ideas grow and mushroom. Forty-one years ago his local historical interest was seeded by four old postcards in an out-of-town newspaper. Twenty thousand photos and pieces of memorabilia later, the collection now landscapes the entirety of a 30'x50' room. ¶ Here are the photographs of Portsmouth under the seige of the 1937 flood; Portsmouth as a canal town, a steel town, a shoe manufacturing town. The room shifts and changes like a garden in four seasons so visitors can return again and again for changing views of the past. As his collection gains in reputation, he is convinced that more outsiders than locals know of its magnitude.

Some people just don't know what's growing in their own backyard.   ¶ The room has a street entrance but, if you may, with permission, enter through the Washington Hotel where the room outside Carl's has a glass case filled with the last remaining vestiges of the famous, world-wide **Williams Shoe Company**, manufacturer of women's shoes and a company almost everyone in Portsmouth worked for at one time or another. Although the local Selby Shoe Company made more expensive shoes, Williams was the company known for heart and sole. Once, when the child of an employee was lost in the woods of surrounding Portsmouth, they closed down the factory for the day and 1600 employees went on the child hunt. The happy ending is one of many stories that still brings tears to the eyes of former employees.

YE OLDE LANTERN RESTAURANT/PORTSMOUTH — It's a small colorful cafe with no fern-bar pretense. The food is very good and inexpensive and most of the patrons are from the neighborhood. Eavesdropping, then, becomes the traveler's sport. The big beef on one day was not between two slices of bread, but between two construction workers regarding the virility of their hunting dogs. One claimed that the baritone nature of his dog's bark was enough to prove the canine's virility, while the other said if that were so, than Pavarotti could have populated Portsmouth solo. No one said if Pavarotti had ever *been* to Portsmouth or, if he had, if he could really do this entirely alone. But a story such as this is nice fodder for a visit to that great monument to Portsmouth stamina, the flood wall.
Corner of Second and Court Streets, 614/353-6638. Mon-Th 11-10; Fri-Sat 11-11; Closed Sun. Inexpensive.

ASIDE You can tell that Portsmouth takes the Ohio River seriously by the three-mile-long massive reinforced concrete flood wall that prohibits any pastoral river view from the streets of downtown. While walking down 2nd Street it's the only southerly view at the crosstreets. First built in 1908, it was raised during the Depression to control a 62-foot flood stage of the river. The 1937 flood, however, rose to 71 feet and citizens can still find mud to pick out of attic corners. Recently, it's become a tourist attraction. During the city's susquecentennial, the city painted over a hundred five-foot white stars on the "river side" of the wall. Now, when famous natives return to town, they are hoisted by the fire department ladder truck to an ascending star and directed to autograph in large script. The ceremony is attended by the city's colorful, sashed, robust mayor, Franklin Gerlach, Portsmouth's biggest booster, whose "Forgiveness Campaign" was written up in The *Wall Street Journal*. "Mr. Gerlach, a lawyer who owns three Rolls-Royces," it said, "has launched a full-blown media campaign. Billboards about town tout forgiveness as the 'key to a prosperous Portsmouth'. Citizens are laughing more, he says. And, he reports, one divorced dry cleaner is considering forgiving her former husband and remarrying him." Three stars have already been signed and to see them, walk south on Court Street through the entrance to the Landing, turn around and look up. High above are the signatures of country music star Earl Thomas Conley; opera singer Kathleen Battle; and professional ex-Pirate ballplayer, Al Oliver. Roy Rogers and Dan Quayle (he was supposedly christened in a Portsmouth church) are on the list of invitees.

ACCESS — It may seem a small thing, but it's funny how simple choices create complex results. Second Street runs into Chillicothe, the main north-south street of Portsmouth. By staying to the left on 2nd, turning left onto Chillicothe is a simple matter. The heart of the business center will appear. By staying to the right on 2nd, you will, in a matter of seconds, be swiftly ushered over the skinny U.S. Grant Bridge to an entirely different land of trees, hills and highway...Kentucky. It's a disorienting move with only one benefit. On the return trip, there's a great view of the flood wall.

THE LEADING LADY/PORTSMOUTH — This shop was opened years ago by the mayor's wife, Cynthia, which now, we suppose, makes The Leading Lady synonymous with The First Lady. She had a strong affinity for Royal Doulton figurines and, as one very expensive piece of porcelain led to another, her collection got so large that the Royal Doulton representative suggested she have an open house. The last remaining heir to the Doulton family was invited, and as he neared Portsmouth, inquired in his most reserved British tone whether the patronage would be coming in by farm tractor. In the end, *how* they arrived didn't matter. They sold more Royal Doulton products on that one Sunday than Marshall Fields of Chicago did in three days. The store also carries Royal Crown Derby, Lladro, Cybis and Goebel and has a habit of keeping its customers' purchases very confidential. After all, what a lady does with her "pin" money is entirely up to her. *620 Chillicothe Street, 614/353-0700. Mon-Sat 10:30-5. Closed Sun.*

MUSEUMS/PORTSMOUTH — The **Southern Ohio Museum and Cultural Center** *(825 Gallia Street, 614/354-5629. Tu-Fri 10-5; Sat-Sun 1-5; Closed Jan & Aug)* is in a beautiful old 1918 bank building with interior columns and mezzanine still intact. Traveling exhibits from the Smithsonian, Ohio Historical Society collections, and Carl Ackerman photos are some of the changing exhibits. It's airy and classy, has a wall of things for sale and the feel of a big city museum. Just down the street is its alter ego, **The Murray Military Museum** *(950 Gallia Street, 614/354-8899. Open Fri-Sat Noon-6)*, the results of private collector, Bill Murray of Newton. Murray has collected several thousand military uniforms from all over the world that date from 1776 to the present. It's become known nationwide as the largest collection of its kind, is presently worth about $4 million, and Murray's expansion plan includes tanks, transports, and large weapons to add to the medals and equipment already there. Don't wear anything magnetic. You may never get out.

TOURING/PORTSMOUTH — The Post Office on Gay Street is probably closed by now, so you can't see Donald Gordley's private collection of **Roy Rogers' memorabilia** *(610 Gay Street, 614/353-5203 or 614/353-0900. By apointment)*. It's too late in the day to take a tour of the **Mitchellace Shoestring Factory** *(830 Murray Street, 614/354-2813. Tours by appointment)* farther down the street. And to be honest, it's too late in the season for the April tour buses that head to **Koenig's Tulip Farm** *(714 Diehlman Road, McDermott 45752, (614/372-4392. April-early May, 9 -6 . Call before you make the trip and get a "bulb check")* up north on Route 1 in McDermott, where 74-year-old Arthur Koenig has planted eight acres of bulbs to give thanks for his second chance of life when he was legally dead for forty-six minutes after a heart attack. And it's too early in the season to join the thousands of tourists who pour into Portsmouth waiting for the sun to go down so that they may head to **Rudd's Christmas Farm** *(1205 Cassel Run Road, Blue Creek 45616 513/544-3500. Day after Thanksgiving-Dec 21; 5:30pm-10:30pm)* in Adams County to see over 190,000 lights and 150 figures covering hills and valleys and telling the *true* Christmas story. So, before heading west to pick up your things at Shawnee State Park Lodge, it's up to you if you want to hang around another day, grab a hot dog at **Ron Nichol's Hot Dog Stand** *(Corner of Gallia and Chillicothe. Open 9-4 or 5, depending on whether conversations have been exhausted)*, see the **1810 House** *(1926 Waller Street, 614/353-6344 or 614/354-3760. May-Dec, Sat & Sun 2-4 or by appointment. Special Christmas displays)* that houses Julia Marlowe's costumes, the actress born over a Portsmouth saloon who played in more Shakespearian plays before more people than anyone in history, or head over to State Route 239 to the oldest house in Scioto County, the **Phillip Moore, Jr. Stone House** *(614/353-5605. By appointment only)* on the tow path of the Ohio-Erie Canal where one stone has the inscription, "D. Boone 1771". Certainly now, well-posed and nourished, it is time to ride the landscape downstream on what was once a mere Indian trace, then a road, then a major highway to Cincinnati, and, after a better one (State Route 32) was built to the north, became, once again, just a road.

BUENA VISTA — The first village past Friendship is the length of a football field. Vic's Grocery is in the west end zone, the Buena Vista Little Grocery was, until recently, in the east. They battled for customers with two yellow blinking signs, one saying the Little grocery carried the *Daily Times*, while Vic's held ground with the *Cincinnati Enquirer*. The *Enquirer* is a sure draw this far away from the city. So, with the play called, the traveler goes for the press. Too bad. "We only carry the *Enquirer* on Sundays, honey," says the clerk. "That's when it's got the coupons in it." Vic's, apparently, won anyway. Three dollars buys a sandwich and a drink. *(Vic's, 614/858-*

9903. Mon-Sat 7am-9:30pm; Sun 8am-9:30pm.)

ACCESS — U.S. 52 swells and curves as it plays hide and seek with the Ohio. The hills to the north separate the lowlanders who live in these tiny road towns from the flatlanders who are regarded as everyone north of the hills. The hills were once covered with grapevines, an extension of the industry begun by Nicholas Longworth of Cincinnati. Disease killed them off and tobacco replaced them. The towns themselves were almost all part of the underground railroad stations that helped transport slaves to freedom in Canada. A rest area with a hand pump that says "safe drinking water" makes a good stop to eat Vic's sandwich. There's a long view of the valley with fields that stretch to the Ohio. The hills of Kentucky take on a purplish hue in the fall late afternoon, and hints of a spectacular sunset are in the atmosphere to the west. But the most striking mental image is of slaves escaping across the river. This yo-yo effect between past and present makes U.S. 52 a schizophrenic ride. Beyond Rome is the giant **Killen Electric Generating Station** that takes up acres of land and horizon with miles of chain link fence. Next thing you know the **Buckeye Station Historical Marker**, a mere pull-off on the north side of the road, appears. In 1940, Indian graves could still be seen on the plateau above, but, if willing to make the climb, one might see the remains of a house that in 1797, General Nathaniel Massie built because, well, he just relished the view. It's said to be the oldest continuously lived-in house in the state. That is until now, unless you want to count the squirrels.

MANCHESTER — The fourth white settlement in Ohio and the next town west, it founded by General Massie in 1791. The town that is most well-known presently for its bars and dance floors had, in 1940, a button factory, a garment factory, and a bakery that delivered 12,000 loaves of bread daily and, in the last decade of the nineteenth century, had showboats and riverboats pulling up to its wharfs. As with all of the towns along U.S. 52, its river town status changed with its way of life. Ranked now as a road town, it, and the rest, for better or worse, will remain the same.

 MOYER VINEYARDS WINERY & RESTAURANT/MANCHESTER — For Ken Moyer, a vigorous, white-haired, goateed gentleman in his 70s who usually gets his way, that's just fine. When he left Mexico City 18 years ago in search of a new challenge, he came upon an old truck stop just west of Manchester that was filled with pool tables and pinball machines. It sat on a 60-acre tract along the Ohio River. He bought it within 15 minutes. His wife, Mary, saw it after the deal was closed. His consolation to her was that they'd work on the house first, but the tiny restaurant opened soon after and on the first day one girl ran the kitchen and Ken ran the front end. They had only three or four things on the menu, but business was so good that the second day he spent trying to hire more help. (Only one thing still remains from the first menu – a delicious cheese, bean and bacon soup sprinkled with Parmasan cheese.) Meanwhile, Ken built a 12,000 gallon winery to accommodate his acres of grapevines and today, in season, the whole operation includes Ken and three more in the winery and Mary and 30-plus people working the gourmet restaurant that seats 150. That

Moyer Vineyards bottles 30,000-50,000 bottles in a year and feeds local as well as international diners, has become a travelers' destination point, is history. The fact that it's on U.S. 52 is sheer good fortune. *2957 U.S. 52, 513/549-2957. Mon-Th 11:30-9; Fri & Sat 11:30-10; Closed Sun. Moderate. V, MC, Discover.*

SIDE TRIPS — Aberdeen's mark was made on the Ohio map when it became the terminus of Zane's Trace, the first continuous Ohio road southwest from Wheeling. It had a hundred years of healthy river economy as it played sister-city to what was then Limestone and what is now Maysville, Kentucky, just across the river. Side trips to **Maysville** and **Washington, Kentucky**, should not be overlooked. Across the Simon Kenton Bridge, Maysville, called the Gateway to Kentucky, has innate charm left over and rescued from its fast food alley. Retail is alive and well. The early 1800s architecture, the cobbled streets, the bookstore, terraced hillsides, the Mason County Museum and 18 active tobacco warehouses — making it the second largest burley tobacco market in the world — are enough of an enticement. Then, as long as you crossed the state line, a five-minute drive south on U.S. 68 through an abysmal twentieth century fast food and commercial district, you find the fossil of a town called **Washington**, a place frozen in time. Were this a guide to Kentucky, lengthy discourse would follow on this place that carries on like nothing peculiar is happening here. So trust is the key word. Just go. For here, four miles up a buffalo trace where Simon Kenton bought land for 50 cents an acre, are log and chink buildings that are the present-day post office and Washington Branch bank. And where, in 1829, the Postmaster General planned a mail stage route that went from Zanesville to New Orleans that the UPS drivers use, and men in blue mechanic shirts fix lawn mowers in open barns on the main street as if the blacksmith was just off taking a lunch break.

The Baird House

THE BAIRD HOUSE BED & BREAKFAST/RIPLEY — Just eight miles down the road, Ripley has been described as "a wonderful heap of burnished bricks and rooftops and towers caught between a mountain and a river, ironically preserved in a flood district where it is unlikely any expansion will ever occur other than the river itself." It also had no place to spend the night unless you counted the city jail. But Ripley is enjoying a renaissance of sorts and two Bed & Breakfast homes are well worth the stay. Those travelers who like U.S. 52 so much that they'd like to sleep practically *on* it should stay at The Baird House Bed and Breakfast, occupied in 1849 by a Civil War paymaster of that name and kept in the family for 100 years. It sits right on the edge of the highway in downtown Ripley and the second floor rear porch has a view of the river. It mixes an eclectic collection of the present owners' homey taste with the regal splendor of its past owners' pocketbook. The end result is a sense of warmth and comfort and a six-course gourmet breakfast prepared by owners, Glenn and Patricia Kittles. They've had guests from 17 countries who find the B&B by chance while traveling "the blue roads" across America. And late into the evening the sound of Pat on the organ and Glenn on his saxophone wax and wane through the summer air for guests so musically inclined.

201 North 2nd Street, 513/392-4918. $60, $70, $80. No credit cards.

The Signal House

THE SIGNAL HOUSE BED & BREAKFAST/RIPLEY — By contrast, sounds coming from this home so close to the river that you could catch breakfast by casting a line from a second story window, are the lyrical tones of Betsy Billingsly. Her good nature and bubbly laugh echo off the 12-foot-high ceilings of the 1830's Italianate home that once had to endure the humiliation of being rowed *over* by some local boys during the 1937 flood. These boys are now the men who work next door in the tobacco warehouse and who, undoubtedly, eye the evolution of the Signal House skeptically, as there are no guarantees that they wouldn't get to do it again. Betsy is not nearly as pessimistic. The Signal House is, perhaps, even more pristine today than when it was used to signal to Reverend John Rankin, by lantern in the attic skylight, that the waterfront was safe to lead slaves to freedom. Request the front room with the four-poster (you can watch the river from bed) and, after dark, try not to fall asleep until you see the lights of at least one barge glide by. In the fall, with the windows still open, waking up to the distant sound of river traffic, a Kentucky rooster, and fish jumping by the dock below, is a close encounter with *Gone With the Wind*, Buckeye-style, and there's still Miss Betsy's breakfast waiting for you downstairs.

234 North Front Street, 513/392-1640. $68/river view, $58/other. No credit cards.

Old Piano Factory Forte

TOURING/RIPLEY — By now, it appears that traveling U.S. 52 is nothing but a preoccupation with repose and repast. This, happily, is largely correct. The rebirth of Ripley, however, does offer several things to do between breakfast, lunch, dinner and bed. First, stop by the **U.S. Shoe Factory Outlet Store** *(One mile east on US52, 513/ 392-4630. Mon-Sat 10-6; Sun 1-6)*. The U.S. Shoe Factory recently closed, but you can buy $70 shoes for $20 at the outlet. These, you then take to **The Old Man at Ripley** *(113 Main Street, 513/392- 4221. Daily except Tu & Wed 9-5)*, who will make you a leather purse, or leather anything, to match. If you shop in the afternoon, stay in downtown Ripley for the morning and visit several fine antique stores. Make sure you get to the **Olde Piano Factory Antique Mall** (307 North 2nd Street, 513/392-9243. Mon-Sat 10-5; Sun 12-6). The Ohio Valley Piano Company manufactured grand and upright pianos here from 1870-1885. The dealers in this building have interesting and high quality merchandise, including several pianos for sale.

COHEARTS/RIPLEY — In the fall, the sunset from a second-floor screened porch on Front Street is romantic and soothing. Four tables overlook the Front Street dock. Alas. It's time to eat again. JoAnn May and Roberta Gaudio, the two sisters who own Cohearts Restaurant, worked two years shoveling out pigeons, cleaning and restoring the 1840s house. They left Cincinnati to find a sense of home, community and neighborhood and found instead the hard task of trying to bridge the gap between natives and newcomers. No one can deny their good intention, hard work, freshly baked bread, fresh house dressings and pasta specials. They would like to have the locals feel at home here, but there is an air of speciality in the polished wood floors and freshly painted walls, quite unlike the Dairy Yum-Yum where a recent mayor held court. And so the town brings *their* visitors who, in turn, tell *their* friends, until pretty soon, on a weekend night, the entire two stories is filled with travelers and the multilingual twangs of Kentucky, West Virginia, Ohio, and an errant U.S. 52 traveling Swede. On the porch, as the sun sets behind the Kentucky hills, tall candles in brass candlesticks cast a warm glow over the Brownie Pie. Bring your own bottle.

18 North Front Street, 513/392-4819. Mon 11:30-8; Closed Tu; Wed-Th 11:30-8; Fri-Sat 11:30-9; Sun 11:30-7. Moderate. Cash or checks.

TOBACCO — And speaking of warm glows over things brown, let's mention the warm glow of tobacco dollars over Brown County. Because the **Ohio Tobacco Museum** *(Contact Jim Arnold for a tour. PO Box 61 Ripley, 45167. 513/392-4746)*, a brick Italianate home built by John Espey in 1860 and sitting across from the cemetery on the east side of town, has erratic hours, here are some important notes of interest from within. Almost six million pounds of tobacco get shipped out of Brown County each year. This burley tobacco, first discovered by tenants on a farm near Higginsport, now supplies income to about 9,600 farm quotas in Southern Ohio on 10,000 acres. (Farm quotas today are how many pounds an acre can produce as compared to originally how many acres are produced. Each farm is on a quota that goes back to the history of that farm.) Tobacco gross income to Ohio's tobacco growers in 25 Ohio counties total $32 million. Two hundred man-hours of labor are needed to handle one acre of tobacco. It is painstaking work. Hence, it is, for many, easier to remain on the welfare dole than work in a tobacco field. The **tobacco auctions** in Ripley, the only place in Ohio where tobacco can be sold, begin around Thanksgiving in the four local warehouses, last until February, stand on ceremony and, it's said, are fun to watch. For a different view of how tobacco effects the area, show up for the **Tobacco Festival** *(last weekend in August)*, when people who've never touched a tobacco leaf in their life pack the streets in the name of entertainment.

ASIDE There are some other very straightforward things about Ripley that even the most twentieth century-minded visitor, unable to entirely ignore the plethora of historical markers around town, should assimilate before leaving. While "New Ripley's" residents are pleasant, a few colorful, and one or two, eccentric (Bill Perry, the police chief for 25 years, now retired, once brought in Jesus Christ on a traffic violation and a recent mayor, Roddy Scott, owned a bear cub named Sid, who accompanied the mayor around town in his pickup truck), "Old Ripley's" residents were downright exotic. A visitor once found in the town history, "a professional opera singer, a cannon maker, several politicians, two tightrope walkers, a private secretary to two chief justices of the U.S. Supreme Court, a number of writers, songwriters, manufacturers, inventors, engineers, a World War I flying ace, the first American female hospital physician, a noted educational reformer, and an English immigrant described as 'Ripley's most noted author, linguist, sailor, surveyor, explorer, miner, sheepherder, musician, railroad executive and adventurer'. And, lest we have to be reminded, there is John Parker, ex-slave and Abolitionist, who patented, among other things, the tobacco press, and finally, the famous Presbyterian minister-Abolitionist, John Rankin.

THE RANKIN HOUSE/RIPLEY — The last thing to do before leaving Ripley for the final leg along U.S. 52 to New Richmond is to wind your way up to **Liberty Hill** where Rankin burned the light from his lantern every evening in the Pre-Civil war era border town so runaway slaves could follow the beacon and pick their way to freedom on the Ohio shore. The **Rankin House**, where over 2000 slaves passed, was restored in 1948 and is only open from Memorial Day to Labor Day, so by mid-September, when the gate to the parking lot is closed, there's nothing to do but park on the hill, set the brake, and walk to the small brick house. Chances are, no one else will be there, a nice change for visiting a state memorial. On a clear day, the bends of the Ohio River, the blue hills of Kentucky, and the steeples of Ripley give more weight to people who molded the great events that surrounded their lives. It was here that Harriet Beecher Stowe heard Rankin's story of the slave, Eliza, carrying her children across the frozen Ohio River, and who, after incorporating the story into her book, *Uncle Tom's Cabin*, was supposedly greeted by President Lincoln as "the little woman that wrote the book that started this big war."

J. DUGAN 1830 OHIO RIVER HOUSE/HIGGINSPORT — However, the road west to **LAVENNA** and **HIGGINSPORT** is gently curved and full of long Kentucky vistas. It's soothing, all those trees and hills, and so it's become a natural sport to count the Mail Pouch tobacco barns along the way. A road called Brown, just before the town of Higginsport, leads to the river and a Bed and Breakfast called J. Dugan 1830 Ohio River House. Robert and Pat Costa, serious Florida-based antique dealers by trade, found the empty shell of a house, wanted it badly, and realized for once, here was something they couldn't fit in the truck. So they moved north and spent nine years restoring the Greek Revival home that, with the long brick warehouse, was its own tiny mid-1800 river port on the Ohio. Mr. Dugan was a man who dealt in the commodities of the day, and people would come and store them in his warehouse waiting for the riverboats to pick up and drop off wares at his wharf. Pork, stacked like wood, waited for loading under the now ancient elm tree. Bricks for the house were handmade on the property and after the 1937 flood took out one warehouse that was attached to the back of the home, the bricks were left in a rubble and the warehouse foundation became a walled back yard. The Costas dug through, uncovering and cleaning thousands of them, and built on an addition, three bricks thick, to match the rest of the house. The view, property, home and superior antique collection creates the atmosphere more characteristic of a museum than a B&B, so if you've ever had the desire to sleep in one, know now that the opportunity exists.
4 Brown Street, 513/375-4395.

AUGUSTA — A concentrated look downriver from the Dugan House and you can see the ferry that crisscrosses the Ohio between a dirt parking lot next to U.S. 52 and a landing in **AUGUSTA, KENTUCKY**.

Augusta, like Ripley, is sprucing up for *its* commodity, the import and export of tourists, who come for mystery weekends at the **Lamplighter Inn** *(103 West 2nd Street, 606/756-2603)*, the art galleries and the antique shops. The ferry ride is the last of the great bargains: $1 for walk-ons, $2 for motorcycles, $5 for cars and pick-ups, $5 for RV's, $5 for straight trucks, $8 for tractor trailers. Compare that, if you will, with the ferry ride from Woods Hole on Cape Cod to Martha's Vineyard: $6 for walk-ons and $68, reservation-only, for cars. Why the discrepancy? Ohio and Kentucky charm is cheap.

JOE'S RESTAURANT/NEW RICHMOND — Joe's is a fine terminus to U.S. 52 (though it continues on unceremoniously towards Cincinnati for several more miles) in a town that still has trouble living down its soggy past even though it hasn't had a major flood since 1964. Joe's Place has been on Front Street since 1902, and a strong eyewitness to the river's ups and the town's downs. Bobbie Abbott has been a waitress here for 22 years. Of late, she started coming in at 5:30 a.m. to tend bar for the regulars who come in for shantyboat hash and beer. The previous bartender died after 62 years at Joe's. Like Ripley and Augusta, New Richmond is trying to entice the tourists, so Front Street is getting spruced up, and an antique and ice cream and bakery have opened and the 3rd weekend in August thousands of outsiders flood the town during River Days. At Joe's, Bobbie just wants to cook and feed the customers. And she likes to *please*. One poor fellow would come in regularly and never know *what* he wanted for breakfast. So Bobbie just cooked him one bacon, one sausage, one egg up, one scrambled, one white toast, one rye toast, one coffee, one juice.
100 Front Street, 513/553-3660. Mon-Th 6 a.m.-7p.m.; Fri-Sat 6 a.m.-9 p.m.; Sun 1-8. Inexpensive.

1853 HOLLYHOCK BED AND BREAKFAST/NEW RICHMOND — There's another place for breakfast and that's for the traveler who began at *this* end of U.S. 52. Two turns and one-and-a-half miles up the hillside from the highway, 15 sheep come by the breakfast deck as if on cue at the 1853 Hollyhock Bed and Breakfast. The shepherdess, Evelyn Cutter, acquired her flock to avoid mowing ten acres. As it turns out, the flock prefers the bushes to the grass, so Evelyn still has to hire a man to bushhog the field. Hollyhock's uniqueness lies in its privacy. Only one queen-sized room with parlor and bath is available. Like Shawnee State Park Lodge, then, the veritable task each day will be merely to leave.
1610 N. Altman Road, 513/553-6585.

ACCESS — Having done so, the traveler, now at a beginning or an ending, and either well-fortified or well-versed, has the pleasures of the *best* of U.S. 52, the "eye of the road" so to speak, before or behind him. In the fall of the year, to follow this road, by a broad river, across streams and history, past stuffed tobacco barns and chartreuse fields, through white eyelet sheets and red bottles of wine, over pie and dale, the traveler cannot deny truth – the journey along U.S. 52 feels very good indeed.

A*SIDE* Not only is it cheap, the landscape is so soothingly thick along the next 25 miles that three years after the devastating 1937 flood, the WPA made their American Guide Series and actually included this ride along U.S. 52 as one of its tours mixing history with accounts of devastation, thus offering the traveler a rather macabre ride.

One writer made these observations: "Utopia is a handful of houses strung along the highway...In 1844 Judge Wade Loofborough acquired land here and established a communistic village of 12 families. The enterprise lasted two years before internal troubles...broke it up. It was sold to a spiritualistic community of 100 souls...who made the tragic error of building their living quarter below the high-water level of the river. In December of 1847 the rains came, the flood struck a dormitory, the walls collapsed and 17 people were drowned".

And: "The highway hugs the river to Chilo, a village of tiny frame houses, some a dingy white, some of green and egg-yolk orange, colors favored by the river folk. U.S. 52 stays on higher ground; the village itself hugs the river, so that a person driving down the graveled street in Chilo on a dark night risks toppling over the bank. Of the 55 houses in Chilo only 14 remained on their foundations after the flood."

Now the town has a well-hidden, beautifully manicured park under huge sycamores and maples. Playground equipment, volleyball nets and a boat ramp, and what looks like a park manager's house leaves only Victorian ladies in white dresses and parasols out of the scene. Much of what was left of Neville after the 1937 flood, was scattered over the roads, highway and farm lands.

"In less troubled times Neville was a popular mooring place for the shanty boatman, to whom, by traditional right, belong 'the first three rows of vegetables nearest the river bank, and all the chickens which stray under the bluff.'" Replacing these vegetables and chickens is now the Captain Anthony Meldahl Locks and Dam. This enormous engineering marvel is a educational canal field trip and puts the visitor on the business end of the river. Climb the steps to the observation platform and watch how a lock system works.

Moscow, one of the first Underground Railroad stations and a large producer of brandy, lost what little it had left to the flood. "Of the 90 houses in Moscow, 44 were knocked from their foundations, 112 collapsed and 20 were washed away. Seven store buildings were destroyed, two tobacco warehouses and the post office were displaced, and the town hall was carried off..."

The 1940 tour of U.S. 52 differs from the 1992 tour of U.S. 52 only slightly. While *that* writer spent a lot of time counting houses left on foundations, *this* writer guaged the quality of life along the highway by the distances between meritable places to eat. That means, not much time was spent in **POINT PLEAS-ANT**, where, during the flood, the entire town took refuge in three buildings and the Grant Memorial Church. It still stands. So does the cottage where Grant was born — because the townspeople placed a huge boulder on it to keep it from drifting away.

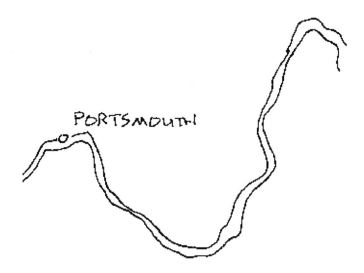

PORTSMOUTH

The Delta Queen

Delta Queen

She is the grande dame of the Ohio and
Mississippi Rivers, the oldest working paddle
wheel steamboat in the world, and a National
Historic Landmark. Her ancestors were the grand
steamers that moved sugar and cotton and transported wealthy plantation owners in extravagant
style. She was born in a Scottish shipyard, had a
reckless youth in California, and matured into a
treasured piece of American history in Cincinnati.
Today, the Delta Queen offers one of the rarest of
vacation experiences — overnight cruises on an
honest-to-goodness paddle wheel steamboat.
¶ Make no mistake, she is a boat and not a ship,
for she was made to travel only on the nation's
interior rivers. A Delta Queen cruise, therefore, is
a very American vacation that takes travelers past
the charming small towns and busy river cities
that lie at the very heart of the country. Though
the Delta Queen is world-famous and has played

hostess to a princess and a president, one crew member says the secret of her popularity is that as a remarkable, floating blend of a first class hotel, gourmet restaurant, and ongoing travelogue, she offers travelers the "three e's" — eating, entertainment, and education.   ¶ Since she is a small boat, passengers get to know the Delta Queen quickly and appreciate the charms of this national icon. Almost inevitably, they fall in love, and people have been known to take twenty and thirty trips on the boat. Though the Delta Queen travels several of the nation's inland waterways, a cruise on the Ohio River between Cincinnati and Pittsburgh is an especially fitting itinerary. Both cities gave her a new lease on life after she served a stint with the Navy during World War II. Pittsburgh provided the "makeover" that restored her beauty; Cincinnati was her home until 1984. In tribute to her Ohio years, the Delta Queen's transom still says "Port of Cincinnati," and thus accompanying her on a trip up the Ohio River is a sentimental journey well worth taking.

THE CRUISES — Steamboatin' vacations on the *Delta Queen* depart February through December from the cities of Cincinnati, New Orleans, St. Louis, St. Paul, Memphis, Nashville, Pittsburgh, and Chattanooga. Cruises last from three to twelve nights, and the assorted itineraries include sights, cities, and points of interest on the Ohio, Mississippi, Cumberland, and Tennessee Rivers. Fares, which will vary depending on the category of cabin you choose, begin at about $250 per person per night, double occupancy, and include all on-board accommodations, meals, and entertainment. Gratuities and charges for beer, wine, liquor, gift shop purchases, and tours on shore are extra. Theme cruises – Dixie Fest, Mardi Gras, Kentucky Derby, Fall Foliage, Old-Fashioned Holidays, and others – are popular vacation options. Arrangements can also be made for steamboat vacations that incorporate air travel to and from most U.S. cities or for deluxe hotel and tour packages in any of the departure cities. Contact the *Delta Queen's* headquarters for information, fares, and reservations.
The Delta Queen Steamboat Company, 30 Robin Street Wharf, New Orleans, LA 70130-1890; 800/543-7637. Personal checks, travelers' checks, all major credit cards.

ASIDE This small glossary of boating terms should help to ease your passage on the *Delta Queen*:

Bow — the front of the boat, which is generally the pointed end and in the case of the *Delta Queen*, the place where they keep the gangplank

Stern — the back of the boat, which in the case of the *Delta Queen*, is where they put the paddle wheel

Port — the left side of the boat as you're facing the bow

Starboard — the right side of the boat as you're facing the bow

Galley — the kitchen on a boat

Head — the bathroom on a boat

Staterooms — passenger cabins named after various states

Main Deck — the *Delta Queen's* first deck, where you'll find the engine room and multi-purpose Orleans Room used for meals, activities, and entertainment

Cabin Deck — the *Delta Queen's* next higher deck, which serves as the boat's lobby and contains most of the public areas and nicer staterooms

Texas Deck — the *Delta Queen's* third deck; tradition has it that this deck got its name because it was added about the time that Texas became a state

Sun Deck — the *Delta Queen's* top deck, where the calliope and Pilot House are located

Chokin' a stump — an impromptu docking of the boat by tying it to a tree along the river bank

THE BOAT — The *Delta Queen* harkens to the heyday of the paddlewheelers, which began in 1811, when the first steamboat, the New Orleans, traveled from Pittsburgh to its namesake city at the mouth of the Mississippi. As the technological descendants of the flatboats that carried the first pioneers westward into the Ohio frontier and beyond, steamboats transported mountains of cargo as well as multitudes of passengers. By 1850, more than 700 paddlewheelers were traveling the Ohio and Mississippi rivers, serving as proud midwives to the birth of the nation's commerce and industry in the nineteenth century. The writings of Mark Twain, of course, immortalized the paddlewheelers and helped make the steamboat era one of the most fabled periods in American history. Today, there are but five authentic steam-powered paddle wheel boats left in the United States, and of those, only the *Delta Queen* and her younger sister steamer, the *Mississippi Queen*, can accommodate passengers overnight. The *Mississippi Queen* is modern – she was commissioned in 1976 – and comes with such comforts as a spa and beauty shop, but the *Delta Queen* is the true queen of the waters, a legendary boat that has been listed on the National Register of Historic Places since 1970. The *Delta Queen* was launched in 1927 at the very twilight of the packet boat era, when a California company that wanted to provide luxury river transportation between Sacramento and San Francisco spent the then-astronomical sum of $875,000 to build her. The *Delta Queen's* steel hull was made at the Isherwood Shipyard in Glasgow, Scotland; the paddle wheel cranks and shaft came from the Krupp factory in Germany; and her four-deck superstructure was fashioned from the finest oak, teak, mahogany, and Oregon cedar. For a while, the *Delta*

Queen was a party boat on the Sacramento River, a floating palace where revelers could legally gamble and drink during Prohibition. But after Pearl Harbor, the Navy drafted the *Delta Queen.* Her shiny white decks were painted battleship grey, and the Navy used her to shuttle troops across San Francisco Bay. Officially, she was renamed *Yard Ferry Boat 56,* but the young soldiers and sailors on board nicknamed her the *U.S.S. Delta Queen.* After World War II, the *Delta Queen* went on the auction block, and she was purchased for the bargain basement price of $46,250 by Captain Tom Greene of the famed Cincinnati family whose Greene Steamboat Company was the forerunner of the *Delta Queen* Steamboat Co. Since the *Delta Queen* had been built for freshwater rivers and not salt water oceans, Captain Greene had to solve the problem of how to safely get her from California to the Mississippi River across the Pacific Ocean and Gulf of Mexico. In the spring of 1947, a novel solution was attempted: the steamboat was boxed in waterproof crating then towed across the oceans to New Orleans. No less than Lloyd's of London insured the venture, which not only succeeded in getting the *Delta Queen* to the Mississippi, but also made her the first – and so far only – paddle wheel steamboat to pass through the Panama Canal. From New Orleans, the *Delta Queen* traveled under her own steam to Cincinnati, where a huge crowd at the Ohio River landing greeted her like visiting royalty. Then it was on to a Pittsburgh shipyard, where the gray paint was stripped away, and within a year, the remodeled *Delta Queen* was prettier than ever – a vision in white with well-appointed cabins and dining rooms ready for overnight passengers. On June 30, 1948, the *Delta Queen* departed from Cincinnati on her first postwar cruise, and she has been taking passengers in grand style on the nation's inland rivers ever since. Like any beauty, the *Delta Queen* cuts a fine figure wherever she goes. Therefore, a few of her vital statistics are herewith presented so that boaters and landlubbers alike can size her up:

Length: 285 feet
Beam (width): 60 feet
Height: 57 feet, five inches to the top of her smoke stack
Paddle wheel width: 19 feet
Paddle wheel diameter: 28 feet
Paddle wheel weight: 44 tons
Displacement: 2,700 short tons
Machinery: Cross compound condensing steam engine with two water-tubed boilers
Fuel: Bunker C oil
Fuel consumption: 11 tons per day
Horsepower: 2,000
Steam pressure: 200 pounds per square inch
Speed: 12 miles per hour (peak); 7 miles per hour (average)
Passenger cabins: 91
Total Passengers: 182
Total Crew: 80

ASIDE The Greene Steamboat Company was started in 1890 by Captain Gordon Christopher Greene, who had the good sense marry Mary Becker. If ever there were a riverwoman, it was Mary "Ma"

Greene, who was as wedded to steamboatin' as she was to her husband. Ma Greene was the first woman licensed as both a riverboat pilot and captain, and she raised her family aboard the steamboats that she and her husband owned. When their river freight business dwindled, the Greenes stayed in business by originating the steamboat vacation: taking passengers on leisurely river cruises complete with lively entertainment and fine food. When her son Tom brought the *Delta Queen* to Cincinnati in 1948, the then-widowed and elderly Ma was the first person to move aboard. She ensconced herself in a stateroom on the cabin deck and spent her time amusing passengers with stories such as how she once beat her husband by an hour in a steamboat race to Cincinnati. Ma died in her stateroom on the *Delta Queen* in 1949, and many folks — including past and present members of the crew — believe that her spirit is still aboard the steamboat. Ma's ghost, they claim, plays the calliope in the middle of the night, turns back the sheets on made-up beds, and haunts her old cabin. Those who doubt Ma's presence would do well to remember the *Delta Queen's* towboat accident. As a staunch Presbyterian, Ma had been less than thrilled when the library on the *Delta Queen's* Texas Deck was replaced by a bar so that passengers could enjoy alcoholic drinks. Several years after Ma died, a towboat hit the *Delta Queen* precisely at the location of the bar and badly damaged it. The towboat was the *Mary B.*, which had been named after none other than Ma Greene.

THE RIVER — The *Delta Queen* affords a unique — and surprisingly pretty — view of the Ohio River. The boat offers not only scenic vistas of towns, farms, and factories, but also a moving perspective on the history, geography, sociology, and economy of the liquid road that for 200 years has been a main artery in the nation's growth and development. The Ohio River begins at the famed "Point" in Pittsburgh, where the Allegheny and Monongahela rivers meet at the apex of the Steel City's triangular downtown. It ends 981 statute miles later at Cairo, Illinois, where it joins the mighty Mississippi. Since Pittsburgh is the benchmark that rivermen use to measure distance on the Ohio, mile 0 of the river is located at the "Point." Colorful mile markers — green triangles and red squares — that can be easily seen from the *Delta Queen* dot the banks of Ohio and indicate the distance from Pittsburgh. The Ohio/Pennsylvania state line is at mile 40; the West Virginia/Kentucky state line, where the Big Sandy River joins the Ohio, is at mile 317; and Cincinnati is at mile 463.5. When the *Delta Queen* departs Cincinnati, she is flying the State Flag of Ohio, but as she heads east toward Pittsburgh, a different state flag is raised whenever she docks in Kentucky, West Virginia, and Pennsylvania. Navigation charts in the Forward Cabin Lounge allow passengers to follow the course of the *Delta Queen* through every bend of the Ohio as the boat winds past the cities and towns that hug the river. Since the Ohio River is significantly higher at Cincinnati than it is at Pittsburgh, the *Delta Queen* must pass through several locks during the cruise, and most passengers find them fascinating. As the *Delta Queen* churns eastward, the urban landscape of Cincinnati quickly gives way to the neat houses and church steeples of small towns on the green and often wooded banks of both the Ohio and Kentucky sides of the river.

Farmers tend crops in the bottomlands, horses and cattle graze on hillside meadows, and a series of brawny power plants with formidable cooling towers give mute but mighty testimony to the economic importance of the Ohio. In the eighty miles between Marietta, Ohio, and Wheeling, West Virginia, the terrain becomes mountainous, and the river narrows. The first factories appear, and the character of the Ohio changes from agricultural to industrial as the boat approaches Pittsburgh and the rounded, rugged foothills of the Alleghenies. Since the Ohio is a working river, towboats pushing barges constantly pass the *Delta Queen,* and very often, you can easily deduce what the barges are hauling. Completely covered barges are probably carrying grain, while petroleum barges have flat tops with lots of pipes peaking skyward. Barges moving anhydrous ammonia are outfitted with refrigeration units to keep the compound cold and liquid. Open barges are piled high either with black coal that is most likely headed for the power plants, with grey riprap used along the river banks as a stony fortification against erosion, or with rusty scrap metal on its way to Japan. Privately owned pleasure boats, of course, are everywhere along the river, but passengers will see runabouts and cabin cruisers most often in the more populated areas such as Cincinnati and the heavy factory belt between Wheeling and Pittsburgh. Boaters seem to be drawn to the *Delta Queen.* They slowly circle the steamboat or pull up alongside as close as they dare, to photograph her and yell out questions — "Where do you live?" "Where are you going?" — to the passengers. Jet skiers come racing out of the river banks and romp like a school of playful dolphins in the *Delta Queen's* broad wake. At the risk of being swamped, some of the more adventurous souls even take their small, open boats *through* the rolling crests of the powerful wake, a bold, into-the-belly-of-the-whale antic that seems to alternately amaze and terrify the passengers cheering them on from the *Delta Queen's* Sun Deck.

THE MYSTIQUE — Even if Mr. Twain had never put his practiced pen to paper and exalted the steamboat, chances are the *Delta Queen* would still be regarded as a great lady on the nation's rivers. Simply put, there's romance in her tall smokestack and cherry red paddle wheel, and the excited cry of "Steamboat's comin'!" still sends people flocking to the river banks just as it did in Twain's time. One of the most pleasurable aspects of taking a *Delta Queen* cruise is that you will never feel more popular, simply because you're aboard that steamboat. Everywhere she goes, the *Delta Queen* gets a wonderful reception. At Cincinnati's Public Landing, people wait on benches or park their cars and watch until she docks. At Maysville, schoolchildren line up on the levee and welcome her by singing "My Old Kentucky Home" in clear, sweet voices, while adults greet debarking passengers with mint julep and lemonade. Motorists and truckers blow their horns when she goes under bridges; passing trains sound their whistles; men camped on Blennerhassett Island for an historical reenactment fire their muzzleloaders in a smoky salute; and one family near Belpre rings a bell and puts up a sign saying "Welcome *Delta Queen.*" At Marietta, the coming of the *Delta Queen* touches off a minor civic celebration. People take blankets down to the river banks, bring a picnic lunch, and spend an afternoon eyeing the boat and those on board. Children wave and shout salutations, and the museums stay open late. When the *Delta Queen* leaves Marietta, everyone gathers on the levee to watch, and even the folks eating underneath the striped awnings at the Levee House Cafe stop their supper to witness her departure and listen to the tunes rollicking from her calliope. The love and respect that the *Delta Queen* elicits along the Ohio River borders on reverence. Not only is she a relic from a precious part of the river's — and nation's — past, but because she has been traveling its waters for almost half a century, generations of river folks have grown up and grown old watching her comings and goings. Her appearance — like the first robin of spring or the last rose of summer — is a both a harbinger and a reassurance that some things — like time, the river, and the turning of her paddle wheel — are eternal. Captain John Davitt says the *Delta Queen* is so beloved that he doesn't worry much about collisions with other boats. "Nobody wants to be known as the person who damaged the *Delta Queen*," he says. "Pilots will do just about *anything* to avoid hitting this steamboat." More than twenty years ago when the Safety of Life at Sea Laws were passed, the *Delta Queen's* wood superstructure and passenger berths almost put her in mothballs until her many fans rallied to her cause. By vote of the U.S. Congress, the *Delta Queen* operates under a special exemption that keeps her on the river, and thus she remains the oldest wooden vessel that carries the American flag.

ASIDE It has been this writer's observation that every queen has her own peculiar wave. The Queen of England, for example, waves from the wrist only in order to create the slightest and most restrained of horizontal hand motions. Beauty queens use a similar movement, but the wave is a more enthusiastic wave since it starts at the elbow and incorporates the entire forearm. The *Delta Queen* wave, however, is the most exuberant of all. It uses the entire arm and is employed whenever passengers wish to convey greetings to passing towboat crews, boaters, lock keepers, or folks on the river banks. To properly execute the *Delta Queen* wave, move your whole arm, beginning in at the shoulder joint, to and fro in a 180 degree arc in front of your body. This broad motion inevitably attracts attention, and your wave will be returned in kind. Shouting "Ahoy!" is optional.

THE ACCOMMODATIONS — Life aboard the *Delta Queen* seems frozen in time somewhere between the Gay Nineties and the Roaring Twenties. It might be because of the ladies in sweeping, full-skirted dresses who greet you as you board; or the banjo players strumming Stephen Foster tunes in the Texas Lounge; or the waiters crisply clad in vests and armbands. From the moment the gangplank is raised, you're removed from modern civilization. There are no telephones or televisions in the cabins. You're notified when meals are ready not by a loudspeaker but by a crew member who walks about the deck subtly tapping on a melodious hand chime. You arrange for a morning wake-up call by writing your cabin number on a chalkboard beside the Purser's Office, and at the appropriate hour, someone not only discretely raps on your cabin door, but also deliver coffee, tea, or a Danish as you've requested. The *Delta Queen* has 91 passenger cabins, all of which accommodate two people and have private baths with showers and views of the water. The kind of cabin you choose determines your fare, and there are seven different categories of cabins that vary in size and amenities. The least expensive are the Outside Staterooms that have either two single beds or a single bed and a berth. The most expensive are the Outside Superior Suites, which offer queen-sized beds and a sitting area. Since the *Delta Queen* is a boat and space is at a premium, none of the cabins can be considered huge, but even the smaller, less expensive ones have fine appointments — hardwood paneling on the walls, brass beds, wall-to-wall carpeting, and stained glass windows. The staterooms on the Cabin Deck are particularly desirable because they have entrances inside the boat and are convenient to the Purser's Office, the Gift Shop, and the Betty Blake Lounge, which has elegant Chippendale furnishings and serves as the boat's formal "living room." The centerpiece of the boat is the Grand Staircase on the Cabin Deck, where you can picture turn-of-the-century ladies in evening gowns floating down the carpeted stairs to have dinner at the Captain's table. The man who built the Grand Staircase supposedly tore it down twice just to get it right, but the resulting extravaganza of rich wood and fancy metal scrollwork was certainly worth the effort. In effect, the *Delta Queen* is a floating luxury hotel. From the exquisite crystal chandeliers that hang in the lounges and dining room to the small brass plaques on the stateroom doors that tell of the famous people — President Jimmy Carter, Princess Margaret, Lady Bird Johnson, Helen Hayes, Van Johnson — who slept there, everything aboard the boat *Delta Queen* is ship shape, having been cleaned, dusted, polished, waxed, and shined to a fare-thee-well. Like any old lady who has been around since the 1920s, the *Delta Queen* has her share of creaky joints. Particularly near the paddle wheel, she shakes and rattles a bit, causing beds in cabins close to the stern to tremble. Yet considering the power being generated by the boilers and the huge pistons that push the paddle wheel's axle, the steamboat is surprisingly quiet. On those still nights when the river is calm enough to reflect the moon and clouds, you can sit outdoors in one of the rocking chairs that line the decks and just relax. All you'll be aware of is the slight splash of the turning paddle boards, an occasional fish jumping in the water, and the fresh scent of lilacs blooming on the shore.

THE FOOD — A *Delta Queen* cruise is a moveable feast during which an ongoing array of gourmet foods is beautifully prepared and flawlessly presented. Since the eating begins at six in the morning and doesn't stop until midnight, you should definitely plan on gaining weight (thankfully, the cabins lack scales as well as televisions). Indeed, this paddlewheeler may well be one of the last places left in America where conspicuous consumption is still accepted — if not *expected* — behavior. A typical day in the culinary life of the *Delta Queen* begins at 6 a.m. with a **continental breakfast** of pastries, assorted muffins, and fresh fruit in the Forward Cabin Lounge. The four-hour-long continental breakfast overlaps the **sit-down breakfast**, which is served in the elegant Orleans Room from 7 a.m. to 9 a.m. At the sit-down breakfast, you can choose either the extensive buffet or order from a menu that includes pancakes, French toast, eggs cooked to order, lox, bagels, fresh biscuits, and custom-made omelettes filled with an assortment of vegetables, cheeses, meats, and seafoods. After breakfast is finished, the menus for lunch and dinner are posted near the entrance to the Orleans Room, where they are served. Both meals feature such a variety of continental, regional, and traditional American dishes that you'll never see the same menu twice during any cruise. **Lunch**, which usually begins at 11:30, offers you the option of either a buffet loaded with main dishes, salads, and desserts, or ordering a four-course meal — soup, salad, entree, and dessert — from the menu. The menu selections range from sophisticated Lasagna Florentine to familiar Southern favorites such as red beans and rice or fried chicken with cornbread. **Afternoon Tea** consists of sweets, finger sandwiches, and light snacks. It is served at about 4 p.m. in the Forward Cabin Lounge. Then in the early evening, **dinner** is an elaborate, five-course affair with each course offering different and tempting items from which to choose. On an Ohio River cruise, you can expect to encounter the following delights at dinner: appetizers that include smoked salmon, frog legs in mushroom sauce, and escargot; soups such as seafood gumbo, black bean, white chile, or cheddar cheese with black bread; Caesar, spinach, and asparagus vinaigrette salads; entrees of leg of lamb, lobster tails, Veal Francais, Fettucine Alfredo, Beef Wellington, or catfish stuffed with crabmeat; and scrumptious desserts consisting of chocolate truffle, Kahlúa crêpes, cheesecake with raspberry sauce, pecan mocha glacé and Cherries Jubilee. The final food fest of the day begins at 10:30 p.m. with the **Moonlight Buffet** in the Forward Cabin Lounge. Every buffet seems to have a different theme — seafood, desserts, Chinese, Italian, Mexican — and you can help yourself to goodies such as shrimp cocktail, egg rolls, enchiladas, sausages in pepper and tomato sauce, blueberry cobbler, coconut cake, and apple torte until 12 a.m. (By then you'll undoubtedly want to retire to your cabin and rest for the food marathon that awaits you on the morrow.) For those folks who must watch what they eat — or have incredible willpower — tasty and imaginative "Heart Smart" selections are available at all meals, so dieters need not feel deprived while everyone else is feasting. Breakfast and lunch have open seating, which gives you an opportunity to mingle with other passengers or snag a window table where you can see the river. Although you will be assigned to a specific table for dinner, you can choose from two separate seatings. The early "A" seating usually begins at 5:45 p.m., while the "B" seating is at 7 p.m. Conservative sportswear is acceptable attire for daytime meals. The evening meal is more formal, but the only time you'll really have to "dress" is when the *Delta Queen* captain hosts his gala **Champagne Dinner**, which is typically held on the last evening of the cruise.

THE SERVICE — Since the *Delta Queen* has a ratio of about one crew member for every two passengers, you would expect the service to be outstanding, and it is. Prepare yourself to be spoiled and pampered. Ice buckets in the cabins are filled every morning; beds are turned down every evening; and sweets are always left on the pillows. The entire crew from Captain to cabin attendants is unfailingly polite, and the mealtime ministrations of the *maitre d*, wine stewards, busboys, bar tenders, waiters, and waitresses are so solicitous that they border on the obsequious. An elderly English passenger happened to mention one evening that he had forgotten his walking stick and was having some difficulty getting about the boat. By the next morning, the *Delta Queen's* carpenter had fashioned a new one for him, complete with the Englishman's initials engraved on the handle. With attention like that, it is no wonder passengers sometimes hope that the boat will break down, just so they could stay a while longer in the lap of luxury, steamboat style.

THE ENTERTAINMENT — Although the food and the shore excursions are diversions in themselves, the entertainment and activities on board never stop. Aside from being a great lady, the *Delta Queen* is a great party. To make sure that the passengers have a good time, she comes equipped with a Steamboatin' Director, an Interlocutor, a Riverlorian, a Texas Lounge Entertainer, and the accomplished musicians of the band known as the *Riverboat Five*. The Riverlorian is a combination tour director, historian, trivia expert, and culture buff who regales passengers with information about the industry, lore and literature of both the river and the towns along its banks. The other entertainers provide passengers with music and amusements from the time they board until they debark. Every evening, there is a different musical show with a different theme – country western, jazz, ragtime – in the Orleans Room, followed by dance music. Since many of the passengers are over 55, the band caters to their tastes and plays a lot of standards and Big Band numbers. One of more popular guest performers is Lewis Hankins, a consummate storyteller who does a fine and witty portrayal of Mark Twain. The singer at the piano in the Texas Lounge performs in the late afternoon and nighttime hours. Daytime activities include bingo, trivia games, sing-alongs, mock steamboat races, and films about the *Delta Queen*. The Captain gives an informative navigational talk, and technically minded passengers can also take tours of the pilot house (which, alas, no longer has a wheel, but does have all manner of intriguing instruments), the boiler room (which is very, very hot and packed tight with equipment), the galley (which is almost as hot as the boiler room and incredibly small for the volume of food prepared there), and the engine room (which is much cooler, smoothly running, and immaculate). Of course, the *Delta Queen's* most obvious and unique entertainment is its steam-operated calliope and the merry tunes – "When the Saints Go Marchin' In," "Dixie," "Take Me Out To The Ball Game – that it produces wherever the steamboat travels. Passengers get at least one opportunity to sit down at the calliope keyboard, and a highlight of each cruise is the Colored Steam Concert, when jets of steam illuminated by pink, yellow, and green lights puff out of the instrument as its being played.

ASIDE The *Delta Queen's* calliope is always played when the steamboat passes by the town of Pomeroy, Ohio. Someone who once worked on the boat now lives there, and the music is the crew's way of saying "Hello."

THE EXCURSIONS — Tours of the towns and sights on shore vary with each cruise and can change because of weather and navigational conditions on the river. Happily, however, they are always scheduled around meal times on the *Delta Queen*, so you won't miss a bite...or a calorie. You can register and buy tickets for guided shore tours from the Riverlorian, but be sure to sign up as soon as possible after you board the boat, because the tours are popular and the limited spaces fill up quickly. The Riverlorian also has maps and background information available for most towns so that you can take a self-guided walking tour or do some shopping on your own. A typical Ohio River trip from Cincinnati to Pittsburgh probably will include stops at Maysville, Kentucky; Blennerhassett Island, West Virginia; Marietta, Ohio; Wellsburg, West Virginia; and, of course, Pittsburgh, Pennsylvania. At the Public Landing in Cincinnati the *Delta Queen* is docked practically in the shadows of Riverfront Stadium and the beautiful blue Suspension Bridge that links the downtown to the green hills of Covington, Kentucky. When the boat reaches **Maysville**, the small Kentucky town with its subtle Southern atmosphere is a subdued contrast to the hustle of Cincinnati. Tobacco has been inspected, shipped, and received in Maysville since 1787, and the town is now the second largest burley tobacco market in the world. Graced by many parks and magnolia trees, the pretty downtown is only a short walk from the river, but you can get a panoramic view that puts the whole place in perspective simply by walking out on the lofty Simon Kenton Bridge between Kentucky and Ohio. Maysville has many old buildings with interesting architecture, the oldest bank in the state, a fine courthouse, and the Mason County Museum, where you can learn

Mason County Museum

all about the town's proud past and the famous folks – frontiersmen Daniel Boone and Simon Kenton, singer Rosemary Clooney, Supreme Court Justice Stanley Reed – who once called Maysville home. Tours to nearby Old Washington, an historic restored frontier village with numerous antique shops, are also available. The *Delta Queen* docks at **Blennerhassett Island*** simply by chokin' a stump on one of the enormous old trees along the river bank. The peaceful island is now a West Virginia state park, but it was once the domain of Harman and

Margaret Blennerhassett, two transplanted Irish aristocrats who led an idyllic life there until they became involved in the land-grabbing schemes of Aaron Burr. You can tour this beautiful and romantic place via a horse-drawn wagon and visit a replication of the Blennerhassett's classic Palladian mansion. As the first authorized settlement in the Northwest Territory, **Marietta*** served as the nation's blueprint for civilized settlement beyond the Allegheny Mountains. This historic town has two outstanding museums – the Campus Martius, which honors the ex-Revolutionary War soldiers who founded Marietta, and the Ohio River Museum, which is the home of the **W.P. Snyder, Jr.**, the last remaining steam-powered paddle wheel towboat. Marietta's levee is the front door to its vintage downtown, and tours – guided or walking – will take you through scenic streets lined with beautiful old homes and interesting shops. **Wellsburg** is in the coal country of West Virginia and the oldest town in the state's northern panhandle. Once a mecca for quick marriages, it has a long manufacturing history, and you can still obtain hand-painted glass – and a glimpse of the glass-blowing process – at the Brooke Glass factory. You can also get guided tours of nearby **Wheeling**, West Virginia, which is noted for its glittering Christmas light festival, neighborhoods of splendid Victorian houses, and magnificent Oglebay Park. A gift to his hometown from industrialist Earl Oglebay, the park has top-notch recreational and resort facilities, an outstanding arboretum, and formal gardens. Mr. Oglebay's grand mansion has been turned into a period museum, and the carriage house now serves as an excellent retail store and museum for decorative glass made in West Virginia. If you're fortunate enough to be aboard the *Delta Queen* when she approaches **Pittsburgh** at night, you're in for a treat. As the boat glides under graceful bridges through the river's velvet darkness, the city ahead dances with sparkling lights spread up and down the steep hillsides and across the downtown "Golden Triangle" where its three rivers join. The tall turrets atop the crystal corporate castle that is the home of Pittsburgh Plate Glass (a.k.a. PPG) glow like beacons in the distance, while the lights of the vertical streetcars known as inclines snake up steep Mt. Washington, where dwellings built on stilts overlook the city. You may even see brilliant fireworks shooting high into the sky above Three Rivers Stadium. Be advised, however, that the fireworks are to celebrate the Pirates winning a baseball game, and the display is *not* yet another rousing welcome for the *Delta Queen*.

*(*For detailed travel information about Blennerhassett Island and Marietta, Ohio, please consult **Particular Places,** volume I.)*

ASIDE Ten tips for first time travelers on the *Delta Queen*:
1. Start a tab so you won't have to carry pocket money on the boat. With a major credit card, you can open an account at the Purser's Office and will be able to simply sign for your tour tickets, drinks at the bar, and gift shop purchases. Before you debark, you'll receive a statement with all the charges.
2. Dress in comfortable clothes and in layers. Temperatures outside on the decks can range from hot in the noonday sun to chilly in the midnight moonlight. Interchangeable slacks, sweaters, and shorts work well. Ladies who pack clothing with pockets where they can stow their sunglasses

and cabin key won't have to be bothered with lugging a handbag around the boat. You'll do plenty of walking on the shore tours, sensible shoes are a must.

3. Bring maps of the states along the route of the boat. You'll be able to track your cruise from your cabin or a deck chair and will have the answer when someone wants to know if that's Ohio or West Virginia off the port bow.

4. Read your daily copy of the *Steamboatin' Times*, an extremely helpful newsletter that not only provides tour schedules and an hour-by-hour account of what is happening on the boat, but also is crammed with interesting information about the places on shore. Better yet, keep a copy with you, so you'll always be on time for activities and won't miss anything.

5. The best place to miss as little as possible is the open bow on the Texas Deck. You can sit outside at one of the tables, get some sun, take in all the shoreline scenery, and still be able to enjoy the jazz and Dixieland being played in the Texas Lounge. Bonus: you're only a few steps away from the lounge's complimentary hot dogs and popcorn.

6. Unless you're unusually attached to them, leave your binoculars at home. The Riverlorian will lend you a pair for the length of the cruise, which means you'll have more room in your suitcase for souvenirs.

7. Mail something, anything from the letterbox located near the Purser's Office on the Cabin Deck. The *Delta Queen* has the nation's oldest moving post office, and your philatelic friends will appreciate the unique *Delta Queen* postmark. Mail a postcard to yourself for a unique souvenir.

8. Buy some of the fake *Delta Queen* money in the gift shop. The inexpensive "doubloons" are highly prized by folks along the river, and you can quickly make friends wherever the *Delta Queen* stops by tossing them from the boat to the wide-eyed children on the levees.

9. Take advantage of the Riverlorian's small library on the Cabin Deck. You'll find many classic novels, travel books, and natural histories about the Ohio and Mississippi valleys that will add significantly to your appreciation of the rivers.

10. Learn what the boat's whistles signify. To wit: One blast — boats are passing each other port side to port side; two blasts — boats are passing each other starboard side to starboard side; three blasts — the boat is backing up; five blasts — danger; six short blasts followed by one long blast — abandon the boat; one long blast followed by two short ones — "hello" or greetings.

Adams County Courthouse

Adams County

No one wants to talk much about Adams County. Like a down-and-out cousin at the family wedding, you hope he eats fast and leaves early, without a pocketful of chicken legs. Adams County's per capita income is the lowest in the state, and more than half the landowners are absentee. And, since public opinion likes to make up its mind and freeze it, until Adams County puts on a good suit, it's always going to get that sidelong glance.   ¶ Silly people. Get over it.
¶ The truth is, Adams County is where small farm owners, clever entrepreneurs, Amish crafts-men, local historians, and far-flung botanists perfectly integrate with farmland and forest and prairie. It is "the country" personified, recog-nized by crackerjack travelers and nature experts alike.   ¶ It has a noble lineage, too. Five of the earth's thirteen different geologic time periods show evidence in Adams County. And it has four physiographic regions. There's the last lump of

dirt from the Illinoian Glacier in the northwestern corner. The Appalachian uplift rises in the east. There's a Bluegrass region in the southwestern triangle and a "little non-descript" region joins the other three. ¶ Through the middle of the county lies a twelve-mile long green corridor created by the Nature Conservancy and the Cincinnati Museum of Natural History to preserve the only place in Ohio where prairie, hardwood forest, oak savannas, and wetlands are within walking distance of one another. It is a place so untouched that new flora and new waterfalls are still being found. ¶ Six groups of prehistoric people lived here. Some left unusual fluted points, some left spear points, some left mounds and most notably, one group left the world's largest serpent. Then it became the Iroquois and Shawnee hunting ground until Nathaniel Massie, American Revolution war veteran, offered land to the first twenty-five families that would help him settle Massie's Station, the future Manchester and the fifth white settlement in the Ohio territory. Thomas Kirker was the first to venture outside the stockade. He became Ohio's second governor and his 1805 home, still standing, remains in the family. The first botanists arrived in the mid-1800s. One, John Locke of Cincinnati, also a physician and instrument-maker, made Ohio's first geologic map, of Adams County, and one of the earliest in the country. General John Hunt Morgan and his raiders galloped through in 1863; 250,000 people attended the 5th Annual World's Plowing Match and Conservation Exposition in 1957; and the Amish decided to resettle here in the 70's. ¶ Actually, it's this "Amish Seal of

Approval" that's infused Adams County with new economy. For where Amish go, good bread and pies and hungry tourists follow. But it's that fecundity of greenspace that begs ecotourism. For where ten forests, parks, and preserves are, a rural adventure awaits. ¶ Exposure is education and education reduces stereotypes. Adams County, once only known for the prehistoric Serpent Mound and unemployment figures, now fuses its history with pie, an unparalleled landscape, and a stellar night's rest. It's a traveling epiphany for the hurried Ohioan and a natural antidote for the judgmental native.

Murphin Ridge Inn

MURPHIN RIDGE INN/WEST UNION — If you're thinking of running away, run here. Listed as one of the top country inns in America, the four-year-old venture by Cincinnatians, Bob and Mary Crosset and landscape architect, Mike Conoway, is Ohio's best kept hideaway. The ten guest rooms, some with fireplaces, are in a striking, contemporary guest house that overlooks the Appalachian uplift to the east. Cathedral ceilings and handmade furniture by the Ohio artisan, David T. Smith, fill the rooms. A full breakfast is included, and lunch and dinners, open to the public by reservation, are served in the 1810 Virginia-style brick farmhouse next door. Washington, D.C., Chef Natasha Shishkevish creates innovative, healthy meals and likes using the local produce. Plan on spending two hours at the table. Upstairs is a gallery that exhibits and sells the work of Adams County artists, but the best all-around display is the hummingbird-like Bob Crosset, an exuberant personality who permeates every air molecule within his radius making Murphin Ridge his personal magnum opas. The poised and composed Mrs. Crosset can only understate, "Living with Bob *is* an adventure..."

750 Murphin Ridge Road; 513/544-2263. Rooms $75. You can rent the entire guest house for $750. Closed Mon & Tu, Christmas Day, all of January and the first two weeks of February. Lunch Wed-Sat 11:30-1; Dinner 5:30-8. Sun 11:30-4. Reservations recommended. Moderate. No credit cards.

DOGWOOD FARM BED & BREAKFAST/WEST UNION — Fern Wilson has the energy of a cheerleader and the culinary skills of a gourmet chef. Combined with a handsome, well-appointed contemporary estate on 62 acres, it makes a worthy overnight stay. There are four lovely guest rooms, one is a suite, two bedrooms have private baths. The second floor view of the pond and thirty acres of woods and hay fields looks like the English countryside and has attracted visitors from overseas as well as Miami University professors hunting tree frogs. But the best view is from close up across Fern's huge kitchen island. As the home economics teacher in the local schools, her tutelage has produced award-winning cakes, pies, and breads at the Ohio State Fair. In fact, in the last five years, her students have won more first-places than any other school in the state. "I can teach anyone to make the perfect pie crust," she says. Not wanting to rest on rising dough, she begins, this fall, Murder Mystery weekends, at the farm, on the first and third weekends of the month. Professional actors and guests gather on Friday night, the murder occurs Saturday — in between Fern's gourmet meals — and guests depart, intact, after Sunday breakfast.

7070 State Route 125; 513/544-5227. Rooms: Weekends $65. Weekdays $50. Murder Mystery Weekends for two including two nights and most meals $200. No smoking. No pets.

The Bayberry Inn

BAYBERRY INN BED & BREAKFAST/PEEBLES – If you miss your mother or grandmother and ache for a good wrap in a quilt and the aroma of eggs, sausage, homemade bread and muffins wafting up the staircase, make a reservation with Marilyn Bagford, Adams County's designated wayside mom. Her pretty, blue, 11-room Victorian has three cozy guest bedrooms filled with lots of quilts, candles, flowers, and books, lending an air of Marilyn-ness to every corner. Guests from Canada, Switzerland, and the West Coast have rejoiced at the hominess, hospitality, and rocking chairs on the front veranda. Marilyn is a good guide to the local attractions and will happily choreograph your day for you...just like mom.

25675 State Route 41N; 513/587-2221. Rooms May-Oct: Double $45. Single $35. Students with parents $12. Under 4 Free. No smoking.

HICKORY RIDGE BED & BREAKFAST/MANCHESTER – This bed and breakfast wins two unofficial awards, first, for the most romance stuffed into and around a small space, and second, for the longest driveway. Hickory Ridge is a dreamy rustic cottage tucked among 150 acres of hickory, oak, and multiple flora and fauna. Sue Bradley lives here, surrounded by distinctive linens and heirloom china and a mountain of meals she miraculously prepares out of a kitchen the size of a hollowed tree. The two bedrooms are upstairs and one leads to the other. So it pays to know all the guests. The most private room looks like it was made for Sleeping Beauty – white carpet; white linen sheets; white, handpainted lamps and tables. The one bath is down-stairs. If you'd like to just take over the whole place, Sue will happily turn over the key. On the other hand, just mention, when making reservations, you'd like to have a full meal, a picnic, afternoon teas or hors d'ourves and snacks, and she will send you a six-page list of menu choices. In the spring the hillsides are covered in wildflowers. The fall foliage will make you weep. You can watch a stunning sunset over the ledges down to the Ohio River. Or, just stay inside and play a tune on the baby grand.
1418 Germany Hill Road; 513/549-3563 or 800/686-3563. The address says Manchester but it's closer to Wrightsville off US247 near the Ohio River. Drive almost three miles east on Germany Hill Road. Turn right at the B&B sign, then it's 7/10 mile on dirt road to the cottage. Rooms: $65. Entire cottage weekly: $350.

MOYER VINEYARDS WINERY & RESTAURANT/MANCHESTER — One of the two (the other is Murphin Ridge Inn) notable restaurants in Adams County, Ken and Mary Moyer's restaurant and winery is already a famous stop on US52. Sixty acres sit along the Ohio River to accommodate the grapevines, the 12,000 gallon winery, and the 150-seat restaurant. Ken bottles between 30,000 and 50,000 bottles of wine a year, enough to feed the locals, the international diners, and the intrepid travelers who drop down from the north to feast on Shrimp Fettucini, Eggs Benedict, Poached Scallops, and Filet Mignon, and wash it down with a bottle of their favorite Moyer wine.
3895 US52; 513/549-2957. Mon-Th 11:30-9; Fri & Sat 11:30-10; Closed Sun. Moderate. V, MC, Discover.

THE OLDE WAYSIDE INN/WEST UNION — This 180-year-old inn, a Blueplate Highway stop on the northeast corner of Main and Cherry Streets (along Zane's Trace), was once The Bradford Tavern and served Andrew Jackson on his way to his inauguration in 1829, Mexican General Santa Anna after his defeat to Sam Houston, and Statesman Henry Clay, likely after a lengthy speech. The food is home-cooked and well-cooked, served cafeteria-style at noon. If you have a liking for whipped potatoes, skillet gravy, old fashioned dressings, homemade noodles, homemade apple dumplings, homemade fruit and creme pies, and history, eat here.
222 Main Street; 513/544-7103. Tu-Sun 8-3. Closed Mon. Inexpensive. V, MC.

BLAKE PHARMACY/WEST UNION — A mild-mannered drugstore outside, Blake Pharmacy on Courthouse Square harbors one of Ohio's few remaining soda fountains and specializes in nickel Cokes, an early

incentive to local schoolchildren who read their library books. That kept Blakes hopping for awhile, but it wasn't nearly as exciting as when 30 or 40 weddings were performed in the sundry and Radio Shack aisle during Bob Blake's tenure as mayor. Bob is still there and will be happy to make you an ice cream soda, malt, shake, or flavored Coke. Flavored Coke is five cents extra...
206 North Market Street; 513/544-2451. Mon-Sat 9 a.m.-8 p.m., Sun 1-5.

FIRST PRESBYTERIAN CHURCH/WEST UNION — The Scotch-Irish were the early settlers of Adams County and their thriftiness shows up largely in the county architecture...there is none. So, in lieu of dressy Victorians and stately mansions, visit West Union's First Presbyterian Church, built of hewn stone in 1810 and the oldest continuously used church in Ohio. The stone mason, Thomas Metcalf, later became the governor of Kentucky. The hefty rope dangling in the narthex rings the church bell. Visitors are welcome.
Corner of South Second and East Walnut Streets; 513/544-2066. Sunday School 9:30, Worship 10:30.

ADAMS COUNTY HERITAGE CENTER/WEST UNION — Originally used as a church, you can hardly tell that the crisp looking, well-landscaped brick heritage center also spent a good portion of its life as a funeral home, with entries widened for caskets and casket-bearing horse-drawn hearses. Like King Tut's tomb, this small center guards the jewels of the county's lifetime, from prehistoric Indian relics, to Nathaniel Massie's surveying equipment (they fought for legal rights to it and removed it from the Warren County Historical Society), to a cornet from the oldest band in Ohio (Liberty Band), to genealogical records, to Sheriff Ben Perry's murder exhibit. Buy a brick ($35) and become a permanent part of Adams County history. Your engraved brick will become an Adams County sidewalk.
Two blocks north of the Adams County Courthouse on State Route 247. PO Box 306, West Union, 45693. Open Th & Sat 12-4.

ASIDE It's appealing to fantasize about taking a very private guided tour of the eclectic Adams County with someone who can entertain, enlighten, and organize 586 square miles of landscape, history, and pie and leave you at day's end simultaneously lighter and heavier. In reality, the person exists but his free time does not. Stephen Kelley has spent half his lifetime collecting, sorting, and synthesizing Adams County. The tangible results are in a collection of ancient Indian relics he has found, bought, or traded, a volume of newspaper columns, four years of his published quarterly, *Ohio Southland*, the formation of the Adams County Heritage Center, and the linguistic talent for informal, painless historical enlightenment. Kelley is the Johnny Appleseed of Adams County, sprinkling stark acreage into life and form with wit and a bagful of charm. Write PO Box 208, Seaman, OH 45679-0208 for information.

COUNTERFEIT HOUSE — If you like "drive-by chillings" wander past the house that Oliver Tompkins built in 1840. It was here that Tompkins made his "funny" fifty cent pieces and $500 bills. Special doorlocks could only be operated by the "right" people, secret compartments hid coins, five false chimneys gave off smoke and were used as spy towers to check on visitors, trap doors and hidden rooms concealed his money-making rooms. Mr. and Mrs. Johnson own it now and still maintain that people were killed at the house. Mrs. Johnson continues to be annoyed by the bloody fingerprints appearing through the painted walls. Human bones discovered in a barbecue pit remain displayed by the front door.
1580 Gift Ridge Road, five miles south of West Union off SR 247 513/549-2309. By appointment only.

KEIM FAMILY MARKET — Seventeen years ago the first Amish family settled in Adams County from Indiana. Roy Keim brought his family from Holmes County five years later. That's how the new brought back the old to Adams County. And since old is in vogue these days, Roy Keim and his family's bakery couldn't be a bigger hit. They're in their 11th year of selling home-baked breads, pies, cookies, and nut breads. Their business, of course, is not electrically driven, it's *personality* driven, by Roy himself, a curbside philosopher, farmer, and gentleman with lots of heart and business soul. Tour buses are regulars at his wooden shelter on the Appalachian Highway. His wife was the original baker but the work's been turned over to his oldest daughter who, with several other Keim daughters spend their days baking the goods at the family farm that are sold the very next day at the stand. During tourist season, Roy's presence behind the counter is required. He's almost as big a draw as the baked goods, cheese, and crafts as he muses about life, culture, economics, his community – kind of an Old Order guru, whose soothing voice and Amish ways calm the hurried masses stopping by.
2621 Burnt Cabin & East Ohio 32; No telephone. You can write to Keim Family Bakery, 2132 Tater Ridge, West Union, 45693. Mar-Dec, Mon-Sat, Daylight hours. Open on most holidays.

MILLER'S BAKERY/WEST UNION — Gerold Miller's father was part of the first generation of Amish who settled in Adams County from Indiana. He raised beef and crops. The children were the ones who started baking and in the old bakery it wasn't unusual to bake for ten or eleven hours. Besides, Gerold liked it better than behind a plow where he'd often fall asleep. Now he's married with a family of his own and his wife's baking skills propelled what was once a small business into an enormous enterprise. In a huge kitchen, the baking starts a 6 a.m. on Friday and Saturday mornings and six or eight people get to work at making 100 dozen glazed donuts, 200 loaves of bread and 200 pies. So the best time to stop at Miller's is on Friday and Saturday. The donuts disappear immediately. The newly remodeled 5000 square foot building holds bulk food, 16 different jams and jellies, homemade crafts and lawn furniture, Texas brand boots, and Minnitonka moccasins. There are days now, Gerold admits, that behind a plow appears to be an attractive option.
960 Wheat Ridge Road, West Union, 45693; 513/544-8524 (between noon and 1 p.m.). Mar-Dec, Mon-Sat, Daylight hours. Most holidays.

ZANE'S TRACE/STATE ROUTE

41 — Cutting diagonally through Adams County is the road generally credited to Ebenezer Zane. Although he did survey and map the route that originated near Wheeling on the Ohio River and went across southeastern Ohio to Maysville, Kentucky, the original path should be credited to bison. Great Plain bison wandered eastward looking for traces between open grassy areas. Salt licks altered their paths, too. Their wandering through this region etched the first path, followed by other game, then Indians, early traders, settlers, important travelers, inns to accommodate them, and finally, asphalt. In 1863, Morgan's Raiders followed Zane's Trace for part of their ride through the county. Watch for these taverns and inns, still standing, but privately owned, along State Route 41: **The Wickerham Tavern (1801)**, just north of Peebles and in the same family until two years ago, is said to be haunted. A coachman was presumably killed and beheaded by the owner for the money he was carrying. His body wasn't found until 1928 when the inn was sold and the basement was torn up to put in a furnace. The new owners found all the bones, minus the head.

The Treber Inn (1793) was built by the local gunsmith John Treber, because so many travelers pestered him for a place to stay. It's one of the oldest log buildings in Ohio and has its own gruesome tale. The skull of local man killed by Shawnee was kept for years as a conversation piece. One night, after peace was declared with the Indians, three Shawnee stopped in, drank heavily, and bragged about killing Ashael Edgington three years before. Later that night, they were shot. The Treber Inn served as an inn and stagecoach stop for forty years.

Governor Kirker's Home (1805) is in its seventh generation of family ownership. He was the first to leave Nathaniel Massie's fort in Manchester and build a home in the Adams County wilderness. Located on the original trace that veers off State Route 41, you can see it at the intersection of State Route 136 and Township Road 12. The hand-hewn stone part of the house was the original home of Ohio's second Governor. Drive up the road a bit farther and see the **Kirker Covered Bridge**, the second-to-last covered bridge to be used in the state highway system, although no longer in use.

Olde Wayside Inn, formally Bradford Tavern (1806) See Olde Wayside Inn/West Union.

Wickerham Inn

ASIDE Adams County Amish are in their third generation. In 1976 there were seven families living on Wheat Ridge Road and in 1989 there were thirty-four families throughout the county. These Old Order Amish are divided into two congregations, Wheat Ridge East and Wheat Ridge West, with church services taking place, by turn, in family homes. The first generation is now in their 50s and 60s and they brought a new life and productive order to an otherwise sagging countryside. They began growing wheat and corn, began a cedar wood business, raised dairy cows, and built homes. Now their children are taking over and bringing in the tourists that bring in thousands of dollars of added income. And where is the first generation? Well, many are off on their own tourist trips. It's not unusual for Mom and Dad to head for Washington, D.C., on an Amish-filled tour bus, while we English do the same to visit those still at home. Wherever they are, they take with them their "highest sense of right" and are living examples of a hopeful future.

AMISH BUSINESSES — Mr. Atlee Hochstetler and four of his five sons buy cedar logs for **The Cedar Works, Inc.,** *19 Cedar Drive.* They make red cedar mail boxes and red cedar shavings for pet litter. Cedar logs used to come from Adams County, but now they come out of Kentucky. When the logs are cut, many go to **Cedar Products,** *180 Measley Ridge Road,* where almost two dozen Amish work with Moses Keim to make thousands of mail boxes and bird feeders for K-Mart and Wal-Mart stores across the U.S. **Aden Yutzy & Sons Cedar Hill Pallet,** *4830 Unity Road,* build wooden pallets for businesses and industry. In 1990 the place went up in flames. The next day, the neighbors cleared everything away by nightfall and they began to rebuild. **Troyer's Quilt Shop,** *1246 Wheat Ridge Road,* is run by Dan and Anna Troyer. It's not unusual to find $700 quilts and $100 wall hangings of excellent quality. They also sell nice oak furniture and Amish crafts. Willis Stutzman owns **Stutzman Carriage Shop,** *1245 Deffey Road,* specializes in restoration of buggies and sleighs as well as repair work on the local buggies. **Raber Shoe Shop,** *5212 Unity Road,* is run by Roy and Betty Raber. Their work started as a sideline to hog farming. They sell name brand shoes, running shoes and straw hats. **The Harshaville General Store,** *6766 Graces Run Road,* **and the Harshaville Repair Shop,** *6688 Graces Run Road,* are run by Atlee and Emma Hershberger. They fix buggy wheels and do general repair and sell bulk products. Emma works on quilts and sells home-made jellies and jams, simple toys, yard goods and baked goods. Emery (Junior), Mary Stutzman and family own **Hillcrest Farms Green-house,** *2260 Bailey Road.* They do general farming, raise hogs and shoe horses in the blacksmith shop. The greenhouse raises flowers and vegetable plants.

ANNUAL WHEAT RIDGE AMISH SCHOOL CONSIGNMENT AUC-TION AND SALE — You can hear the bidding over the hills for miles when, in the fall, the Adams County Amish hold their most impressive event. In its 17th year, the auction raises money to support their private schools. The fields and barns along Wheat Ridge Road are filled with Amish buggies and tourist vehicles. The big pole barn at the

Cedar Hill Pallet Company has its basketball hoop raised and Rumpke Port-a-Potties stand guard outside. The rolling fields across the street are lined with buggies and spotted with collections of things for auction. The schedule runs something like this: small items at 9 a.m.; small animals at 10 a.m.; antiques and furniture at 10:30 a.m.; quilts, harness tack, and horse-drawn equipment at 11 a.m.; horses at 3 p.m. One half of the huge pole barn is devoted to about 115 handmade quilts hanging on clotheslines strung back and forth so potential bidders can get a good close look at the patterns and stitch quality. The auction goes quickly so write down your numbered choices and be prepared to let go of some sizable coin. If you'd rather spend your money on Amish baked goods, get in line at the other side of the barn where hundreds of loaves of breads and an Amish lunch of pressed meats and cheese will round out a day and a waist.
4830 Unity Road. September.

LEWIS MOUNTAIN HERBS & EVERLASTINGS — The Amish aren't the only big tourist draw in the county. John and Judy Lewis have been growing herbs and everlastings (the "now" term for dried flowers) for almost 15 years. Their modest beginning has expanded to eight acres and six greenhouses. In the spring they sell over 150,000 live herbs in three months in Ohio, Kentucky, Indiana, and West Virginia. They carry over 600 varieties of herbs and everlastings and all are available if you stop by in the spring. The gardens contain over 60 varieties of scented geraniums. The grounds, greenhouses, gift shop, and Melrose apple gazebo are host to a couple of tour buses a week, garden club meetings, and an occasional wedding. It's a sensated oasis and the perfect stop for the blossom-loving hikers who are forbidden to touch the flowers in the 11 Adams County preserves.
2345 State Route 247, Manchester. (The Manchester address is misleading. It's just south of West Union.); 513/549-2484. Mon-Sat 9-4. Closed Sunday. Call about group tours and craft classes.

OLDE THYME HERB FAIR — Over 4000 people show up at Lewis Mountain in the fall for two days of summer harvest. There are over 50 booths by herb clubs, herbal related antiques, Amish crafts and food, herbal snacks, the Fire Department's Pig Roast, The Adams County Liberty Band, Peach Mountain's Bluegrass Boys, the Adams County Cloggers, and enough herbs and everlastings to heal, spice, freshen, and decorate unbounded floral cravings. Arrive with an empty car trunk.
2nd Weekend in Oct, 10-5. Other exhibitors welcome. Call 513/549-2484.

EDGE OF APPALACHIA — As Adams County struggles under a black economic mist, there lies on the east side of Ohio Brush Creek a land unique, beautiful, and *protected*. It's an Ohio Galapagos, so-to-speak, where the unbridled enthusiasm of botanists collides with about 75 potentially threatened, threatened or endangered species and where the rare Allegheny wood rat, mollusks, and green and four-toed salamanders live on where farmers couldn't. Here, at the very brim of the Appalachian Plateau, are 11,000 acres protected by the Cincinnati Museum of Natural History and the Nature Conservancy. They cover a 12-mile long, north-south stretch of land, the largest privately owned

group of nature preserves in the state and a whopping piece of real estate for Chris Bedel, director, to keep an eye on. Bedel works for the Cincinnati Museum of Natural History and lives in a cabin year round. He's the guy who chases motorcycles off, does PR, creates a budget, deals with illegal dumping, writes the grants, raises money, repels root diggers, and runs 11 sessions of summer science camp. It helps to be 29, enthusiastic, and in good shape. But he's always looking for volunteers to help make trails, do repair work, check for unwanted debris, or share a spontaneous wonderment.
For more information write: Edge of Appalachia Preserve, 19 Abner Hollow Road, Lynx, OH 45650; 513/544-2880.

The Preserve system offers **two public access sites**. That means they may be visited *without* permission. Understand that the Preserves exist for research, education, passive recreation and preservation, so please stay on the paths and *don't pick or dig the flowers.* Save the picnic for Adams Lake State park two miles north of West Union on SR41 and Shawnee State Forest, 10 miles east of Lynx on SR125.

BUZZARD ROOST ROCK – This 75 X 81 X 36 foot block of Peebles dolomite attracts more people for the view than for the 21 species of plants upon it. Almost trampled to death, the flora is now protected by a wooden walkway and deck made by volunteers who carried 296 unassembled pieces of treated lumber to the top of the roost. Originally called Split Rock Hill by the early settlers of the 1700s, it got its new name for the turkey and black vultures who are often seen roosting there or flying overhead. The rock rises 500 feet above the Ohio Brush Creek Valley. The trail to the rock is a shade less than three miles round trip with just one huffing and puffing hill.
Take State Route 125 east towards Lynx. Turn left on Weaver Road to parking area (north side of State Route 125). Trail then crosses State Route 125 heading south and zigzags. Watch for sharp right turn in path to the rock.

LYNX PRAIRIE — The best time to visit is during July, August, and September when the prairie is in full bloom. The best way to under-stand it is through an interpretive tour. But if you merely want to experience the romance of your pioneer forbearers, try this: Put on jeans, hiking boots or sturdy tennis shoes, insect repellent (chiggers and ticks can be aggressive) and sunglasses. Bring a canteen and camera. Let your sentimental journey begin. Look for signs of over 250 plant species on these ten prairie openings, some of these yawnings no bigger than a livingroom. Watch every step you take to avoid crushing something rare. When you get home, take a hot, soapy shower or bath to get rid of the chiggers and ticks. Envision your pioneer forbearers with a cold, soapy bucket of water and no calamine.
Take State Route 125 east through Lynx. Take the first hard-paved road to your right, Tulip Road. Go 1/2 mile to East Liberty Church on the left. Turn into the drive and go past the church to the cemetery. The trail begins beyond the headstones.

ADAMS COUNTY NATURE YIN AND YANG — Seven different agencies own numerous different natural areas (including Edge of Appalachia). What's legal at one will get you arrested at another. So, before you dig for ginseng, hunt for squirrels, collect fossils, or pick a plant, call these numbers for a set of rules and directions:

Adams Lake State Park (614/858-6652). This day-use park offers fishing, picnicking, hiking, and boating (no gasoline engines). If you visit between May 29 and September 26, stop in at **Flamingo Ice**, a tidy flavored-ice stand by the entranceway. It's owned and run by a pleasant high school student, Christopher Beam. Chris offers 30 flavors of refreshment. $1 regular quenches the thirst from a good hike.
North of West Union on State Route 41. Dawn to dusk. Flamingo Ice: Mon-Sat 3-10. Sun 3-9.

Adams Lake Prairie State Nature Preserve (513/544-9750). Adjacent to Adams Lake State Park, these 25 acres have two, short, loop trails. Post Oak Trail goes through the forest. Prairie Dock trail goes through the xeric Prairie Remnant which includes fourteen species of rare prairie plants.

Edwin H. Davis State Memorial (614/297-2633). Scientists from all over the world have visited the 88-acre Davis Memorial. There are caves, rugged cliffs, rich forests, prairie openings, even a sink hole. There are two trails plus a portion of The Buckeye Trail.
Southeast of Peebles off of Davis Memorial Road.

Shawnee State Forest (614/858-6685). Here's a handsome piece of forest that covers mostly Scioto County but spills into Adams nonetheless. Together, there are 62,00 acres, 8,000 designated as a wilderness, meaning no motorized vehicles and no timber harvesting. There's 60 miles of hiking and 70 miles of bridle trails with hitching posts for overnighters.
Follow Churn Creek Road to the farthest southeast corner of the county.

Tranquility Wildlife Area (513/372-9261). 3,818 acres of public hunting, fishing and hiking.
Northwest of Tranquility between State Route 770 and State Route 32.

Brush Creek State Forest (614/372-3194). Hiking, picnicking, and horseback riding predominate this 12,000-acre day-use park. It has a nice hardwood forest and one public hiking trail and is usually thick with deer hunters in open season.
State Route 73 South, about five miles south of State Route 32.

Chaparral Prairie State Nature Preserve (513/544-9750). One of the least known nature preserves, this 66 acres is spotted with prairie vegetation and mixed forests. It has one three-quarter mile loop trail called Hawk Hill Loop. Stay on the path. Private land is interwoven.
Three miles northwest of West Union on Hawk Hill Road, just off of Chaparral Road.

MUSEUM OF NATURAL HISTORY SCIENCE CAMPS – There's a camp for adults rated R for relaxing and one for teens and pre-teens rated E for exhausting. Because the Edge of Appalachia Preserve is largely closed to the general public, this is an opportunity to observe its natural minutia first hand. (Ask specifically about the **Swirl Hole** and **Cedar Falls**.) Sessions last for five days and are limited to 12 campers. You get to stay in the lovely, stone Rieveschl Chalet and sleep in nice bunks. Chris Bedel, and an assistant, cook all of the meals. Adult sessions begin on Friday afternoon and end on Monday evening avoiding interrupting work schedules. It's a unique opportunity for the novice and serious amateur botanist. In between bird walks, hikes, fossil hunts, owl calls, and prairie walks, Chris likes to schedule at least one meal at the Murphin Ridge Inn. The Spring Camp is a study in phenomenal wildflowers and returning spring birds. The Fall Camp is for foliage lovers. Pre-teen camps satisfy lots of healthy curiosities. The large telescopes are pointing at the stars, not the neighbors' windows.
Address all inquiries to Chris Bedel at above address. Adult camp $165. Includes four days food and lodging and transportation from Cincinnati. Teen and Pre-teen camps $185. Includes five days food and lodging, transportation from Cincinnati, plus t-shirts.

BUCKEYE TRAIL — The Buckeye Trail is 1,200 miles of Sherwin Williams' #2408 "Sweeping Blue" paint blazes circling inside the Ohio borders. According to the very specific manual for Buckeye Trail Maintenance Volunteers, a hiker should be able to see the double blazes and access blazes looking forward and backward from any point. And, on each off-road stretch, the trail should be a "pathway with sound footing, reasonably free of vegetative hindrances and at least three feet wide." There are 24 detailed section maps and two of them are in Adams County – 4 miles in the Sinking Spring Section and 59 miles in the West Union Section. Both spill over a bit into surrounding counties. The maps are wonderfully detailed with markings for campsites and points of interest. We recommend the **Sinking Spring Section**. It's loaded with history as it winds through the Serpent Mound, the ghost town of Louisville, across Ohio Brush Creek, through the ghost town of Marble Furnace, down Zane's Trace, past the Wickerham Tavern, through the Davis Memorial Nature Preserve (88 acres), along the shoreline of Mineral Springs Lake (largest privately owned lake in Ohio), past the entrance to the General Electric Proving Grounds, into the ruins of the former resort town of Mineral Springs and ending at the remains of the 1900 Wamsleyville grist mill.
Contact: Buckeye Trail Association, Inc., PO Box 254, Worthington, OH 43085.

SERPENT MOUND STATE MEMORIAL — Now listed as one of the ten most endangered sites in the United States, perhaps this is a good time to visit the Serpent Mound, before a 1,100 acre man-made lake and convention center appear. The 1,348-foot Serpent Mound's been around, likely, since 800 B.C. when the Adenas built their conical mounds nearby. It's been owned and protected by the Ohio Historical Society since 1900. The history versus economics fight has just begun. Adams County tops the state with a 18.3 percent unemployment rate and sees money and jobs in the housing and recreational development. OHS sees several thousands years of historical mysteries sinking to the bottom of a lake. In the middle is the Army Corps of Engineers, permit holders for a dam. This could be a lesson in favor of county zoning. (For more history of the Serpent Mound, see *Particular Places, Volume I, p. 72.*)

3850 State Route 73, Peebles; 513/587-2796. Apr-mid-May: Park, Sat & Sun 10-7; Museum, Sat & Sun 10-5. Memorial Day weekend-Labor Day: Park, Daily 9:30-8; Museum, Daily 9:30-5. After Labor Day - October: Park, 10-7; Museum, Sat & Sun 10-5.

GENERAL ELECTRIC AIRCRAFT ENGINE PEEBLES OUTDOOR TEST FACILITY

— Maybe, several thousand years from now, scientists and tourists will wander through what was once Adams County, ponder the remains of jet engines, and their test cells, and wonder if they demand a genuflect. Right now, this very private "Steelhenge" sits on 7000 acres of thickly wooded land in eastern Adams County that includes a stocked and fed wild turkey game preserve. In 1955, GE carved out a $120 million star wars facility with eight simulating test cells and 60,000 square feet of assembly space for 225 employees to test an average of 250 airplane engines each year. And test they do. On certain nights this northeastern point of Adams County lights up like an Appalachian aurora borealis. If you're within earshot, the sound is like a tornado. Why? Because someone has to test these engines *before* they're attached to the planes. So they reproduce conditions that might adversely effect an engine in flight like: hail, monsoon rains, dust or sand, severe ice, and, *gulp*, flocks of birds. Besides a Pratt-Whitney engine testing ground in Florida, this GE Proving Ground, a federally regulated industry, is the only one in the U.S..

They have an Open House every year or two. It's announced in the local newspaper, The People's Defender, or write for information at GE, attention Dave Lane, 1 Neuman Way, N-109, Cincinnati, Ohio 45215-6301.

RUDD'S CHRISTMAS FARM/BLUE CREEK

— GE isn't the only thing that lights up the county's nighttime skies. One-half million Christmas lights radiate quite a glow. For 22 years Carl Rudd has been quietly stringing Christmas lights through the woods around his farm in an effort to illuminate the life of Christ from birth to ascension. We suggest he's succeeded and so do the enormous crowds that take the 35-minute walk down the lighted path. Dress for the weather and wear non-slick shoes. More fun than a weeping Madonna on a water tower.

1205 Cassel Run Road; 513/544-3500. Take State Route 125 East to Blue Creek Road. Turn west onto Cassel Run and drive to the end of the road. There's a gravel parking lot. Open the day after Thanksgiving to Dec 21; 5:30-10:30. Donations appreciated.

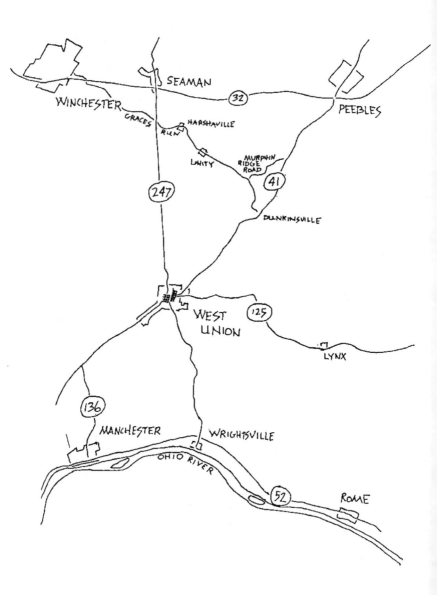

Index